Sustainable Transportation Networks

Sustainable Transportation Networks

Anna Nagurney

John F. Smith Memorial Professor, Isenberg School of Management, University of Massachusetts at Amherst, USA

Edward Elgar

Cheltenham, UK • Northampton, MA, USA

Published by
Edward Elgar Publishing Limited
Glensanda House
Montpellier Parade
Cheltenham
Glos GL50 1UA
UK

Edward Elgar Publishing, Inc.
136 West Street
Suite 202
Northampton
Massachusetts 01060
USA

A catalogue record for this book
is available from the British Library

Library of Congress Cataloguing in Publication Data

Nagurney, Anna.
Sustainable transportation networks / Anna Nagurney.
Includes bibliographical references and index.
1. Urban transportation—planning. 2. Urban transportation—environmental aspects.

HE305.N83 2000
388.4—dc21 99–059384

ISBN 1 84064 357 9

Printed and bound in Great Britain by Bookcraft (Bath) Ltd.

Contents

List of Figures

List of Tables

Preface

Networks form the infrastructure for the functioning of today's societies and economies. Transportation networks, in particular, provide the foundation for the movement of people and goods across space and time. The existence of transportation networks and their utilization are so fundamental to today's modern societies that such associated negative externalities with their usage as congestion and pollution are demanding increasing attention. Indeed, even with the advent of telecommuting and electronic commerce through telecommunication networks the demand for transportation resources is not expected to decrease in the foreseeable future.

Given societal, as well as governmental, recognition of the growing problems of congestion and pollution associated with the transportation sector, one may ask whether or not transportation networks are *sustainable*, that is, according to the definition, *can they last*? Are environmental quality standards even achievable in the context of today's transportation networks and the demand for their usage?

In this book, I develop a framework for the study, analysis, and design of sustainable transportation networks and answer the above question positively in a spectrum of settings. The focus here is rigorous since it is my belief that it is only through clearly defined concepts and methodologies that one can tackle this complex and timely issue. The topic is particularly challenging for several reasons:

1. What environmental and transportation planners may have considered to be improvements to a transportation network leading to expected reductions in pollution emissions may actually have the opposite effect. Indeed, the book motivates the problem of sustainability of transportation networks by presenting emission paradoxes which demonstrate that so-called "improvements" to a transportation network may actually result in an increase in the total number of emissions generated by the vehicles.
2. Transportation networks are spatial in nature as are the deleterious effects of the emissions generated. Hence, any associated environmental analysis must consider the network topology as well as the spatial nature of pollution

dispersion. Since transportation networks are large-scale in nature, analytical tools must be able to handle the dimensionality of the problem.

3. The behavior of the users of a transportation network and their interaction on the network must be taken into consideration in both the modeling and analysis of sustainable transportation networks. Indeed, flows on different links on a network may influence the travel time or cost on other links. Consequently, policy instruments must be such that they apply to the appropriate behavioral setting and achieve the desired environmental goals.

The above points emphasize one of the major themes of this book which is that the study and analysis of sustainable transportation networks and the underlying policies cannot be divorced from the networks nor from the behavior of the users of the networks. Specifically, in this book, I present formulations of sustainable transportation networks which explicitly consider what I believe are such critical issues as the network topologies themselves as well as the behavior of the users of the transportation networks. The possibility of distinct behaviors of users on the transportation networks are considered, who may operate according to their own best interests, that is, in a *user-optimizing* fashion or acccording to what is best from a societal perspective and, hence, in a *system-optimizing* manner.

This book presents models, accompanied by analyses, and numerous illustrative examples which, through a variety of policy instruments, guarantee that the transportation network in question will be sustainable, that is, given the behavior of the travelers on the networks, the environmental goals can be achieved. The book is the first to develop an integrated theory of sustainable transportation networks and establishes the foundations for this important area of research and practice.

Although the focus of the book is on urban transportation networks, the concepts, models, qualitative analysis, as well as the computational procedures described herein are also relevant in other transportation network contexts in which congestion and/or pollution issues are of increasing practical importance. For example, transportation networks such as freight networks, airline networks, as well as certain water networks, especially those close to ports, are increasingly characterized by the dual problems of congestion and pollution.

The book is divided into five parts, beginning with Part I, which provides an introduction and overview of the contents of the book, and contains the necessary background for the transportation and environmental topics covered in the remainder of the book. This part also presents emission paradoxes which illustrate that counterintuitive phenomena may occur in the case of so-called improvements to a transportation network in regards to the total emissions generated. I provide here definitions for both viable and sustainable transportation networks, with viability being a precursor to sustainability. Part I, hence, lays the foundation for the rest of the book and establishes its scope and focus.

Part II focuses on transportation networks in which travelers behave in a user-optimizing fashion in traveling from their origins to their destinations. Thus, it is assumed in this part of the book that the travelers act individually in a unilateral manner in order to determine their optimal routes of travel. Here both transportation networks with fixed travel demands and those with elastic travel demands are modeled and studied and pricing policies developed for such networks to be sustainable. Alternative pollution permit systems are also devised.

In addition, in Part II, transportation networks are studied in different situations, where, for example, the long-term perspective is addressed where travelers may choose not only their travel paths, but, respectively, their destinations (such as their places of work), their origins (such as their residential locations), or, in the most general case, their origins, their destinations, as well as their routes of travel between the origins and destinations. Here it is shown how to transform such networks in order to be able to apply directly the tools that are developed for networks in which travelers have fixed origins and destinations and select only their routes of travel.

Part III then turns to system-optimized transportation networks, which are subject to a central controller or transportation authority who can direct the flows from the origins to the destinations in a manner that is optimal from a societal perspective. Note that the flows in such networks may be travelers or flows such as freight. In such networks, I add another dimension to the analysis, in that I not only develop models which guarantee that the environmental goals are achieved, but also that the total cost in the network, as reflected by the total congestion, is minimized. Here I consider both pricing policies to ensure that system-optimized networks are sustainable, and also pollution permit systems. In the case of the latter, models are developed in which trading of the permits takes place. Moreover, I establish how the permits or licenses should be allocated in order to achieve the environmental quality standard. The trading can take place across regions or nations/states.

In addition, this part of the book then considers the scenario in which travelers behave in a user-optimizing manner, but the transportation authority (or authorities in the case of several jurisdictions) wishes to implement policies which guarantee that the user-optimizing flow patterns are, at the same time, system-optimized. I provide policy instruments in the form of tolls to show how this goal can be achieved, while, simultaneously, ensuring that the transportation networks are also sustainable.

Part IV of this book considers special topics, beginning with sustainable spatial price networks, in which the firms are assumed to compete in an oligopolistic manner. For such oligopolistic networks, it proposes a pollution permit system associated with the shipment of the commodity from the firms to the demand markets that guarantees that such networks will be sustainable. It then models perfectly competitive spatial price network problems in which the producers, the shippers, and the consumers are now subject to environmental quality standards and determines emission pricing policies that guarantee that such trade networks are sustainable. Subsequently, design and technology issues are studied in the context of sustainable transportation networks.

Finally, Part V concludes with the last chapter of this book, which provides a recapitulation of the main points of the book, highlights promising directions for research, and gives some personal reflections.

For the convenience of the reader, the book also contains appendices which cover the basics of the methodologies used in this book, as well as an appendix which contains some sample problems that may be used for pedagogical purposes or for self-study.

The book is intended for researchers and practitioners in the area of transportation and the environment, and especially for students of the subject, and any other interested parties.

The book was written while I was on sabbatical leave from the University of Massachusetts at Amherst and visiting the Division of Transportation and Location Analysis at the Royal Institute of Technology (KTH) in Stockholm, Sweden. Acknowledgment of both institutions is given for their support in this endeavor.

Finally, I acknowledge the support of John F. Smith Jr., the Chairman of the Board, the Chief Executive Officer, and the President of the General Motors Corporation, for his endowment in memory of his father of the John F. Smith Memorial Professorship of Operations Management, which I hold.

Parts of Chapter 3 appear in A. Nagurney, "Congested Urban Transportation Networks and Emission Paradoxes," to appear in *Transportation Research D*. Parts of Chapter 7 appear in A. Nagurney (1999), "Alternative Pollution Permit Systems for Transportation Networks Based on Origin/Destination Pairs and Paths," *Transportation Research D* **5**, 37-58. Acknowledgments are extended to Elsevier Science Ltd, the publisher of *Transportation Research D*, for the use of the material in this book.

Part I Introduction and Overview

1 Introduction

The physical movement of humans and commodities over space and time is essential to the functioning of societies and economies. Fundamental to the movement is the existence of infrastructure networks, in particular, transportation networks, which allow for the physical movement to take place. Indeed, the very organization of societies and economies themselves is increasingly taking on the structure of networks with both transportation and telecommunication networks forming the underlying foundations.

The transportation of humans and commodities cannot be realized without vehicles and their production comprises the biggest manufacturing industry in the world today. In the middle of the twentieth century there were 2.6 billion people on the earth and 50 million cars. Half a century later, the number of people has risen to 6 billion and the total number of cars to 500 million with the total number of vehicles including trucks and motorcycles being 777 million. The tenfold increase in the number of cars has occurred in only a couple of generations.

Vehicles and, in particular, cars have provided the medium for enhanced mobility and freedom for individuals and access to cars has been pivotal in shaping modern urban forms. Indeed, there are few aspects of today's modern life that have been untouched by the car, and the production of cars, as well as their usage, has revolutionized modern industry and has led to the evolution of the spatial structure of cities and regions as we know them today.

Moreover, ground transportation alone, as a sector of the United States economy, provided \$277 billion contribution to the 1992 gross domestic product (GDP) and in 1994 this figure, which measures all expenditures for moving goods and passengers, was in excess of \$900 billion. In 1995, it was estimated that the United States had 30% of the world's motor vehicles and yet only 4.5% of the world's population. Furthermore, the total number of passenger miles traveled annually in the United States alone was estimated to be 3.7 trillion passenger miles over 4 million miles of roads and highways (see Dower, et al. 1997). In Figure 1.1, the trend in vehicle miles traveled in

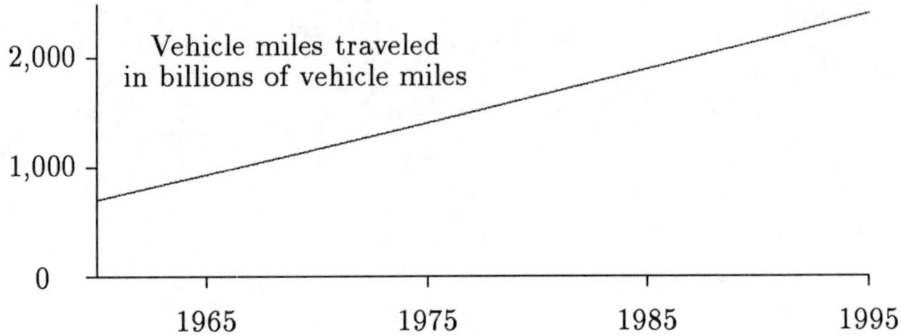

Fig. 1.1. Trend for vehicle miles traveled in the United States

Source: Oak Ridge National Laboratories (1993)

the United States is presented.

Nevertheless, despite the positives of vehicle ownership and use, the negative effects, notably, traffic congestion and pollution associated with vehicular travel and with increasing vehicular use, are now well-recognized. For example, in the United States alone, congestion results in $100 billion in lost productivity annually, whereas the figure in Europe is estimated to be $150 billion. The average American car driver travels approximately 12,000 miles annually, with a typical trip being of average length about 8.4 miles, whereas the European driver travels only about 8,400 miles annually. In the United States, buses and trains account for only about 3% of the travel mileage, whereas in Europe the percentage exceeds 15% (*The Economist* 1996). In Figure 1.2, the percentage of passenger travel by different modes of travel in the United States is given.

In addition, in the United States, the increasing suburban sprawl results in greater distances between residences and places of work as well as stores, schools, and other amenities. Furthermore, the traffic and congestion in many metropolitan areas in both the United States and abroad are growing annually with conditions expected to only worsen in the future.

Moreover, environmental pollution is one of the most pressing public policy problems faced by our societies today and the degradation of the environment due to adverse environmental effects such as air pollution from

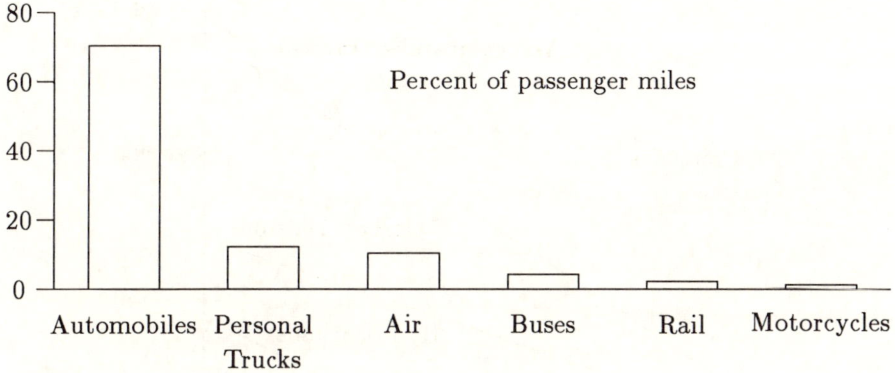

Fig. 1.2. Passenger travel in the United States

Source: American Automobile Manufacturers Association (1996)

vehicular exhaust emissions is well-documented. The average car during its lifetime travels 100,000 miles, uses over 3,000 gallons of gas and over 50 gallons of oil. It discharges through its exhaust more than 35 tons of carbon, with the world's 500 million cars producing 10 trillion cubic meters of exhaust fumes annually (*The Economist* 1996).

Despite 25 years of engineering progress and efforts and substantial reductions in transportation-related emissions, motor vehicles remain important sources of emissions of carbon monoxide, organic compounds, nitrogen oxides, and other forms of air pollution, mainly due to the growth of vehicular fleets. Presently, about 15% of the world's emissions of carbon dioxide, the principal global warming gas, is generated by motor vehicles. Furthermore, transportation is responsible for approximately 50% of the nitrogen oxide emissions, which, in combination with other pollutants, form nitric acid which then falls to earth as acid rain. Finally, 90% of the carbon monoxide generated comes from emissions from the transportation sector (Button 1990). Cars and other motor vehicles are responsible for at least 50% of the air pollution in urban areas (*The Economist* 1996, 1997). The number of cars is expected to rise by 50% by the year 2010 and to double by the year 2030. Figure 1.3 illustrates the travel and emission forecasts for all countries through the year 2030, given current 1990 policies. Indeed, even with potential reductions in vehicular emissions due, for example, to engineering innovations, without intervention congestion will not be reduced.

The World Health Organization (WHO) has conducted studies which reveal that only about 20% of the town dwellers on our earth enjoy good enough air quality as measured by the levels of emissions, such as nitrogen oxides. Indeed, the United Nations has estimated that people residing in approxi-

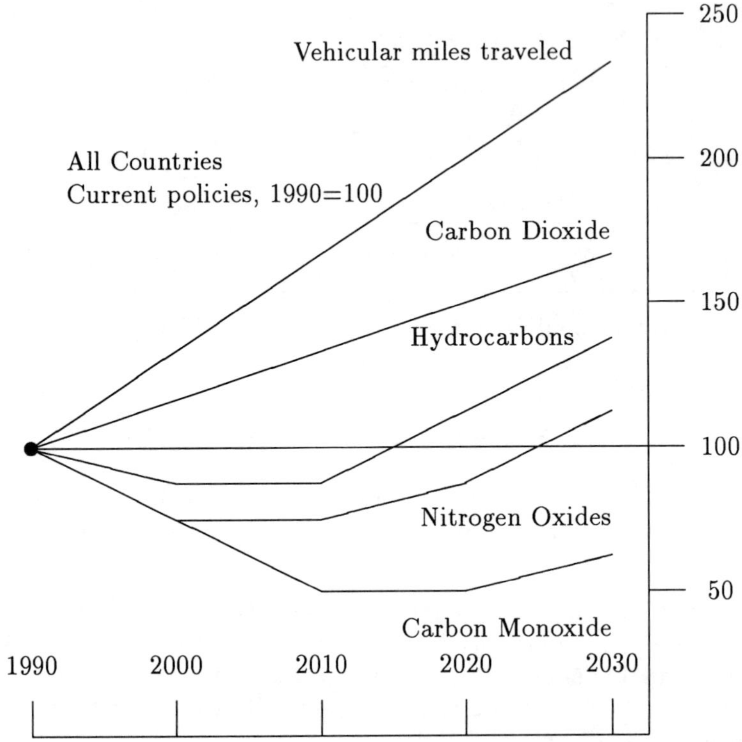

Fig. 1.3. Travel and emission forecasts for all countries through the year 2030, given current 1990 policies

Source: Adapted from *The Economist* (1996) obtained from OECD

mately one half of the world's cities are breathing more carbon monoxide than is good for them (*The Economist* 1996).

In light of the above figures, and the recognition of the negative effects of the dual problems of congestion and pollution by both individuals as well as their governments, one may ask the question whether or not the existing transportation networks are *sustainable*, that is, *can they last*? Indeed, with the seemingly conflicting forces of demand for transportation resources on the one hand and pressures to attain environmental quality standards on the other, as increasingly mandated by governmental legislation, and to also reduce congestion, one wonders whether there even exists a viable solution.

In this book, I develop a framework for the formulation, study, analysis, and design of sustainable transportation networks. Figure 1.4 presents a depiction of the major theme of this book, which is the achievement of sustainability of transportation networks through appropriate policies. The topic of

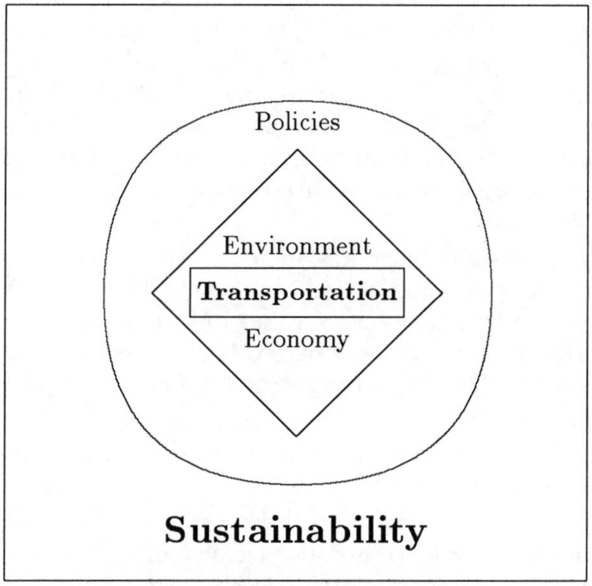

Fig. 1.4. Depiction of major theme of this book

sustainability, which explicitly considers the integration of economic, environmental, and social goals, has been the subject of increasing attention, as well as debate, since the 1987 Brundtland Commission Report (World Commission on Environment and Development 1987) defined *sustainable development* as development that meets the needs of the present without compromising the ability of future generations to meet their needs.

This book is the first to focus on sustainable transportation from a network perspective and to demonstrate – in a rigorous manner – how a spectrum of policy interventions, ranging from pricing policies to tradable pollution permits, and, finally, network design and technology can be applied in order to attain environmental goals. The topic is especially timely due to increasing interest in the subject on local, regional, national, as well as global levels.

Furthermore, with the advances in both analytical techniques, as well as the availability of computer technology, the theoretical results established in this book can be implemented in practice. Indeed, a recent report by the World Bank (1996) contends that "A policy for sustainable transport is one that identifies and implements the win–win policy instruments and explicitly confronts the tradeoffs so that the balance is chosen rather than accidentally arrived at. It is a policy of informed, conscious choices."

The book is written against the backdrop of increasing activity in the transportation field as regards environmental issues and, in particular, the notion of sustainability, as evidenced from recent conferences, papers, and studies that have addressed such issues (see, for example, Replogle 1991; Roseland 1992; Whitelegg 1993; OECD 1995; Sperling and Shaheen 1995; World Bank 1996; President's Council on Sustainable Development 1996a, b; Nijkamp, Rienstra, and Vleugel 1998). A recent report by the Transportation Research Board (1997) addressed the nature of long-term threats to the environment due to transportation infrastructure development and operation in the United States.

The notion of sustainability has roots at least as early as the work of the eighteenth-century economist and philosopher Thomas R. Malthus, who, however, focused on growth limits (see also Meadows et al. 1974). As regards transportation, sustainability has evolved, according to a recent World Bank report (see also Transportation Research Board 1997), to include such principal components as:

- the economic and financial component, which concerns the adequacy of the transportation infrastructure;
- the environmental as well as the ecological component, which concerns issues of how investments in transportation and mode choice options affect transportation and land use patterns and how these, in turn, affect, for example, emissions, air and water quality, and energy consumption; and
- the social component, which focuses on adequate access to transportation services by all members of society.

The book aims to develop a rigorous theoretical framework for the study of sustainable transportation networks, which encompasses various facets of the above components. It is by no means, however, meant to be all-encompassing, but, rather, to set the foundations for further research, discussion, and policy analysis and implementation. The structure of the book is given in Table 1.1.

The book is organized into five parts, beginning with Part I, entitled "Introduction and Overview," which provides the introductory material and an overview of the subject matter and book contents. In particular, this, the first, chapter describes the general setting and motivation for the book and overviews the book's contents. Chapter 2 then lays out the foundations for the transportation and environmental topics that follow and familiarizes the reader with the network concepts, the alternative perspectives of travelers' behavior, as well as the environmental issues and how they relate to transportation networks and their users. It also gives an overview of the basic environmental economic issues that arise in the transportation setting and provides a brief historical overview of policies aimed at congestion reduction and/or vehicular emission control.

Subsequently, Chapter 3 identifies emission paradoxes that may occur in transportation networks through concrete examples. These paradoxes, which illustrate certain counterintuitive phenomena in that so-called "improvements" to a transportation network, be they in the form of a road addition, a decrease in travel demand, or a transfer of travelers from a mode with

Table 1.1. Structure of the book

Part I: Introduction and Overview			
1. Introduction	2. Foundations	3. Emission Paradoxes	4. Viable and Sustainable Transportation Networks
Part II: Policies for Sustainable User-Optimized Transportation Networks			
5. Emission Pricing	6. Permits for Fixed Demand Networks	7. Permits for Elastic Demand Networks	
Part III: Policies for Sustainable System-Optimized Transportation Networks			
8. Sustainable Networks	9. Tradable Pollution Permits		
Part IV: Special Topics			
10. Spatial Oligopolies and Permits	11. Spatial Price Networks and Emission Policies	12. Technology and Network Design	
Part V: Summary and Conclusions			
13. Concluding Comments			

higher emissions to a mode with lower emissions, among others, may result in an increase in total emissions generated. The examples emphasize that policy makers must integrate the network topology, the travel cost and demand structure with the behavior of the users/travelers on the transportation network in order to appropriately assess any policies aimed at environmental quality standards attainment.

Chapter 4 provides rigorous definitions of viable and sustainable transportation networks which are utilized in the book for policy instrument design, analysis, and evaluation. Viable networks are defined as those on which (in the particular situation under consideration) the demand and flow constraints on the network can be satisfied by a flow pattern in the presence of an environmental quality standard. A sustainable transportation network is then defined as a viable network which achieves the environmental quality standard, given the behavior of the travelers on the network (and the presence, oftentimes, of an appropriate policy). Cost considerations and traveler behavior enter explicitly into the investigation of sustainability. Furthermore, a sustainable system, by its definition, implies a system "that lasts." Hence, viability is a *feasibility* concept, whereas sustainability is an *equilibrium* or *optimality* concept, depending on the behavior and operating principles of the transportation network.

Chapter 4 considers viability of transportation networks in distinct situations, beginning with one which may be interpreted as having a short-term perspective, in that the origins and destinations of the travelers have already been determined and travelers seek their optimal routes of travel. The chapter then formulates the viability problem in three other situations in which, respectively, the origin nodes are known, as well as the total number of trip productions at the origins, and travelers select both their destinations and their routes of travel; the destination nodes are known and the associated trip attractions, and both the origins and the travel routes are to be determined; and, finally, what may be viewed as the most general case in a sense, in that the total number of trips in the network is known and the origins, the destinations, and the routes of the travelers are to be determined. Lastly, Chapter 4 defines sustainable transportation networks. It is important to emphasize at the outset that sustainability of a transportation network may involve the imposition of regulatory policies to ensure that the behavior of the users of the network complies with the environmental goals.

Part II of the book, entitled, "Policies for Sustainable User-Optimized Transportation Networks," considers transportation networks in which the behavior of the travelers is that of user-optimization that is, the travelers seek to determine their optimal routes of travel where optimality is from the individual traveler's perspective rather than that of the system (or society as a whole). In Chapter 5, both fixed travel demand as well as elastic travel demand networks are considered. Moreover, I demonstrate how to recast the sustainability question for the different network situations described in Chapter 4 as sustainability for the network with known origin and destination pairs and associated travel demands. Specifically, I show how to construct the problem over expanded, abstract networks. Here pricing schemes are provided which guarantee that the user-optimized transportation networks, be they of fixed or elastic demand, are sustainable.

Chapter 6, subsequently, considers pollution permits for user-optimized fixed travel demand transportation networks and shows that the networks can achieve sustainability under this policy instrument. In particular, it is established that the environmental quality standard is achieved, provided that the initial license (or permit) allocation is set accordingly. Qualitative properties of existence and uniqueness of the equilibrium pattern are discussed and an algorithm is proposed, along with convergence results. The algorithm is then applied to numerical examples to illustrate both the permit model and the computational procedure.

Chapter 7 turns to elastic demand transportation networks which are user-optimized. Here a hierarchy of three pollution permit systems is constructed for such networks: a permit system by origin/destination pairs; a permit system by paths; and a link-based permit system. Each of these systems is guaranteed to achieve the environmental quality standard, provided that the sum of the initial license allocations is set to that value. Such a portfolio of possible permit systems provides transportation and environmental planners with the flexibility of selecting the appropriate one for the particular network with its characteristic topology.

Chapter 8 begins Part III of this book, entitled, "Policies for Sustainable System-Optimized Transportation Networks." In this part of the book, system-optimized networks are considered in which it is assumed that there is a central authority or controller who can route the flows on the network in a manner that is optimal from a societal or system point of view. In this part of the book, the total cost of traveling in the network enters explicitly into the objective function of the central authority and, hence, here the total congestion is treated in addition to the environmental quality goal.

In particular, Chapter 8 presents models for sustainable system-optimized transportation networks in which the policy instruments include road pricing. It then considers the more complex scenario in which travelers behave in a user-optimizing manner, but the transportation authority wishes to alter their behavior so that the flow pattern on the network is, at the same time, system-optimized. I propose emission/congestion tolls to accomplish precisely this and which, furthermore, ensure that the transportation network under study is sustainable.

Chapter 9 turns to the scenario in which there are now several transportation networks (these can be local or regional, for example), each of which is under the control of its own authority. It first develops a model in which a supra authority, such as the federal authority, for example, determines the desired environmental quality standard and allocates the licenses accordingly among the transportation networks. The pollution permit system model developed here is link-based and allows for trading to take place. Here each transportation authority with particular network jurisdiction now considers not only the total cost on his own network but also the (potential) net revenue associated with license or permit trading.

The framework is then further extended to allow for user-optimized behavior on the part of the travelers or users of the transportation networks. Specifically, it is demonstrated, in Chapter 9, how pricing should be carried out in the presence of a tradable pollution permit system scheme. Note that, in contrast to the permit system models in Part II of this book, here system-optimization is now considered in conjunction with user-optimization.

Part IV of this book is focused on special topics, beginning with sustainable spatial price networks. In such *trade* networks, producers are involved with the production of a commodity which is then shipped to consumers. Both the producers, located at the supply regions, and consumers, located at the demand regions, are spatially separated. One seeks to determine the equilibrium production, consumption, and trade patterns on such networks. Note that here I consider not only mobile sources of pollution occurring during the shipment of the good but also stationary sources corresponding to the producers at the production or supply nodes and consumers at the consumption or demand nodes.

Specifically, in Chapter 10, I develop an oligopolistic model of spatial competition in which the policy instrument is that of marketable pollution permits associated with the emissions generated during the shipment of the commodity from the firms to the demand markets. It is established here that, under such a policy, such a trade network is sustainable, that is, that the environmental quality standard is achieved. In Chapter 11, I then consider perfectly competitive spatial price networks, in which now the stationary sources at the production nodes and at the consumption nodes emit pollutants as well, in addition to those emitted through the shipment of the commodity from the producers to the consumers. Here I establish emission pricing policies which guarantee that such spatial price trade networks are sustainable. Here I also explicitly consider the situation that the emissions generated by the producers, the shippers, and/or the consumers can be distinct.

Chapter 12 returns to congested urban transportation networks and presents models for addressing sustainability issues through network design and technology improvements. It also discusses some practical issues in regards to the implementation of policies described in this book.

The final chapter of this book, Chapter 13, which comprises Part V, recapitulates the main points, describes promising areas for research, and presents a personal prospectus.

2 Foundations

Transportation networks are complex, typically large-scale systems and the study of their efficient operation, often through some outside intervention, has attracted much interest from economists, engineers, as well as transportation and urban planners and operations researchers. The subject dates to ancient times with such classical examples including the publicly provided Roman road network and the "time of day" chariot policy, whereby chariots were banned from the ancient city of Rome at particular times of the day (see Banister and Button 1993).

From an economic perspective, some of the earliest contributions to the subject date to Pigou (1920), who is also viewed as the forefather of road pricing. In particular, his idea of using road pricing to regulate traffic congestion on a simple two-node, two-link network has spawned additional research, discussion, and practical applications. Pigou (1920) (see also Knight 1924) used the example of a congested road to illustrate the concepts of externality and optimal tolls as congestion charges. Specifically, Pigou argued that travelers should be charged according to their marginal external congestion costs. Note that an *externality* is present when the actions of some economic agents (such as travelers) affect the utility (typically travel time or cost in the case of transportation) or production set of another without that person's consent or compensation. An externality is seen as *negative* when the harm done to others is considered to be uncompensated. In the case of transportation networks, the harm may include, for example, increased travel time due to congestion, or increased pollution. See Figure 2.1 for a depiction of externality relationships in a transportation system.

Earlier in 1844, Dupuit had used a bridge as an illustration of the concept of efficient pricing of public goods. Coase (1960), in turn, utilized a transportation example, among others, in the form of sparks from a railway, when he addressed the absence of property rights in relation to the existence of externalities. *Property rights* refer to the group of entitlements comprising the property owner's rights and privileges plus the constraints imposed for the use of the resource. Property rights are typically distinguished as to whether

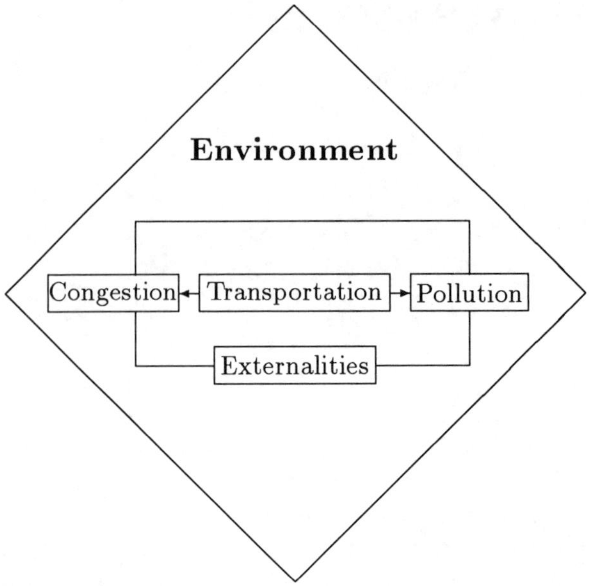

Fig. 2.1. Some externality relationships in a transportation system

they are: *private*, that is, held by individuals or firms; *common*, that is, held by an identifiable group; *state*, that is, held by the government; or of *open access*, in which no explicit ownership applies and, hence, the property is open or available to all.

As early as the 1960s, Vickrey (1960, 1963) emphasized that the cost of congestion was high, with the real economic cost of transportation infrastructure in the United States at that time being estimated to be approximately three times the total vehicular and gasoline taxes generated by car use on urban streets. Moreover, he argued in 1959 (see Hau 1998) that the results of not charging travelers for their rush-hour usage could be "disastrously expensive."

Engineers were also concerned about the operation of transportation networks. In particular, Wardrop (1952) explicitly recognized alternative possible behaviors of users of transportation networks and stated two principles, which are commonly named after him:

First Principle: The journey times of all routes actually used are equal, and less than those which would be experienced by a single vehicle on any unused route.

Second Principle: The average journey time is minimal.

The first principle corresponds to the behavioral principle in which travel-

Table 2.1. Distinct behavior on transportation networks

User-Optimization	System-Optimization
⇓	⇓
Equilibrium Principle:	Optimality Principle:
User travel costs on used paths for each O/D pair are equalized and minimal.	Marginals of the total travel cost on used paths for each O/D pair are equalized and minimal.

ers seek to (unilaterally) determine their minimal costs of travel whereas the second principle corresponds to the behavioral principle in which the total cost in the network is minimal.

Beckmann, McGuire, and Winsten (1956) were the first to rigorously formulate these conditions mathematically, as had Samuelson (1952) in the framework of spatial price equilibrium problems in which there were, however, no congestion effects. Specifically, Beckmann, McGuire, and Winsten (1956) established the equivalence between the *traffic network equilibrium* conditions, which state that all used paths connecting an origin/destination pair will have equal and minimal travel times (or costs) (corresponding to Wardrop's first principle), and the Kuhn-Tucker conditions of an appropriately constructed optimization problem, under a symmetry assumption on the underlying functions. Hence, in this case, the equilibrium link and path flows could be obtained as the solution of a mathematical programming problem. Their approach made the formulation, analysis, and subsequent computation of solutions to traffic network problems based on actual transportation networks realizable.

Dafermos and Sparrow (1969) coined the terms *user-optimized* (U-O) and *system-optimized* (S-O) transportation networks to distinguish between two distinct situations in which, respectively, users act unilaterally, in their own self-interest, in selecting their routes, and in which users select routes according to what is optimal from a societal point of view, in that the total cost in the system is minimized. In the latter problem, marginal costs rather than average costs are equilibrated. The former problem coincides with Wardrop's first principle, and the latter with Wardrop's second principle.

See Table 2.1 for the two distinct behavioral principles underlying transportation networks. The concept of "system-optimization" is also relevant to other types of "routing models" in transportation (as well as in communications), including those concerned with the routing of freight. Dafermos and Sparrow (1969) also provided explicit computational procedures, that is, *algorithms*, to compute the solutions to such network problems in the case where the user travel cost on a link was an increasing (in order to handle congestion) function of the flow on the particular link and linear.

For definiteness, and for easy reference, I present both the classical system-optimized traffic network model in Section 2.1.1 and then the classical user-optimized network model in Section 2.1.2. Subsequently, in Section 2.1.3, I discuss toll policies which guarantee that the user-optimized flow pattern is also system-optimizing. Note that at this point in the discussion in this chapter no environmental concerns have as yet been raised. I return to this topic in Section 2.3.

In Section 2.2, I consider more general models, in which the user link travel cost functions are no longer separable and are also asymmetric. In Section 2.2.1, I construct link- and path-toll policies for such transportation networks. In Section 2.2.3, I then consider the U-O traffic network problem with general user link travel cost functions and provide the variational inequality formulations of the governing equilibrium conditions, since, in this case, the conditions can no longer be reformulated as the Kuhn-Tucker conditions of a convex optimization problem (see also Appendices A and B). Finally, in Section 2.2.4, I present the variational inequality formulations in the case of elastic travel demands.

Section 2.3, subsequently, focuses on transportation and the environment, and describes some basic policy instruments drawn from environmental economics. Section 2.4 highlights some unique characteristics of transportation networks as regards environmental issues.

2.1 System-Optimization Versus User-Optimization

In this section, the basic traffic network models are reviewed, under distinct assumptions of their operation and distinct behavior of the travelers or users of the network. The models are classical and due to Beckmann, McGuire, and Winsten (1956) and Dafermos and Sparrow (1969).

2.1.1 System-Optimization

Consider a general network $G = [N, L]$, where N denotes the set of nodes, and L the set of directed links. Let a denote a link of the network connecting a pair of nodes, and let p denote a path consisting of a sequence of links connecting an O/D pair. In transportation networks, nodes correspond to origins and destinations, as well as to intersections. Links, on the other hand, correspond to roads/streets. A path, thus, is a sequence of roads which comprise a route from an origin to a destination. P_w denotes the set of paths connecting the origin/destination (O/D) pair of nodes w. Let P denote the set of all paths in the network and assume that there are J origin/destination pairs of nodes.

Let x_p represent the flow on path p and let f_a the load on link a. The path flows on the network are grouped in the column vector $x \in R_+^{n_P}$, where n_P denotes the number of paths in the network. The link loads, in turn, are grouped into the column vector $f \in R^n_+$, where n denotes the number of links in the network.

The following conservation of flow equation must hold:

$$f_a = \sum_{p \in P} x_p \delta_{ap}, \quad \forall a \in L, \tag{2.1}$$

where $\delta_{ap} = 1$, if link a is contained in path p, and 0, otherwise. Expression (2.1) states that the load on a link a is equal to the sum of all the path flows on paths p that contain (traverse) link a.

Moreover, if one lets d_w denote the demand associated with O/D pair w, then one must have that

$$d_w = \sum_{p \in P_w} x_p, \quad \forall w \in W, \tag{2.2}$$

where $x_p \geq 0$, $\forall p \in P$; that is, the sum of all the path flows between an origin/destination pair w must be equal to the given demand d_w.

Let c_a denote the user link travel cost associated with traversing link a, and let C_p denote the user cost associated with traversing the path p.

Assume that the user link travel cost function is given by

$$c_a = c_a(f_a), \quad \forall a \in L, \tag{2.3}$$

where c_a is assumed to be an increasing function of the link load f_a in order to model the effect of the link load on the travel cost.

The total cost on link a, denoted by $\hat{c}_a(f_a)$, hence, is given by:

$$\hat{c}_a(f_a) = c_a(f_a) \times f_a, \quad \forall a \in L, \tag{2.4}$$

that is, the total cost on a link is equal to the user link travel cost on the link times the flow on the link. Here the travel cost is interpreted in a general sense but often principally from a transportation engineering perspective, the travel cost on a link is assumed to coincide with the travel time on a link.

See Figure 2.2, for such a typical user link travel time function, where the free flow travel time refers to the travel time to traverse a link when there is zero load on the link (or zero vehicles).

In the system-optimized problem, there exists a central controller who seeks to minimize the total cost in the network system, where the total cost is expressed as

$$\sum_{a \in L} \hat{c}_a(f_a), \tag{2.5}$$

where the total cost on a link is given by expression (2.4).

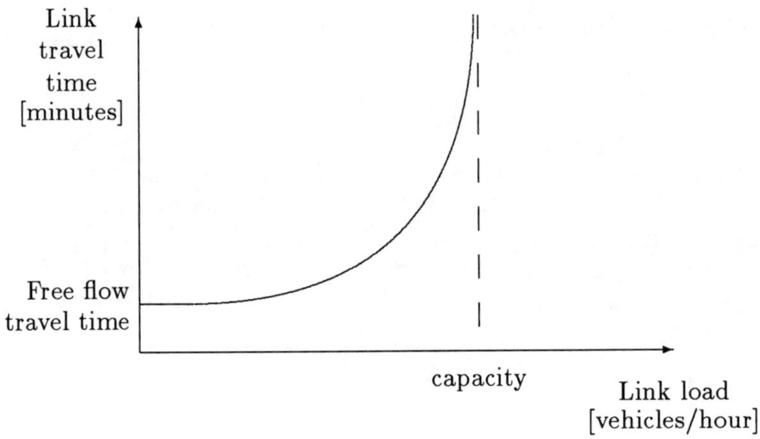

Fig. 2.2. A graph of a typical user link travel time function

The System-Optimized Problem

The system-optimization problem is, thus, given by:

$$\text{Minimize} \quad \sum_{a \in L} \hat{c}_a(f_a) \tag{2.6}$$

subject to:

$$\sum_{p \in P_w} x_p = d_w, \quad \forall w \in W, \tag{2.7}$$

$$f_a = \sum_{p \in P} x_p, \quad \forall a \in L, \tag{2.8}$$

$$x_p \geq 0, \quad \forall p \in P. \tag{2.9}$$

The constraints (2.7) and (2.8), along with (2.9), are commonly referred to in network terminology as *conservation of flow equations*. In particular, they guarantee that the flow in the network, that is, the travelers, do not "get lost."

The total cost on a path, denoted by $\hat{C}_p$, is the user link travel cost on a path times the flow on a path, that is,

$$\hat{C}_p = C_p x_p, \quad \forall p \in P, \tag{2.10}$$

where the user travel cost on a path, C_p, is given by the sum of the user link travel costs on the links that comprise the path, that is,

$$C_p = \sum_{a \in L} c_a(f_a)\delta_{ap}, \quad \forall a \in L. \tag{2.11}$$

In view of (2.8), one may express the cost on a path p as a function of the path flow variables and, hence, an alternative version of the above system-optimization problem can be stated in path flow variables only, where one has now the problem:

$$\text{Minimize} \quad \sum_{p \in P} C_p(x) x_p \tag{2.12}$$

subject to constraints (2.7) and (2.9). In this text, hence, without any loss of generality, I express the travel cost on a path as a function of either the path flow or the link load pattern.

System-Optimality Conditions

Under the assumption of increasing user link cost functions, the objective function in the S-O problem is convex, and the feasible set consisting of the linear constraints is also convex. Therefore, the optimality conditions, that is, the Kuhn-Tucker conditions (see Appendix A) are: For each O/D pair $w \in W$, and each path $p \in P_w$, the flow pattern x (and link load pattern f), satisfying (2.7)–(2.9) must satisfy:

$$\hat{C}'_p \begin{cases} = \mu_w, & \text{if} \quad x_p > 0 \\ \geq \mu_w, & \text{if} \quad x_p = 0, \end{cases} \tag{2.13}$$

where $\hat{C}'_p$ denotes the marginal of the total cost on path p, given by:

$$\hat{C}'_p = \sum_{a \in L} \frac{\partial \hat{c}_a(f_a)}{\partial f_a} \delta_{ap}, \tag{2.14}$$

and in (2.13) is evaluated at the solution.

Note that in the S-O problem, according to the optimality conditions (2.13), it is the marginal of the total costs on each used path connecting an O/D pair which are equalized and minimal. Indeed, conditions (2.13) state that a system-optimized flow pattern is such that for each origin/destination pair the incurred marginals of the total cost on each used path are equal and minimal.

2.1.2 User-Optimization

In this subsection, the user-optimized traffic network problem is considered, also commonly referred to as the *traffic assignment* problem or the *traffic network equilibrium* problem. Again, as in the system-optimized problem of Section 2.1.1, the network $G = [N, L]$, the travel demands associated with the origin/destination pairs, as well as the user link travel cost functions are assumed as given. Recall that user-optimization follows Wardrop's first principle.

Traffic Network Equilibrium Conditions

Now, however, one seeks to determine the path flow pattern x^* (and link load pattern f^*) which satisfies the conservation of flow equations (2.1), (2.2) and the nonnegativity assumption on the path flows, and which also satisfies the traffic network equilibrium conditions given by the following statement.

For each O/D pair $w \in W$ and each path $p \in P_w$:

$$C_p \begin{cases} = \lambda_w, & \text{if} \quad x_p^* > 0 \\ \geq \lambda_w, & \text{if} \quad x_p^* = 0. \end{cases} \tag{2.15}$$

Hence, in the user-optimization problem there is no explicit optimization concept, since now travelers act independently, in a noncooperative manner, until they cannot improve on their situations unilaterally and, thus, an equilibrium is achieved, governed by the above equilibrium conditions. Indeed, conditions (2.15) are simply a restatement of Wardrop's (1952) first principle mathematically and mean that only those paths connecting an O/D pair will be used which have equal and minimal user travel costs. Otherwise, a traveler could improve upon his situation by switching to a path with lower travel cost.

In order to obtain a solution to the above problem, Beckmann, McGuire, and Winsten (1956) established that the solution to the equilibrium problem, in the case of separable user link travel cost functions, could be obtained by solving the following optimization problem:

$$\text{Minimize} \quad \sum_{a \in L} \int_0^{f_a} c_a(x)dx \tag{2.16}$$

subject to:

$$\sum_{p \in P_w} x_p = d_w, \quad \forall w \in W, \tag{2.17}$$

$$f_a = \sum_{p \in P} x_p \delta_{ap}, \quad \forall a \in L, \tag{2.18}$$

$$x_p \geq 0, \quad \forall p \in P. \tag{2.19}$$

Note that the conservation of flow equations are identical in both the user-optimized network problem (see (2.17)–(2.19)) and the system-optimized problem (see (2.7) – (2.9)). The behavior of the travelers, however, is different.

The objective function given by (2.16) is simply a device constructed to obtain a solution using general purpose convex programming algorithms. It does not possess the economic meaning of the objective function encountered in the system-optimization problem given by (2.6), equivalently, by (2.12).

Remark 2.1

A simplified user function, used in practice, sometimes also referred to as a common link performance function (see Sheffi 1985), is the expression developed by the Bureau of Public Roads (BPR). This equation is given by

$$c_a = c_a^0 \left[1 + \alpha (\frac{f_a}{t'_a})^\beta \right],$$

where, in this formula, c_a and f_a are the travel time and link load, respectively, on link a, c_a^0 is the free-flow travel time, and t'_a is the "practical capacity" of link a. The quantities α and β are model parameters, for which the values $\alpha = 0.15$ minutes and $\beta = 4$ are typical values. For example, these values imply that the practical capacity of a link is the flow at which the travel time is 15% greater than the free-flow travel time.

2.1.3 Toll Policies

In this subsection, it is described how tolls, either in the form of path tolls or link tolls, can be imposed in order to make the system-optimizing solution also user-optimizing. Tolls serve as a means for modifying the travel cost as perceived by the individual travelers and are considered a powerful pricing policy instrument.

Recall that the system-optimizing flow pattern is one that minimizes the total travel cost over the entire network, whereas the user-optimized flow pattern has the property that no user has any incentive to make a unilateral decision to alter his/her travel path. One would expect the former pattern to be established when a central authority dictates the paths to be selected, so as to minimize the total cost in the system, and the latter, when travelers are free to select their routes of travel so as to minimize their individual travel cost. The latter solution, however, typically results in a higher total system cost and, in a sense, is an underutilization of the transportation network. In order to remedy this situation tolls can be applied with the recognition that imposing tolls will not change the travel cost as perceived by society since tolls are not lost.

In particular, in this subsection, it will be shown how tolls can be collected on a *link basis*, that is, every traveler on a link will be charged the same toll, irrespective of origin or final destination, or on a *path basis*, in which every traveler traveling from an origin to a destination on a particular path will be charged the same toll. (Note that one can construct multimodal versions of such a toll policy in which the pricing on links or paths is according to mode; see Dafermos 1973 and Nagurney 1999a).

Let t_a denote a toll associated with link a in the link-toll collection policy and let t_p denote the toll on path p associated with the path-toll collection policy. Of course, even in the link-toll collection policy one may define a "path toll" through the expression

$$t_p = \sum_{a \in L} t_a \delta_{ap}, \quad \forall p \in P. \tag{2.20}$$

Observe that, after the imposition of tolls, the travel cost as perceived by society remains $c_a(f_a)$, for all links $a \in L$. The travel cost on a path p as perceived by the individual, however, is modified to

$$\bar{C}_p = C_p(f) + t_p, \quad \forall p \in P. \tag{2.21}$$

Consequently, a system-optimizing flow pattern is still defined as before, that is, it is one that solves the problem

$$\text{Minimize}_{f \in K} \sum_{a \in L} \hat{c}_a(f_a), \tag{2.22}$$

where $K \equiv \{f |\, \text{there exists an}\, x \geq 0,\, \text{satisfying}\, (2.7)\, \text{and}\, (2.8)\}$.

In particular, the solution to (2.22), under the assumption that each $\hat{c}_a(f_a)$ is convex, is equivalent to the conditions (2.13). Note that conditions (2.13), in turn, are equivalent to the statement For every O/D pair $w \in W$, there exists an ordering of the paths $p \in P_w$, such that

$$\hat{C}'_{p_1}(f) = \ldots = \hat{C}'_{p_{s_w}}(f) = \mu_w \leq \hat{C}'_{p_{s_{w+1}}}(f) \leq \cdots \leq \hat{C}'_{p_{n_w}}(f) \tag{2.23}$$

$$x_{p_{r_w}} > 0, \quad r_w = 1, \ldots, s_w$$

$$x_{p_{r_w}} = 0, \quad r_w = s_{w+1}, \ldots, n_w,$$

where n_w denotes the number of paths for O/D pair w.

On the other hand, in view of equilibrium conditions (2.15), one can deduce that the system-optimizing flow pattern x, after the imposition of a toll policy, is at the same time user-optimizing if: For every O/D pair $w \in W$, every path $p \in P_w$:

$$\bar{C}_{p_1}(f) = \ldots = \bar{C}_{p_{s_w}}(f) = \bar{\lambda}_w \leq \bar{C}_{p_{s_{w+1}}}(f) \leq \cdots \leq \bar{C}_{p_{n_w}}(f) \tag{2.24}$$

$$x_{p_{r_w}} > 0, \quad r_w = 1, \ldots, s_w$$

$$x_{p_{r_w}} = 0, \quad r_w = s_{w+1}, \ldots, n_w.$$

The following proposition (see Dafermos (1973)) enables the construction of toll policies which render an S-O flow pattern also a U-O one:

Proposition 2.1

A toll-collection policy renders a system-optimizing flow pattern user-optimizing if and only if for each O/D pair $w \in W$:

$$
\begin{aligned}
t_{p_1} &= \bar{\lambda}_w - C_{p_1}(f) \\
\vdots \quad & \qquad \quad \vdots \\
t_{p_{s_w}} &= \bar{\lambda}_w - C_{p_{s_w}}(f)
\end{aligned}
\tag{2.25}
$$

$$
\begin{aligned}
t_{p_{s_w+1}} &\geq \bar{\lambda}_w - C_{p_{s_w+1}}(f) \\
\vdots \quad & \qquad \quad \vdots \\
t_{p_{n_w}} &\geq \bar{\lambda}_w - C_{p_{n_w}}(f).
\end{aligned}
\tag{2.26}
$$

Proof:
It is clear that if (2.23) and (2.24) are satisfied for the same flow pattern x, then (2.25) and (2.26) follow. Conversely, if (2.25) and (2.26) are satisfied, then any f that satisfies (2.23) also satisfies (2.24). □

I now turn to the determination of the link-toll and the path-toll collection policies.

2.1.3.1 Solution of the Link-Toll Collection Policy

Using (2.23), (2.24), (2.25), and (2.26), one reaches the conclusion that the link-toll collection policy is determined by

$$t_a = \frac{\partial \hat{c}_a(f_a)}{\partial f_a} - c_a(f_a), \quad \forall a \in L, \tag{2.27}$$

where both the first and the second terms on the right-hand side of expression (2.27) are evaluated at the system-optimizing solution f.

Hence, to determine the link-toll policy, one first must compute the system-optimizing solution. This can be accomplished using a general-purpose convex programming algorithm, an appropriate nonlinear network code, or, in the case of separable linear user cost functions, the equilibration algorithm of Dafermos and Sparrow (1969). Once the system-optimizing solution is established, one then substitutes the S-O load pattern f into equation (2.27) to compute the link toll t_a for all links $a \in L$.

2.1.3.2 Solution of the Path-Toll Collection Policy

It is clear from (2.25) and (2.26) that one may construct an infinite number of solutions of the path-toll collection problem. For example, one may select, a priori, for each $w \in W$, the level of personal travel cost $\bar{\lambda}_w$, as well as the values of $t_{p_{s_w+1}}, \ldots, t_{p_{n_w}}$, subject to only constraint (2.26), and then determine a path-toll pattern according to (2.25) and (2.26). Hence, in this case

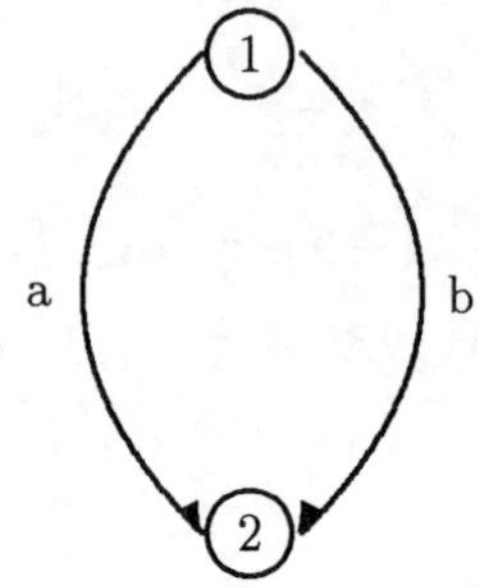

Fig. 2.3. Network topology for a link-toll policy example

there is some flexibility in selecting a toll pattern, and one can incorporate additional objectives. Certain possibilities are:

(i) One may wish to ensure that some, if not all, travelers are charged with a nonnegative toll; in other words, no subsidization is allowed. This can be accomplished by choosing the corresponding $\bar{\lambda}_w$ sufficiently large.

(ii) Suppose one wishes a "fair" policy. A possible one would be to ensure that the level of personal travel cost $\bar{\lambda}_w$ is equal to the personal travel cost λ_w before the imposition of tolls.

In summary, one computes the path-toll policy as follows. First, compute the system-optimizing solution. Then determine the user travel cost C_p, for all paths $p \in P$, evaluated at the system-optimizing solution and $\bar{\lambda}_w$, $\forall w \in W$, so that an objective is met. Finally, compute the path tolls t_p, $\forall p \in P$, according to (2.25) and (2.26).

A simple example is now presented in order to illustrate how one computes a link-toll policy.

Example 2.1

Consider the network depicted in Figure 2.3 in which there are two nodes: 1, 2; two links: a, b; and a single O/D pair $w_1 = (1, 2)$. Let path $p_1 = a$ and path $p_2 = b$.

Assume, for simplicity, the user link travel cost functions:

$$c_a(f_a) = 2f_a + 5, \quad c_b(f_b) = f_b + 10,$$

and the travel demand:

$$d_{w_1} = 10.$$

In the absence of any policies, travelers operating in a user-optimized manner will select the paths as follows: $x_{p_1} = 5$, and $x_{p_2} = 5$ with induced link load patterns of: $f_a = 5$ and $f_b = 5$. The incurred user travel costs on the paths under this user-optimized flow pattern will be:

$$C_{p_1} = c_a = 15, \quad C_{p_2} = c_b = 15,$$

which satisfies the traffic equilibrium conditions (2.15). This path flow pattern, in turn, will yield a total cost on the network given by $c_a \times f_a + c_b \times f_b = 75 + 75 = 150$.

The system-optimized flow pattern satisfying conditions (2.13) is, however, given by: $x_{p_1} = 4\frac{1}{6}$, $x_{p_2} = 5\frac{5}{6}$, which induces the link load pattern: $f_a = 4\frac{1}{6}$, $f_b = 5\frac{5}{6}$ and the marginals of the total travel costs on the paths are:

$$\hat{C}'_{p_1} = \hat{c}'_a = 21\frac{2}{3}, \quad \hat{C}'_{p_2} = \hat{c}'_b = 21\frac{2}{3},$$

with a total cost in the network under the S-O pattern equal to $131\frac{7}{18}$, which is clearly lower than the total cost under the U-O flow pattern above, which was 150.

I now turn to the computation of the link-toll policy (cf. (2.27)) which will render the S-O flow pattern also a U-O flow pattern. The link-toll policy that renders the system-optimizing flow pattern also user-optimized is given by:

$$t_a = 8\frac{1}{3}, \quad t_b = 5\frac{5}{6},$$

with the induced user costs (cf. (2.21)) $\bar{C}_{p_1} = \bar{C}_{p_2} = 21\frac{2}{3}$.

2.2 Models with Asymmetric Link Costs

The past several decades have been witness to much dynamic research activity in both the modeling and the development of methodologies to enable the formulation and computation of more general traffic network equilibrium models. Examples of general models include those that allow for multiple modes of transportation or multiple classes of users, who perceive cost on a link in an individual way. In this section, I consider traffic network models in which the user travel cost on a link is no longer dependent solely on the flow on that link. Other traffic network models, including dynamic traffic models, can be found in Mahmassani et al. (1993), and in the books by Ran and Boyce (1996) and Nagurney and Zhang (1996), and the references therein.

2.2.1 Link- and Path-Toll Policies

For example, I now consider user link travel cost functions which are of the general form (refer to (2.3)), where the travel cost on a link may depend also on the load of this as well as other loads on the network, that is,

$$c_a = c_a(f), \quad \forall a \in L. \tag{2.28}$$

In the case where the symmetry assumption exists, that is, $\frac{\partial c_a(f)}{\partial c_b(f)} = \frac{\partial c_b(f)}{\partial c_a(f)}$, for all links $a, b \in L$, one can still reformulate the solution to the traffic network equilibrium problem satisfying equilibrium conditions (2.15) as the solution to an optimization problem (cf. Nagurney 1999a and the references therein), albeit, again, with an objective function that is artificial and simply a mathematical device. However, when the symmetry assumption is no longer satisfied, such an optimization reformulation no longer exists and one must appeal to *variational inequality theory* (see Appendix B).

Indeed, it was in the problem domain of traffic network equilibrium problems that the theory of finite-dimensional variational inequalities realized its earliest success, beginning with the contributions of Smith (1979) and Dafermos (1980). For an introduction to the subject, as well as applications ranging from traffic network equilibrium problems to financial equilibrium problems, see the book by Nagurney (1999a). The methodology of finite-dimensional variational inequalities is utilized in this book in order to develop a spectrum of policy models.

The system-optimization problem, in turn, in the case of nonseparable user link travel cost functions becomes (see also (2.6)–(2.9)):

$$\text{Minimize} \quad \sum_{a \in L} \hat{c}_a(f), \tag{2.29}$$

subject to (2.7)–(2.9), where $\hat{c}_a(f) = c_a(f) \times f_a$, $\forall a \in L$.

The system-optimality conditions remain as in (2.13) but where now the marginal of the total cost on a path becomes, in the more general case:

$$\hat{C}'_p = \sum_{a,b \in L} \frac{\partial \hat{c}_b(f)}{\partial f_a} \delta_{ap}, \quad \forall p \in P. \tag{2.30}$$

The link-toll collection policy (see (2.27)) is now given by:

$$t_a = \sum_{b \in L} \frac{\partial \hat{c}_b(f)}{\partial f_a} - c_a(f), \quad \forall a \in L. \tag{2.31}$$

The path-toll policy, in turn, can still be computed according to formulas (2.25) and (2.26), where $\bar{C}_p$ is given by (2.21).

See also Bergendorff, Hearn, and Ramana (1997) for other toll policies for traffic networks with asymmetric user link travel cost functions.

2.2.2 Practical Considerations

Tolls, hence, provide an example of road pricing for congestion management. As noted by Small and Gomez-Ibanez (1998), public officials have become

Table 2.2. Various road pricing schemes in practice

Source: Small and Gomez-Ibanez (1998)

Type of road pricing	In place	Under study
City center: congestion pricing	Singapore, 1975	Hong Kong Cambridge, UK
City center: tolling	Bergen, 1986 Oslo, 1990 Trondheim, 1991	Stockholm
Single facility: congestion pricing	Autoroute A1, France, 1992 Route R1, California, 1995 Interstate 15, San Diego, 1996	
Area-wide: congestion pricing		Ramstad London

increasingly interested in congestion pricing as a means to stem the growth of traffic congestion. Refer to Table 2.2 for various road pricing schemes in practice.

Indeed, the practical experience with road pricing has been increasing globally, with notable examples including those of Singapore, Hong Kong, and Cambridge, England. Singapore's area license scheme was initiated in 1975 and is still operational. It has recently adopted an electronic version. Hong Kong has an electronic road pricing scheme, whereas Cambridge has investigated congestion pricing schemes which have included also rigorous modeling and theoretical underpinnings. Scandinavian cities, in turn, have adopted a type of road pricing which, although the systems do not represent congestion pricing, do support highway financing. Specifically, toll rings now surround the three Norwegian cities of Oslo, Trondheim, and Bergen and such a ring is also in the planning stages for Stockholm.

France on Autoroute A1, which is an expressway connecting Paris to Lille, instituted congestion pricing, as did California in Riverside County. Indeed, the first site of congestion pricing in the United States is a section of highway in southern California which opened in 1995.

During the past decade, interest has grown both in the United States and abroad, especially in Europe, to utilize advanced computer, electronics, and communication technologies (collectively referred to as intelligent transportation systems or ITS) in order to improve transportation efficiency (as well as safety). With the advent of such associated developments as electronic toll technology, as well as intelligent vehicle highway systems (IVHS) and advanced traffic information management systems (ATIMs) (cf. Boyce, Kirson, and Schofer 1994), it is becoming increasingly pragmatic to implement both the tolls described in this chapter, as well as other road pricing and and permit schemes that are described in this book and which focus both on congestion reduction and emission abatement.

2.2.3 Variational Inequality Formulations of Fixed Demand Problems

As mentioned in the preceding section, in the case where the user link travel cost functions are no longer symmetric, one cannot compute the solution to the U-O, that is the traffic network equilibrium, problem using standard optimization algorithms. Such cost functions are very important from an application standpoint since they allow for asymmetric interactions on the network. For example, allowing for asymmetric cost functions permits one to handle the situation when the flow on a particular link affects the cost on another link in a different way than the cost on the particular link is affected by the flow on the other link. Returning to the network depicted in Figure 2.1, an example of an asymmetric user link travel cost structure would be:

$$c_a(f) = 5f_a + f_b + 10, \quad c_b(f) = 3f_b + 2f_a + 15,$$

since $\frac{\partial c_a}{\partial f_b} = 1 \neq \frac{\partial c_b}{\partial f_a} = 2$.

The allowance for such asymmetric interactions enables also the more realistic modeling of multimodal traffic networks in which a particular flow of a mode affects the costs of other modes in a different manner than it is affected by the other modes.

Since in this book equilibrium is such a fundamental concept in terms of sustainable transportation networks and since variational inequality theory is one of the basic ways in which to study such problems I now, for completeness, also give variational inequality formulations of the traffic network equilibrium conditions (2.15). These formulations are presented without proof (for derivations, see Smith 1979 and Dafermos 1980, as well as Florian and Hearn 1995 and the book by Nagurney 1999a). Moreover, appropriate variational inequalities for the specific models are derived later in this book.

First, the definition of a variational inequality problem is given (see also Appendix B). I then give both the path flow formulation as well as the link load formulation for the traffic network equilibrium conditions.

Specifically, the variational inequality problem (finite-dimensional) is defined as follows:

Definition 2.1 (Variational Inequality Problem)
The finite-dimensional variational inequality problem, VI$(F, \mathcal{K})$, *is to determine a vector* $X^* \in \mathcal{K}$ *such that*

$$\langle F(X^*)^T, X - X^* \rangle \geq 0, \quad \forall X \in \mathcal{K}, \tag{2.32}$$

where F *is a given continuous function from* $\mathcal{K}$ *to* R^N, $\mathcal{K}$ *is a given closed convex set, and* $\langle \cdot, \cdot \rangle$ *denotes the inner product in* R^N.

Variational inequality (2.32) is referred to as being in *standard form*. Hence, for a given problem, typically an *equilibrium* problem, one must determine the function F that enters the variational inequality problem, the vector of variables X, as well as the feasible set $\mathcal{K}$.

The variational inequality problem contains, as special cases, such well-known problems as systems of equations, optimization problems (see Appendices A and B), and complementarity problems. Hence, it is a powerful unifying methodology for equilibrium analysis and computation.

Theorem 2.1 (Variational Inequality Formulation of Traffic Network Equilibrium with Fixed Demands – Path Flow Version)
A vector $x^* \in K^1$ is a traffic equilibrium path flow pattern, that is, it satisfies equilibrium conditions (2.15) if and only if it satisfies the variational inequality problem:

$$\sum_{w\in W}\sum_{p\in P_w} C_p(x^*)\times(x-x^*)\geq 0, \quad \forall x\in K^1, \tag{2.33}$$

or, in vector form:

$$\langle C(x^*)^T, x-x^*\rangle \geq 0, \quad \forall x\in K^1, \tag{2.34}$$

where C is the n_P-dimensional column vector of path user travel costs and K^1 is defined as: $K^1 \equiv \{x\geq 0,$ such that (2.17) holds$\}$.

Theorem 2.2 (Variational Inequality Formulation of Traffic Network Equilibrium with Fixed Demands – Link Load Version)
A vector $f^* \in K^2$ is a traffic equilibrium link load pattern if and only if it satisfies the variational inequality problem:

$$\sum_{a\in L} c_a(f^*)\times(f_a-f_a^*)\geq 0, \quad \forall f\in K^2, \tag{2.35}$$

or, in vector form:

$$\langle c(f^*)^T, f-f^*\rangle \geq 0, \quad \forall f\in K^2, \tag{2.36}$$

where c is the n-dimensional column vector of link user travel costs and K^2 is defined as: $K^2 \equiv \{f \mid$ there exists an $x\geq 0$ and satisfying (2.17) and (2.18)$\}$.

Note that one may put variational inequality (2.34) in standard form (2.32) by letting $F\equiv C$, $X\equiv x$, and $\mathcal{K}\equiv K^1$. Also, one may put variational inequality (2.36) in standard form where now $F\equiv c$, $X\equiv f$, and $\mathcal{K}\equiv K^2$.

2.2.4 Variational Inequality Formulations of Elastic Demand Problems

In this subsection, the general traffic network equilibrium model with elastic travel demands due to Dafermos (1982) is recalled. Specifically, it is assumed that now one has associated with each O/D pair w in the transportation network a travel disutility λ_w, where here the general case is considered in which the travel disutility may depend upon the entire vector of travel demands, which are no longer fixed, but are now variables, that is,

$$\lambda_w = \lambda_w(d), \quad \forall w \in W, \tag{2.37}$$

where d is the J-dimensional column vector of the travel demands.

The notation, otherwise, is as described in Section 2.1, except that here I also consider user link travel cost functions which are general, that is, of the form (2.28). The conservation of flow equations (see also (2.1) and (2.2)), in turn, are given by

$$f_a = \sum_{p \in P} x_p \delta_{ap}, \quad \forall a \in L, \tag{2.38}$$

$$d_w = \sum_{p \in P_w} x_p, \quad \forall w \in W, \tag{2.39}$$

$$x_p \geq 0, \quad \forall p \in P. \tag{2.40}$$

Hence, in the elastic travel demand case, the travel demands in expression (2.39) are now variables and no longer given, as was the case for the fixed travel demand expression in (2.2).

Traffic Network Equilibrium Conditions in the Case of Elastic Travel Demand

The traffic network equilibrium conditions (see also (2.15)) now take on in the elastic travel demand case the following form: For every O/D pair $w \in W$, and each path $p \in P_w$, a vector of path flows and travel demands (x^*, d^*) satisfying (2.39)–(2.40) (which induces a link load pattern f^* through (2.38)) is a traffic network equilibrium pattern if it satisfies:

$$C_p(x^*) \begin{cases} = \lambda_w(d^*), & \text{if} \quad x_p^* > 0 \\ \geq \lambda_w(d^*), & \text{if} \quad x_p^* = 0. \end{cases} \tag{2.41}$$

Equilibrium conditions (2.41) state that the travel costs on used paths for each O/D pair are equal and minimal and equal to the travel disutility associated with that O/D pair. Travel costs on unutilized paths can exceed the travel disutility.

In the next two theorems, both the path flow version and the link load version of the variational inequality formulations of the traffic network equilibrium conditions (2.41) are presented. These are analogues of the formulations (2.33) and (2.34), and (2.35) and (2.36), respectively, for the fixed demand model.

Theorem 2.3 (Variational Inequality Formulation of Traffic Network Equilibrium with Elastic Demands – Path Flow Version)
A vector $(x^*, d^*) \in K^3$ is a traffic equilibrium path flow pattern, that is, it satisfies equilibrium conditions (2.41) if and only if it satisfies the variational inequality problem:

$$\sum_{w \in W} \sum_{p \in P_w} C_p(x^*) \times (x - x^*) - \sum_{w \in W} \lambda_w(d^*) \times (d_w - d_w^*) \geq 0, \quad \forall (x, d) \in K^3, \tag{2.42}$$

or, in vector form:

$$\langle C(x^*)^T, x - x^* \rangle - \langle \lambda(d^*)^T, d - d^* \rangle \geq 0, \quad \forall (x, d) \in K^3, \tag{2.43}$$

where λ is the J-dimensional vector of travel disutilities and K^3 is defined as: $K^3 \equiv \{x \geq 0,$ such that (2.39) holds$\}$.

Theorem 2.4 (Variational Inequality Formulation of Traffic Network Equilibrium with Elastic Demands – Link Load Version)
A vector $(f^*, d^*) \in K^4$ is a traffic equilibrium link load pattern if and only if it satisfies the variational inequality problem:

$$\sum_{a \in L} c_a(f^*) \times (f_a - f_a^*) - \sum_{w \in W} \lambda_w(d^*) \times (d_w - d_w^*) \geq 0, \quad \forall (f, d) \in K^4, \tag{2.44}$$

or, in vector form:

$$\langle c(f^*)^T, f - f^* \rangle - \langle \lambda(d^*)^T, d - d^* \rangle \geq 0, \quad \forall (f, d) \in K^4, \tag{2.45}$$

where $K^4 \equiv \{(f, d),$ such that there exists an $x \geq 0$ satisfying (2.38), (2.39)$\}$

Note that, under a symmetry assumption on the travel disutility functions, in addition to such an assumption on the user link travel cost functions, one can obtain (see Beckmann, McGuire, and Winsten 1956) an optimization reformulation of the traffic network equilibrium conditions (2.41), which in the case of separable user link cost functions and travel disutility functions takes is given by:

$$\text{Minimize} \quad \sum_{a \in L} \int_0^{f_a} c_a(x)dx - \sum_{w \in W} \int_0^{d_w} \lambda_w(y)dy \tag{2.46}$$

subject to: (2.38)–(2.40).

I now present an example of an elastic demand traffic network equilibrium problem.

Example 2.2

Consider the network depicted in Figure 2.4 in which there are three nodes: 1, 2, 3; three links: a, b, c; and a single O/D pair $w_1 = (1, 3)$. Let path $p_1 = (a, c)$ and path $p_2 = (b, c)$.

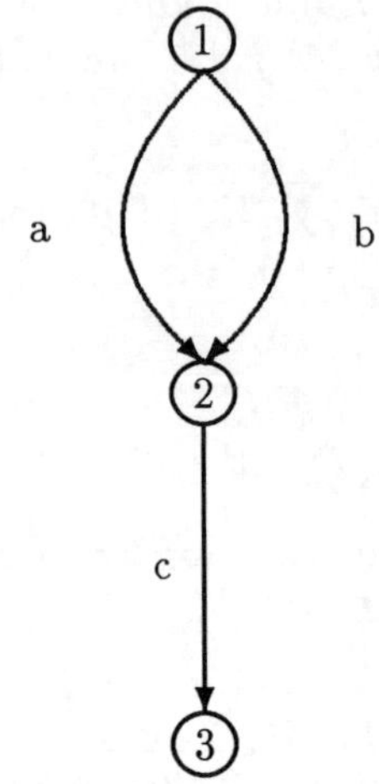

Fig. 2.4. An elastic demand example

Assume that the user link travel cost functions are:

$$c_a(f) = 5f_a + 2f_b + 5, \quad c_b(f) = 7f_b + f_a + 5, \quad c_c(f) = 3f_c + f_a + f_b + 7,$$

and the travel disutility is:

$$\lambda_{w_1}(d_{w_1}) = -2d_{w_1} + 99.$$

The U-O flow and demand pattern that satisfies equilibrium conditions (2.41) is:

$$x^*_{p_1} = 5, \quad x^*_{p_2} = 4,$$
$$d^*_{w_1} = 9,$$

with associated link load pattern:

$$f^*_a = 5, \quad f^*_b = 4, \quad f^*_c = 9.$$

The incurred user travel costs on the paths are:

$$C_{p_1} = C_{p_2} = 81,$$

which is precisely the value of the travel disutility λ_{w_1}. Hence, this flow and demand pattern satisfies equilibrium conditions (2.41).

2.3 Transportation and the Environment

Road pricing as a concept, even more than seventy-five years after Pigou (1920) and more than thirty-five years after the work of Walters (1961) and Vickrey (1963), is still used principally in regards to congestion problems. Surveys of road pricing include the works of Morrison (1986), Johansson and Mattsson (1995), and Verhoef (1996) (see also Arnott et al. 1994). Recently, however, there has been a growing interest in exploring road pricing not only as a tool for congestion management but also as a tool for environmental management since there has occurred an increase in environmental awareness both on the part of citizens as well as government officials. Indeed, the interest in utilizing road pricing as a policy instrument is now being investigated in such areas as the reduction of environmental effects including global warming, as well as noise abatement, and accident reduction (see Verhoef 1996; Button and Verhoef 1998, and the references therein).

Moreover, governments have introduced a variety of legislation that has spurred the further development of policy instruments aimed at pollution reduction. In 1955, the United States Congress passed legislation in order to tackle the policy problem of increasingly polluted air (cf. Clean Air Act 1955). However, the legislation was primarily focused on supporting research into air quality issues and the next decade and a half, although filled with legislative activity, did not yield much practical impact. The Clean Air Act Amendments of 1970 signaled a new thrust in the United States, with the federal government playing a more significant role. This led to the creation of the United States Environmental Protection Agency (EPA) with the mission of controlling the emission of pollutants into the air.

The Clean Air Act and, in particular, its amendments (cf. CAAA 1990, US Department of Transportation 1992a) addresses two classes of pollutants – *criteria* pollutants and *hazardous* pollutants. The seven criteria pollutants are: sulfur dioxide, carbon monoxide, nitrogen oxides, hydrocarbons, ozone, lead, and total suspended particulates. These pollutants are commonly found in most parts of the world and are regarded to be dangerous in high concentrations. The seven hazardous pollutants listed by the EPA in the United States are: asbestos, beryllium, mercury, arsenic, vinyl chloride, benzene, and radionuclides. Even limited exposure to these pollutants can be harmful.

The EPA has set legal standards, known as *ambient air quality standards*, for each criteria pollutant. The *primary standard* has the earliest deadline for compliance and is set for each pollutant separately. The *secondary standard* governs other aspects such as aesthetics and, hence, only two pollutants, sulfur dioxide and total suspended particulates, have separate secondary standards.

In the United States, hence, the 1990 Clean Air Act Amendments (cf. US DOT 1992a) and the 1991 Intermodal Surface Transportation Efficiency Act (US DOT 1992b) have stimulated a growing interest in the development, analysis, and application of environmental transportation policies.

Table 2.3. Some policy instruments for regulating externalities due to transportation studied in this book

Demand-side oriented policies	Supply-side oriented policies
• Marginal cost pricing • Emissions pricing • Tradable pollution permits • Mode switching	• Technology policies • Infrastructure (network design) policies

Various transportation control measures have also been applied around the globe in such cities as Athens, Amsterdam, Barcelona, and Munich, as well as urban road pricing, as already mentioned in Section 2.2, in Singapore (see, e.g., Jones and Hervik 1992; Goddard 1997; *The Economist* 1997). It is becoming increasingly evident that transportation policies to reduce pollution must be coupled with congestion reduction. Indeed, this point has been reiterated by many studies (cf. Lawson et al. 1990; Ingalls 1989).

2.3.1 Environmental Policy Instruments

The interest in pollution reduction, in general, has given rise to a large body of literature in the field of environmental economics and in the regulation of externalities. Indeed, the optimal solution from a firm's or other pollution source's perspective does not coincide, typically, with the optimal solution from society's point of view. In this subsection, I discuss policy instruments which have had a thorough investigation in the literature and which have also been implemented in practice. For a survey on environmental economics, see Cropper and Oates (1992).

The emphasis here is on economic-incentive policy instruments which are fundamental to the models developed and studied in this book. Table 2.3 summarizes some of the policy instruments for regulating externalities that are studied in this book.

In particular, in this subsection, the focus is on two fundamental economic policy instruments, that is, Pigouvian taxes and subsidies, as well as marketable pollution permits. Such economic-incentive approaches to environmental policy and decision-making are to be contrasted with an earlier common approach to environmental regulation known as *command and control*, which was lacking in positive incentives. The command and control aspect set the emission standards for the sources, specified how the pollution was to be reduced, for example, through the adoption of particular technologies, and no trading of pollution allowances was permitted.

Indeed, historically, most pollution control has been in the form of a command and control approach in the form of regulation. However, it is now being recognized that such an approach with the regulations being designed with little or no regard for the cost of abatement has not been successful. For example, a joint report by the US Department of Transportation and the Environmental Protection Agency in 1993 noted that traditional transportation control measures aimed at decreasing motor vehicle trips, the number of vehicle miles traveled, and congestion by encouraging off-peak travel or the use of alternative transportation modes have "not generated significant air quality benefits." The same report suggests that "economic-market-based" transportation control measures and incentives such as congestion pricing and emission charges which affect the demand for travel may be more promising for emissions reduction.

2.3.1.1 Taxes and Subsidies

Environmental taxes such as those charged to polluters are a form of economic-incentive policy instrument in that something negative, in the form of pollution, for example, is taxed in order to provide an incentive for it to be reduced. A Pigouvian or a per-unit tax on emissions set equal to marginal social damage at the optimal level of emissions, is a particular form of pollution tax and aims to internalize the external costs imposed by the polluting source onto the victims (cf. Baumol and Oates 1988). Although the per-unit tax was proposed in the early twentieth century by Pigou (1920), these instruments of policy control are a *new* concept in pollution control and the status quo very often is inclined to resist taxes.

In several chapters of this book, I propose pricing policies, which can be interpreted as Pigouvian taxes, in the context of congested urban transportation networks, in which environmental quality standards are also imposed. Button and Verhoef (1998) provide, in their edited volume, a collection of papers that examine Pigouvian taxes, as well as other policies under the topic of road pricing.

Subsidies, on the other hand, may be granted based on the amount of pollution that is reduced. Under this approach, rather than coercing the polluters to pay a tax for exceeding a standard, the polluters are encouraged to reduce pollution, for example, by installing pollution-abatement technologies. Of course, subsidies may be used in conjunction with taxes.

2.3.1.2 Marketable Pollution Permits

The idea of pollution permits can be traced to Crocker (1966), who focused on air pollution permits, and Dales (1968), whose work was on water permits. In this policy setting, the regulatory agency specifies a certain level of pollutants, and then issues permits, with the trading of permits triggering this system.

The marketability of permits is the main appeal of this approach. First, this approach is cost-effective since the polluter, who faces higher pollution-abatement costs, may be able to buy additional permits in order to cover the excess emissions, whereas another polluter, who faces lower abatement costs, may be able to sell the excess permits in the market. In the case where there are new entrants in the market, in order that the same environmental standard is maintained, the new entrants may buy permits or invest in technologies aimed at limiting emissions. The regulatory agency can potentially release more permits into the market or buy back some permits, depending upon the level of environmental quality desired.

Montgomery (1972) provided the rigorous theoretical foundations of marketable pollution permits and proposed two systems: a system of "pollution licenses" that defines allowable pollution concentrations at a set of receptor points and a system of "emission licenses" that confers the right to emit pollutants at a certain rate at the sources. The former system is known as the ambient-based permit system (APS), whereas the latter is known as the emission-based permit system (EPS). Further, he established that markets can attain equilibrium that achieves the externally set environmental quality standards. He also explicitly recognized the spatial nature of pollution dispersion and introduced a diffusion matrix. Montgomery (1972) focused on *stationary* sources of pollution, that is, those which are fixed in location, as opposed to *mobile* sources of emissions, such as motor vehicles.

Nagurney and Dhanda (1996) considered both perfectly competitive firms as well as oligopolistic firms and developed variational inequality-based models to study and determine the equilibrium problems. Nagurney, Dhanda, and Stranlund (1997) subsequently proposed a multiproduct, multipollutant, perfectly competitive firm model with pollution permits. Nagurney and Dhanda (1997a) devised a variational inequality framework for the study of multiproduct, multipollutant, oligopolistic firms in the presence of marketable pollution permits with opportunities for investment in production technology and/or emission/abatement technology. Nagurney and Dhanda (1997b) then addressed compliance versus noncompliance behavior in oligopolistic markets, again, with ambient-based pollution permits. Nagurney and Dhanda (1997c), in turn, considered oligopolistic markets and pollution permits in the presence of transaction costs.

The system of marketable pollution permits was given credibility as an economic incentive-based environmental regulation approach to address pollution by Title IV of the 1990 amendments to the Clean Air Act (CAAA). Under Title IV, for example, electricity generating facilities can trade allowances or permits for the emissions of sulfur dioxide.

The principal appeal of the economic incentive approach versus the traditional command and control approach is that the former system encourages firms to employ pollution control technologies. For example, a firm participating in a permit market may install emission reducing technologies, lower its level of emissions, and sell the excess entitlements of permits for revenue. For a detailed discussion of other advantages of permits, see Tietenberg (1985), Baumol and Oates (1988), and Pearce and Turner (1990).

Nagurney, Ramanujam, and Dhanda (1998) were the first to rigorously

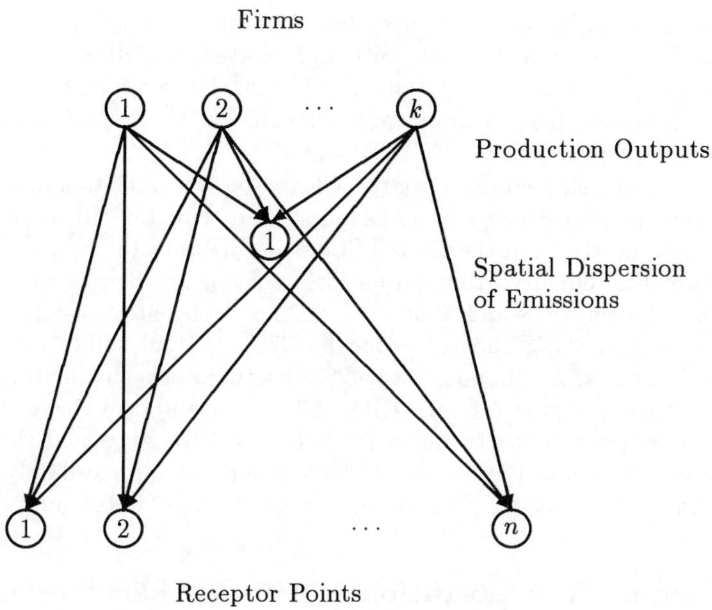

Fig. 2.5. Spatial dispersion of emissions due to firms

construct a system of pollution permits for congested transportation networks. They also considered the issue of compliance versus noncompliance. The book by Dhanda, Nagurney, and Ramanujam (1999) describes a variety of economic-incentive-base approaches for emission abatement through the prism of *environmental networks*, which provide a graphical and, hence, visual approach to the study of economic activity and its environmental affects. In Figure 2.5, a graphical depiction of pollution dispersion by firms is presented in a network format. In this system, there are k firms, which produce a single commodity, and n receptor points for the single pollutant emissions. For further details, see Dhanda, Nagurney, and Ramanujam (1999). What is important to note is that the pollution emitted by firms may affect locations distinct from those where the firms are located and also distinct from where the consumers are located.

A practical application of tradable permits in transportation was the vehicle quota system in Singapore (Koh and Lee 1994). Another example of a tradable permit system related to transportation is the lead trading program in the United States, which was designed to reduce lead in large refineries (Hahn 1989). Button (1993) considers the United States Corporate Average Fuel Economy Standards (CAFE) program, introduced in 1975, as another example of tradable permits in the transportation sector, albeit one in which the trading is internal to a firm, rather than external. Goddard (1997) describes the applicability of a permit system for transportation in the Mexico City area. *Feebates*, an alternative, although related, incentive approach for pollution reduction, denotes a system of fees and rebates applied to new cars and trucks based on their emission rates, fuel efficiency, or other characteristics (see Train, Davis, and Levine 1997).

It is important to mention that the Clean Air Act and its amendments have resulted in major progress in terms of the reduction in ambient air pollution concentrations in the United States, as documented by the Council on Environmental Quality (1991). Indeed, according to their report, during the period between 1978 and 1990, the ambient concentration of nitrogen oxides declined by 24%, that of ozone by 27%, that of sulfur dioxide by 39%, and that of carbon monoxide by 42%. Furthermore, an Environmental Protection Agency report (cf. US EPA 1997) analyzing the Clean Air Act and its amendments in the two decades following 1970 suggested that each dollar of compliance cost is estimated to have generated approximately $15.60 in such areas as agricultural production, property values, and human health.

2.4 Unique Transportation Network Characteristics

A transportation network may be viewed as an economic system in which the demand side corresponds to potential travelers or consumers of the network, whereas the supply side is represented by the network itself, with incurred prices corresponding to the travel costs. As already noted, two negative externalities associated with such networks include both congestion and pollution.

Presently, almost all urban regions in the United States are faced with inducing major changes in current transportation choices in order to achieve the objectives of reducing congestion and improving air quality. In Europe, on the other hand, the European Commission's Green Paper on *Fair and Efficient Pricing* (Commission of the European Communities 1996) reflects the current reassessment of transportation policy and states that "transport policy is at a crossroads." Indeed, since it has become increasingly clear that enhanced emission control technologies may not be sufficient to achieve air quality goals, interest in how policies can affect the utilization of transportation networks and the associated negative effects has increased.

Since transportation networks are complex systems in which individuals interact typically unilaterally but, nevertheless, affect the cost and travel time of others, policies which fail to incorporate the behavior of the users of the system may lead to contrary results from that intended. Indeed, this possibility has been increasingly noted. For example, Hall (1995), in discussing a class of transportation policies known as transport control measures (TCMs), has noted that better understanding of actual behavior coupled with new scientific and technical observations of how emissions actually relate to patterns of vehicle use has challenged the conventional wisdom that reduced vehicle miles travelled and/or improved traffic flow means less congestion and cleaner

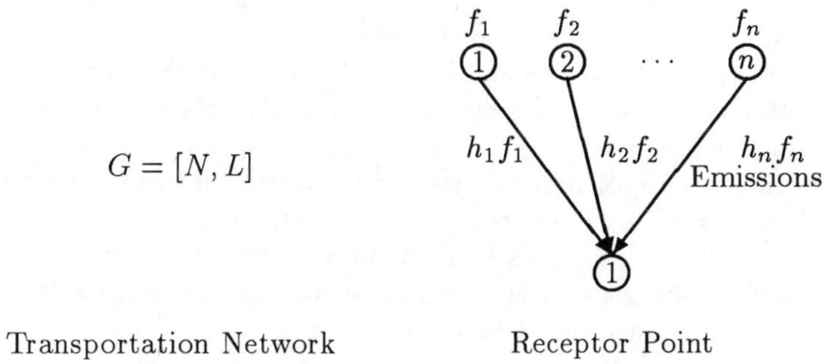

Fig. 2.6. Spatial dispersion of vehicular emissions

air. TCMs are a broad grouping of diverse alternatives that seeks to modify light-duty vehicle use either by increasing the cost in terms of money or time, or by providing improved, that is, lower, cost or more convenient, transportation alternatives.

Sevigny (1998) notes that her design of an emission tax for automobiles for pollution control could, in fact, have the perverse consequence of increasing vehicle emissions by encouraging more short trips to reduce taxable vehicle miles traveled. Further, she notes that a trip generation model, which would also account for trip cost (and, hence, require the network topology and travel cost structure) would be a useful addition to her policy modeling schema. Indeed, as regards transportation policies, their effectiveness can only be determined when the influence on human behavior (and the interaction between fuel/vehicle technology, if any) is also calculated.

A Transportation Research Board (1995) study examined the effect of highway capacity improvement on motor vehicle travel, energy use, and emissions and found that the relationships among them are highly complex because of secondary effects on travel demand. Another Transportation Research Board (1997) report focused on transportation in the context of a sustainable environment and noted that there is a lack of and a need for policy research on this topic.

In this book, I explicitly develop policy models for emission and/or congestion abatement, which determine flows on the transportation network endogenously, operating under a particular behavioral assumption. The key in the calculation of the mobile source emission estimates (see Figure 2.6) is the relationship that the volume of emissions is equal to the product of a composite emission factor times the vehicular activity at the link levels (cf. DeCorla-Souza et al. 1995), which is also herein used in the technical analyses. The emission factor may be interpreted as a term in the diffusion matrix introduced by Montgomery (1972) in his marketable pollution permit work. Indeed, in Figure 2.6, the spatial dispersion of vehicular emissions is represented as a network where the flow on the links are then converted into emissions (after multiplication by an emission factor on each link). In this case, there is a single receptor point associated with the emissions. On the other hand, in the case of multiple receptor points, one would need to add additional lower nodes to the network on the right of the figure and to also draw links from the upper nodes to those new nodes. Note that in the case of transportation networks, in contrast to firms, the emissions are now due to mobile rather than stationary sources.

3 Emission Paradoxes in Transportation Networks

In this chapter, I identify several distinct paradoxical phenomena that can occur in congested urban transportation networks as regards the total emissions generated. In particular, I show that so-called "improvements" to the transportation network may actually have an opposite effect, that is, they may induce increases in the total emissions generated.

The emission paradoxes are presented through specific illustrative examples and reinforce the fundamental importance of the structure of the transportation networks themselves as well as that of the travelers' behavior on the networks in the study and analysis of environmental issues. Hence, in order to be able to appropriately evaluate the effects of environmental policies aimed at pollution reduction one must consider such critical network parameters as: the network topology, the user travel cost structure, the travel demand structure, and the behavior of the travelers on the network, in addition to such environmental factors as emissions. Indeed, such network constructs must be taken into consideration in any policy system aimed at the reduction of emissions due to motor vehicles.

In particular, I illustrate, through specific examples, the following counterintuitive phenomena:

1. the addition of a road may result in an increase in total emissions with no change in travel demand;
2. a decrease in the travel demand may result in an increase in total emissions;
3. the improvement of a road in terms of travel cost reduction may result in an increase in total emissions without a change in the travel demand;
4. a transfer of travel demand from a mode with higher total emissions to a mode with lower total emissions on a network may result in an increase in the total emissions; and
5. making travel less attractive between an origin/destination pair as revealed through its travel disutility function may result in an increase in total

Table 3.1. Summary of emission paradoxes examples

Paradox 1	
• Addition of road ⇒ with no change in demand	total emissions can ↑
Paradox 2	
• A decrease in travel demand ⇒	total emissions can ↑
Paradox 3	
• A road improvement⇒ with no change in demand	total emissions can ↑
Paradox 4	
• A mode transfer from a ⇒ higher emitting mode to a lower one	total emissions can ↑
Paradox 5	
• Making travel less attractive ⇒ for an O/D pair	total emissions can ↑

emissions.

In Table 3.1, a summary of the emission paradoxes is provided.

Note that there is a growing body of literature based, in part, on models developed by the National Environmental Protection Agency (NEPA), that deals with the conversion of traffic data into an account of the pollutants emitted. The key in the estimation of air pollution due to vehicular emissions is the relationship that the volume of emissions is equal to the product of an emission factor and the vehicle activity (or link load) (cf. DeCorla-Souza et al. 1995; Anderson et al. 1996; and Allen 1996).

Specifically, in this book, the emissions from vehicles traveling on different links on paths between origin/destination pairs are assumed to pollute at a certain receptor point. Let h_a denote the emission factor on link $a \in L$, which is assumed to be given for all links; such emission factors are utilized in modeling efforts throughout this book. For example, as noted in DeCorla-Souza et al. (1995), emission factors vary depending on several characteristic travel activities, such as: vehicle type and age mix, vehicle speed, trip length distribution, operating mode, and ambient temperature. In Table 3.2, a listing of variables affecting vehicular emissions is provided.

Hence, if multiple modes, multiple classes of users of the transportation system, and/or multiple pollutants are to be considered, then the framework developed here is still applicable, but one needs to expand the notation accordingly.

This chapter is organized as follows. In Section 3.1, three examples of fixed travel demand networks with a single mode of transportation are presented, which illustrate, respectively, the occurrence of counterintuitive phenomena

Table 3.2. Variables affecting vehicular emissions

Source: Compiled by Hall (1995)

• Age distribution of vehicular fleet
• Number of miles each age cohort is driven
• Average emissions by cohort
• Rate of decay of emissions controls
• Degree of tampering
• Inspection and maintenance effectiveness
• Ambient temperature
• Driving speed
• Frequency of open-loop (off-cycle) operation
• Number of cold starts
• Idling time
• Type of fuel utilized

1 through 3 above. In Section 3.2, I then turn to multimodal networks with fixed travel demands and reveal through a specific example the occurrence of phenomenon 4. Finally, in Section 3.3, I again consider single modal traffic networks, but now with elastic travel demands, and illustrate through an example the occurrence of phenomenon 5. I assume, in this chapter, that travelers operate in a user-optimizing (U-O) manner, according to the principles laid out in Chapter 2.

3.1 Paradoxes in Single Modal, Fixed Demand Networks

In this section, I demonstrate, through three network examples, distinct counterintuitive phenomena which can occur as regards the total emissions generated. The models are single modal, fixed, travel demand models in which it is assumed that travelers act independently in a user-optimized fashion as described in Chapter 2. I assume here that the emission factors associated with the links are given.

3.1.1 Paradox 1

In this subsection, I identify, through a specific transportation network example, that the addition of a link to a network may result in an increase in the total emissions with no change in the travel demand. This example may be viewed as an analogue of the Braess (1968) Paradox in which the addition of a road makes all travelers worse off in terms of the travel cost associated with traveling from their origin to their destination. In the case of emissions,

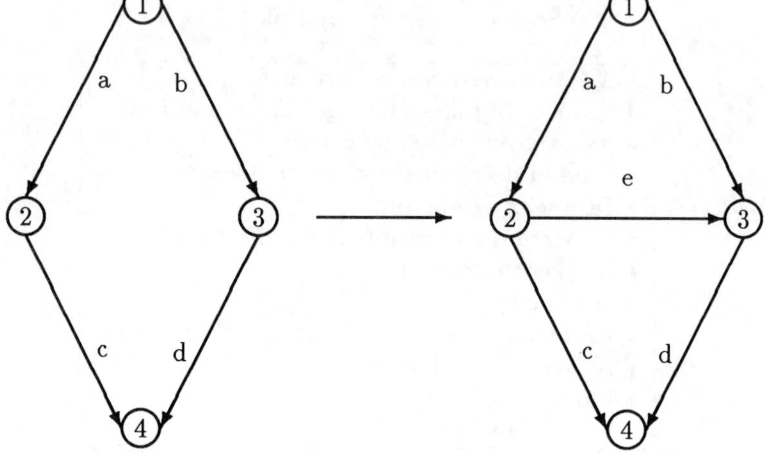

Fig. 3.1. Network topology for Paradox 1: Braess network

however, I show that if one adds a road to a network then all the travelers may be worse off not only in terms of their travel cost but the total emissions may also increase without any change in the travel demand.

For completeness, I first recall the Braess example and then show that the paradox carries through also in terms of emissions. For easy reference, see the two networks depicted in Figure 3.1.

Assume a network as the first network depicted in Figure 3.1 in which there are four nodes: 1, 2, 3, 4; four links: a, b, c, d, and a single O/D pair $w_1 = (1,4)$. There are, hence, two paths available to travelers between this O/D pair: $p_1 = (a,c)$ and $p_2 = (b,d)$.

The user link travel cost functions are:

$$c_a(f_a) = 10f_a, \quad c_b(f_b) = f_b + 50, \quad c_c(f_c) = f_c + 50, \quad c_d(f_d) = 10f_d,$$

and the fixed travel demand $d_{w_1} = 6$.

It is easy to verify (see also (2.15)) that the equilibrium path flows are:

$$x^*_{p_1} = 3, \quad x^*_{p_2} = 3,$$

the equilibrium link loads are:

$$f^*_a = 3, \quad f^*_b = 3, \quad f^*_c = 3, \quad f^*_d = 3,$$

with associated equilibrium user path travel costs:

$$C_{p_1} = 83, \quad C_{p_2} = 83.$$

Assume now that the emission factors on the links are: $h_a = h_b = h_c = h_d = 0.1$. The total emissions generated are, hence, equal to: $h_a f_a^* + h_b f_b^* + h_c f_c^* + h_d f_d^*$=0.3 + 0.3 + 0.3 + 0.3=1.2.

Suppose now that, as depicted in Figure 3.1, a new link e, joining node 2 to node 3, is added to the original network, with user cost $c_e(f_e) = f_e + 10$. The addition of this link creates a new path $p_3 = (a, e, d)$ that is available to the travelers. The travel demand d_{w_1} remains at 6 units of flow. Note that the original flow distribution pattern with path flows given by: $x_{p_1} = 3$ and $x_{p_2} = 3$ is no longer an equilibrium pattern, since at this level of flow the cost on path p_3, $C_{p_3} = 70$. Hence, users from paths p_1 and p_2 would switch to path p_3.

The equilibrium flow pattern on the new network is:

$$x_{p_1}^* = 2, \quad x_{p_2}^* = 2, \quad x_{p_3}^* = 2,$$

with equilibrium link loads:

$$f_a^* = 4, \quad f_b^* = 2, \quad f_c^* = 2, \quad f_d^* = 4, \quad f_e^* = 2,$$

and with associated equilibrium path travel costs:

$$C_{p_1} = 92, \quad C_{p_2} = 92.$$

Note that the travel cost increased for every user of the network from 83 to 92! Indeed, one can verify that *any* reallocation of the path flows would yield a higher travel cost on a path and, hence, this flow pattern is user-optimized.

Assume now that the emission factor on the new link e is $h_e = 0.1$. Indeed, the total emissions generated in the new network without any change in the travel demand are now equal to $h_a f_a^* + h_b f_b^* + h_c f_c^* + h_d f_d^* + h_e f_e^* =$ 0.4 + 0.2 + 0.2 + 0.4 + 0.2= 1.4, which is greater than the total generated in the original network. Hence, the addition of the new road makes everyone worse off in terms of both travel cost and the total emissions generated.

3.1.2 Paradox 2

In this subsection, I demonstrate, through another transportation network example, that a decrease in travel demand associated with an origin/destination pair may result in an increase in emissions.

Consider the transportation network depicted in Figure 3.2, consisting of three nodes: 1, 2, 3, and three links: a, b, c.

There are two origin/destination pairs: $w_1 = (1, 2)$ and $w_2 = (1, 3)$. The path connecting O/D pair w_1, p_1, consists of the single link a. The paths connecting O/D pair w_2 are: $p_2 = (a, c)$ and $p_3 = b$. The travel demands in the original problem are: $d_{w_1} = 1$ and $d_{w_2} = 2$.

The user link travel cost functions are:

$$c_a(f_a) = f_a + 1, \quad c_b(f_b) = f_b + 4, \quad c_c(f_c) = f_c + 1.$$

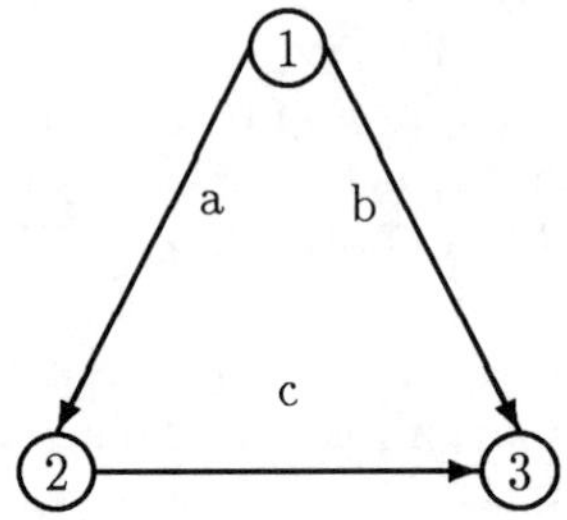

Fig. 3.2. Network topology for Paradox 2

The emission factors on the links are: $h_a = 0.01$, $h_b = 0.01$, and $h_c = 0.5$. The traffic equilibrium path flow pattern is:

$$x^*_{p_1} = 1; \quad x^*_{p_2} = 1, \quad x^*_{p_3} = 1,$$

with induced link load pattern:

$$f^*_a = 2, \quad f^*_b = f^*_c = 1.$$

The path travel costs are: For O/D pair w_1: $C_{p_1} = 3$, and for O/D pair w_2: $C_{p_2} = C_{p_3} = 5$.

The total emissions generated are equal to: $h_a f^*_a + h_b f^*_b + h_c f^*_c = .02 + .01 + .5 = .53$.

Consider now a decrease in travel demand associated with O/D pair w_1 with the new demand $d_{w_1} = 0.5$ and all other data remain the same.

The new traffic equilibrium path flow pattern is:

$$x^*_{p_1} = 0.5, \quad x^*_{p_2} = 1.6666..., \quad x^*_{p_3} = 0.833...,$$

with induced equilibrium link load pattern:

$$f^*_a = 1.5666..., \quad f^*_b = 0.833..., \quad f^*_c = 1.166...$$

The new path travel costs are: For O/D pair w_1: $C_{p_1} = 2.666...$, and for O/D pair w_2: $C_{p_2} = C_{p_3} = 4.833...$.

The total emissions now generated by the new equilibrium pattern are equal to: $h_a f^*_a + h_b f^*_b + h_c f^*_c = 0.0166... + 0.00833... + 0.583 = 0.6079...$.

Hence, the total emissions have increased from 0.53 to 0.6079... even though the travel demand has decreased. Note that the travel cost, however, associated with traveling between each O/D pair has decreased.

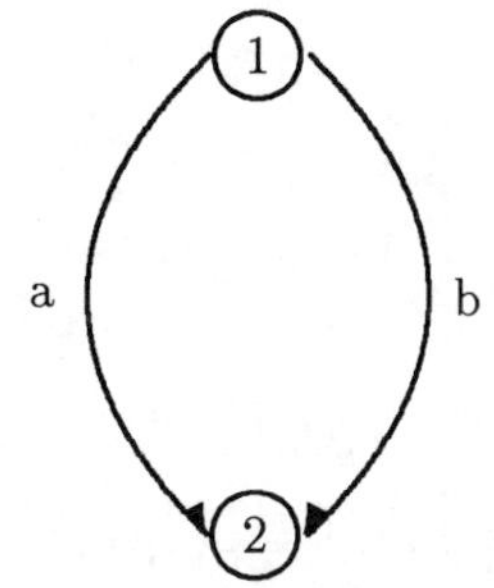

Fig. 3.3. Network topology for Paradox 3

3.1.3 Paradox 3

In the final example in this subsection, I show that an improvement in the cost structure in the network, through the reduction of the user travel cost on a link, may result in an increase in total emissions.

Consider now the transportation network depicted in Figure 3.3 consisting of two nodes: 1, 2, and two links: a, b.

The user link travel cost functions are given by:

$$c_a(f_a) = f_a + 5, \quad c_b(f_b) = f_b + 9.$$

There is a single origin/destination pair $w_1 = (1, 2)$ with an associated travel demand $d_{w_1} = 6$. There are two paths: $p_1 = a$ and $p_2 = b$.

The emission factors are: $h_a = 0.5$ and $h_b = 0.4$.

The traffic equilibrium path flow pattern is:

$$x^*_{p_1} = 5, \quad x^*_{p_2} = 1,$$

which induces the equilibrium link load pattern:

$$f^*_a = 5, \quad f^*_b = 1,$$

and travel costs on the paths:

$$C_{p_1} = C_{p_2} = 10.$$

The total emissions generated are, hence, equal to: $h_a f^*_a + h_b f^*_b = 2.5 + 0.4 = 2.9$.

Consider now the following improvement in the cost structure, which may represent, for example, a repaving of the road or link a. Let the new cost function on link a be given by:

$$c_a(f_a) = f_a + 4.$$

Assume that all the other data are as previously described for this example.

The new traffic equilibrium path flow pattern is:

$$x^*_{p_1} = 5.5, \quad x^*_{p_2} = 0.5,$$

with induced equilibrium link load pattern:

$$f^*_a = 5.5, \quad f^*_b = 0.5.$$

The new user travel costs on the paths are:

$$C_{p_1} = C_{p_2} = 9.5.$$

The total emissions generated by the new equilibrium flow pattern are equal to: $h_a f^*_a + h_b f^*_b = 2.75 + 0.20 = 2.95$. Hence, with no change in travel demand, an improvement in a road resulted in an increase in total emissions from 2.9 to 2.95! In this network what occurred was that the travelers switched to the reduced cost path which had a higher emission factor, resulting in an overall increase in emissions.

3.2 A Paradox in Multimodal, Fixed Demand Networks

I now turn to the presentation of a paradox which may occur in multimodal traffic networks with fixed travel demands. Multimodal networks may include such modes as private cars as well as public transit, for example. As in Section 3.1, I assume that the travelers behave in a user-optimized fashion. Of course, the paradoxes that have been presented in Section 3.1 for single modal transportation networks are also relevant in the case of multimodal traffic networks.

3.2.1 Paradox 4

Specifically, I present an example which illustrates the following phenomenon: the reallocation of travelers from a mode with higher total emissions to that of a mode with lower total emissions may result in an increase in the total emissions.

The network topology in the example is identical to that of the network depicted in Figure 3.3 but now there are two modes traveling on the network, rather than a single mode as was the case in the example in Section

3.1.3. Let the superscript of 1 on the demands, flows, costs, and emission factors refer to mode 1 and the superscript of 2 to mode 2. Denote the single origin/destination pair $w_1 = (1,2)$ and let path $p_1 = a$ and path $p_2 = b$. Assume that the travel demands for the modes are given by:

$$d^1_{w_1} = 10, \quad d^2_{w_1} = 5.$$

The user link travel cost functions are:

$$c^1_a(f^1_a) = f^1_a + 5, \quad c^1_b(f^1_b) = f^1_b + 5,$$

$$c^2_a(f^2_a) = f^2_a + 10, \quad c^2_b(f^2_b) = f^2_b + 5.$$

The emission factors associated with the links and modes are:

$$h^1_a = 0.2, \quad h^1_b = 0.2, \quad h^2_a = 0.4, \quad h^2_b = 0.1.$$

The multimodal traffic network equilibrium conditions, which are a generalization of the single modal ones given in (2.15), simply require that the conditions also hold for each mode separately where the conservation of flow equations are also satisfied for each mode individually.

It is easy to verify that the traffic equilibrium pattern is given by:

$$x^{1\ *}_{p_1} = 5, \quad x^{1\ *}_{p_2} = 5, \quad x^{2\ *}_{p_1} = 0, \quad x^{2\ *}_{p_2} = 5,$$

with associated equilibrium link load pattern:

$$f^{1*}_a = 5, \quad f^{1*}_b = 5, \quad f^{2*}_a = 0, \quad f^{2*}_b = 5,$$

and user path travel costs:

$$C^1_{p_1} = C^1_{p_2} = 10, \quad C^2_{p_1} = C^2_{p_2} = 10.$$

The total emissions due to travelers using mode 1 are: $h^1_a f^{1*}_a + h^1_b f^{1*}_b = 1 + 1 = 2$, whereas the total emissions due to travelers using mode 2 are: $h^2_a f^{2*}_a + h^2_b f^{2*}_b = 0 + 0.5 = 0.5$ with the total emissions generated equal to 2.5.

Consider now the transfer of 2.5 units of travel demand from mode 1 to mode 2 (which may correspond, for example, to a reallocation of a subset of travelers by car to public transit) so that the new travel demands are given by:

$$d^1_{w_1} = 7.5, \quad d^2_{w_1} = 7.5.$$

The new traffic equilibrium pattern is then:

$$x^{1\ *}_{p_1} = 3.75, \quad x^{1\ *}_{p_2} = 3.75, \quad x^{2\ *}_{p_1} = 1.25, \quad x^{2\ *}_{p_2} = 6.25,$$

with associated link load pattern:

$$f^{1*}_a = 3.75, \quad f^{1*}_b = 3.75, \quad f^{2*}_a = 1.25, \quad f^{2*}_b = 6.25,$$

and user path travel costs:

$$C^1_{p_1} = C^1_{p_2} = 8.75, \quad C^2_{p_1} = C^2_{p_2} = 11.25.$$

The total emissions are now equal to 2.625, which exceed those prior to the mode transfer.

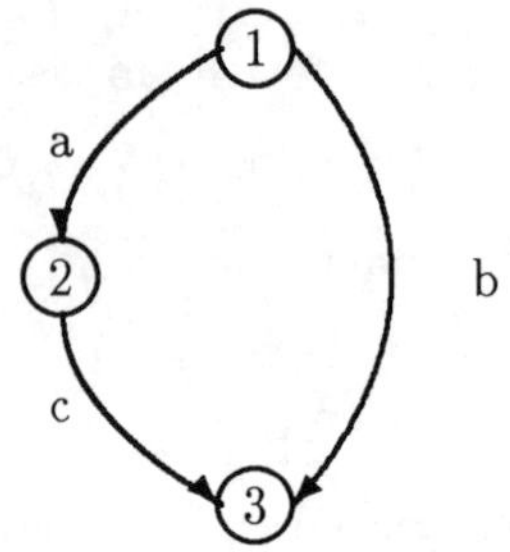

Fig. 3.4. Network topology for Paradox 5

3.3 A Paradox in Elastic Demand Networks

I now turn to elastic demand traffic networks, but in the case of a single mode of transportation, and demonstrate, through an example, that decreasing the attractiveness associated with traveling between an origin/destination pair may result in an increase in total emissions. As in the preceding two sections, it is assumed that travelers behave in a user-optimized manner.

3.3.1 Paradox 5

Consider the transportation network depicted in Figure 3.4 in which there are three nodes: 1, 2, 3, and three links: a, b, c. Assume two origin/destination pairs of travel: $w_1 = (1,2)$ and $w_2 = (1,3)$. The travel disutility functions associated with traveling between the origin/destination pairs are:

$$\lambda_{w_1}(d_{w_1}) = -d_{w_1} + 4, \quad \lambda_{w_2}(d_{w_2}) = -d_{w_2} + 7.$$

The paths are: For O/D pair w_1: $p_1 = a$, and for O/D pair w_2: $p_2 = (a, c)$, and $p_3 = b$.

The user link travel cost functions are:

$$c_a(f_a) = f_a + 1, \quad c_b(f_b) = f_b + 4, \quad c_c(f_c) = f_c + 1.$$

The emission factors are: $h_a = 0.02$, $h_b = 0.02$, and $h_c = 0.6$.

The traffic network equilibrium path flow and demand pattern is:

$$x^*_{p_1} = 1, \quad x^*_{p_2} = 1, \quad x^*_{p_3} = 1,$$

and

$$d^*_{w_1} = 1, \quad d^*_{w_2} = 2,$$

with induced link load pattern:

$$f_a^* = 2, \quad f_b^* = 1, \quad f_c^* = 1.$$

The path travel cost and travel disutility for O/D pair w_1 are:

$$C_{p_1} = \lambda_{w_1} = 3,$$

and for O/D pair w_2:

$$C_{p_2} = C_{p_3} = \lambda_{w_2} = 5.$$

The total emissions generated are: $h_a f_a^* + h_b f_b^* + h_c f_c^* = 0.04 + 0.02 + 0.6 =$ .66.

Now, suppose that the travel disutility associated with O/D pair w_1 is modified as follows:

$$\lambda_{w_1}(d_{w_1}) = -d_{w_1} + 3.5$$

with all other data remaining as above.

The new traffic network equilibrium path flow and demand pattern is then:

$$x_{p_1}^* = 0.6875, \quad x_{p_2}^* = 1.1250, \quad x_{p_3}^* = 0.9375,$$

with

$$d_{w_1}^* = 0.6875, \quad d_{w_2}^* = 2.0625,$$

and new link loads given by:

$$f_a^* = 1.8125, \quad f_b^* = 0.9375, \quad f_c^* = 1.1250.$$

The path travel costs and travel disutilities are: For O/D pair w_1:

$$C_{p_1} = \lambda_{w_1} = 2.8125,$$

and for O/D pair w_2:

$$C_{p_2} = C_{p_3} = \lambda_{w_2} = 4.9375.$$

The total emissions now generated at the new equilibrium flow pattern are equal to 0.73, which exceed the emissions in the network prior to the travel disutility modification.

Hence, in this chapter, it has been demonstrated, through specific numerical examples, that so-called "improvements" to a transportation network may actually result in increases in the total emissions generated. Such counterintuitive phenomena suggest that policy makers must use caution and careful quantitative analysis before any policy implementations for environmental emissions reductions in transportation networks. Indeed, the network topology, the demand structure, the link travel cost structure, as well as the behavior of the travelers on the network must all be incorporated into any environmental modeling schema for transportation network environmental policy analysis.

The paradoxes described in Section 3.1 were previously identified by Nagurney (1999b). The paradoxes presented in Sections 3.2 and 3.3 are new.

4 Viable and Sustainable Transportation Networks

In this chapter, I make explicit the fundamental concepts of *viability* and *sustainability* of transportation networks. These concepts are rigorously defined through formal definitions and rest against the backdrop of environmental goals. Roughly speaking, in this framework, viability is concerned with whether or not the environmental goals are achievable, given the transportation network topology and travel demands as well as the environmental parameters. Sustainability, on the other hand, is concerned with the attainment of the goals through a variety of policy instruments, given not only the transportation network and the environmental parameters, but also the cost structure and the travel behavior. Clearly, in this framework, viability of a transportation network is a precursor to sustainability.

In Section 4.1, I consider viability of a transportation network, given that the origin/destination pairs are known as well as the associated travel demands. In Section 4.2, I take what may be viewed as a longer perspective and provide formal definitions of viability in the following situations:

Situation 1

Given the origin nodes and the total number of trips produced in each origin node, the travelers select their destinations as well as their travel paths.

Situation 2

Given the destination nodes and the total number of trips attracted to each destination, the travelers select both their origins and their travel paths.

Situation 3

Given the origin nodes, the destination nodes, and the total number of trips generated in all the origin nodes, which is equal to the number of trips attracted to each destination, the travelers are free to select their origins, their destinations, as well as their travel paths.

Table 4.1. Classification of fixed demand networks in different situations

Given		To be Determined
Baseline:	• O/D pairs and demands	• routes of travel
Situation 1:	• Origin nodes and trip productions	• destinations and routes of travel
Situation 2:	• Destination nodes and trip attractions	• origins and routes of travel
Situation 3:	• Origins nodes, destination nodes, and total number of trips	• origins, destinations, and routes of travel

Situation 1 models the scenario in which travelers have predetermined origins, typically places of residence, and seek to determine their work destinations as well as the routes of travel to the destinations. Situation 2, on the other hand, models the scenario in which travelers have predetermined destinations, such as places of work, and seek to determine their residential locations, as well as their paths of travel. Finally, Situation 3 is the most flexible one in a sense in that travelers determine their places of employment, their places of residence, as well as the routes of travel between the origin/destinations. In Table 4.1, I summarize the classification of fixed demand networks in distinct situations.

In Section 4.2, I also illustrate, through examples, how a network may not be viable in the case of fixed origin/destination pairs and associated travel demands but may be viable in one of the three situations noted above.

In Section 4.3, I discuss viable transportation networks in the case of elastic, rather than fixed, travel demands in the three situations highlighted above for fixed demand networks. In the elastic problems, in contrast to the fixed demand problems, the demands, the trip productions, the trip attractions, or the total number of trips are now variables.

In Section 4.4, I move from viability of transportation networks to that of sustainability and set the foundation for the policies that follow in subsequent chapters.

4.1 Viability of Networks with Known O/D Pairs and Travel Demands

In this, and the subsequent section, transportation networks with fixed travel demands are considered. In this section, however, I assume, as in the classical traffic network models (see Chapter 2), that the origin/destination pairs are known and given a priori as are the associated travel demands. Note that, in regards to viability of a transportation network, I do not consider the travel cost structure on the network nor the behavior of the travelers. The cost parameters and behavior of the travelers enter into the equation when we investigate sustainability of a network in Section 4.4.

I motivate the definition of viability by first presenting two problems.

Problem 4.1 (Determination of the Tightest Achievable Environmental Quality Standard)

Given a network topology $G = [N, L]$, the set of origin/destination pairs W, the vector of travel demands d, and the vector of link emissions h, what is the tightest environmental quality standard, denoted by Q^*, that can be achieved by the transportation network?

The solution to this question can be formulated as a mathematical programming problem, in particular, a *linear programming* problem, given by:

$$\text{Minimize} \quad Q \tag{4.1}$$

subject to:

$$\sum_{p \in P_w} x_p = d_w, \quad \forall w \in W, \tag{4.2}$$

$$\sum_{a \in L} h_a \sum_{p \in P} x_p \delta_{ap} \leq Q, \tag{4.3}$$

$$x_p \geq 0, \quad \forall p \in P. \tag{4.4}$$

The first set of constraints (4.2) guarantees that the path flow pattern satisfies the travel demands, whereas the second one (4.3) guarantees that the path flow pattern does not exceed the tightest environmental quality standard (which is endogenous to this problem). Finally, the last set of constraints ensures that the path flows are nonnegative.

I now solve this problem for a specific network example depicted in Figure 4.1.

Example 4.1

I present a small example for illustrative purposes. The network is depicted in Figure 4.1 and consists of two nodes: 1, 2; three links: a, b, c, and one origin/destination pair: $w_1 = (1, 2)$. There are three paths connecting the O/D pair, each of which consists of a single link, that is, $p_1 = a$, $p_2 = b$, and $p_3 = c$. The travel demand is $d_{w_1} = 10$. The emission factors are: $h_a = 0.1$, $h_b = 0.2$, and $h_c = 0.3$.

A straightforward application of the simplex method (see Bazarra, Jarvis, and Sherali (1990)) to Problem 4.1 for this example, where one seeks to solve:

$$\text{Minimize} \quad Q$$

subject to:

$$x_{p_1} + x_{p_2} + x_{p_3} = 10,$$

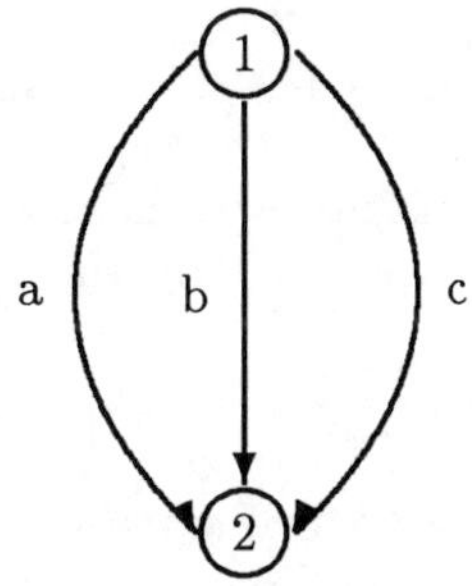

Fig. 4.1. Network topology for Example 4.1

$$0.1x_{p_1} + 0.2x_{p_2} + 0.3x_{p_3} \leq Q,$$

$$x_{p_1} \geq 0, \quad x_{p_2} \geq 0, \quad x_{p_3} \geq 0,$$

yields: $Q^* = 1$, that is, the tightest emission quality standard that is achievable by this network is given by 1.

I next ask the question as to what is the maximum demand that is achievable, given a desired environmental quality standard.

Problem 4.2 (Determination of the Maximum Achievable Travel Demand, Given the Environmental Quality Standard)

Given a network topology $G = [N, L]$, the set of origin/destination pairs W, the vector of link emissions h, and the desired environmental quality standard $\bar{Q}$, what is the maximum total demand that is achievable?

The solution to this question can also be formulated as a linear programming problem given by:

$$\text{Maximize} \quad \sum_{w \in W} d_w \tag{4.5}$$

subject to:

$$\sum_{p \in P_w} x_p = d_w, \quad \forall w \in W, \tag{4.6}$$

$$\sum_{a \in L} h_a \sum_{p \in P} x_p \delta_{ap} \leq \bar{Q}, \tag{4.7}$$

$$x_p \geq 0, \quad \forall p \in P. \tag{4.8}$$

Note that, in this problem, the constraints (4.6) (as (4.2) in Problem 4.1) guarantee that the path flow pattern satisfies the travel demands, but now the travel demands are no longer known but are variables whose optimal values are to be determined. Constraint (4.7) guarantees that the environmental quality standard is met by the path flow pattern, but now, in contrast to the analogous constraint in Problem 4.1, there is a known environmental quality standard, denoted by $\bar{Q}$, which one wishes not to exceed. Hence, in this problem, the travel demands, rather than the environmental quality standard, are endogenous and to be determined by the solution of the optimization problem.

Example 4.2

I now consider, again, the network in Figure 4.1, with emission factors: $h_a = 0.1$, $h_b = 0.2$, and $h_c = 0.3$. The desired environmental standard, denoted by $\bar{Q}$, is equal to 1. Problem 4.2 applied to the example, is given by:

$$\text{Maximize} \quad d_{w_1}$$

subject to:

$$x_{p_1} + x_{p_2} + x_{p_3} = d_{w_1},$$

$$0.1x_{p_1} + 0.2x_{p_2} + 0.3x_{p_3} \leq 1,$$

$$x_{p_1} \geq 0, \quad x_{p_2} \geq 0, \quad x_{p_3} \geq 0,$$

and its solution is obtained via an application of the simplex method yielding: $d^*_{w_1} = 10$. Hence, the highest achievable travel demand for the network, given the desired environmental standard of 1, is equal to 10.

Henceforth, I will term a transportation network with given origin/destination pairs and travel demands *viable* if there exists a solution to the following linear system:

Linear System 4.1

Determine a vector x satisfying:

$$\sum_{p \in P_w} x_p = d_w, \quad \forall w \in W, \tag{4.9}$$

$$\sum_{a \in L} h_a \sum_{p \in P} x_p \delta_{ap} \leq \bar{Q}, \tag{4.10}$$

$$x_p \geq 0, \quad \forall p \in P. \tag{4.11}$$

Note that the existence of a solution to this linear system of equations and inequalities guarantees that the demand associated with the O/D pairs can be satisfied by a path flow pattern, which also simultaneously satisfies the environmental quality standard. Clearly, there may be more than one such path flow pattern.

Moreover, if, for a particular transportation network, the imposed environmental quality standard is not smaller than the tightest achievable standard for the network, that is: $\bar{Q} \geq Q^*$ (where Q^* is the solution to Problem

4.1), then the network is viable. In other words, there exists a feasible path flow pattern, that is, one that is nonnegative and satisfies the travel demands, while, at the same time, not exceeding the imposed environmental quality (emissions) standard for the network equal to $\bar{Q}$.

The focus in this book is on environmental quality standards as regards air quality and vehicular emissions. Of course, the definition of viability may be modified to capture other environmental quality standards (and goals) as well, provided that the system of equations and inequalities are modified/expanded accordingly.

Hence, one has the following definition:

Definition 4.1 (Viable Transportation Network with Known O/D Pairs and Travel Demands)
A transportation network with known origin/destination pairs and fixed travel demands associated with the origin/destination pairs is viable if there exists a solution to the Linear System 4.1. Alternatively, a transportation network is viable if $Q^* \leq \bar{Q}$.

Note that viability is an achievability/feasibility concept and it is relative to the desired environmental target or quality standard $\bar{Q}$ under the given demand structure and network topology.

Returning to the network depicted in Figure 4.1, and assuming now that the emission parameters remain as in Example 4.1, but the travel demand doubles to 20, one can see that the network is no longer viable, given an environmental quality standard of 1.

In the next section, I present a transportation network example which is not viable under the fixed O/D pair and travel demand scenario but is viable in Situation 1. This suggests that environmental goals may be achievable if one allows for an additional degree of flexibility such as, for example, by also allowing for the selection of destination nodes.

4.2 Viability of Traffic Networks in Other Situations

In this section, I consider the viability of transportation networks in the three distinct situations outlined above, each of which is discussed separately in its respective subsection. As mentioned earlier, these situations reflect a longer time perspective for the network since travelers now select not only their travel paths but also their destinations, or their origins, or both their origins and their destinations. Note that, as in Section 4.1, I do not consider the cost structure on the network or the behavior of the travelers in making their decisions. Such issues enter in when one assesses whether or not a network is sustainable. Hence, the determination of the precise travel demands associated with the ultimate O/D pairs (as well as the "ultimate" path flows from the portfolio of feasible flows) can only be accomplished after the cost structure and travelers' behavior are superimposed on the network.

4.2.1 Known Origins and Trip Productions

Given known origins corresponding to particular nodes in a fixed demand traffic network, and which correspond to locations in which trips are produced, and the total number of trips produced at the origin nodes, we are interested in determining whether such a network is viable or not. Specifically, I assume as given the origin nodes, with a typical origin node denoted by y, and the number of trips at each origin node, with the number of trips at origin node y denoted by O_y. Let P_{O_y} denote the set of paths originating at origin node y and ending at any of the destination nodes. Let Y denote the set of such paths in the network.

Assuming, as in Section 4.1, that one is given the environmental quality standard $\bar{Q}$ for the network, one can define the following linear system:

Linear System 4.2

Determine a vector x satisfying the following linear system:

$$\sum_{p \in P_{O_y}} x_p = O_y, \quad \forall y \in Y, \tag{4.12}$$

$$\sum_{a \in L} h_a \sum_{y \in Y} \sum_{p \in P_{O_y}} x_p \delta_{ap} \leq \bar{Q}, \tag{4.13}$$

$$x_p \geq 0, \quad \forall p \in P_{O_y}, \quad \forall y \in Y. \tag{4.14}$$

Also, consider the solution to Problem 4.3.

Problem 4.3 (Determination of the Tightest Achievable Quality Standard in the Case of Known Origins and Trip Productions)

$$\text{Minimize} \quad Q \tag{4.15}$$

subject to:

$$\sum_{y \in P_{O_y}} x_p = O_y, \quad \forall y \in Y, \tag{4.16}$$

$$\sum_{a \in L} h_a \sum_{y \in Y} \sum_{p \in P_{O_y}} x_p \delta_{ap} \leq Q, \tag{4.17}$$

$$x_p \geq 0, \quad \forall y \in P_{O_y}, \quad \forall y \in Y, \tag{4.18}$$

and denote the solution to this problem by Q^{1^*}.

Then one can state the following definition of viability of a transportation network in the case of Situation 1:

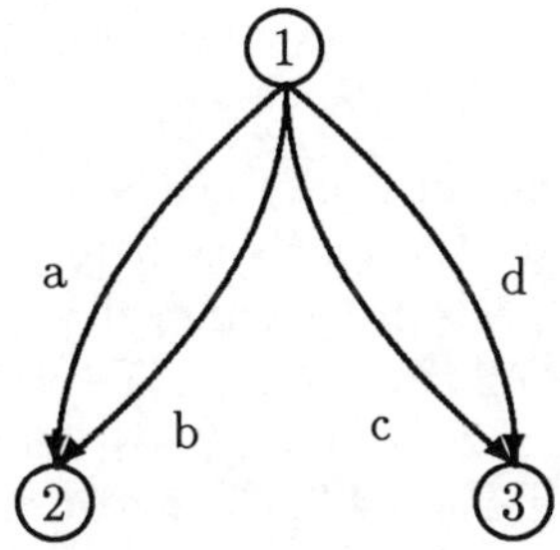

Fig. 4.2. Network topology for Example 4.3

Definition 4.2 (Viability of a Transportation Network with Known Origins and Trip Productions)
A network is said to be viable in the case of known origins and trip productions if there exists a solution to Linear System 4.2; equivalently, if $Q^{1^*} \leq \bar{Q}$.

I now present an example which illustrates that a network may not be viable in the case of fixed origin/destination pairs and travel demands but, nevertheless, may be viable in the case of known origins and trip productions.

Example 4.3

This example illustrates the fact that a network may not be viable in the case of known O/D pairs and travel demands but, nevertheless, may be viable in Situation 1.

Consider the network depicted in Figure 4.2, in which there are three nodes: $1, 2, 3$, and 4 links: a, b, c, d. There are two O/D pairs: $w_1 = (1,2)$ and $w_2 = (1,3)$. The paths connecting O/D pair w_1 are: $p_1 = a$ and $p_2 = b$, whereas the paths connecting O/D pair w_2 are: $p_3 = c$ and $p_4 = d$. The travel demands are: $d_{w_1} = 6$ and $d_{w_2} = 4$. The emission factors are: $h_a = 0.5$, $h_b = 0.5$, $h_c = 0.3$, and $h_d = 0.3$.

It is straightforward to verify that the minimum total emissions, that is, the solution to Problem 4.1, are equal to $Q^* = 4.2$ for this network. Assume, however, that the desired environmental quality standard is $\bar{Q} = 4$. Then, clearly, since $\bar{Q} < Q^*$, according to the definition of viability given in Definition 4.1, the network is not viable. Indeed, the environmental quality standard of 4 cannot be achieved by this network.

Suppose now that, rather than having the O/D pairs being fixed with known travel demands, one now has Situation 1 applying to the network example. There is only a single origin node and that is node 1 (since it was the origin for both O/D pairs in the original problem) and the travelers are free to choose their destinations, which can be either node 2 and/or node 3. The total number of trips at node 1 is given by the sums of the original travel demands and, hence, $O_1 = 6 + 4 = 10$.

If one can provide one solution to Linear System 4.2, then the network is viable under Situation 1 since one only needs to establish the existence of a solution. One can enumerate the paths as before. Let $x_{p_1} = x_{p_2} = 2.5$ and $x_{p_3} = x_{p_4} = 2.5$. This flow pattern is nonnegative, and satisfies both the first equation in Linear System 4.2 since $2.5 + 2.5 + 2.5 + 2.5 = 10$ as well as the second constraint since $0.5 \times 2.5 + 0.5 \times 2.5 + 0.3 \times 2.5 + .3 \times 2.5 = 4 = \bar{Q}$.

Hence, according to Definition 4.2, the network (which was not originally viable in the case of known O/D pairs and associated travel demands) is now viable in Situation 1.

4.2.2 Known Destinations and Trip Attractions

Now consider the problem in which the destinations are predetermined, but the travelers select their origins (and their travel paths). Hence, I assume now that one has, as given, the total number of trips D_z attracted to each destination z and let P_{D_z} denote the paths from the origin nodes to the destination node z. Let Z denote the set of such paths in the network. In order to determine whether a network is viable in Situation 2, I consider the following linear system, which is analogous to Linear Systems 4.1 and 4.2, but for the case when only the destinations and the trip attractions are given.

Linear System 4.3

Determine a vector x satisfying the following linear system:

$$\sum_{p \in P_{D_z}} x_p = D_z, \quad \forall z \in Z, \tag{4.19}$$

$$\sum_{a \in L} h_a \sum_{z \in Z} \sum_{p \in P_{D_z}} x_p \delta_{ap} \leq \bar{Q}, \tag{4.20}$$

$$x_p \geq 0, \quad \forall p \in P_{D_z}, \quad \forall z \in Z. \tag{4.21}$$

Also, consider the solution to the following problem:

Problem 4.4 (Determination of the Tightest Achievable Environmental Quality Standard in the Case of Known Destinations and Trip Attractions)

$$\text{Minimize} \quad Q \tag{4.22}$$

subject to:

$$\sum_{p \in P_{D_z}} x_p = D_z, \quad \forall z \in Z, \tag{4.23}$$

$$\sum_{a \in L} h_a \sum_{z \in Z} \sum_{p \in P_{D_z}} x_p \delta_{ap} \leq Q, \tag{4.24}$$

$$x_p \geq 0, \quad \forall p \in P_{D_z}, \quad \forall z \in Z, \tag{4.25}$$

and denote the optimal value of the objective function by Q^{2^*}.

One can now state the definition of viability of a transportation under Situation 2.

Definition 4.3 (Viability of a Transportation Network with Known Destinations and Trip Attractions)
A network is said to be viable in the case of known destinations and trip attractions, if there exists a solution to Linear System 4.3; equivalently, if $Q^{2^*} \leq \bar{Q}$*, where recall that* $\bar{Q}$ *denotes the environmental quality standard.*

4.2.3 Known Total Number of Trips

In this subsection, I assume now that the total number of trips T generated in all origin nodes of the network (and equal to the total number of trips attracted to the destination nodes in the network) is given. I am interested in determining whether or not the transportation network is viable in Situation 3. The linear system that one needs to investigate the existence of a solution to, hence, is:

Linear System 4.4

Determine a vector x satisfying:

$$\sum_{p \in P} x_p = T, \tag{4.26}$$

$$\sum_{a \in L} h_a \sum_{p \in P} x_p \delta_{ap} \leq \bar{Q}, \tag{4.27}$$

$$x_p \geq 0, \quad \forall p \in P. \tag{4.28}$$

Equivalently, one can investigate the solution to the following problem and see whether the solution exists and whether the optimal value of the objective function, denoted by Q^{3^*}, satisfies: $Q^{3^*} \leq \bar{Q}$.

Problem 4.5 (Determination of Tightest Achievable Environmental Quality Standard in the Case of Known Total Number of Trips)

$$\text{Minimize} \quad Q \tag{4.29}$$

subject to:

$$\sum_{p \in P} x_p = T, \tag{4.30}$$

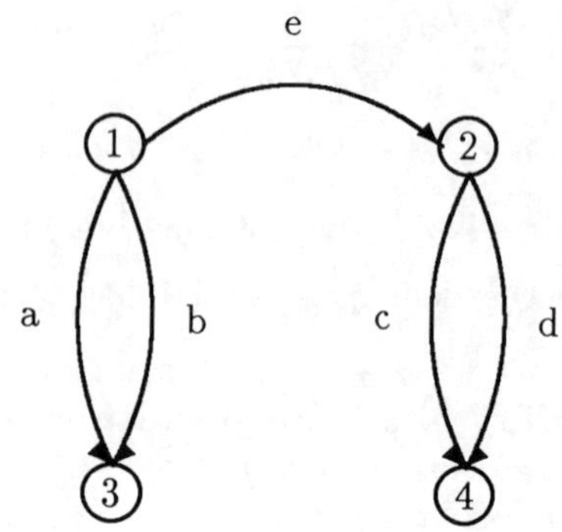

Fig. 4.3. Network topology for Example 4.4

$$\sum_{a\in L} h_a \sum_{p\in P} x_p \delta_{ap} \leq Q, \tag{4.31}$$

$$x_p \geq 0, \quad \forall p \in P. \tag{4.32}$$

The optimal value of the objective function is denoted by Q^{3^*}.

Analogously to the definitions of viability of a network in Situations 1 and 2 above, I now state:

Definition 4.4 (Viability of a Transportation Network in the Case of Known Total Number of Trips)
A network is said to be viable in the case of known total number of trips if there exists a solution to Linear System 4.4; equivalently, if $Q^{3^*} \leq \bar{Q}$.

I now present an example which illustrates that a transportation network may not be viable in the case of given travel O/D pairs and travel demands; may not be viable in the case of known origins and trip productions: but, nevertheless, may be viable in the case of known total number of trips.

Example 4.4

Consider the transportation network depicted in Figure 4.3 consisting of four nodes: 1, 2, 3, 4, and five links: a, b, c, d, and e. Consider, first, the case of known O/D pairs and travel demands and assume that there are 3 O/D pairs: $w_1 = (1,3)$, $w_2 = (1,2)$, and $w_3 = (2,4)$. Assume that the travel demands are: $d_{w_1} = 2$, $d_{w_2} = 2$, and $d_{w_3} = 2$. Let the paths be as follows: For O/D pair w_1: $p_1 = a$, $p_2 = b$; for O/D pair w_2: $p_3 = e$, and for O/D pair w_3: $p_4 = c$, and $p_5 = d$.

The emission factors are: $h_a = 0.1$, $h_b = 0.1$, $h_c = 0.2$, $h_d = 0.2$, and $h_e = 0.7$. Assume that the desired environmental quality standard $\bar{Q} = 0.6$.

It is easy to see that this environmental quality standard is not achievable by this network under fixed O/D pairs by noting that the emissions generated just by travelers between O/D pair w_2 are equal to 1.4.

Suppose now that one wishes to investigate whether the network is viable in Situation 1. Note that one now has two origin nodes: 1 and 2 (which corresponded to the origin nodes in the O/D pairs originally), and three possible destination nodes: 2, 3, and 4. The trip production at node 1, O_1, is equal to $d_{w_1} + d_{w_2}$ since O/D pairs w_1 and w_2 both had origin nodes 1 or $2 + 2 = 4$, whereas the trip production at node 2, O_2, is equal to 2.

One notes that the solution to Problem 4.3 yields $Q^{1^*} = 0.8$, which still exceeds the desired environmental quality standard of 0.6.

Finally, consider Situation 3, where the total number of trips $T = 2+2+2 = 6$ (and corresponds to $d_{w_1} + d_{w_2} + d_{w_3}$ in the original network). It is easy to verify that the environmental quality standard of 0.6 is now achievable. For example, a path flow pattern that satisfies Linear System 4.4 is given by: $x_{p_1} = x_{p_2} = 3$, with all other path flows equal to 0. Hence, the first equation in Linear System 4.4 is satisfied as well as the second constraint. Furthermore, the path flows are nonnegative. Alternative path flow patterns which would satisfy the system are: $x_{p_1} = 6$, with all other path flows being zero, and $x_{p_2} = 6$, with all other path flows being zero.

Note that viability of transportation networks was defined in the context of the network topology, the given emission factors, as well as the environmental quality standard. Examples 4.3 and 4.4 illustrate that a network may be viable in one situation but not in another situation. Of course, one may also make a network viable through technological improvements such as through the reduction of the emission factors. We leave the discussion of technological and network design issues to Part IV of this book.

4.3 Viability of Elastic Demand Traffic Networks

In both Sections 4.1 and 4.2 it was assumed that, be it the travel demands, or the trip productions, or the trip attractions, or the total number of trips, the values were known and fixed. Here, in contrast, I consider transportation networks in which these take on no longer fixed values but are now variables. Hence, in the case of known origin/destination pairs, the associated travel demands would now be variables. In the case of Situation 1, the trip productions would no longer be fixed but would be allowed to vary. Similarly, in the case of Situation 2, the trip attractions would no longer be fixed but could vary, and in Situation 3, the total number of trips would also be allowed to vary.

Indeed, one may immediately write down the elastic counterparts to the Linear Systems 4.1–4.4, given, respectively, by Linear Systems 4.5–4.8. In Table 4.2, I provide a summary of the classification of elastic demand networks in different situations (analogous to Table 4.1, but for the elastic case).

Table 4.2. Classification of elastic demand networks in different situations

Given		To be Determined
Baseline:	• O/D pairs	• demands and routes of travel
Situation 1:	• Origin nodes	• destinations, trip productions, and routes of travel
Situation 2:	• Destination nodes	• origins, trip attractions, and routes of travel
Situation 3:	• Origins nodes and destination nodes	• origins, destinations, total number of trips, and routes of travel

Linear System 4.5

Determine a vector of travel demands d and a vector of path flows x satisfying:

$$\sum_{p \in P_w} x_p = d_w, \quad \forall w \in W, \tag{4.33}$$

$$\sum_{a \in L} h_a \sum_{p \in P} x_p \delta_{ap} \leq \bar{Q}, \tag{4.34}$$

$$x_p \geq 0, \quad \forall p \in P. \tag{4.35}$$

Note that, in contrast to Linear System 4.1, one now needs to determine not only the vector of path flows x but also the vector of travel demands d.

Linear System 4.6

Determine a vector of trip productions O and a vector of path flows x satisfying the following linear system:

$$\sum_{p \in P_{O_y}} x_p = O_y, \quad \forall y \in Y, \tag{4.36}$$

$$\sum_{a \in L} h_a \sum_{y \in Y} \sum_{p \in P_{O_y}} x_p \delta_{ap} \leq \bar{Q}, \tag{4.37}$$

$$x_p \geq 0, \quad \forall p \in P_{O_y}, \quad \forall y \in Y. \tag{4.38}$$

Linear System 4.7

Determine a vector of trip attractions D and a vector of path flows x satisfying the following linear system:

$$\sum_{p \in P_{D_z}} x_p = D_z, \quad \forall z \in Z, \tag{4.39}$$

$$\sum_{a \in L} h_a \sum_{z \in Z} \sum_{p \in P_{D_z}} x_p \delta_{ap} \le \bar{Q}, \tag{4.40}$$

$$x_p \ge 0, \quad \forall p \in P_{D_z}, \quad \forall z \in Z. \tag{4.41}$$

Linear System 4.8

Determine the total number of trips T and a vector of path flows x satisfying:

$$\sum_{p \in P} x_p = T, \tag{4.42}$$

$$\sum_{a \in L} h_a \sum_{p \in P} x_p \delta_{ap} \le \bar{Q}, \tag{4.43}$$

$$x_p \ge 0, \quad \forall p \in P. \tag{4.44}$$

It is clear that there *always* exists a solution to each of the Linear Systems 4.4–4.8, since the trivial solution of setting the path flows equal to zero (with the demands, or trip productions or attractions, also equal to zero) will always guarantee that even the tighest environmental quality standard is met. However, this implies that there will be no travel on the transportation network! One can also establish that there always exists a nontrivial solution to each of the Linear Systems 4.5–4.8, although the total number of demands, or trip productions, or trip attractions, or total number of trips may be very small. Hence, we have the following observation:

Observation 4.1

A transportation network in the case of elastic demands, or elastic trip productions, or elastic trip attractions, or elastic total number of trips is always viable in that the corresponding linear system always has a solution.

In the case of such "elastic" traffic networks, Problem 4.2, and its counterparts to the elastic versions of Situations 1, 2, and 3, are relevant. Indeed, a transportation authority may wish, for example, to solve Problem 4.2 in order to determine whether or not the total demand would be sufficient in order to maintain the transportation network. In the case of the elastic version of Situation 1 (see also Linear System 4.5) the relevant problem would be the following:

Problem 4.6 (Determination of Maximum Achievable Trip Productions, Given the Environmental Quality Standard)

Determine a vector of trip productions O and a vector of path flows x satisfying:

$$\text{Maximize} \quad \sum_{y \in Y} O_y \tag{4.45}$$

subject to:

$$\sum_{p \in P_{O_y}} x_p = O_y, \quad \forall y \in Y, \tag{4.46}$$

$$\sum_{a \in L} h_a \sum_{y \in Y} \sum_{p \in P_{O_y}} x_p \delta_{ap} \leq \bar{Q}, \tag{4.47}$$

$$x_p \geq 0, \quad \forall p \in P_{O_y}, \quad \forall y \in Y. \tag{4.48}$$

The solution to this problem would determine the total number of trip productions that can be handled by the network, given the emission factors and the desired environmental quality standard.

Analogously, one can construct the mathematical programming problems in order to determine the maximal trip attractions, or the maximal total number of trips that can be handled by the network.

4.4 Sustainable Transportation Networks

In this section, I turn to the presentation of one of the most fundamental concepts in this book, that of *sustainability*. The term "sustainability" necessarily implies that a system will *last*. Moreover, it should last in the context of the environmental setting in which it is situated and within the framework of the users of the system, which, unless an authority imposes some policies in order to modify their behavior, may be in conflict with the environmental goals which serve to determine the ultimate existence and usage of the system itself.

In the context of a transportation network, sustainability of the network is crucially linked to the behavior of the users of the network system, which are the travelers, and their interaction on the network through the travel demand structure, the cost structure, as well as any environmental policies. I motivate what follows through an example.

Example 4.5

I return to the network depicted in Figure 4.1, consisting of two nodes, three links, and a single O/D pair $w_1 = (1, 2)$. Assume, as in Examples 4.1 and 4.2, that the emission factors are: $h_a = 0.1$, $h_b = 0.2$, and $h_c = 0.3$, and the desired environmental quality standard, as in Problem 4.2, is $\bar{Q} = 1$.

I now impose a cost structure on the network consisting of user travel link cost functions as follows:

$$c_a(f_a) = 2f_a + 5, \quad c_b(f_b) = f_b + 8, \quad c_c(f_c) = 1.5f_c + 5.$$

Assuming the behavioral principle (also commonly referred to as Wardrop's first principle) of user-optimization (see also Chapter 2), the travelers, in order to minimize their path travel costs (and in the absence of any policy interventions in order to guarantee that the behavior complies with the desired environmental quality standard), select their paths, where $p_1 = a$, $p_2 = b$, and $p_3 = c$, as follows:

$$x^*_{p_1} = 3, \quad x^*_{p_2} = 3, \quad x^*_{p_3} = 4,$$

which corresponds to the link load pattern:

$$f^*_a = 3, \quad f^*_b = 3, \quad f^*_c = 4,$$

and incurred user travel costs on the paths:

$$C_{p_1} = C_{p_2} = C_{p_3} = 11.$$

Indeed, this path flow pattern satisfies the traffic network equilibrium conditions given in (2.15).

Note, however, that the total emissions under this user-optimized path flow pattern is: $h_a f^*_a + h_b f^*_b + h_c f^*_c = 0.3 + 0.6 + 1.2 = 2.1$, which clearly exceeds the environmental quality standard of $\bar{Q} = 1$. Nevertheless, we know that the network is viable in that there exists a solution to the Linear System 4.1, with the path flow pattern: $x_{p_1} = 10$, $x_{p_2} = x_{p_3} = 0$.

Suppose now that one considers a policy of adding tolls to the roads so that the travelers still behave in a user-optimized manner, but now one also wishes to guarantee that the environmental quality standard will be met.

If one assigns tolls t_a, t_b, and t_c, on links a, b, and c, respectively, as: $t_a = 0$, $t_b = 17$, and $t_c = 20$, then the new user-optimized pattern will be: $x^*_{p_1} = 10$, $x^*_{p_2} = x^*_{p_3} = 0$, with associated *generalized* user path travel costs: $\bar{C}_{p_1} = C_{p_1} + t_a = 25$, $\bar{C}_{p_2} = C_{p_2} + t_b = 25$, and $\bar{C}_{p_3} = C_{p_3} + t_c = 25$.

Hence, in the presence of tolls as assigned above, this user-optimized path flow pattern satisfies the environmental target since the total emissions generated are equal to 1. However, note that travelers on link a, although they emit all the emissions, are not tolled since the toll on link a, t_a, is equal to zero. In subsequent chapters, I provide policy instruments, including tolls and pollution permits, which make users of the transportation networks pay according to their emissions.

I am now ready to state the definition of a sustainable transportation network.

Table 4.3. Relationship between viability and sustainability of a network

Viability + **Behavioral Principle**	**Appropriate Policy** ⇒	**Sustainability**

Definition 4.5 (Sustainable Transportation Network)
Henceforth, a transportation network is said to be sustainable if the flow pattern satisfies the conservation of flow equations and does not exceed the imposed environmental quality standard, subject to the operating behavioral principle(s) underlying the network.

Note that the definition of a sustainable transportation network does not exclude the imposition of policies; in fact, policies will be viewed as an essential tool in directing transportation networks to sustainability and are the topic of Parts II–IV of this book. Indeed, Table 4.3 emphasizes this important point.

This chapter introduced the concepts of viability and sustainability of transportation networks in the case of fixed demand traffic networks as well as elastic demand traffic networks. It described different situations of traffic networks which may lead to viability. The ideas described in this chapter are original, with a preliminary approach to the topic of sustainability reported earlier in Nagurney (1999c).

Part II Policies for Sustainable User-Optimized Transportation Networks

5 Emission Pricing for Sustainability – User-Optimized Perspective

With this chapter, I begin Part II of this book, which focuses on policy instruments for sustainable transportation networks when the travelers behave in a user-optimized fashion. In Part III, on the other hand, policies for sustainable system-optimized networks are proposed.

In this chapter, it is assumed that the networks are viable in that they satisfy the appropriate definition of viability for the given situation. In Section 5.1, I first consider traffic networks with given origin/destination pairs and fixed travel demands, and provide an emission pricing scheme which guarantees that the network will be sustainable, that is, that the environmental quality standard will be met and that the traffic flow pattern will be in equilibrium. In Section 5.2, I extend the pricing concept for the case of Situations 1 through 3 discussed in Section 4.2, in the preceding chapter.

In Section 5.3, I turn to elastic demand traffic network problems and provide a mechanism for emission pricing for such networks which guarantees sustainability, that is, that the environmental quality standard is met and the traffic flow pattern is in equilibrium.

In Section 5.4, I discuss a computational procedure which can be applied to compute the equilibrium patterns in both the fixed demand and the elastic demand traffic network policy models presented in this chapter. The algorithm is then applied to several numerical examples. The results in this chapter are original.

Table 5.1 provides a summary of the policy instruments developed in this chapter for the sustainability of user-optimized transportation networks.

Table 5.1. Summary of policy instruments for sustainability of U-O networks developed in Chapter 5

	Fixed demand networks	
Emission pricing for:	Baseline:	• Known O/D pairs and demands
	Situation 1:	• Known origin nodes and trip productions
	Situation 2:	• Known destination nodes and trip attractions
	Situation 3:	• Known origin nodes, destination nodes, and total number of trips
	Elastic demand networks	
Emission pricing for:	Baseline:	• Known O/D pairs

5.1 Pricing for Sustainable Fixed Demand Networks

In this section, I develop a traffic network policy model which guarantees sustainability of the network in question, under the assumption that the travelers behave in a user-optimized manner. The policy that is presented is that of emission pricing but, unlike the tolls discussed for Example 4.5 in the preceding chapter, here it is guaranteed that the tolls are equitable, in that the travelers pay according to their emissions.

In order to fix ideas, a simplified model is first presented, which is classical in the sense that the user link travel cost functions are assumed to be separable, akin to the model described in Section 2.1.2. From the optimality conditions for this problem, I then argue that they are also appropriate as equilibrium conditions for the more general case in which the user travel cost function on each link may depend not only on the flow on a particular link but also on the flows on other links in the network, as was the case in the more general traffic network equilibrium model in Section 2.2.3.

The notation utilized in this chapter is the same as in previous chapters, except where noted.

5.1.1 A Simple Model

As throughout this book, consider a traffic network consisting of the graph $G = [N, L]$, where N denotes the set of nodes and L the set of links. In this subsection, it is assumed, as given, a vector of travel demands d associated with the origin/destination pairs. Also, in this subsection I consider the "classical" form of the user link travel cost functions, due to Beckmann, McGuire, and Winsten (1956), where the user travel cost on link a, denoted by c_a (see also (2.3)), is separable, that is:

$$c_a = c_a(f_a), \quad \forall a \in L. \tag{5.1}$$

Moreover, I assume that this function is increasing in the flow for each link in the network.

The travel cost on a path p, hence, is equal to the sum of the travel costs on links that comprise that path, that is:

$$C_p = \sum_{a \in L} c_a(f_a)\delta_{ap}, \quad \forall a \in L. \tag{5.2}$$

Recall that, in the case of such functions (see Section 2.1.2), the traffic network equilibrium conditions (cf. (2.15)), which state that, in equilibrium, all used paths for each O/D pair have equal and minimal travel costs, can be reformulated as a solution to an optimization problem, where the objective function is given by:

$$\text{Minimize} \quad \sum_{a \in L} \int_0^{f_a} c_a(x)dx. \tag{5.3}$$

In the simple pricing model for sustainability one retains, hence, the objective function of the classical traffic network equilibrium model, as well as the constraints, but now one adds the environmental quality constraint. After making the substitution for the link load $f_a = \sum_{p \in P} x_p \delta_{ap}$ in the objective function (in order to simplify the derivation), one obtains the following problem:

$$\text{Minimize} \quad \sum_{a \in L} \int_0^{\sum_{p \in P} x_p \delta_{ap}} c_a(x)dx \tag{5.4}$$

subject to:

$$\sum_{p \in P_w} x_p = d_w, \quad \forall w \in W, \tag{5.5}$$

$$\sum_{a \in L} h_a \sum_{p \in P} x_p \delta_{ap} \leq \bar{Q}, \tag{5.6}$$

$$x_p \geq 0, \quad \forall p \in P. \tag{5.7}$$

Observe that conditions (5.5)–(5.7) correspond precisely to Linear System 4.1, the existence of a solution to which guarantees viability of a transportation network with given O/D pairs and travel demands.

Optimality Conditions

I now derive the optimality conditions for the optimization problem given by (5.4)–(5.7). Note that since the user travel cost functions are increasing functions of the flow, the objective function is convex and the constraints, which are linear, are also convex. Hence, the Kuhn-Tucker optimality conditions (see Appendices A and B) can be stated as follows: $x^* \in R^{n_P}_+$ is an optimal solution if it satisfies the travel demands and satisfies the following system of equalities and inequalities: For each O/D pair $w \in W$ and each path $p \in P_w$:

$$\bar{C}_p(x^*, \tau^*) = C_p(x^*) + \tau^* \sum_{a \in L} h_a \delta_{ap} \begin{cases} = \lambda_w, & \text{if } x_p^* > 0 \\ \geq \lambda_w, & \text{if } x_p^* = 0, \end{cases} \tag{5.8}$$

where τ^* is the Lagrange multiplier associated with the environmental quality constraint (5.5) with τ^* having the interpretation here as being the marginal cost of emission abatement.

In addition, one must have that:

$$\bar{Q} - \sum_{a \in L} h_a \sum_{p \in P} x_p^* \delta_{ap} \begin{cases} = 0, & \text{if } \tau^* > 0 \\ \geq 0, & \text{if } \tau^* = 0. \end{cases} \tag{5.9}$$

Note that $\bar{C}_p$ in (5.8) denotes the *generalized* cost associated with traveling now on path p after the imposition of the tolls, where the toll on a path p is equal to $\tau^* \sum_{a \in L} h_a \delta_{ap}$. Hence, the higher the emission factors on a utilized path, the higher the toll payment for travelers on that path.

Of course, the optimization problem can be solved by any general purpose convex programming algorithm. However, in Section 5.4, I will present an algorithm which can be applied to solve all the models presented in this chapter.

Emission Pricing Policies

According to (5.8) and (5.9), the following emission toll policies satisfy the equilibrium conditions:

Link Pricing Policy

The link pricing policy given by $t_a = \tau^* h_a$, $\forall a \in L$, where τ^* is the equilibrium marginal cost of emission abatement and t_a denotes the toll on link a, guarantees that the transportation network is sustainable.

Path Pricing Policy

The path pricing policy given by $t_p = \tau^* \sum_{a \in L} h_a \delta_{ap}$ for all $p \in P$, where t_p denotes the toll on path p guarantees that the network will be sustainable.

An example is now presented, in which the tolls can be solved for explicitly, as well as the equilibrium flow pattern.

Example 5.1

I return to the network in Example 4.5, whose network topology is depicted again, for convenience, in Figure 5.1. The network consist of two nodes, denoted by 1 and 2; three links, denoted by a, b, and c, and a single O/D pair $w_1 = (1, 2)$. Let $p_1 = a$, $p_2 = b$, and $p_3 = c$. The travel demand $d_{w_1} = 10$. Recall that the user link travel cost functions are:

$$c_a(f_a) = 2f_a + 5, \quad c_b(f_b) = f_b + 8, \quad c_c(f_c) = 1.5f_c + 5.$$

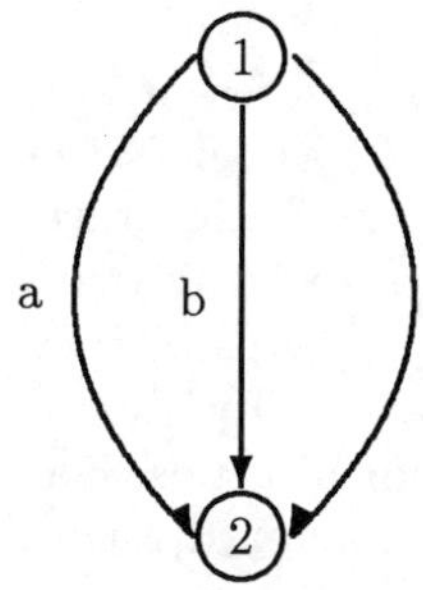

Fig. 5.1. Network topology for Example 5.1

The emissions are: $h_a = 0.1$, $h_b = 0.2$, and $h_c = 0.3$, with the environmental quality standard $\bar{Q} = 1$.

One is interested in determining a pricing policy, as described above. First, note that the viable solution $x_{p_1} = 10$, and $x_{p_2} = x_{p_3} = 0$ is, in fact, the only feasible solution with conditions (5.9) holding as an equality.

Hence, one has, from conditions (5.8), that for path p_1, which is the only path that will be utilized, that

$$\hat{C}_{p_1} = c_a + \tau^*.1 = 2f_a^* + 5 + \tau^*.1 = 25 + \tau^*.1.$$

Moreover, since paths p_2 and p_3 will not be utilized, one has also that:

$$\bar{C}_{p_2} = c_b + \tau^*.2 = f_b + 8 + \tau^*.2 = 8 + \tau^*.2 \geq \bar{C}_{p_1} = 25 + \tau^*.1.$$

In addition, one has that:

$$\bar{C}_{p_3} = c_c + .3\tau^* = 1.5f_c + 5 + .3\tau^* = 5 + .3\tau^* \geq \bar{C}_{p_1} = 25 + \tau^*.1.$$

But these two inequalities imply that:

$$17 \leq .1\tau^* \quad \text{and} \quad 20 \leq .2\tau^*,$$

or that $\tau^* \geq 170$.

Letting then $\tau^* = 170$, one obtains the following link emission toll policy: $t_a = h_a\tau^* = 17$, $t_b = h_b\tau^* = 34$, and $t_c = h_c\tau^* = 51$, yielding generalized path travel costs of:

$$\bar{C}_{p_1} = 42, \quad \bar{C}_{p_2} = 42, \quad \bar{C}_{p_3} = 56.$$

Note that, unlike the toll policy described for the problem in Example 4.5, one has equity here since the travelers who travel on path p_1 do now pay a positive toll according to their emissions.

In the subsequent subsection, I present a general model which explicitly utilizes conditions (5.8) and (5.9) as *equilibrium conditions*. Indeed, conditions (5.8) state that for each O/D pair travelers will stop switching their paths, provided that the generalized travel costs on utilized path (after the imposition of the tolls) are equal and minimal. Conditions (5.9), in turn, state that, if the environmental quality standard is met precisely, then the marginal cost of emission abatement is positive; if the total emissions are less than the environmental quality standard, then the marginal cost of emission abatement is zero.

5.1.2 The General Model

Observe that conditions (5.8) and (5.9), although derived from an optimization problem, may be interpreted as equilibrium conditions. I henceforth consider these conditions as equilibrium conditions, and present a generalized version of the model in Subsection 5.1.1, which considers user link travel cost functions which are no longer separable. Moreover, the equilibrium conditions will be shown to satisfy a variational inequality problem.

Indeed, I now consider user link travel cost functions, which may, in general, depend upon the entire vector of link loads; that is, I assume that now

$$c_a = c_a(f), \quad \forall a \in L. \tag{5.10}$$

I first formally state the definition and then derive the variational inequality formulation of the equilibrium conditions.

Definition 5.1 (Traffic Network Equilibrium in the Presence of Emission Tolls)
Given O/D pairs and fixed travel demands, in the presence of emission tolls and user-optimized behavior, a path flow pattern and the marginal cost of emission abatement (x^*, τ^*) is said to be in equilibrium if it satisfies equilibrium conditions (5.8) and (5.9). Moreover, such a traffic network is sustainable.

I now establish that the solution to the systems of equations and inequalities (5.8) and (5.9) satisfies a variational inequality problem.

Theorem 5.1 (Variational Inequality Formulation of Traffic Network Equilibrium in the Presence of Emission Tolls)
A traffic flow pattern and marginal cost of emission abatement $(x^*, \tau^*) \in \mathcal{K}^1$ is an equilibrium of the traffic network toll policy model described above if and only if it is a solution to the variational inequality problem:

Path Flow Formulation:

$$\sum_{w\in W}\sum_{p\in P_w}\left[C_p(x^*)+\tau^*\sum_{a\in L}h_a\delta_{ap}\right]\times[x_p-x_p^*]$$

$$+\left[\bar{Q}-\sum_{a\in L}h_a\sum_{p\in P}x_p^*\delta_{ap}\right]\times[\tau-\tau^*]\geq 0,\quad\forall(x,\tau)\in\mathcal{K}^1,\tag{5.11}$$

where $\mathcal{K}^1\equiv\bar{K}^1\times R^1_+$ *and* $\bar{K}^1\equiv\{x|x\geq 0$ *and satisfies* (5.5)$\}$, *or, equivalently,* $(f^*,\tau^*)\in\mathcal{K}^2$ *is an equilibrium link load and marginal cost of emission abatement pattern if and only if it satisfies the variational inequality problem:*

Link Load Formulation:

$$\sum_{a\in L}[c_a(f^*)+\tau^*h_a]\times[f_a-f_a^*]$$

$$+\left[\bar{Q}-\sum_{a\in L}h_af_a^*\right]\times[\tau-\tau^*]\geq 0,\quad\forall(f,\tau)\in\mathcal{K}^2,\tag{5.12}$$

where $\mathcal{K}^2\equiv\bar{K}^2\times R^1_+$, *and* $\bar{K}^2\equiv\{f|$ *there exists an* $x\geq 0$ *satisfying* (5.5)$\}$.

Proof:
I first establish that if a path flow pattern and marginal cost of emission abatement are in equilibrium, that is, they satisfy equilibrium conditions (5.8) and (5.9), then this pattern also satisfies variational inequality (5.11), equivalently, variational inequality (5.12).

Note that from (5.8) one has that, for a fixed O/D pair w and a fixed path $p\in P_w$:

$$\left[C_p(x^*)+\tau^*\sum_{a\in L}h_a\delta_{ap}-\lambda_w\right]\times[x_p-x_p^*]\geq 0.\tag{5.13}$$

Indeed, since if $x_p^*>0$, then the left-hand side of inequality (5.13) must be precisely equal to zero, in which case (5.13) must hold. On the other hand, if $x_p^*=0$, then $[x_p-x_p^*]\geq 0$, since the path flows must be nonnegative, and the left-hand side of (5.13) is also nonnegative due to (5.8) and, hence, since the product of two nonnegative terms is also nonnegative, the inequality in (5.13) is also satisfied.

Furthermore, since (5.13) holds for all paths connecting O/D pair w, we can sum the inequality in (5.13) over all such paths, that is:

$$\sum_{p\in P_w}\left[C_p(x^*)+\tau^*\sum_{a\in L}h_a\delta_{ap}-\lambda_w\right]\times[x_p-x_p^*]\geq 0,\tag{5.14}$$

but since the path flows must sum up to the travel demands (cf. (5.5)), (5.14) reduces to:

$$\sum_{p\in P_w}\left[C_p(x^*)+\tau^*\sum_{a\in L}h_a\delta_{ap}\right]\times\left[x_p-x_p^*\right]\geq 0. \tag{5.15}$$

But (5.15) also holds for any O/D pair and, hence, summing over all O/D pairs, yields the inequality:

$$\sum_{w\in W}\sum_{p\in P_w}\left[C_p(x^*)+\tau^*\sum_{a\in L}h_a\delta_{ap}\right]\times\left[x_p-x_p^*\right]\geq 0, \quad \forall x\in \bar{K}^1. \tag{5.16}$$

Using now the relationships between the path travel cost and the link travel costs (see (5.2)), as well as the path flow pattern and the link load pattern, inequality (5.16) is equivalent, in link loads, to the inequality:

$$\sum_{a\in L}\left[c_a(f^*)+\tau^*h_a\right]\times\left[f_a-f_a^*\right]\geq 0, \quad \forall f\in \bar{K}^2. \tag{5.17}$$

I now turn to equilibrium conditions (5.9) and, arguing as above, but for τ^*, note that these equilibrium conditions imply the inequality:

$$\left[\bar{Q}-\tau^*\sum_{a\in L}h_a\sum_{p\in P}x_p^*\delta_{ap}\right]\times\left[\tau-\tau^*\right]\geq 0, \quad \forall\tau\in R_+^1. \tag{5.18}$$

Summing now inequality (5.16) and (5.18), one obtains variational inequality (5.11) (which is in path flows since path flows are the variables). Similarly, summing inequality (5.17) and (5.18), and using the relationship: $f_a=\sum_{p\in P}x_p\delta_{ap}$, $\forall a\in L$, one obtains variational inequality (5.12).

I now show that a solution to variational inequality (5.11) and, equivalently, a solution to variational inequality (5.12), satisfies the equilibrium conditions (5.8) and (5.9).

Indeed, consider first variational inequality (5.11), and make the following substitutions: Let $\tau=\tau^*$, and let $x_p=x_p^*$, for all paths $p\in P_\omega$, for all $\omega\neq w$. Further, for paths $p\in P_w$, let r denote some path such that $x_r>0$ (we know that such a path must exist since the travel demand for each O/D pair is positive), and select some path $q\in P_w$; for all paths $p\neq q\subset r$, let $x_p=x_p^*$. Let $x_r=x_r^*-\delta$, for some small $\delta>0$, and let $x_q=x_q^*+\delta$. Clearly, such a constructed path flow pattern is feasible. Substitution into variational inequality (5.11), after some algebraic simplifications, yields then:

$$C_q(x^*)+\tau^*\sum_{a\in L}h_a\delta_{aq}\leq C_r(x^*)+\tau^*\sum_{a\in L}h_a\delta_{ar}. \tag{5.19}$$

Now, if $x_q^*>0$, one can construct an analogous path flow (and marginal cost of emission abatement pattern) but with a δ reallocation from path q to path

r yielding:

$$C_q(x^*) + \tau^* \sum_{a \in L} h_a \delta_{aq} \geq C_r(x^*) + \tau^* \sum_{a \in L} h_a \delta_{ar}. \tag{5.20}$$

However, in order for (5.19) and (5.20) to hold simultaneously, one must have that they hold with an equality and, thus, I have shown the first part of equilibrium conditions, that is, if the flows on paths are positive then their generalized path travel costs must be equal. On the other hand, inequality (5.19) holds even if the path flow on q is zero (in this case one cannot make a construction such as (5.11) since it would mean that the resulting flow on q would be negative and, hence, infeasible), which implies the second condition of (5.8), that is, that unused paths or those with zero flow have generalized path travel costs that cannot be less than those on used paths.

In order to establish that a solution to variational inequality (5.11) also satisfies equilibrium conditions (5.9), I make the following construction: set $x_p = x_p^*$, for all paths $p \in P$, and substitute into variational inequality (5.11), which yields:

$$\left[\bar{Q} - \tau^* \sum_{a \in L} h_a \sum_{p \in P} x_p^* \delta_{ap}\right] \times [\tau - \tau^*] \geq 0, \quad \forall \tau \in R_+^1. \tag{5.21}$$

It is easy to see that (5.21) implies equilibrium conditions (5.9), since if $\tau^* = 0$, one knows that $\tau - \tau^* = \tau \geq 0$, and for the entire expression to be nonnegative, it must be that $\bar{Q} - \tau^* \sum_{a \in L} h_a \delta_{ap} \geq 0$. On the other hand, if $\tau^* > 0$, then since the inequality must hold for any $\tau \geq 0$, one can let $\tau = \tau^* + \delta$ and substitute the resultant into (5.21), yielding:

$$\left[\bar{Q} - \tau^* \sum_{a \in L} h_a \sum_{p \in P} x_p^* \delta_{ap}\right] \times \delta \geq 0. \tag{5.22}$$

Similarly, one can let $\tau = \tau^* - \delta$ for the same small $\delta > 0$, in which case substitution into (5.21) yields:

$$\left[\bar{Q} - \tau^* \sum_{a \in L} h_a \sum_{p \in P} x_p^* \delta_{ap}\right] \delta \leq 0. \tag{5.23}$$

However, for both (5.22) and (5.23) to hold, one must conclude that for $\tau^* > 0$:

$$\bar{Q} - \tau^* \sum_{a \in L} h_a \sum_{p \in P} x_p^* \delta_{ap} = 0. \tag{5.24}$$

I have, thus, also verified the second part of equilibrium conditions (5.8).

Hence, the proof of equivalence in the case of the path flow variational inequality (5.11) is complete. What remains to be shown only is that a solution to the link load formulation (5.12) also satisfies equilibrium conditions (5.8), since in the course of establishing the proof for (5.11), I have already established, since $f_a = \sum_{p \in P} x_p \delta_{ap}$, $\forall a \in L$, that (5.9) must hold. But the first term of variational inequality (5.12) is derived from the first term of variational inequality (5.11) and, thus, the conclusion must follow. □

I now put both variational inequality problems (5.11) and (5.12) into standard form given by (2.32).

I first consider variational inequality (5.11), which is in path flow variables, and define the column vector $X \equiv (x, \tau) \in \mathcal{K}^1$ and the column vector $F(X)$, where

$$F(X) \equiv (C(X), T(X)).$$

$C(X)$ is the n_P-dimensional vector with component p given as follows:

$$C_p(X) : C_p(x) + \tau \sum_{a \in L} h_a \delta_{ap},$$

whereas $T(X)$ is the one-dimensional vector with component:

$$T(X) : \bar{Q} - \sum_{a \in L} h_a \sum_{p \in P} x_p \delta_{ap}.$$

Clearly, the variational inequality (5.11) can now be put into standard form (2.32) where $\mathcal{K} \equiv \mathcal{K}^1$.

Next, consider variational inequality (5.12), which is in link load variables and define the column vector $X \equiv (f, \tau)$ and the column vector $F(X)$, where

$$F(X) \equiv (c(X), T(X)).$$

$c(X)$ is the n-dimensional vector with component a given by:

$$c_a(X) = c_a(f) + h_a \tau,$$

whereas $T(X)$ is as defined for the variational inequality in path flow variables above.

5.2 Pricing in Alternative Situations

In this section, I develop pricing policies, analogous to the one in Section 5.1, but now I address transportation networks in the alternative situations discussed in Section 4.2. Specifically, in Subsection 5.2.1, I return to Situation 1, in which one is given known origins and trip productions. In Section 5.2.2, I consider Situation 2, in which one is given, instead, known destinations and trip attractions. Finally, in Section 5.2.3, I regard the most general situation,

Situation 3, in which one is given the total number of trips. Recall that, in Section 4.2, in the discussions of viability of a network in such situations, no travel cost structure was imposed on the network and no behavior was assumed for the travelers on the network. In this section, in contrast, since the focus is on pricing schemes for sustainability, I assume that the travel behavior is that of user-optimization, as was done in Section 5.1.

Furthermore, I introduce, for the first time, the concept of an *expanded* network, which is based on the original transportation network in the given situation but which allows one to determine not only the equilibrium path flow akin to those in the networks with fixed travel demands, but also the travel demands themselves. In this section, as in Section 5.1, it is assumed that the given networks are viable according to the respective definition in Section 4.2. The notion of an expanded network was also utilized in Nagurney (1999a) to transform multimodal networks under distinct situations into a multimodal traffic network equilibrium problem with known O/D pairs and travel demands. That work was an extension of the idea developed for single modal networks by Dafermos (1976) who called such network problems *integrated* traffic network equilibrium problems. The models therein, however, in contrast to those described here, were not concerned with sustainability issues in an environmental setting.

5.2.1 Emission Pricing for Networks with Known Origins and Trip Productions

Consider now traffic networks in Situation 1 in which the origins are known as well as the trip productions. Assume user-optimized behavior on such networks and a general user link travel cost function on each link $a \in L$ given by (5.10).

I first state the equilibrium conditions for a network in such a situation (in the absence of any policies such as tolls). I then provide a construction of the network in expanded form which allows one to reduce either the equilibrium problem without or with tolls to the corresponding problem with known O/D pairs and travel demands discussed in Section 5.1.

Definition 5.2 (Equilibrium Conditions for User-Optimization in Situation 1)
A traffic flow pattern on a transportation network in Situation 1 is said to be in equilibrium if all used paths emanating from each origin node are equal and minimal, that is, one has that for each $y \in Y$, and $p \in P_y$:

$$C_p(x^*) \begin{cases} = & \lambda_y, & \text{if } x_p^* > 0 \\ \geq & \lambda_y, & \text{if } x_p^* = 0, \end{cases} \tag{5.25}$$

where $\sum_{p \in P_{O_y}} x_p^* = O_y$, $\forall y \in Y$.

I now need to introduce the expanded network concept in this situation, that is, when one is given known origins and trip productions (and not O/D pairs and associated travel demands as in the networks in Section 5.1).

Construction of Expanded Network for Situation 1

I do the network construction as follows: Construct a "super" demand or sink node, denoted by ψ, and from each destination node construct then a single link terminating in the destination node ψ. Associate with each link a in the original network a user travel cost c_a, which is assumed to take on the general form given by (5.10). Associate with each of the artificial links terminating in node ψ a user travel cost equal to zero.

I now denote by $\hat{p}$ the path, which consists of the links in path p plus the artificial link terminating in ψ. In addition, define then the O/D pairs on the expanded network consisting, respectively, of each of the original origin nodes y and with destination node ψ. Associate with each such O/D pair $\hat{w}$ the corresponding "travel demand," given by O_y. Note that, in the model with known origins and trip productions, it is path travel costs on paths emanating from each origin to all the destinations that are equalized for all used paths.

Equilibrium conditions (5.8) and (5.9) are then applied to the expanded network. Equivalently, in order to obtain the equilibrium path flows and marginal cost of emission abatement, one can solve variational inequality (5.11) or (5.12). Note that, once, the solution is obtained to the pricing problem on the expanded network, one can then recover the travel demands to the original network in Situation 1, by simply summing the resulting path flows on the paths between each origin y and the respective destination nodes.

An example is now given.

Example 5.2

I return now to Example 4.3, whose network topology is depicted for convenience again in Figure 5.2, along with the expanded network construction.

In this network there are three nodes: 1, 2, 3, and four links: a, b, c, d, in the original network and four nodes and six links in the expanded network. There are two destinations: 2 and 3 and, hence, according to the network expansion construction, one has a single "O/D" pair denoted by $\hat{w}_1 = (1, \psi)$ and four paths connecting the O/D pair: $\hat{p}_1 = (a, e)$, $\hat{p}_2 = (b, e)$, $\hat{p}_3 = (c, f)$, and $\hat{p}_4 = (d, f)$.

Recall that the emission factors are: $h_a = 0.5$, $h_b = 0.5$, $h_c = 0.3$, and $h_d = 0.3$, and that the desired environmental quality standard $\bar{Q} = 4$.

I now impose a travel cost structure as follows:

$$c_a(f_a) = f_a + 5, \quad c_b(f_b) = f_b + 5, \quad c_c(f_c) = 2f_c + 1, \quad c_d(f_d) = 2f_d + 1,$$

with user travel costs on the "new" links given by:

$$c_e(f_e) = c_f(f_f) = 0.$$

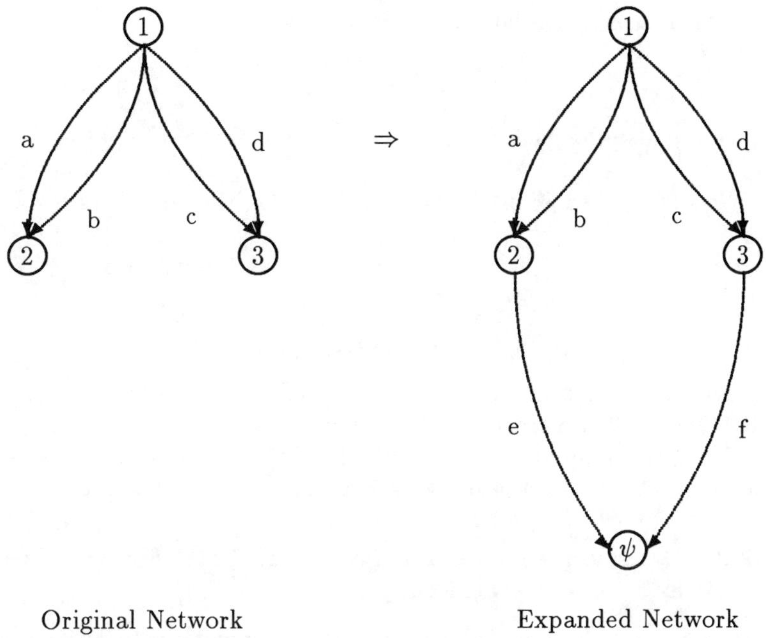

Fig. 5.2. Expanded network for Example 5.2

Furthermore, from $O_1 = 10$ one constructs the travel demand on the expanded network given by $d_{\hat{w}_1} = 10$.

Utilizing the equilibrium conditions (5.8) and by the "symmetry" in the network and the user link travel cost functions, one can conclude that $f_a^* = f_b^*$ and $f_c^* = f_d^*$. Further, I posit that, since the emissions factors are low on the links relative to the travel demand and the environmental quality standard, $\tau^* = 0$. Hence, the solution of the emission pricing problem collapses to the solution of a variational inequality problem governing the well-known traffic network equilibrium conditions without any policies (see (2.34) or (2.36)), or, equivalently, since the user travel cost functions on the links are separable, to the solution of the optimization reformulation of the conditions given by (2.16)–(2.19).

Due, however, to the simplicity of the example, solutions of the resulting algebraic equations (see also (5.25)) yields:

$$x^*_{\hat{p}_1} = 2, \quad x^*_{\hat{p}_2} = 2, \quad x^*_{\hat{p}_3} = 3, \quad x^*_{\hat{p}_4} = 3,$$

with induced link loads:

$$f_a^* = f_b^* = 2, \quad f_c^* = f_d^* = 3,$$

and

$$f_e^* = 4, \quad f_f^* = 6.$$

The incurred generalized path travel costs are:

$$\bar{C}_{\hat{p}_1} = \bar{C}_{\hat{p}_2} = \bar{C}_{\hat{p}_3} = \bar{C}_{\hat{p}_4} = 7,$$

which are also the path travel costs, respectively, on the paths p_1, p_2, p_3, and p_4.

Note that, hence, in the original network, the equilibrium solution must be:

$$x_{p_1}^* = 2, \quad x_{p_2}^* = 2, \quad x_{p_3}^* = 3, \quad x_{p_4}^* = 3,$$

and

$$d_{w_1} = 4, \quad d_{w_2} = 6.$$

The total emissions generated are: $h_a f_a^* + h_b f_b^* + h_c f_c^* + h_d f_d^* = 1 + 1 + 0.6 + 0.6 = 3.2$, which is less than $\bar{Q} = 4$.

Thus, both equilibrium conditions (5.8) and (5.9) hold, respectively, for the flow pattern and the marginal cost of emission abatement.

5.2.2 Emission Pricing for Networks with Known Destinations and Trip Attractions

In this subsection, I consider transportation networks in Situation 2, as discussed in Section 4.2, in which now one is given the known destinations and the trip attractions associated with the destinations. I assume user-optimized behavior in that the travelers will select their origins as well as their paths to the given destinations so that the path travel costs on used paths to each destination are equal and minimal. The statement of the equilibrium conditions is, hence, as follows (refer to Section 4.2.2):

Definition 5.3 (Equilibrium Conditions for User-Optimization in Situation 2)
A traffic network is said to be in equilibrium in Situation 2 if the following conditions hold: For each destination node $z \in Z$, and each path $p \in P_z$:

$$C_p(x^*) \begin{cases} = & \lambda_z, \quad \text{if } x_p^* > 0 \\ \geq & \lambda_z, \quad \text{if } x_p^* = 0, \end{cases} \tag{5.26}$$

where $\sum_{p \in P_{D_z}} x_p^* = D_z, \forall z \in Z$.

Analogously to Situation 1, one can construct an expanded network in Situation 2, which can be used to: (1) determine the user-optimized traffic flow pattern without any policies and (2) determine the user-optimized traffic flow pattern in the presence of toll policies.

Construction of Expanded Network for Situation 2

The construction of the expanded network is as follows: Construct a super origin or source node denoted by ξ and from node ξ construct as many links as there are origin nodes, with each such link originating at the supersource node and terminating at the origin node. These links are artificial links. Let the new paths in the network, which originate at the supersource node and terminate in one of the destination or attraction nodes, be denoted by $\hat{p}$, where $\hat{p}$ consists of the appropriate artificial link in addition to the links on path p.

The user link costs on the artificial links are set equal to zero. The O/D pairs on the expanded network become $\hat{w} = (\xi, z)$ for each destination node z with associated demand $d_{\hat{w}} = D_z$. The equilibrium conditions in the case of tolls according to (5.8) and (5.9) are now applicable to the expanded network where we make the substitutions of $\hat{w}$ for w and $\hat{p}$ for p. Moreover, as in Situation 1, one can recover the path flows and travel demand for the original network in this case.

5.2.3 Pricing for Networks with Known Number of Trips

In this subsection, I turn to networks in Situation 3, in which the known number of trips for the entire network is given and denoted by T. I assume that the network is viable in this situation and I first state the equilibrium conditions without the imposition of any toll policy. In this situation, travelers select their origins, their destinations, as well as their travel paths. Hence, in this situation, it is the travel costs on used paths from each origin to each destination which are equalized and minimal in equilibrium. Formally stated, one has the following:

Definition 5.4 (Equilibrium Conditions for User-Optimization in Situation 3)
A traffic flow pattern is said to be in equilibrium in Situation 3 if for all $p \in P$*:*

$$C_p(x^*) \begin{cases} = & \lambda, \quad \text{if } x_p^* > 0 \\ \geq & \lambda, \quad \text{if } x_p^* = 0, \end{cases} \tag{5.27}$$

where $\sum_{p \in P} x_p^* = T$.

Construction of Expanded Network in Situation 3

In order to construct an expanded network, which enables one to reduce this equilibrium problem to that governing the case of known O/D pairs and travel demands, one proceeds as follows: Construct a supersource node ξ and a super sink node ψ. Then construct an artificial link from the supersource node to each origin node. In addition, construct a link from each destination node to the supersink node. Denote by $\hat{p}$ for this situation a path which consists of p but has the appropriate artificial link from the supersource node attached to it as well as the artificial link at its terminus ending at the

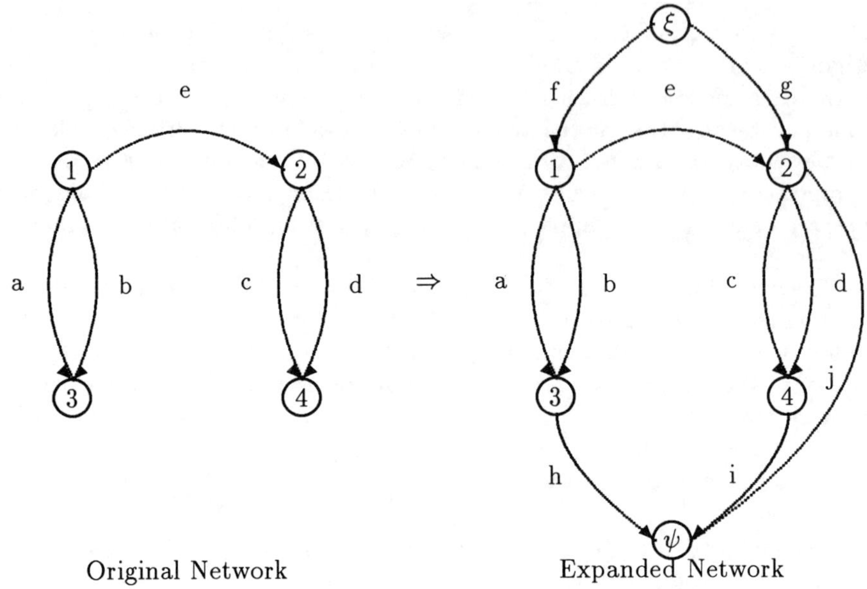

Fig. 5.3. Expanded network for Example 5.3

supersink node. There is then defined to be a single artificial O/D pair on the expanded network given by $\hat{w} = (\xi, \psi)$. The equilibrium conditions (5.27) are then subsumed by the equilibrium conditions (2.15) for the expanded network (with only a single O/D pair).

Furthermore, the equilibrium conditions (5.8) and (5.9) can be now applied directly to the expanded network with the appropriate substitutions for paths and O/D pair to obtain the equilibrium conditions for the emission pricing problem in the case of Situation 3.

I now, for illustration purposes, present an example.

Example 5.3

Consider the network in Example 4.4, consisting of four nodes: 1, 2, 3, 4, and five links: a, b, c, d, and e. Construct the expanded network, which is depicted in Figure 5.3, as follows: Add a single supersource node ξ and a supersink node ψ and links f and g originating in node ψ and terminating, respectively, in the origin nodes 1 and 2. Also, construct links h, i, and j originating in the destination nodes 2, 3, and 4 and terminating in the super sink node ψ. There is then a single (artificial) O/D pair on the expanded network $\hat{w} = (\xi, \psi)$ with an associated (artificial) travel demand $d_{\hat{w}} = T = 6$.

Both the orignal network and the expanded network for this example are illustrated in Figure 5.3.

Table 5.2. Summary of expanded network constructions

	Situation 1
Known origins and trip productions:	Construct a supersink node ξ and add a zero cost link from each destination node to ξ.
	Situation 2
Known destinations:	Construct a supersource node ψ add a zero cost link from ψ to each origin node.
	Situation 3
Known total number:	Construct a supersource node ψ and a supersink node ξ and add a zero cost link from ψ to each origin node and a zero cost link from each destination node to ψ.

The emission factors are: $h_a = 0.1$, $h_b = 0.1$, $h_c = 0.2$, $h_d = 0.2$, and $h_e = 0.7$. Assume that the desired environmental quality standard $\bar{Q} = 0.6$.

The cost structure is now described. The user link cost functions are:

$$c_a(f_a) = f_a + 1, \quad c_b(f_b) = f_b + 1, \quad c_c(f_c) = f_c + 1,$$

$$c_d(f_d) = f_d + 1, \quad c_e(f_e) = 2f_e + 5,$$

with the travel costs on the artificial links f, g, h, and i being set equal to zero, by construction.

The paths, hence, on the expanded network are: $\hat{p}_1 = (f, a, h)$, $\hat{p}_2 = (f, b, h)$, $\hat{p}_3 = (f, e, j)$, $\hat{p}_4 = (g, c, i)$, and $\hat{p}_5 = (g, d, i)$.

It is straightforward to verify that the path flow pattern: $x^*_{\hat{p}_1} = x^*_{\hat{p}_2} = 3$, with all other path flows equal to zero, and $\tau^* = 0$ is an equilibrium solution for the problem.

In Table 5.2, a summary of the expanded network constructions is given for the different transportation network situations. Again, I emphasize that the expanded network constructions allow one to transform the traffic network model into the baseline model and then to determine the emission pricing policy in order to assure sustainability of the network. Note that it has been explicitly assumed that the network is first viable according to the appropriate definition for the corresponding situation. In the next section, I turn to elastic demand networks, which, as established in Section 4.3, are always viable.

5.3 Pricing for Sustainable Elastic Demand Traffic Networks

In this section, the topic is that of pricing of elastic demand traffic networks for sustainability where the behavior is that of user-optimization. As in Section 5.1, I assume that the travel cost on a link may depend upon, in general, the entire link load pattern, that is, we assume user link travel cost functions of the form given by (5.10). In addition, since the demand is no longer fixed, as in the elastic demand traffic network models, I assume now that one has associated with each O/D pair w a travel disutility λ_w, such that

$$\lambda_w = \lambda_w(d), \quad \forall w \in W, \tag{5.28}$$

that is, I assume that, in general, the travel disutility associated with traveling between O/D pair w may depend upon the vector of travel demands. In this case, one may adapt equilibrium conditions (5.8) directly and equilibrium conditions (5.9) are still applicable, yielding the following definition:

Definition 5.5 (Traffic Network Equilibrium with Elastic Demands in the Presence of Emission Pricing)
For each O/D pair $w \in W$, and each path $p \in P_w$:

$$\bar{C}_p(x^*, \tau^*) = C_p(x^*) + \tau^* \sum_{a \in L} h_a \delta_{ap} \begin{cases} = & \lambda_w(d^*), \quad \text{if } x_p^* > 0 \\ \geq & \lambda_w(d^*), \quad \text{if } x_p^* = 0, \end{cases} \tag{5.29}$$

In addition, one must have that:

$$\bar{Q} - \sum_{a \in L} h_a \sum_{p \in P} x_p^* \delta_{ap} \begin{cases} = & 0, \quad \text{if } \tau^* > 0 \\ \geq & 0, \quad \text{if } \tau^* = 0, \end{cases} \tag{5.30}$$

where the path flow pattern must satisfy (2.39).

Hence, in this problem, one also needs to determine the travel demands, in addition to the path flows and the marginal cost of emission abatement.

I now provide the variational inequality formulations in path flows and in link loads of the equilibrium conditions (akin to (5.11) and (5.12) for the model with fixed travel demands). They are presented without proof since the proofs are similar to that of Theorem 5.1.

Theorem 5.2 (Variational Inequality Formulations of Elastic Demand Traffic Network Emission Pricing Policy Model)
A traffic flow and demand pattern and marginal cost of emission abatement $(x^*, d^*, \tau^*) \in \mathcal{K}^3$ is an equilibrium of the traffic network emission pricing policy model with elastic demands if and only if it is a solution to the variational inequality problem:

Path Flow Formulation:

$$\sum_{w\in W}\sum_{p\in P_w}\left[C_p(x^*)+\tau^*\sum_{a\in L}h_a\delta_{ap}\right]\times[x_p-x_p^*]-\sum_{w\in W}\lambda_w(d^*)\times(d_w-d_w^*)$$

$$+\left[\bar{Q}-\sum_{a\in L}h_a\sum_{p\in P}x_p\delta_{ap}\right]\times[\tau-\tau^*]\geq 0,\quad \forall(x,\tau,d)\in\mathcal{K}^3, \tag{5.31}$$

where $\mathcal{K}^3\equiv\bar{\mathcal{K}}^3\times R^1_+$ *and* $\bar{\mathcal{K}}^3\equiv\{(x,d)|x\geq 0,\ and\,(2.39)\ holds\}$, *or, equivalently,* $(f^*,d^*,\tau^*)\in\mathcal{K}^4$ *is an equilibrium link load, travel demand, and marginal cost of emission abatement pattern if and only if it satisfies the variational inequality problem:*

Link Load Formulation:

$$\sum_{a\in L}[c_a(f^*)+h_a\tau^*]\times[f_a-f_a^*]-\sum_{w\in W}\lambda_w(d^*)\times(d_w-d_w^*)$$

$$\left[\bar{Q}-\sum_{a\in L}h_af_a^*\right]\times[\tau-\tau^*]\geq 0,\quad \forall(f,d,\tau)\in\mathcal{K}^4, \tag{5.32}$$

where $\mathcal{K}^4\equiv\bar{\mathcal{K}}^4\times R^1_+$ *and* $\bar{\mathcal{K}}^4\equiv\{f|\ there\ exists\ an\ x\geq 0,\ so\ that\,(2.39)\ holds\}$.

I now show that variational inequalities (5.31) and (5.32) can be put into standard form (2.32). I first establish this for variational inequality (5.31) which is in path flow variables. Define the column vector $X\equiv(x,d,\tau)\in\mathcal{K}^3$ and the column vector $F(X)\equiv(C(X),L(X),T(X)$, where $C(X)$ and $T(X)$ are as defined for the fixed demand model and $L(X)$ is the J-dimensional vector with component w given by:

$$L_w(X):\lambda_w(d).$$

For variational inequality (5.32) in link load variables, define the column vector $X\equiv(f,d,\tau)\in\mathcal{K}^4$ and the column vector

$$F(X)\equiv(c(X),L(X),T(X)),$$

where $c(X)$ is as defined for the fixed demand emission pricing model, and $L(X)$ and $T(X)$ are as defined above.

In the special case in which the user link travel cost functions are separable and given by (5.1), and the travel disutility functions are also separable, that is,

$$\lambda_w=\lambda_w(d_w),\quad \forall w\in W, \tag{5.33}$$

one may obtain a solution to the simple case of the traffic network policy model with elastic travel demands. Indeed, one has:

Corollary 5.1 (Optimization Reformulation in a Special Case)
The solution to the traffic network equilibrium policy model in the case of separable user link travel cost functions and travel disutility functions can be obtained by solving the optimization problem:

$$\text{Minimize} \quad \sum_{a\in L} \int_0^{\sum_{p\in P} x_p\delta_{ap}} c_a(x)dx - \sum_{w\in W} \int_0^{d_w} \lambda_w(y)dy \tag{5.34}$$

subject to:

$$\sum_{p\in P_w} x_p = d_w, \quad \forall w \in W, \tag{5.35}$$

$$\sum_{a\in L} h_a \sum_{p\in P} x_p\delta_{ap} \leq \bar{Q}, \tag{5.36}$$

$$x_p \geq 0, \quad \forall p \in P. \tag{5.37}$$

In the next section, I describe a general algorithm for the solution of variational inequality problems in which the function that enters the variational inequality is monotone and Lipschitz continuous.

5.4 A Computational Procedure

In this section, an algorithm is presented which can be applied to solve any variational inequality problem (see (2.32)) in which the function F that enters the variational inequality is monotone and Lipschitz continuous, provided that a solution exists. The algorithm is the modified projection method of Korpelevich (1977).

Recall that *monotonicity* of a function F (see also Appendix B) requires that F satisfies the following condition:

$$\langle (F(X^1) - F(X^2))^T, X^1 - X^2\rangle \geq 0, \quad \forall X^1, X^2 \in \mathcal{K}, \tag{5.38}$$

whereas *Lipschitz continuity* of a function F requires that there exists a positive constant $\bar{L}$, such that

$$\|F(X^1) - F(X^2)\| \leq \bar{L}\|X^1 - X^2\|, \quad \forall X^1, X^2 \in \mathcal{K}. \tag{5.39}$$

The statement of the modified projection method is as follows, where $\mathcal{T}$ denotes an iteration counter:

Modified Projection Method

Step 0: Initialization
Set $X^0 \in K$. Let $\mathcal{T} = 1$ and let α be a scalar such that $0 < \alpha < \frac{1}{L}$, where L is the Lipschitz continuity constant (cf. (5.39)).

Step 1: Computation

Compute $\bar{X}^{\mathcal{T}}$ by solving the variational inequality subproblem:

$$\langle (\bar{X}^{\mathcal{T}} + \alpha F(X^{\mathcal{T}-1})^T - X^{\mathcal{T}-1})^T, X - \bar{X}^{\mathcal{T}} \rangle \geq 0, \quad \forall X \in \mathcal{K}. \tag{5.40}$$

Step 2: Adaptation

Compute $X^{\mathcal{T}}$ by solving the variational inequality subproblem:

$$\langle (X^{\mathcal{T}} + \alpha F(\bar{X}^{\mathcal{T}})^T - X^{\mathcal{T}-1})^T, X - X^{\mathcal{T}} \rangle \geq 0, \quad \forall X \in \mathcal{K}. \tag{5.41}$$

Step 3: Convergence Verification

If max $|X_l^{\mathcal{T}} - X_l^{\mathcal{T}-1}| \leq \epsilon$, for all l, with $\epsilon > 0$, a prespecified tolerance, then stop; else, set $\mathcal{T} =: \mathcal{T} + 1$, and go to Step 1.

I now discuss the modified projection method more fully (see also Appendix B). I first recall the definition of the projection of X on the closed convex set $\mathcal{K}$, with respect to the Euclidean norm, and denoted by $P_{\mathcal{K}}X$, as

$$y = P_{\mathcal{K}}X = \arg\min_{z \in \mathcal{K}} \|X - z\|. \tag{5.42}$$

In particular, note that $\bar{X}^{\mathcal{T}}$ generated by the modified projection method as the solution to the variational inequality subproblem (5.40) is actually the projection of $(X^{\mathcal{T}-1} - \alpha F(X^{\mathcal{T}-1})^T)$ on the closed convex set $\mathcal{K}$. In other words,

$$\bar{X}^{\mathcal{T}} = P_{\mathcal{K}}\left[X^{\mathcal{T}-1} - \alpha F(X^{\mathcal{T}-1})^T\right]. \tag{5.43}$$

Similarly, $X^{\mathcal{T}}$ generated by the solution to variational inequality subproblem (5.41) is the projection of $X^{\mathcal{T}-1} - \alpha F(\bar{X}^{\mathcal{T}})^T$ on $\mathcal{K}$, that is,

$$X^{\mathcal{T}} = P_{\mathcal{K}}\left[X^{\mathcal{T}-1} - \alpha F(\bar{X}^{\mathcal{T}})^T\right]. \tag{5.44}$$

I now give an explicit statement of the modified projection method for the solution of variational inequality problem (5.12) for the fixed demand traffic network equilibrium model with emission pricing.

Modified Projection Method for the Solution of Variational Inequality (5.12)

Step 0: Initialization

Set $(f^0, \tau^0) \in \mathcal{K}^2$. Let $\mathcal{T} = 1$ and set α such that $0 < \alpha < \frac{1}{\bar{L}}$, where $\bar{L}$ is the Lipschitz constant for the problem.

Step 1: Computation

Compute $(\bar{f}^{\mathcal{T}}, \bar{\tau}^{\mathcal{T}}) \in \mathcal{K}^2$ by solving the variational inequality subproblem:

$$\sum_{a \in L} (\bar{f}_a^{\mathcal{T}} + \alpha(c_a(f^{\mathcal{T}-1}) + h_a \tau^{\mathcal{T}-1}) - f_a^{\mathcal{T}-1}) \times (f_a - \bar{f}_a^{\mathcal{T}})$$

$$+(\bar{\tau}^{\mathcal{T}}+\alpha(\bar{Q}-\sum_{a\in L}h_a f_a^{\mathcal{T}-1})-\tau^{\mathcal{T}-1})\times(\tau-\bar{\tau}^{\mathcal{T}})\geq 0,\quad \forall(f,\tau)\in\mathcal{K}^2. \quad (5.45)$$

Step 2: Adaptation

Compute $(f^{\mathcal{T}},\tau^{\mathcal{T}})\in\mathcal{K}^2$ by solving the variational inequality subproblem:

$$\sum_{a\in L}(f_a^{\mathcal{T}}+\alpha(c_a(\bar{f}^{\mathcal{T}})+h_a\bar{\tau}^{\mathcal{T}})-f_a^{\mathcal{T}-1})\times(f_a-f_a^{\mathcal{T}})$$

$$+(\tau^{\mathcal{T}}+\alpha(\bar{Q}-\sum_{a\in L}h_a\bar{f}_a^{\mathcal{T}})-\tau^{\mathcal{T}-1})\times(\tau-\tau^{\mathcal{T}})\geq 0,\quad \forall(f,d)\in\mathcal{K}^2. \quad (5.46)$$

Step 3: Convergence Verification

If $\mid f_a^{\mathcal{T}}-f_a^{\mathcal{T}-1}\mid\leq\epsilon$, for all $a\in L$ and $\mid\tau^{\mathcal{T}}-\tau^{\mathcal{T}-1}\mid\leq\epsilon$, with $\epsilon>0$, a pre-specified tolerance, then stop; otherwise, set $\mathcal{T}:=\mathcal{T}+1$, and go to Step 1.

The decomposed subproblems take on a simple form which can be computed very efficiently. Note that since the feasible set $\mathcal{K}^2$ is a Cartesian product, where $\mathcal{K}^2\equiv\bar{K}^2\times R^1_+$, the above variational inequality subproblems can be decomposed across $\bar{K}^2$, which has the network structure of the problem, and across the nonnegative orthant. In fact, (5.45) yields the subproblem in $\bar{K}^2$ in link variables given by:

$$\text{Minimize}_{f\in\bar{K}^2}\langle\bar{f}^{\mathcal{T}T},\bar{f}^{\mathcal{T}}\rangle+\langle g^{\mathcal{T}},f^{\mathcal{T}}\rangle, \quad (5.47)$$

where $\bar{f}^{\mathcal{T}}$ is the column vector with component $a=\bar{f}_a^{\mathcal{T}}$, g is the column vector with component $g_a=\alpha(c_a(f^{\mathcal{T}-1})+h_a\tau^{\mathcal{T}-1})-f_a^{\mathcal{T}-1})$. Observe that this subproblem is a quadratic programming problem or, equivalently, the optimization reformulation of the traffic network equilibrium conditions in the case of linear and separable user link travel cost functions. Hence, this problem can be solved in numerous ways. I discuss my approach in the subsequent numerical example section.

In addition, (5.45) yields a subproblem in the marginal cost of emission abatement variable, which can be solved explicitly and exactly in closed form as follows: Set

$$\bar{\tau}^{\mathcal{T}}=\max\{0,-\alpha(\bar{Q}-\sum_{a\in L}h_a f_a^{\mathcal{T}-1})+\tau^{\mathcal{T}-1}\}. \quad (5.48)$$

The solution of the induced subproblems in (5.46) can be solved in an analogous fashion.

I now state the convergence result for the algorithm for the fixed demand emission pricing model. It is presented without proof since the proof is similar to the convergence proofs of the modified projection method given in subsequent chapters.

Theorem 5.3 (Convergence)
If the user link travel cost functions c are assumed to be monotone and have bounded first-order derivatives, then the modified projection method described above converges to the solution of the variational inequality (5.12).

I now show the realization of the modified projection method for the solution of the variational inequality in link loads for the elastic demand emission pricing policy model.

Modified Projection Method for the Solution of Variational Inequality (5.32)

Step 0: Initialization
Set $(f^0, d^0, \tau^0) \in \mathcal{K}^4$. Let $\mathcal{T} = 1$ and set α such that $0 < \alpha < \frac{1}{\bar{L}}$, where $\bar{L}$ is the Lipschitz constant for the problem.

Step 1: Computation
Compute $(\bar{f}^{\mathcal{T}}, \bar{d}^{\mathcal{T}}, \bar{\tau}^{\mathcal{T}}) \in \mathcal{K}^4$ by solving the variational inequality subproblem:

$$\sum_{a\in L}(\bar{f}_a^{\mathcal{T}} + \alpha(c_a(f^{\mathcal{T}-1}) + h_a\tau^{\mathcal{T}-1}) - f_a^{\mathcal{T}-1}) \times (f_a - \bar{f}_a^{\mathcal{T}})$$

$$+ \sum_{w\in W}(\bar{d}_w^{\mathcal{T}} - \alpha\lambda_w(d^{\mathcal{T}-1}) - d_w^{\mathcal{T}-1}) \times (d_w - \bar{d}_w^{\mathcal{T}})$$

$$+(\bar{\tau}^{\mathcal{T}} + \alpha(\sum_{a\in L}\bar{Q} - \sum_{a\in L}h_a f_a^{\mathcal{T}-1}) - \tau^{\mathcal{T}-1}) \times (\tau - \bar{\tau}^{\mathcal{T}}) \geq 0, \quad \forall (f,d,\tau) \in \mathcal{K}^4. \tag{5.49}$$

Step 2: Adaptation
Compute $(f^{\mathcal{T}}, d^{\mathcal{T}}, \tau^{\mathcal{T}}) \in \mathcal{K}^4$ by solving the variational inequality subproblem:

$$\sum_{a\in L}(f_a^{\mathcal{T}} + \alpha(c_a(\bar{f}^{\mathcal{T}}) + h_a\bar{\tau}^{\mathcal{T}}) - f_a^{\mathcal{T}-1}) \times (f_a - f_a^{\mathcal{T}})$$

$$+ \sum_{w\in W}(d_w^{\mathcal{T}} - \alpha\lambda_w(\bar{d}^{\mathcal{T}}) - d_w^{\mathcal{T}-1}) \times (d_w - d_w^{\mathcal{T}})$$

$$+(\tau^{\mathcal{T}} + \alpha(\sum_{a\in L}\bar{Q} - \sum_{a\in L}h_a\bar{f}_a^{\mathcal{T}}) - \tau^{\mathcal{T}-1}) \times (\tau - \tau^{\mathcal{T}}) \geq 0, \quad \forall (f,d,\tau) \in \mathcal{K}^4. \tag{5.50}$$

Step 3: Convergence Verification
If $|f_a^{\mathcal{T}} - f_a^{\mathcal{T}-1}| \leq \epsilon$, for all $a \in L$, $|d_w^{\mathcal{T}} - d_w^{\mathcal{T}-1}| \leq \epsilon$, for all $w \in W$, and $|\tau^{\mathcal{T}} - \tau^{\mathcal{T}-1}| \leq \epsilon$, with $\epsilon > 0$, a pre-specified tolerance, then stop; otherwise, set $\mathcal{T} := \mathcal{T} + 1$, and go to Step 1.

The decomposed subproblems (5.48) and (5.49) can be computed very efficiently.

Note that since the feasible set $\mathcal{K}^4$ is again a Cartesian product, where $\mathcal{K}^4 \equiv \bar{K}^4 \times R^1_+$, the above projections can be decomposed across $\bar{K}^4$, which has the network structure of the problem, and across the nonnegative orthant. Hence, (5.49), for example, yields the subproblem in K^4 in link and demand variables given by:

$$\text{Minimize}_{(f,d)\in \bar{K}^2} \langle \bar{f}^{\mathcal{T}T}, \bar{f}^{\mathcal{T}} \rangle + \langle g^T, f^{\mathcal{T}} \rangle + \langle \bar{d}^{\mathcal{T}T}, \bar{d}^{\mathcal{T}} \rangle - r^T, \tag{5.51}$$

where $\bar{f}^{\mathcal{T}}$ is the column vector with component $a = \bar{f}^{\mathcal{T}}_a$, g is the column vector with component $g_a = \alpha(c_a(f^{\mathcal{T}-1}) + h_a\tau^{\mathcal{T}-1}) - f^{\mathcal{T}-1}_a$, $\bar{d}^{\mathcal{T}}$ is the column vector with component $w = \bar{d}^{\mathcal{T}}_w$, and r is the column vector with component $w = \alpha\lambda_w(d^{\mathcal{T}-1}) + d^{\mathcal{T}-1}_w$. This subproblem is a quadratic programming problem or, equivalently, the optimization reformulation of the traffic network equilibrium conditions in the case of linear and separable user link travel cost and travel disutility functions. Hence, this problem can be also solved in numerous ways (see, e.g., Dhanda, Nagurney, and Ramanujam 1999). In addition, one can reformulate the elastic demand problem as a fixed demand problem over an appropriately constructed abstract network (see Gartner 1980) and, therefore, one can apply then the equilibration algorithm of Dafermos and Sparrow (1969) (see Appendix B).

Furthermore, (5.49) yields a subproblem in the marginal cost of emission abatement, which can be solved using the expression (5.48) above.

Convergence for the algorithm is given in the following theorem, which is also presented without proof since the proof is similar to other proofs of convergence given in this book.

Theorem 5.4 (Convergence)
If the user link travel cost functions c and the travel disutility functions $-\lambda$ are assumed to be monotone and have bounded first-order derivatives, then the modified projection method described above converges to the solution of the variational inequality (5.32).

Here the focus has been on the computation of solutions to the variational inequalities in link loads rather than path flow variables and in the next section I provide several numerical examples. In Chapter 7, I present variational inequalities and computational procedures for which the variables are path flow variables, when I investigate alternative pollution permit systems.

5.5 Numerical Examples

In this section, several numerical examples are presented. Specifically, I consider the solution of the fixed demand emission pricing policy model of Section 5.2.1 and apply the modified projection method for solving the governing variational inequality given by (5.12) as outlined in the preceding section. The modified projection method was implemented in FORTRAN and the system utilized was the IBM SP2 located at the Computer Science Department at the University of Massachusetts at Amherst for the numerical work.

For the solution of the standard traffic network equilibrium problem encountered in both the computation and adaptation steps (cf. (5.45) and (5.46)) I utilized the equilibration method (cf. Dafermos and Sparrow 1969 and Appendix B). The convergence criterion used was: $|x_p^{\mathcal{T}} - x_p^{\mathcal{T}-1}| \leq \epsilon$, for all $p \in P$; $|\tau^{\mathcal{T}} - \tau^{\mathcal{T}-1}| \leq \epsilon$. Note that requiring that the absolute difference between the computed path flows for two successive iterations be less than the convergence tolerance is comparable to requiring that the absolute difference between the computed link loads at two successive iterations be less than a related epsilon (as stated in the convergence verification Step 3 of the algorithm following (5.46)).

The modified projection method was initialized by setting the flow on a path equal to the travel demand for the O/D pair that the path belongs to divided by the number of paths. All other variables were initialized to zero.

Example 5.4: Variant of Example 5.1

The first numerical example was identical to Example 5.1 except for the following change: I relaxed the environmental quality standard from $\bar{Q} = 1$ to $\bar{Q} = 1.5$. Note that $\bar{Q} = 1.5$ is still lower than the total number of emissions emitted, which was equal to 2.1, if there is no emission pricing policy system in place. I set $\alpha = 0.4$ in the modified projection method. An application of the modified projection method yielded the following solution:

$$f_a^* = 5.79, \quad f_b^* = 3.40, \quad f_c^* = 0.81.$$

This equilibrium link load pattern was induced by the equilibrium path flow pattern:

$$x_{p_1}^* = 5.79, \quad x_{p_2}^* = 3.40, \quad x_{p_3}^* = 0.81.$$

The generalized user travel costs on the paths were: $\bar{C}_{p_1} = \bar{C}_{p_2} = \bar{C}_{p_3} = 21.62$.

The equilibrium marginal cost of emission abatement was:

$$\tau^* = 51.79.$$

The environmental standard was met since the total emissions: $\sum_{a \in L} h_a f_a^* = \bar{Q} = 1.5$. Clearly, both equilibrium conditions (5.8) and (5.9) are satisfied by the computed flow and marginal cost of emission abatement pattern.

Example 5.5

I then considered the transportation network depicted in Figure 5.4 consisting of ten nodes, thirteen links and two O/D pairs: $w_1 = (1, 8)$ and $w_2 = (2, 10)$ with travel demands $d_{w_1} = 5$ and $d_{w_2} = 5$.

The user link travel cost functions were:

$$c_1(f) = .00005 f_1^4 + 5 f_1 + 2 f_2 + 5, \quad c_2(f) = .00003 f_2^4 + 4 f_2 + f_1 + 2,$$

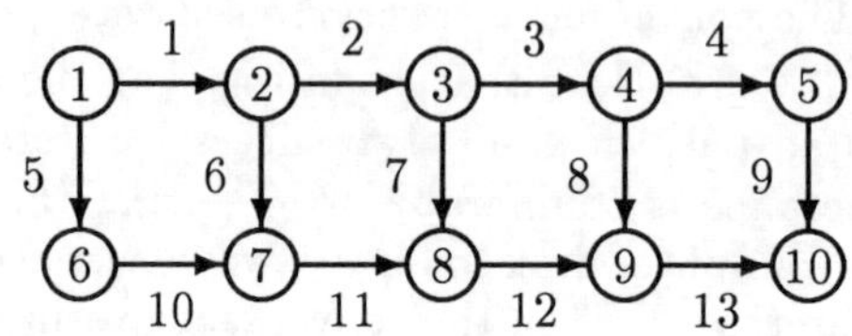

Fig. 5.4. Network topology for Example 5.5

$$c_3(f) = .00005f_3^4 + 3f_3 + f_4 + 3, \quad c_4(f) = .00003f_4^4 + 6f_4 + 3f_5 + 4,$$
$$c_5(f) = 4f_5 + f_{12} + 8, \quad c_6(f) = .00007f_6^4 + 7f_6 + 4f_{12} + 6,$$
$$c_7(f) = 8f_7 + 2f_{13} + 7, \quad c_8(f) = .00001f_8^4 + 7f_8 + 3f_{12} + 6,$$
$$c_9(f) = 8f_9 + 3f_{11} + 5, \quad c_{10}(f) = .00003f_{10}^4 + 6f_{10} + f_1 + 3,$$
$$c_{11}(f) = .00004f_{11}^4 + 4f_{11} + f_2 + 4, \quad c_{12}(f) = .00002f_{12}^4 + 6f_{12} + f_1 + 5,$$
$$c_{13}(f) = .00003f_{12}^4 + 9f_{13} + 2f_4 + 3.$$

The paths were:
For O/D pair w_1:

$$p_1 = (1, 2, 7), \quad p_2 = (1, 6, 11), \quad p_3 = (5, 10, 11)$$

and for O/D pair w_2:

$$p_4 = (2, 3, 4, 9), \quad p_5 = (2, 3, 8, 13), \quad p_6 = (2, 7, 12), \quad p_7 = (6, 11, 12, 13).$$

The parameter α in the modified projection method was set to 0.1, whereas ϵ was set to .0001. The emission parameters were: $h_a = 0.5 \times a$, $\forall a \in L$, and the environmental quality standard $\bar{Q} = 91$.

The modified projection method yielded the equilibrium link load pattern given by:

$$f_1^* = 3.88, \quad f_2^* = 7.36, \quad f_3^* = 5.00, \quad f_4^* = 3.51,$$
$$f_5^* = 1.12, \quad f_6^* = 1.52, \quad f_7^* = 2.36, \quad f_8^* = 1.49,$$
$$f_9^* = 3.51, \quad f_{10}^* = 1.12, \quad f_{11}^* = 2.64, \quad f_{12}^* = 0.00, \quad f_{13}^* = 1.49,$$

with an equilibrium path flow pattern:

For O/D pair w_1:

$$x^*_{p_1} = 2.36, \quad x^*_{p_2} = 1.52, \quad x^*_{p_3} = 1.12,$$

and for O/D pair w_2:

$$x^*_{p_4} = 3.51, \quad x^*_{p_5} = 1.49, \quad x^*_{p_6} = 0.00, \quad x^*_{p_7} = 0.00,$$

and with generalized user travel costs:
For O/D pair w_1:

$$\bar{C}_{p_1} = \bar{C}_{p_2} = \bar{C}_{p_3} = 140.43,$$

For O/D pair w_2:

$$\bar{C}_{p_4} = \bar{C}_{p_5} = 193.14, \quad \bar{C}_{p_6} = 203.16, \quad \bar{C}_{p_7} = 203.16.$$

The equilibrium marginal cost of emission abatement was $\tau^* = 7.41$.

The total emissions generated were precisely equal to the environmental quality standard $\bar{Q} = 91$. The equilibrium conditions (5.8) and (5.9) were also met by the computed flow and marginal cost of emission abatement pattern.

In the next chapter, an alternative economic-incentive-based approach for emission abatement – that of pollution permits – is modeled and analyzed.

6 Permits for User-Optimized, Fixed Demand Networks

In this chapter, I develop a framework for sustainable transportation systems through the perspective of pollution permits. In particular, I consider fixed demand traffic networks in which the travel behavior on the transportation network is that of user-optimization. For such networks, a permit system on links is constructed which guarantees that the environmental quality standard is satisfied. I assume throughout this chapter that the transportation network in question is viable. Specifically, a variational inequality framework is utilized for the modeling, qualitative analysis, and computation of equilibrium patterns in the congested urban transportation systems in the presence of emission pollution permits. Qualitative analysis of the model is conducted and existence and uniqueness results of the solution obtained. I also propose an algorithm, with convergence results, to compute the equilibrium link load, marginal cost of emission abatement, license, and license price pattern. Numerical examples are included to illustrate this approach.

In this chapter, hence, the topic of sustainable transportation systems is explored through the prism of pollution permits. As noted in Chapter 2, the theoretical basis for marketable pollution permits was provided by Montgomery (1972), who showed that perfectly competitive firms could trade permits in an effort to comply with preexisting regional environmental standards with the quantity of pollution fixed by the total number of permits. The system of marketable pollution permits could also address the spatial dimension of the pollution problem by incorporating ambient concentrations within the model. In this chapter, in contrast, I consider users of a transportation network who are mobile, rather than fixed in location, as are firms. Nevertheless, the pollution dispersion is still spatial in nature as it was in the preceding chapters.

The chapter is organized as follows. In Section 6.1, the traffic network equilibrium policy model with pollution permits is developed, which determines the equilibrium flow pattern of travelers, the equilibrium license holdings, as well as the equilibrium marginal costs of emission abatement and the license price. I prove that the equilibrium pattern guarantees that the imposed environmental emission standards are met and formulate the governing equilibrium conditions as a variational inequality problem. I then utilize the theory of variational inequalities to study this new model qualitatively. The theory of variational inequalities has been adopted for environmental policy modeling in the case of firms trading in marketable pollution permits by Nagurney and Dhanda (1996, 1997c). Variational inequality theory has also been used to study a plethora of equilibrium problems ranging from traffic network equilibrium problems and oligopolistic market equilibrium problems to general economic equilibrium problems and financial equilibrium problems (cf. Nagurney and Siokos 1997; Nagurney 1999a) and the references therein). In this model, however, the focus is on vehicular emission permits along roads in order to ensure that emissions along the links do not exceed predetermined limits. Specifically, sustainability issues, pollution permits, and fixed travel demand traffic networks are treated within the same modeling schema.

In Section 6.2, an algorithm for the computation of the equilibrium pattern is presented, along with convergence results, and then applied in Section 6.3 to compute the solution to several numerical examples.

6.1 The Model with Fixed Travel Demands and Pollution Permits

Here, as in Chapter 5, a single pollutant and the case of a single receptor point for emissions are considered. This permit system model readily generalizes to multiple pollutants and multiple receptor points but with an associated increase in notation.

The necessary notation is presented first. As in the preceding chapters, consider a transportation network $G = [N, L]$ consisting of the set of nodes N and a set of directed links L. Let a, b, etc., denote the links and let p, q, etc., denote the paths, which are assumed to be acyclic. Assume that there are J origin/destination (O/D) pairs in the network, with a typical O/D pair denoted by w, and the set of O/D pairs denoted by W. Let P_w denote the set of paths connecting O/D pair w and let P denote the set of paths in the network.

The flow on a link a is denoted by f_a, and the user cost associated with traveling on link a by c_a. Group the link loads into a column vector $f \in R^n$, and the link user travel costs into a row vector $c \in R^n$, where n is the number of links in the network.

The user travel cost on a link will, in general, depend upon the entire link load pattern, that is,

$$c = c(f), \tag{6.1}$$

where c is a known smooth function.

A user traveling on path p incurs a user travel cost C_p, where

$$C_p(f) = \sum_{a\in L} c_a(f)\delta_{ap}, \tag{6.2}$$

where $\delta_{ap} = 1$, if link a is contained in path p, and 0, otherwise.

Here I consider the case of fixed travel demands where the demand for O/D pair is denoted by d_w. The nonnegative flow on path p is denoted by x_p, with the path flows grouped into a column vector $x \in R^{n_P}_+$, where n_P denotes the number of paths in the network. The following conservation of flow equations must be satisfied by the flows in the network:

$$d_w = \sum_{p\in P_w} x_p, \quad \forall w \in W, \tag{6.3}$$

and

$$f_a = \sum_{p\in P} x_p\delta_{ap}, \quad \forall a \in L. \tag{6.4}$$

Recall that the conservation of flow equation (6.3) states that the sum of the path flows on paths connecting an O/D pair must be equal to the travel demand for that O/D pair. Equation (6.4), in turn, states that the flow on a link equals the sum of the path flows on paths that use that link. Let K denote the feasible set defined as follows:

$$K \equiv \{f, \text{ such that there exists a vector } x \geq 0, \text{ satisfying (6.3) and (6.4)}\}.$$

Let l_a denote the number of license permits on link a that allows travelers to emit pollutants at a certain rate. Let l^0_a denote the initial allocation of licenses on link a, which is assumed to be nonnegative. Group the licenses into the column vector $l \in R^n_+$. As in the previous chapters, let h_a denote the emission factor associated with link $a \in L$.

I now discuss the price and cost structure associated with the pollution permits. Let ρ denote the price of a license in the transportation network and let τ_a denote the marginal cost of emission abatement on link a. Note that, in contrast to the emission pricing policy models of Chapter 5, one now has not a single marginal cost of emission abatement for the entire network but one for each link of the network. Without any loss of generality, one can group the marginal costs of abatement into the column vector $\tau \in R^n_+$.

Next, I construct the equilibrium conditions. They consist of systems of equalities and inequalities which must hold, respectively, for the path flows, the marginal costs of emission abatement, the licenses, and the license price.

Subsequently, the variational inequality formulation of the governing equilibrium conditions is derived.

Equilibrium Conditions

The traveler on a path p is now subject not only to the user travel cost, given by (6.2), but also is subject to the payment of the price or cost of emissions. In particular, one now has that the cost on a link a is given by $c_a(f) + h_a \tau_a$, and, hence, the *generalized* cost on a path p, denoted by $\bar{C}_p(f, \tau)$ is given by $\bar{C}_p(f, \tau) = C_p(f) + \sum_{a \in L} h_a \tau_a \delta_{ap}$. Consequently, the traffic network equilibrium conditions, in the presence of the pollution permit system, take on the form: For all O/D pairs $w \in W$ and each path $p \in P_w$:

$$\bar{C}_p(f^*, \tau^*) = C_p(f^*) + \sum_{a \in L} h_a \tau_a^* \delta_{ap} \begin{cases} = & \lambda_w, & \text{if } x_p^* > 0 \\ \geq & \lambda_w, & \text{if } x_p^* = 0, \end{cases} \tag{6.5}$$

where τ_a^* denotes the equilibrium marginal cost of emission abatement associated with link a and discussed further below.

Indeed, equilibrium conditions (6.5) state that a traveler on a path of the network is now subjected to payment of the true cost of his emissions while traveling on the path p. The emission payment for traveling on path p is equal to the sum over all links that comprise the path p of the marginal cost of emission abatement times the emission factor on the links. Note that, in this framework, the transportation authority is responsible for informing the travelers of the license prices and the corresponding payments required, as well as the availability of the licenses or permits on the links.

One also has the following conditions, which must hold in equilibrium, akin to those that must hold in the case of firms and marketable pollution permits (cf. Nagurney and Dhanda 1996). For each link $a \in L$, the equilibrium marginal cost of emission abatement τ_a^* must satisfy the following system: For each link $a \in L$:

$$h_a f_a^* \begin{cases} = & l_a^*, & \text{if } \tau_a^* > 0 \\ \leq & l_a^*, & \text{if } \tau_a^* = 0. \end{cases} \tag{6.6}$$

In other words, if the marginal cost of emission abatement, τ_a^*, is positive in equilibrium for a link a, then the emissions on that link are precisely equal to the pollution license holdings for that link; if the number of licenses exceeds the emissions on a link, then, in equilibrium, the marginal cost of abatement is zero.

The following condition must also be met at equilibrium: For each link $a \in L$:

$$\tau_a^* \begin{cases} = & \rho^*, & \text{if } l_a^* > 0 \\ \leq & \rho^*, & \text{if } l_a^* = 0. \end{cases} \tag{6.7}$$

Hence, in equilibrium, a positive holding of licenses for a link implies that the marginal cost of emission abatement must be equal to the price of the license on a link. However, if the price of the license exceeds the marginal cost of emission abatement, then the number of licenses for that link will be zero.

Finally, the equilibrium price, ρ^*, of a license must satisfy the following equilibrium condition:

$$\sum_{a\in L}(l_a^0 - l_a^*)\begin{cases} = & 0, \quad \text{if } \rho^* > 0 \\ \geq & 0, \quad \text{if } \rho^* = 0. \end{cases} \tag{6.8}$$

Expression (6.8) corresponds to the well-known economic equilibrium conditions that state that, in equilibrium, if a price of a good (which in this case is the license) is positive, then the market for that good must clear; that is, the supply of the licenses, which is equal to $\sum_{a\in L} l_a^0$, must be equal to the demand for the licenses in equilibrium, which is given by $\sum_{a\in L} l_a^*$. On the other hand, if the price of a license in the transportation network is zero, then we may have an excess supply of the licenses in this network.

Let $\mathcal{K}$ denote the feasible set such that $\mathcal{K} \equiv K \times R_+^{2n+1}$, since both vectors l and τ are n-dimensional vectors and ρ is single dimensional.

I am now ready to define the equilibrium state.

Definition 6.1 (Pollution Permit System Traffic Network Equilibrium)
A vector $(f^*, \tau^*, l^*, \rho^*) \in \mathcal{K}$ is an equilibrium of the traffic network equilibrium emission permits market model if and only if it satisfies the systems of equalities and inequalities (6.5), (6.6), (6.7), and (6.8).

The variational inequality formulation of the equilibrium conditions for the model is now derived. Subsequently, a special case is considered.

Theorem 6.1 (Variational Inequality Formulation of Pollution Permit System Traffic Network Equilibrium)
A vector of link loads, marginal costs of emission abatement, licenses, and license price, $(f^*, \tau^*, l^*, \rho^*) \in \mathcal{K}$, is an equilibrium of the traffic network equilibrium problem with emission pollution permits if and only if it is a solution to the variational inequality problem:

$$\sum_{a\in L}(c_a(f^*) + h_a\tau_a^*) \times (f_a - f_a^*) + \sum_{a\in L}(l_a^* - h_a f_a^*) \times (\tau_a - \tau_a^*)$$

$$+\sum_{a\in L}(\rho^* - \tau_a^*)\times(l_a - l_a^*) + \sum_{a\in L}(l_a^0 - l_a^*)\times(\rho - \rho^*) \geq 0, \quad \forall (f, \tau, l, \rho) \in \mathcal{K}. \tag{6.9}$$

Proof:
I first establish that a solution to the equilibrium conditions (6.5), (6.6), (6.7), and (6.8) satisfies the variational inequality problem (6.9).

Equilibrium conditions (6.5) imply that, for a fixed O/D pair $w \in W$ and a fixed path $p \in P_w$:

$$(C_p(f^*) + \sum_{a \in L} h_a \tau_a^* \delta_{ap}) \times (x_p - x_p^*) \geq 0, \quad \forall x_p \in R_+. \tag{6.10}$$

Summing (6.10) over all paths p and O/D pairs w, and using (6.2), (6.3), and (6.4) yields:

$$\sum_{a \in L} (c_a(f^*) + h_a \tau_a^*) \times (f_a - f_a^*) \geq 0, \quad \forall f \in K. \tag{6.11}$$

From (6.6) and (6.7) one has, in turn, that, for a fixed link a:

$$(l_a^* - h_a f_a^*) \times (\tau_a - \tau_a^*) \geq 0, \quad \forall \tau_a \in R_+, \tag{6.12}$$

and

$$(\rho^* - \tau_a^*) \times (l_a - l_a^*) \geq 0, \quad \forall l_a \in R_+. \tag{6.13}$$

Summing now (6.12) and (6.13) over all links a, one obtains:

$$\sum_{a \in L} (l_a^* - h_a f_a^*) \times (\tau_a - \tau_a^*) + \sum_{a \in L} (\rho - \tau_a^*) \times (l_a - l_a^*) \geq 0, \quad \forall (\tau, l) \in R_+^{2n}. \tag{6.14}$$

From equilibrium conditions (6.8), one can conclude that:

$$\sum_{a \in L} (l_a^0 - l_a^*) \times (\rho - \rho^*) \geq 0, \quad \forall \rho \in R_+. \tag{6.15}$$

Summing now (6.11), (6.14), and (6.15) yields variational inequality (6.9).

I now prove that a solution to the variational inequality problem (6.8) also satisfies the equilibrium conditions (6.5), (6.6), (6.7), and (6.8).

Let $(f^*, \tau^*, l^*, \rho^*) \in \mathcal{K}$ be a solution to (6.12). Let $f_a = f_a^*$, for all $a \in L$, $l_a = l_a^*$, for all $a \in L$, and $\rho = \rho^*$, and substitute these values in (6.9). One then obtains:

$$\sum_{a \in L} (l_a^* - h_a f_a^*) \times (\tau_a - \tau_a^*) \geq 0, \tag{6.16}$$

which implies the equilibrium conditions (6.6).

Similarly, if one lets $f_a = f_a^*$, for all $a \in L$, $\tau_a = \tau_a^*$, for all $a \in L$, and $\rho = \rho^*$, and substitutes these values in (6.9), one gets:

$$\sum_{a \in L} (\rho^* - \tau_a^*) \times (l_a - l_a^*) \geq 0, \tag{6.17}$$

which implies the equilibrium conditions (6.7).

Also, if one lets $l_a = l_a^*$, $\tau_a = \tau_a^*$, for all $a \in L$, and $\rho = \rho^*$, and substitutes these values into (6.9), one obtains:

$$\sum_{a \in L} (c_a(f^*) + h_a \tau_a^*) \times (f_a - f_a^*) \geq 0, \tag{6.18}$$

which implies the equilibrium conditions (6.5).

Finally, if one lets $f_a = f^*_a$, for all $a \in L$, $\tau_a = \tau^*_a$, and $l_a = l^*_a$, for all $a \in L$, then upon substitution into (6.9), one obtains:

$$\sum_{a \in L} (l^0_a - l^*_a) \times (\rho - \rho^*) \geq 0, \tag{6.19}$$

which implies the economic equilibrium conditions (6.8). This completes the proof of the theorem. □

The variational inequality (6.9) is now put into standard form (cf. (2.32)). Define column vector $X \equiv (f, \tau, l, \rho) \in \mathcal{K}$ and the column vector $F(X)$, where

$$F(X) \equiv (C(X), T(X), L(X), P(X)).$$

$C(X)$, $L(X)$, $T(X)$ are each n-dimensional vectors with component a given, respectively, as follows:

$$C_a(X) : c_a(f) + h_a \tau_a,$$

$$T_a(X) : l_a - h_a f_a,$$

$$L_a(X) : \rho - \tau_a,$$

whereas $P(X)$ is the one-dimensional vector with the single component:

$$P(X) : \sum_{a \in L} (l^0_a - l_a).$$

Thus, variational inequality (6.9) can be expressed as

$$\langle F(X^*)^T, X - X^* \rangle \geq 0, \quad \forall X \in \mathcal{K}. \tag{6.20}$$

I now turn to studying whether the equilibrium pattern is independent of the initial allocation of the licenses on the links and how to guarantee that the environmental emission standards imposed by the governing body are met in equilibrium. The question as to whether the initial allocation of licenses affects the equilibrium pattern is answered in the following corollary.

Corollary 6.1 (Equilibrium Pattern Independence from Initial License Allocation)
If $l^0_a \geq 0$ for all $a \in L$, and $\sum_{a \in L} l^0_a = \bar{Q}$, with $\bar{Q}$ fixed and positive, then the equilibrium pattern $(f^*, \tau^*, l^*, \rho^*)$ is independent of the initial allocation.

Proof:
The terms in the variational inequality (6.9) are either independent of l^0_a or depend only on the sum, $\sum_{a \in L} l^0_a$. The conclusion follows. □

In the following proposition, it is shown that the environmental standards are met by the equilibrium pattern, provided that the sum of the initial

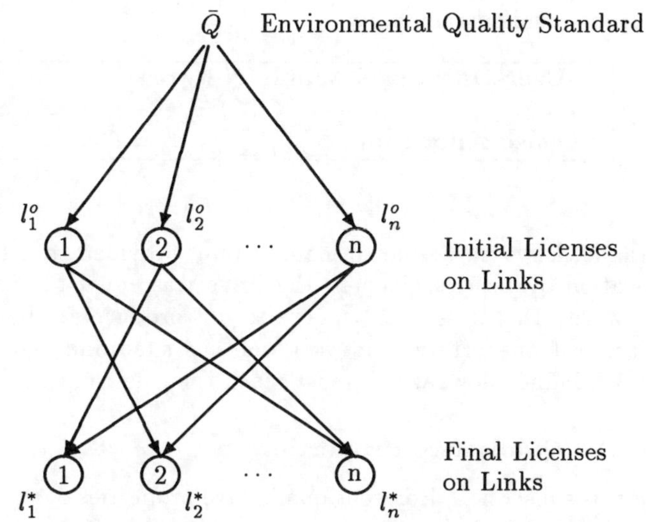

Fig. 6.1. Initial license allocation and final license holdings

allocation of licenses is equal to the imposed environmental standard given by $\bar{Q}$.

Proposition 6.1 (Achievement of Environmental Quality Standard) *If $\sum_{a\in L} l_a^0 = \bar{Q}$, the equilibrium vector achieves the environmental quality standard, $\bar{Q}$, provided that the transportation network is viable.*

Proof:
One has from equilibrium conditions (6.6) and (6.8) that

$$\sum_{a\in L} h_a f_a^* \leq \sum_{a\in L} l_a^* \leq \sum_{a\in L} l_a^0 = \bar{Q}.$$

Hence, the environmental standards are met by the equilibrium pattern. □

In Figure 6.1, a graphical depiction is provided of the initial license allocation summing up to the environmental quality standard, and the final license holdings on the links. In Table 6.1, further reinforcement is provided that sustainability is achieved under the pollution permit system.

In Nagurney and Dhanda (1996), an economic policy model with marketable pollution permits was proposed for oligopolistic and perfectly competitive firms, which were, however, fixed in location. In that paper, it was also shown, under similar conditions, that imposed environmental quality

Table 6.1. Relationship between a viable user-optimized network, pollution permits, and sustainability

User-Optimized Viable Network + **License Allocation:** $\sum_{i\in I}\sum_{a\in L_i} l_a^0 = \bar{Q}$	$\Rightarrow$	**Sustainability**

standards would be met in equilibrium, provided that the sum of initial allocation of licenses given to the firms was equal to the imposed standard. However, the firms could choose to not produce at all, whereas here in this class of transportation network one has fixed and positive travel demands, which induce flows which must reach their destinations.

6.1.1 Qualitative Properties

In this subsection, I present qualitative properties of the equilibrium. In particular, I provide existence and uniqueness results and also establish properties of the function $F(X)$ under which convergence of the algorithm in Section 6.2 is guaranteed.

Theorem 6.2 (Existence)
If $(f^*, \tau^*, l^*, \rho^*) \in \mathcal{K}$ satisfies the variational inequality (6.9), then the equilibrium link load vector f^* is a solution to the variational inequality problem:

$$\sum_{a\in L} c_a(f^*) \times (f_a - f_a^*) \geq 0, \quad \forall f \in K^1, \tag{6.21}$$

where

$$K^1 \equiv \{f, \text{ such that there exist vectors } x \geq 0 \text{ and}$$

$$l \geq 0 \text{ so that} (6.3), (6.4); h_a f_a \leq l_a, \forall a \in L, \text{ and } \sum_{a\in L} l_a^0 \geq \sum_{a\in L} l_a \text{ are satisfied}\}.$$

A solution to (6.21) is guaranteed to exist since K^1 is compact and c is assumed to be continuous. Furthermore, there exist vectors: $l^* \in R_+^n$, $\tau^* \in R_+^n$, and $\rho^* \in R_+$ with $(f^*, \tau^*, l^*, \rho^*)$ being a solution to the variational inequality problem (6.9) and, hence, in equilibrium.

Proof:
I will prove this theorem by contradiction. Assume that (6.21) is not true, that is:

$$\sum_{a\in L} c_a(f^*) \times (f_a - f_a^*) < 0, \quad \text{for some } f \in K^1. \tag{6.22}$$

According to (6.9), one then has that

$$\sum_{a\in L} h_a \tau_a^* \times (f_a - f_a^*) + \sum_{a\in L} (l_a^0 - l_a^*) \times (\rho - \rho^*)$$

$$+\sum_{a\in L}(\rho^* - \tau_a^*) \times (l_a - l_a^*) + \sum_{a\in L}(l_a^* - h_a f_a^*) \times (\tau_a - \tau_a^*) \geq$$

$$-\sum_{a\in L} c_a(f^*) \times (f_a - f_a^*) > 0. \tag{6.23}$$

Letting τ_a and ρ equal zero, substitution into (6.23), after some algebraic manipulations, yields:

$$\sum_{a\in L}[l_a^0 - l_a][-\rho^*] + \sum_{a\in L}[l_a - h_a f_a][-\tau_a^*] > 0. \tag{6.24}$$

However, the inequality on the left-hand side of (6.24) is clearly non-positive and, hence, a contradiction to the initial assumption. Thus, the variational inequality (6.21) must be satisfied.

Moreover, K^1 is compact, since $\sum_{a\in L} l_a \leq \sum_{a\in L} l_a^0$ and the travel demands are bounded. Thus, f and l lie in a compact set. Hence, the existence of f^* and l^* is guaranteed from the standard theory of variational inequalities (cf. Kinderlehrer and Stampacchia 1980). Also, according to the Lagrange Multiplier Theorem, there exist multipliers $t^* \in R_+^n$ and $\rho^* \in R_+$ associated with the constraints of K^1 and these, together, with the (f^*, l^*) above must satisfy the variational inequality (6.9). This completes the proof of the theorem. □

A uniqueness result is presented in the subsequent theorem.

Theorem 6.3 (Uniqueness)
Assume that the user link cost functions c are strictly monotone in f, that is:

$$\langle (c(f^1) - c(f^2))^T, f^1 - f^2 \rangle \geq 0, \quad \forall f^1, f^2 \in K, \quad f^1 \neq f^2. \tag{6.25}$$

Then the equilibrium link load pattern f^* is unique.

Proof:
Assume, on the contrary, that there are two distinct equilibrium patterns, denoted by X^1 and X^2. Then, both must satisfy the variational inequality (6.9). Hence, one must have that

$$\langle F(X^1)^T, X - X^1 \rangle \geq 0, \quad \forall X \in \mathcal{K} \tag{6.26}$$

and

$$\langle F(X^2)^T, X - X^2 \rangle \geq 0, \quad \forall X \in \mathcal{K}. \tag{6.27}$$

Substituting X^2 for X in (6.26) and X^1 for X in (6.27) and adding the two resultant inequalities, after algebraic simplifications, yields:

$$\sum_{a\in L}(c_a(f^1) - c_a(f^2)) \times (f_a^2 - f_a^1)) \geq 0, \tag{6.28}$$

but due to the assumption of strict monotonicity this implies that this inequality must hold as an equality and, hence, one must have that $f^1 = f^2$. □

Certain qualitative properties of the function $F(\cdot)$ are now investigated.

Lemma 6.1
Assume that the user link cost functions c are monotone increasing in the link loads, that is, for every $f^1, f^2 \in K$, we have that:

$$\langle (c(f^1) - c(f^2))^T, f^1 - f^2 \rangle \geq 0, \quad \forall f^1, f^2 \in K. \tag{6.29}$$

Then $F(X)$ is monotone, that is:

$$\langle (F(X^1) - F(X^2))^T, X^1 - X^2 \rangle \geq 0, \quad \forall X^1, X^2 \in \mathcal{K}. \tag{6.30}$$

Proof:
From the definition of $F(X)$ for this model, the left-hand side term of inequality (6.30) is given by

$$\sum_{a \in L} (c_a(f^1) - c_a(f^2)) \times (f_a^1 - f_a^2)$$

$$+ \sum_{a \in L} (\tau_a^1 h_a - \tau_a^2 h_a) \times (f_a^1 - f_a^2) + \sum_{a \in L} ((l_a^1 - h_a f^1) - (l_a^2 - h_a f_a^2)) \times (\tau_a^1 - \tau_a^2)$$

$$+ \sum_{a \in L} ((l_a^0 - l_a^1) - (l_a^0 - l_a^2)) \times (\rho^1 - \rho^2) + \sum_{a \in L} ((\rho^1 - \tau_a^1) - (\rho^2 - \tau_a^2)) \times (l_a^1 - l_a^2). \tag{6.31}$$

After rearranging the terms and simplifying, (6.31) reduces to

$$\sum_{a \in L} (c_a(f^1) - c_a(f^2)) \times (f_a^1 - f_a^2), \tag{6.32}$$

which by the assumption of monotonicity, is greater than or equal to zero. The proof is complete. □

Theorem 6.4 (Lipschitz Continuity)
If the user link travel cost functions and the disutility functions have bounded first-order derivatives, then the function $F(X)$ is Lipschitz continuous, that is, there exists a positive constant $\bar{L}$, such that

$$\| F(X^1) - F(X^2) \| \leq \bar{L} \, \| X^1 - X^2 \|, \quad \forall X^1, X^2 \in \mathcal{K}. \tag{6.33}$$

Proof:
Follows along the same arguments as the proof of Lemma 3 in Nagurney (1994). □

6.2 The Algorithm

In this section, the modified projection method of Korpelevich (1977) is proposed for the solution of variational inequality (6.9) governing the traffic network equilibrium model for pollution permits. The algorithm resolves the problems into simpler variational inequality subproblems. The algorithm was also proposed Section 5.4 for the computation of the emission pricing policy models developed in Chapter 5. Its general statement is given in Section 5.4. Here, for completeness, I show what form the modified projection method takes in the specific application.

Modified Projection Method for the Policy Model with Pollution Permits Satisfying Variational Inequality (6.9)

Step 0: Initialization

Set $(f^0, \tau^0, l^0 \rho^0) \in \mathcal{K}$. Let $\mathcal{T} = 1$ and set α such that $0 < \alpha < \frac{1}{\bar{L}}$, where $\bar{L}$ is the Lipschitz constant for the problem.

Step 1: Computation

Compute $(\bar{f}^{\mathcal{T}}, \bar{\tau}^{\mathcal{T}}, \bar{l}^{\mathcal{T}}, \bar{\rho}^{\mathcal{T}}) \in \mathcal{K}$ by solving the variational inequality subproblem:

$$\sum_{a \in L} (\bar{f}_a^{\mathcal{T}} + \alpha(c_a(f^{\mathcal{T}-1}) + h_a \tau_a^{\mathcal{T}-1}) - f_a^{\mathcal{T}-1}) \times (f_a - \bar{f}_a^{\mathcal{T}})$$

$$+ \sum_{a \in L} (\bar{\tau}_a^{\mathcal{T}} + \alpha(l_a^{\mathcal{T}-1} - h_a f_a^{\mathcal{T}-1}) - \tau_a^{\mathcal{T}-1}) \times (\tau_a - \bar{\tau}_a^{\mathcal{T}})$$

$$+ \sum_{a \in L} (\bar{l}_a^{\mathcal{T}} + \alpha(\rho^{\mathcal{T}-1} - \tau_a^{\mathcal{T}-1}) - l_a^{\mathcal{T}-1}) \times (l_a - \bar{l}_a^{\mathcal{T}})$$

$$+ (\bar{\rho}^{\mathcal{T}} + \alpha(\sum_{a \in L} l_a^0 - \sum_{a \in L} l_a^{\mathcal{T}-1}) - \rho^{\mathcal{T}-1}) \times (\rho - \bar{\rho}^{\mathcal{T}}) \geq 0, \quad \forall (f, \tau, l, \rho) \in \mathcal{K}. \quad (6.34)$$

Step 2: Adaptation

Compute $(f^{\mathcal{T}}, \tau^{\mathcal{T}}, l^{\mathcal{T}}, \rho^{\mathcal{T}}) \in \mathcal{K}$ by solving the variational inequality subproblem:

$$\sum_{a \in L} (f_a^{\mathcal{T}} + \alpha(c_a(\bar{f}^{\mathcal{T}}) + h_a \bar{\tau}_a^{\mathcal{T}}) - f_a^{\mathcal{T}-1}) \times (f_a - f_a^{\mathcal{T}})$$

$$+ \sum_{a \in L} (\tau_a^{\mathcal{T}} + \alpha(\bar{l}_a^{\mathcal{T}} - h_a \bar{f}_a^{\mathcal{T}}) - \tau_a^{\mathcal{T}-1}) \times (\tau_a - \tau_a^{\mathcal{T}})$$

$$+ \sum_{a \in L} (l_a^{\mathcal{T}} + \alpha(\bar{\rho}^{\mathcal{T}} - \bar{\tau}_a^{\mathcal{T}}) - l_a^{\mathcal{T}-1}) \times (l_a - l_a^{\mathcal{T}})$$

$$+ (\rho^{\mathcal{T}} + \alpha(\sum_{a \in L} l_a^0 - \sum_{a \in L} \bar{l}_a^{\mathcal{T}}) - \rho^{\mathcal{T}-1}) \times (\rho - \rho^{\mathcal{T}}) \geq 0, \quad \forall (f, d, l, \tau, \rho) \in \mathcal{K}. \quad (6.35)$$

Step 3: Convergence Verification
If $|f_a^{\mathcal{T}} - f_a^{\mathcal{T}-1}| \leq \epsilon$, $|l_a^{\mathcal{T}} - l_a^{\mathcal{T}-1}| \leq \epsilon$, $|\tau_a^{\mathcal{T}} - \tau_a^{\mathcal{T}-1}| \leq \epsilon$, for all $a \in L$, and $|\rho^{\mathcal{T}} - \rho^{\mathcal{T}-1}| \leq \epsilon$, with $\epsilon > 0$, a pre-specified tolerance, then stop; otherwise, set $\mathcal{T} := \mathcal{T} + 1$, and go to Step 1.

The decomposed subproblems in (6.34) and (6.35) can be computed very efficiently. Observe that since the feasible set $\mathcal{K}$ here is a Cartesian product, where $\mathcal{K} \equiv K \times R_+^{2n+1}$, the above variational inequality subproblems can be decomposed across K, which has the network structure of the problem, and across the coordinates of the nonnegative orthant. Hence, (6.34), for example, yields the subproblem in K in link variables given by:

$$\text{Minimize}_{f \in K} \langle \bar{f}^{\mathcal{T}T}, \bar{f}^{\mathcal{T}} \rangle + \langle g^{\mathcal{T}}, f^{\mathcal{T}} \rangle, \tag{6.36}$$

where $\bar{f}^{\mathcal{T}}$ is the column vector with component $a = \bar{f}_a^{\mathcal{T}}$, g is the column vector with component $g_a = \alpha(c_a(f^{\mathcal{T}-1}) + h_a \tau_a^{\mathcal{T}-1}) - f_a^{\mathcal{T}-1})$. This subproblem is a quadratic programming problem or, equivalently, the optimization reformulation of the traffic network equilibrium conditions in the case of linear and separable user link travel cost functions. Hence, this problem can be solved in many different ways. A possible approach is given in the subsequent numerical example section.

In addition, (6.34) yields subproblems in the marginal cost of emission abatement, the license, and the price variables, which are defined, in turn, on the nonnegative orthant and can be solved explicitly and exactly in closed form as follows.

For each link a, $a \in L$, compute the marginal cost of emission abatement according to:

$$\bar{\tau}_a^{\mathcal{T}} = \max\{0, -\alpha(l_a^{\mathcal{T}-1} - h_a f_a^{\mathcal{T}-1}) + \tau_a^{\mathcal{T}-1}\} \tag{6.37}$$

and for each link a, $a \in L$, compute the license thus:

$$\bar{l}_a^{\mathcal{T}} = \max\{0, -\alpha(\rho^{\mathcal{T}-1} - \tau_a^{\mathcal{T}-1}) + l_a^{\mathcal{T}-1}\}. \tag{6.38}$$

Finally, one can compute the license price as follows:

$$\bar{\rho}^{\mathcal{T}} = \max\{0, -\alpha(\sum_{a \in L} l_a^0 - \sum_{a \in L} l_a^{\mathcal{T}-1})\}. \tag{6.39}$$

The problem (6.35) also yields analogous subproblems to those above, where the first one is simply an optimization reformulation of the classical traffic network equilibrium problem with fixed travel demands, and the other subproblems can be solved exactly and in closed form in a similar manner as described above.

Convergence for the algorithm is given in the following theorem.

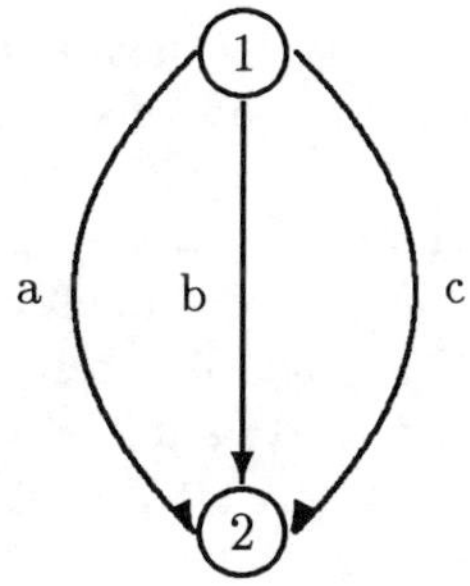

Fig. 6.2. Network topology for Examples 6.1 and 6.2

Theorem 6.5 (Convergence)
If the user link travel cost functions c are assumed to be monotone and have bounded first-order derivatives, then the modified projection method described above converges to the solution of the variational inequality (6.9).

Proof:
From Lemma 6.1, if c is monotone, one has that $F(X)$ is monotone. By Theorem 6.4, $F(X)$ is Lipschitz continuous. Hence, according to Korpelevich (1977), the modified projection method is guaranteed to converge. □

6.3 Numerical Examples

In this section, numerical examples are presented in order to illustrate both the model and the algorithm. Moreover, the results obtained are compared to the numerical results of Section 5.5 of the preceding chapter. In particular, the modified projection method was implemented in FORTRAN and the system utilized for the numerical work was the IBM SP2 located at the Computer Science Department at the University of Massachusetts at Amherst.

For the solution of the standard traffic network equilibrium problem encountered in both the computation and adaptation steps (cf. (6.34) and (6.35)) I utilized the equilibration method (cf. Dafermos and Sparrow 1969 and Appendix B). The convergence criterion was given by $|x_p^{\mathcal{T}} - x_p^{\mathcal{T}-1}| \leq \epsilon$, for all $p \in P$, $|\tau_a^{\mathcal{T}} - \tau_a^{\mathcal{T}-1}| \leq \epsilon$, for all $a \in L$, $|l_a^{\mathcal{T}} - l_a^{\mathcal{T}-1}| \leq \epsilon$, for all $a \in L$, and $|\rho^{\mathcal{T}} - \rho^{\mathcal{T}-1}| \leq \epsilon$.

The modified projection method was initialized by setting the flow on a path equal to the travel demand for the O/D pair that the path belongs to divided by the number of paths. All other variables were initialized to zero.

Example 6.1

The first numerical example was identical to Example 5.1 in the preceding chapter in terms of the data and had the network topology depicted in Figure 5.1, which is reproduced in Figure 6.2, for convenience. Recall that the emission factors were given by: $h_a = 0.1$, $h_b = 0.2$, and $h_c = 0.3$, and the environmental quality standard $\bar{Q} = 1$ with a travel demand $d_{w_1} = 10$. The data for this example, hence, were identical to those of Example 5.1, for comparison purposes, except that the licenses (which do not exist in the models in Chapter 5) also needed to be initialized so I set the initial license allocations to $l_a^0 = l_b^0 = l_c^0 = \frac{1}{3}$ with $l_a^0 + l_b^0 + l_c^0 = 1 = \bar{Q}$. The convergence tolerance $\epsilon = .001$.

An application of the modified projection method with $\alpha = 0.7$ yielded the following solution:

$$f_a^* = 10.00, \quad f_b^* = 0.00, \quad f_c^* = 0.00.$$

This equilibrium link load pattern was induced by the equilibrium path flow pattern:

$$x_{p_1}^* = 10.00, \quad x_{p_2}^* = 0.00, \quad x_{p_3}^* = 0.00.$$

The generalized user travel costs on the paths were: $\bar{C}_{p_1} = \bar{C}_{p_2} = \bar{C}_{p_3} = 41.99$.
The equilibrium licenses were:

$$l_a^* = 1.00, \quad l_b^* = 0.00, \quad l_c^* = 0.00.$$

The equilibrium marginal costs of emission abatement were:

$$\tau_a^* = 169.97, \quad \tau_b^* = 169.96, \quad \tau_c^* = 123.31.$$

The price of a license in equilibrium was:

$$\rho^* = 1.00.$$

In this example, the market for licenses cleared, that is, the excess supply of licenses was zero.

It is easy to verify that, indeed, equilibrium conditions (6.5)–(6.8) are satisfied by this flow, marginal cost, licenses, and price pattern. Moreover, the environmental standard was met since the total emissions $\sum_{a \in L} h_a f_a^* = 1$.

Note that the equilibrium flow pattern was identical to the one determined for Example 5.1 in Section 5.1.1. The marginal costs of emission abatement on the links were also approximately equal to the marginal cost of emission abatement computed for Example 5.1, that is, $\tau^* = 170$.

Example 6.2: Variant of Example 6.1

I then made the following change to Example 6.1, which is identical to the change made in Variant 1 for Example 5.1 and discussed in Example 5.4

in Section 5.5. Specifically, the environmental quality standard was relaxed from $\bar{Q} = 1$ to $\bar{Q} = 1.5$. Recall that $\bar{Q} = 1.5$ is still lower than the total number of emissions emitted, which was equal to 2.1, if there is no permit system in place. Hence, the data were identical to those of Example 6.1 except that now the initial license allocations were changed so that they summed to 1.5, rather than to 1, as follows: $l_a^0 = 0.25$, $l_b^0 = 0.25$, and $l_c^0 = 1.00$. We set $\alpha = 0.4$. An application of the modified projection method yielded the following solution:

$$f_a^* = 5.75, \quad f_b^* = 3.39, \quad f_c^* = 0.85.$$

This equilibrium link load pattern was induced by the equilibrium path flow pattern:

$$x_{p_1}^* = 5.75, \quad x_{p_2}^* = 3.39, \quad x_{p_3}^* = 0.85.$$

The generalized user travel costs on the paths were: $\bar{C}_{p_1} = \bar{C}_{p_2} = \bar{C}_{p_3} = 21.62$.
The equilibrium licenses were:

$$l_a^* = 0.57, \quad l_b^* = 0.68, \quad l_c^* = 0.25.$$

The equilibrium marginal costs were:

$$\tau_a^* = 51.15, \quad \tau_b^* = 51.15, \quad \tau_c^* = 51.15.$$

The price of a license in equilibrium was:

$$\rho^* = 51.15.$$

In this example, the market for licenses cleared, that is, the excess supply of licenses was zero.

It is easy to verify that, indeed, equilibrium conditions (6.5)–(6.8) are satisfied by this flow, marginal cost, licenses, and price pattern. Moreover, the environmental standard was met since the total emissions $\sum_{a \in L} h_a f_a^* = 1.5$.

Moreover, note that the computed equilibrium flow pattern was precisely the one computed for Example 5.4. Furthermore, the computed marginal cost of emission abatement therein was almost precisely equal to the marginal cost of emission abatement on the links for used links computed for this example.

Example 6.3

Assume a network as depicted in Figure 6.3 in which there are five links: a, b, c, d, e; four nodes: 1, 2, 3, 4, and a single O/D pair $w_1 = (1, 4)$. There are, hence, three paths available to travelers between this O/D pair: $p_1 = (a, c)$, $p_2 = (b, d)$, and $p_3 = (a, e, c)$.

The link travel cost functions are:

$$c_a(f_a) = 10 f_a, \quad c_b(f_b) = f_b + 50,$$

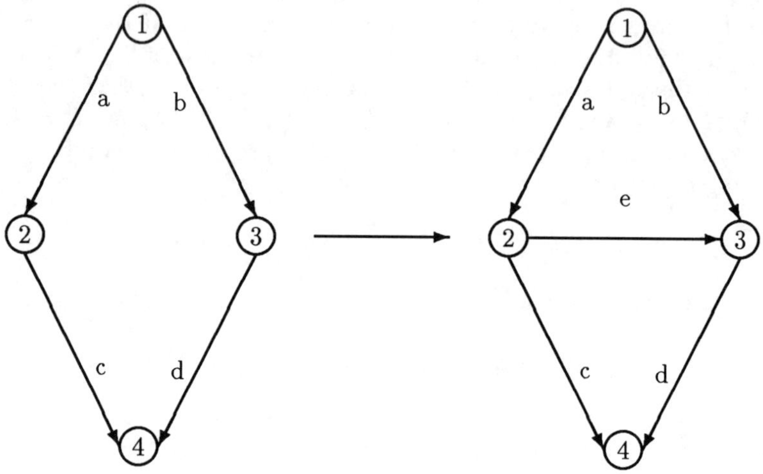

Fig. 6.3. Network topology for Example 6.3: Braess network

$$c_c(f_c) = f_c + 50, \quad c_d(f_d) = 10f_d, \quad c_e(f_e) = f_e + 10.$$

Assume a fixed travel demand $d_{w_1} = 6$. The emission factors were set to $h_a = 0.1$, for all $a \in L$.

I utilized $\alpha = 0.1$ in the modified projection method for this example and allocated the initial licenses as follows: $l_a^0 = l_b^0 = l_c^0 = l_d^0 = l_e^0 = 0.24$ with the total environmental quality standard being equal to 1.2 which was the level in the original network (cf. Figure 6.3) before the addition of the new road e. The convergence tolerance ϵ was set to .00001. The modified projection method yielded the following equilibrium pattern:

$$f_a^* = 3.00, \quad f_b^* = 3.00, \quad f_c^* = 3.00, \quad f_d^* = 3.00, \quad f_e^* = 0.00.$$

This equilibrium link load pattern was induced by the equilibrium path flow pattern:

$$x_{p_1}^* = 3.00, \quad x_{p_2}^* = 3.00, \quad x_{p_3}^* = 0.00.$$

The generalized user travel costs on the used paths were:

$$\bar{C}_{p_1} = \bar{C}_{p_2} = \bar{C}_{p_3} = 108.98.$$

The equilibrium licenses were:

$$l_a^* = 0.30, \quad l_b^* = 0.30, \quad l_c^* = 0.30, \quad l_d^* = 0.30, \quad l_e^* = 0.00.$$

The equilibrium marginal costs of emission abatement were:

$$\tau_a^* = 129.88, \quad \tau_b^* = 126.07, \quad \tau_c^* = 129.88, \quad \tau_d^* = 129.88, \quad \tau_e^* = 129.88.$$

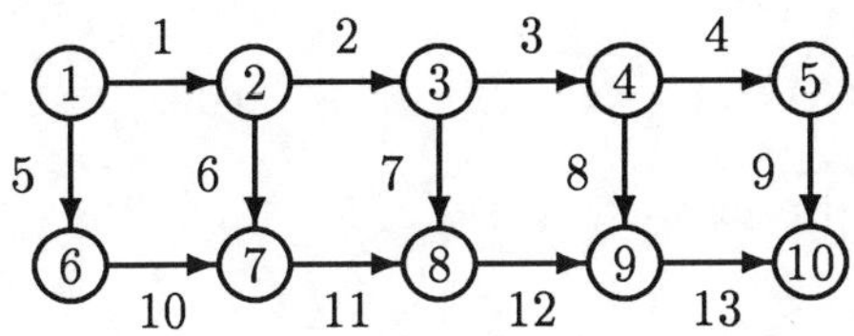

Fig. 6.4. Network topology for Example 6.4

The price of a license in equilibrium was:

$$\rho^* = 129.88.$$

In this example, the market for licenses cleared, that is, the excess supply of licenses was zero. The total calculated emissions were 1.2, which was precisely the imposed environmental quality standard. Note that the use of pollution permits precludes the utilization of the new path p_3 since to do so would increase the emissions over and above the desired environmental quality standard.

Example 6.4

I then returned to Example 5.5, whose network topology is reproduced for convenience in Figure 6.4 and consists of ten nodes, thirteen links and two O/D pairs: $w_1 = (1, 8)$ and $w_2 = (2, 10)$ with travel demands $d_{w_1} = 5$ and $d_{w_2} = 5$.

The user link travel cost functions were as given in Example 5.5. The parameter α in the modified projection method was set to 0.1 and ϵ was set to .0001. We set the emission parameters $h_a = 0.5 \times a$, for all $a \in L$. Hence, the data are identical to those of Example 5.5, except that here we also needed to determine an initial license allocation. Hence, the initial licenses were set as: $l_a^0 = a$, for all links $a \in L$.

The modified projection method yielded the equilibrium link load pattern given by:

$$f_1^* = 3.88, \quad f_2^* = 7.36, \quad f_3^* = 5.00, \quad f_4^* = 3.51,$$

$$f_5^* = 1.12, \quad f_6^* = 1.52, \quad f_7^* = 2.36, \quad f_8^* = 1.49,$$

$$f_9^* = 3.51, \quad f_{10}^* = 1.12, \quad f_{11}^* = 2.64, \quad f_{12}^* = 0.00, \quad f_{13}^* = 1.49,$$

with an equilibrium path flow pattern:
For O/D pair w_1:

$$x^*_{p_1} = 2.36, \quad x^*_{p_2} = 1.52, \quad x^*_{p_3} = 1.12,$$

and for O/D pair w_2:

$$x^*_{p_4} = 3.51, \quad x^*_{p_5} = 1.49, \quad x^*_{p_6} = 0.00, \quad x^*_{p_7} = 0.00,$$

and with generalized user travel costs:
For O/D pair w_1:

$$\bar{C}_{p_1} = \bar{C}_{p_2} = \bar{C}_{p_3} = 140.43,$$

and for O/D pair w_2:

$$\bar{C}_{p_4} = \bar{C}_{p_5} = 193.14, \quad \bar{C}_{p_6} = 203.16, \quad \bar{C}_{p_7} = 203.16.$$

The computed licenses were:

$$l_1^* = 1.93, \quad l_2^* = 7.36, \quad l_3^* = 7.50, \quad l_4^* = 7.02,$$

$$l_5^* = 2.80, \quad l_6^* = 4.56, \quad l_7^* = 8.26, \quad l_8^* = 5.95,$$

$$l_9^* = 15.81, \quad l_{10}^* = 5.61, \quad l_{11}^* = 14.52, \quad l_{12}^* = 0.00, \quad l_{13}^* = 9.67.$$

The equilibrium price was $\rho^* = 7.41$, which was also the value of all the marginal costs on the links with positive license holdings. The equilibrium marginal cost on the link with zero license holdings was:

$$\tau_{12}^* = 7.41.$$

The market for licenses also cleared for this example. The total emissions generated were precisely equal to the environmental quality standard $\bar{Q} = 91$.

Note that the equilibrium flow pattern is identical to the equilibrium flow pattern computed for Example 5.5. Moreover, there the equilibrium marginal cost of emission abatement was computed to be $\tau^* = 7.41$, which is precisely the value computed here for the links.

The results in this chapter are from Nagurney (1999c). Nagurney (1999d) presents alternative permit schemes by O/D pairs and by paths. I consider such permit schemes in the case of elastic travel demands in Chapter 7.

7 Permits for User-Optimized, Elastic Demand Networks

In this chapter, I consider elastic, rather than fixed, travel demand networks, in which the behavior of the travelers is that of user-optimization. For such networks, I present a hierarchy of permit systems based, respectively, on origin/destination pairs, on paths, and on links. The governing equilibrium conditions are derived for each system as are the variational inequality formulations. The O/D pair-based and the path-based permit systems are then compared to the link-based permit system model.

Moreover, as was done for the fixed demand model in Chapter 6, I establish that the proposed permit systems in this chapter also achieve the environmental quality standard provided that the initial license allocations are set accordingly. I also prove that, given the equilibrium solution to the origin/destination permit system problem, one can construct from it a solution to the path-based permit system problem and vice versa. The qualitative properties of the equilibrium solution patterns are discussed in this chapter and an algorithm is proposed for the computation of the patterns for both models. Finally, a numerical example is presented that illustrates the permit systems. In light of this work, transportation planning agencies now have available alternative permit systems for their use for pollution reduction.

The availability of alternative permit systems provides the responsible jurisdictions and planning agencies with greater flexibility in the achievement of environmental quality standards. Moreover, from a management (as well as a computational) perspective, a given transportation network topology may be more conducive to one type of permit system over another. For example, in the case of a network with few origin/destination pairs a permit system based on origin/destination pairs may be preferable to one based on links or paths. In Table 7.1, the hierarchy of pollution permit system models

Table 7.1. Hierarchy of pollution permit systems

Type of permit system:	• Origin/Destination Pair-Based •Path-Based •Link-Based

developed in this chapter for elastic demand traffic networks is given.

The chapter is organized as follows. Section 7.1 introduces the hierarchy of permit system models. Specifically, Subsection 7.1.1 describes the O/D pair-based permit system model, Subsection 7.1.2 develops the path-based permit system model, whereas Subsection 7.1.3 presents the link-based permit system model. Subsection 7.1.4, in turn, establishes that the environmental quality standard is met by the models, provided that the initial license allocation is set accordingly. Hence, the transportation networks are sustainable under these permit systems.

Section 7.2 subsequently presents some qualitative properties of the models. Section 7.3 then describes the computational procedure, which is applied in Section 7.4 to a numerical example.

7.1 The Permit Models

In this section, I develop a hierarchy of transportation network policy models based, respectively, on origin/destination pair licenses or permits, on path licenses, and on link licenses. I also relate the former two models to the link-based permit system model. In these models vehicular travel and, thereby, pollution due to emissions is restrained by the incorporation of emission pollution licenses or permits. The market-based fee, or equilibrium license price, for these emission permits stimulates the reduction in travel and pollution.

Consider a single-modal transportation network in which the travel demands are not fixed but, rather, elastic, and in which both the user link travel cost functions and the travel disutility functions associated with traveling between the O/D pairs can be asymmetric, as was the case in the general traffic network equilibrium model with emission pricing policies, in the form of tolls, described in Section 5.3. It is assumed here, as was done in Chapter 6 as well, that the government informs the users of the transportation system of the initial license allocations, be they for the O/D pairs, the paths, or the links, as well as the total license availability.

For both the O/D pair-based and the path-based permit systems, I give the variational inequality formulations in path flow variables, whereas for the link-based model I recall the link-based variational inequality formulation in link flow variables since it is those that are used for computational purposes.

Notation for the Transportation Network

I begin with the notation that is common to the models. The notation is similar to that in the preceding chapters but is given here for completeness and easy reference. Consider a transportation network $G = [N, L]$ consisting of the set of nodes N and a set of directed links L. Let a, b, etc., denote the links and let p, q, etc., denote the paths, which are assumed to be acyclic. There are J origin/destination (O/D) pairs in the network, with a typical O/D pair denoted by w and the set of O/D pairs denoted by W. Let P_w denote the set of paths connecting O/D pair w and P the set of paths in the network.

The flow on a link a is denoted by f_a, whereas the flow on a path p is denoted by x_p. Group the link flows into a column vector $f \in R^n$, and the path flows into the column vector $x \in R_+^{n_P}$ where n is the number of links in the network and n_P is the number of paths. Let A denote the $n \times n_P$ arc-path incidence matrix whose (a, p)th component is 1 if arc a is contained in path p, and 0, otherwise.

The following conservation of flow equation equation expresses the relationship between the flow on a link a and the path flows:

$$f_a = \sum_{p \in P} x_p \delta_{ap}, \quad \forall a \in L, \tag{7.1}$$

or, in vector form:

$$f = Ax, \tag{7.2}$$

that is, the flow on a link is equal to the sum of the path flows on paths that use that link.

Let d_w denote the travel demand associated with traveling between O/D pair w and group the travel demands into the column vector $d \in R_+^J$. Let B denote the path/OD pair incidence matrix with component (p, w) equal to 1 if path $p \in P_w$, or 0, otherwise. The equation relating the travel demand for an O/D pair to the path flows connecting the O/D pair is:

$$d_w = \sum_{p \in P_w} x_p, \quad \forall w \in W, \tag{7.3}$$

or, in vector form:

$$d = Bx, \tag{7.4}$$

that is, the demand associated with an O/D pair is equal to the sum of the path flows on paths connecting the O/D pair.

Let c_a denote the user travel cost associated with traveling on link a and group the link travel costs into the row vector $c \in R^n$. The user travel cost on a link may, in general, depend upon the entire link load pattern, that is:

$$c_a = c_a(f), \tag{7.5}$$

where c_a is a known smooth function.

A user traveling on path p, hence, incurs a user travel cost C_p, where, in view of (7.2), we may write

$$C_p(x) = \sum_{a \in L} c_a(f)\delta_{ap}, \tag{7.6}$$

where $\delta_{ap} = 1$ if link a is contained in path p, and 0, otherwise.

Here, I treat the case of elastic travel demands where travelers can forgo travel entirely if the cost associated with traveling is too high. The travel disutility function associated with traveling between O/D pair w is denoted by λ_w. I assume that, in general, the travel disutilities can depend on the entire vector of travel demands. In view of (7.3), and without any loss of generality, we may write:

$$\lambda_w = \lambda_w(x). \tag{7.7}$$

Before I introduce the notation necessary for the modeling of the permit market systems I recall the well-known traffic network equilibrium conditions in the case of elastic travel demands (Beckmann, McGuire, and Winsten 1956; Dafermos 1982) (see also (2.41)): For each O/D pair $w \in W$, and each path $p \in P_w$:

$$C_p(x^*) \begin{cases} = & \lambda_w(x^*), \quad \text{if } {x_p}^* > 0 \\ \geq & \lambda_w(x^*), \quad \text{if } {x_p}^* = 0, \end{cases} \tag{7.8}$$

that is, only those paths that have minimal and equal travel costs for each O/D pair are utilized and the used path costs connecting an O/D pair must be equal to the travel disutility for that O/D pair.

Notation for the Permit Systems

I now introduce the notation for the permit systems. Since I am considering here two new permit systems (by O/D pairs and by paths) and relating them to an existing one (by links), I need to present the notation relevant to all. Let h_a denote the emission factor on link a and let $h_p = \sum_a h_a \delta_{ap}$ denote the emission factor on path p.

Hence, here I assume a single pollutant and the case of a single receptor point for emissions (cf. Dhanda, Nagurney, and Ramanujam 1999). The permit system models readily generalize to multiple pollutants and multiple receptor points but with an associated increase in notation.

Let l_w denote the number of licenses or permits for O/D pair w that allows the travelers between O/D pair w to emit pollutants at a certain rate. Similarly, let l_p denote the number of permits for path p and l_a the number of permits for link a. Let l^0_w, l^0_p, and l^0_a denote, respectively, the initial allocation of licenses for O/D pair w, path p, and link a, with these values assumed to be nonnegative. Group the licenses, respectively, into the column vectors $l^W \in R^J_+$, $l^P \in R^{n_P}_+$, and $l^L \in R^n_+$. Later, I discuss how the government should allocate the initial licenses in order to comply with the imposed environmental standards.

Also, let ρ^W, ρ^P, and ρ^L denote, respectively, the price of a license in the O/D pair-based, path-based, and link-based systems. Let τ_w denote the marginal cost of emission abatement for O/D pair w. Similarly, let τ_p denote the marginal cost of emission abatement for path p, and τ_a the marginal cost of emission abatement on link a. Group, respectively, the marginal costs of emission abatement into the column vectors: $\tau^W \in R^J$, $\tau^P \in R^{n_P}$, and $\tau^L \in R^n$.

I now present the equilibrium conditions, respectively, for the O/D pair-based, the path-based, and the link-based systems. I also provide the variational inequality formulations of the governing equilibrium conditions.

7.1.1 O/D Pair-Based Permit System Model

In this subsection, I develop the permit system model based on origin/destination pairs, beginning with a derivation of the equilibrium conditions.

O/D Pair-Based Permit System Equilibrium Conditions

I first present the equilibrium conditions for the O/D pair-based permit system. They consist of systems of equalities and inequalities which most hold for the path flows, the marginal costs of emission abatement, the licenses, and the license price.

The traveler on a path p is now subject not only to the user travel cost, given by (7.6), but also is subject to the payment of the price or cost of his emissions. Consequently, the traffic network equilibrium conditions (7.8), in the presence of the O/D pair-based emission pollution permit system, take on the form: For each O/D pair $w \in W$, and each path $p \in P_w$:

$$C_p(x^*) + h_p \tau_w^* \begin{cases} = & \lambda_w(x^*), & \text{if } x_p^* > 0 \\ \geq & \lambda_w(x^*), & \text{if } x_p^* = 0, \end{cases} \tag{7.9}$$

where τ_w^* denotes the equilibrium marginal cost of emission abatement discussed below. Equilibrium conditions (7.9) state that a traveler on a path of the network is now subjected to payment of the true cost of his emissions while traveling on the path p.

Note that, in this framework, the transportation authority is responsible for informing the travelers of the license price and the corresponding payments required, as well as the availability of the licenses or permits for the O/D pairs. The government then collects the payment $h_p \tau_w^*$ associated with traveling on path $p \in P_w$.

One also has the following conditions which must hold in equilibrium: For each O/D pair w, the marginal cost of emission abatement τ_w, in equilibrium, must satisfy the following system:

$$\sum_{p \in P_w} h_p x_p^* \begin{cases} = & l_w^*, & \text{if } \tau_w^* > 0 \\ \leq & l_w^*, & \text{if } \tau_w^* = 0. \end{cases} \tag{7.10}$$

In other words, if the marginal cost of emission abatement, τ_w^*, is positive in equilibrium for an O/D pair w, then the emissions by that O/D pair are precisely equal to the pollution license holdings of that O/D pair; if the number of licenses held by that O/D pair exceed the emissions then, in equilibrium, the marginal cost of emission abatement is zero.

The following condition must also be met at equilibrium: For each O/D pair $w \in W$:

$$\tau_w^* \left\{ \begin{array}{lll} = & \rho^{W^*}, & \text{if } l_w^* > 0 \\ \leq & \rho^{W^*}, & \text{if } l_w^* = 0. \end{array} \right. \tag{7.11}$$

Hence, in equilibrium, a positive holding of licenses by an O/D pair implies that the marginal cost of abatement must be equal to the price of the license. However, if the price of the license exceeds the marginal cost of abatement, then the number of licenses for that O/D pair will be zero.

I now state the well-known economic equilibrium conditions that express that, in equilibrium, if a price of a good (which here is the license) is positive, then the market clears for that good; if there is an excess supply of the good, then the price is zero in equilibrium. Mathematically, hence, the equilibrium price, ρ^{W^*}, of a license must satisfy the following equilibrium condition:

$$\sum_{w \in W} (l_w^0 - l_w^*) \left\{ \begin{array}{lll} = & 0, & \text{if } \rho^{W^*} > 0 \\ \geq & 0, & \text{if } \rho^{W^*} = 0. \end{array} \right. \tag{7.12}$$

In (7.12), one can see that $\sum_{w \in W} l_w^0$ is the supply of the O/D pair-based licenses available in the network, whereas $\sum_{w \in W} l_w^*$ is the demand for licenses in equilibrium.

Let $\mathcal{K}^1$ denote the feasible set such that $\mathcal{K}^1 \equiv R_+^{n_P+2J+1}$, since the vector x is n_p-dimensional and since both the vectors l^W and τ^W are J-dimensional vectors and ρ^W is single dimensional.

I am now ready to define the equilibrium state.

Definition 7.1 (O/D Pair-Based Permit System Equilibrium)
A vector $(x^*, \tau^{W^*}, l^{W^*}, \rho^{W^*}) \in \mathcal{K}^1$ is an equilibrium of the traffic network equilibrium O/D pair-based emission permits market model if and only if it satisfies the systems of equalities and inequalities (7.9)–(7.12).

The variational inequality formulation of the equilibrium conditions for this model is now given. This and the subsequent variational inequality formulations are presented without proof since the proofs are analogous to that of Theorem 6.1 (see also Nagurney, Nagurney, and Ramanujam 1998 and the proof of Theorem 10.1 in Dhanda, Nagurney, and Ramanujam 1999).

Theorem 7.1 (Variational Inequality Formulation – O/D Pair-Based System)
A vector of path flows, marginal costs of emission abatement for O/D pairs, O/D pair licenses, and license price, $(x^*, \tau^{W^*}, l^{W^*}, \rho^{W^*}) \in \mathcal{K}^1$, is an equilibrium of the traffic network equilibrium problem with O/D pair-based emission

pollution permits if and only if it is a solution to the variational inequality problem:

$$\sum_{w \in W} \sum_{p \in P_W} (C_p(x^*) + h_p \tau_w^* - \lambda_w(x^*)) \times (x_p - x_p{}^*)$$

$$+ \sum_{w \in W} (l_w^* - \sum_{p \in P_w} h_p x_p^*) \times (\tau_w - \tau_w^*)$$

$$+ \sum_{w \in W} (\rho^{W*} - \tau_w^*) \times (l_w - l_w^*) + \sum_{w \in W} (l_w^0 - l_w{}^*) \times (\rho^W - \rho^{W*}) \geq 0,$$

$$\forall (x, \tau^W, l^W, \rho^W) \in \mathcal{K}^1. \tag{7.13}$$

Variational inequality (7.13) can be put into standard form (cf. (2.32)) as follows. Since I will be presenting two other variational inequality formulations for the equilibrium conditions governing the path-based permit system as well as the link-based permit system, I utilize a superscript to distinguish among them.

Define column vector $X^1 \equiv (x, \tau^W, l^W, \rho^W) \in \mathcal{K}^1$ and the column vector $F^1(X^1)$, where:

$$F^1(X^1) \equiv \left(C^1(X^1), T^1(X^1), L^1(X^1), P^1(X^1)\right).$$

$C^1(X^1)$ is the n_P-dimensional vector whose pth component is given by:

$$C_p^1(X^1) : C_p(x) + h_p \tau_w - \lambda_w(x),$$

$T^1(X^1)$ and $L^1(X^1)$ are each J-dimensional vectors with component w given, respectively, by:

$$T_w^1(X^1) : l_w - \sum_{p \in P_w} h_p x_p$$

and:

$$L_w^1(X^1) : \rho^W - \tau_w,$$

whereas $P^1(X^1)$ is the one-dimensional vector with the single component:

$$P^1(X^1) : \sum_{w \in W} (l_w^0 - l_w).$$

Thus, variational inequality (7.13) can be expressed as:

$$\langle F^1(X^{1*})^T, X^1 - X^{1*} \rangle \geq 0, \quad \forall X^1 \in \mathcal{K}^1. \tag{7.14}$$

7.1.2 Path-Based Permit System

In this subsection, I develop a permit system based on paths. As in Section 7.1.1, I begin with the derivation of the governing equilibrium conditions.

Path-Based Permit System Equilibrium Conditions

I now present the equilibrium conditions for the path-based permit system, analogous to (7.9)–(7.12) for the O/D pair-based system.

Recall that the traveler on a path p (see also (7.9)) is subject not only to the user travel cost, given by (7.6), but also is subject to the payment of the price or cost of his emissions. In the presence of the path-based emission pollution permits, the traffic network equilibrium conditions take the form: For each O/D pair $w \in W$, and each path $p \in P_w$:

$$C_p(x^*) + h_p\tau_p^* \begin{cases} = & \lambda_w(x^*), & \text{if } x_p^* > 0 \\ \geq & \lambda_w(x^*), & \text{if } x_p^* = 0. \end{cases} \tag{7.15}$$

Note that equilibrium conditions (7.15) are similar to those in (7.9) with the exception that one now has the equilibrium marginal emission abatement cost τ_p corresponding to a path p multiplying the path emission factor h_p.

The marginal cost of emission abatement equilibrium conditions, analogous to (7.10) in this model are: For each path $p \in P$, the marginal cost of emission abatement τ_p, in equilibrium, must satisfy the following system:

$$h_p x_p^* \begin{cases} = & l_p^*, & \text{if } \tau_p^* > 0 \\ \leq & l_p^*, & \text{if } \tau_p^* = 0. \end{cases} \tag{7.16}$$

In other words, if the marginal cost of emission abatement, τ_p^*, is positive in equilibrium for a path p, then the emissions by that path are exactly equal to the pollution license holdings of that path; if the number of licenses held by that path exceed the emissions, then, in equilibrium, the marginal cost of emission abatement is zero.

The following condition (see also (7.11)) must also be met at equilibrium: For each path $p \in P$:

$$\tau_p^* \begin{cases} = & \rho^{P*}, & \text{if } l_p^* > 0 \\ \leq & \rho^{P*}, & \text{if } l_p^* = 0. \end{cases} \tag{7.17}$$

Hence, in equilibrium, a positive holding of licenses by a path implies that the marginal cost of emission abatement must be equal to the price of the license. However, if the price of the license exceeds the marginal cost of emission abatement, then the number of licenses for that path will be zero.

I now give the analogue of the economic equilibrium conditions (7.12) for the path-based system:

$$\sum_{p \in P}(l_p^0 - l_p^*) \begin{cases} = & 0, & \text{if } \rho^{P*} > 0 \\ \geq & 0, & \text{if } \rho^{P*} = 0. \end{cases} \tag{7.18}$$

Let $\mathcal{K}^2$ denote the feasible set for this model such that $\mathcal{K}^2 \equiv R_+^{3n_P+1}$, since the vectors x, τ^P, and l^P are each of dimension n_P and ρ^P is single dimensional.

The definition of the equilibrium state for the path-based permit system model is:

Definition 7.2 (Path-Based Permit System Equilibrium)
A vector $(x^*, \tau^{P^*}, l^{P^*}, \rho^{P^*}) \in \mathcal{K}^2$ is an equilibrium of the traffic network equilibrium path-based emission permits market model if and only if it satisfies the systems of equalities and inequalities (7.15)-(7.18).

The variational inequality formulation of the equilibrium conditions for this model is now given.

Theorem 7.2 (Variational Inequality Formulation – Path-Based System)
A vector of path flows, marginal costs of emission abatement on paths, path licenses, and license price, $(x^*, \tau^{P^*}, l^{P^*}, \rho^{P^*}) \in \mathcal{K}^2$, is an equilibrium of the traffic network equilibrium problem with path-based emission pollution permits if and only if it is a solution to the variational inequality problem:

$$\sum_{w \in W} \sum_{p \in P_w} (C_p(x^*) + h_p \tau_p^* - \lambda_w(x^*)) \times (x_p - x_p^*) + \sum_{p \in P} (l_p^* - h_p x_p^*) \times (\tau_p - \tau_p^*)$$

$$+ \sum_{p \in P} (\rho^{P^*} - \tau_p^*) \times (l_p - l_p^*) + \sum_{p \in P} (l_p^0 - l_p^*) \times (\rho^P - \rho^{P^*}) \geq 0,$$

$$\forall (x, \tau^P, l^P, \rho^P) \in \mathcal{K}^2. \tag{7.19}$$

I now put the variational inequality (7.19) into standard form akin to (7.14). Define column vector $X^2 \equiv (x, \tau^P, l^P, \rho^P) \in \mathcal{K}^2$ and the column vector $F^2(X^2)$, where:

$$F^2(X) \equiv \left(C^2(X^2), T^2(X^2), L^2(X^2), P^2(X^2)\right).$$

$C^2(X^2)$ is the n_P-dimensional vector whose pth component is given by:

$$C_p^2(X) : C_p(x) + h_p \tau_p - \lambda_w(x),$$

$T^2(X^2)$ and $L^2(X^2)$ are also n_P-dimensional vectors with component p given, respectively, by:

$$T_p^2(X^2) : l_p - h_p x_p$$

and:

$$L_p^2(X^2) : \rho^P - \tau_p,$$

whereas $P^2(X^2)$ is the one-dimensional vector with the single component:

$$P^2(X^2) : \sum_{p \in P} (l_p^0 - l_p).$$

Thus, variational inequality (7.19) can be expressed as

$$\langle F^2(X^{2^*})^T, X^2 - X^{2^*}\rangle \geq 0, \quad \forall X^2 \in \mathcal{K}^2. \tag{7.20}$$

7.1.3 Link-Based Permit System Model

In this subsection, I present a link-based permit system model, which is an elastic demand analogue of the fixed demand link-based permit system model described in Chapter 6. Of course, one may also develop permit system models in the case of fixed travel demands, which are either O/D pair-based or path-based.

Link-Based Permit System Equilibrium Conditions

I now present the link-based permit system equilibrium conditions. These are the single-modal version of the model with compliance discussed in Nagurney, Ramanujam, and Dhanda (1998).

The traffic network equilibrium conditions (akin to (7.9) and (7.15)) are: For each O/D pair $w \in W$, and each path $p \in P_w$:

$$C_p(x^*) + \sum_{a \in L} h_a \tau_a^* \delta_{ap} \begin{cases} = & \lambda_w(x^*), & \text{if } x_p^* > 0 \\ \geq & \lambda_w(x^*), & \text{if } x_p^* = 0. \end{cases} \tag{7.21}$$

The marginal cost of emission abatement equilibrium conditions, which are link-based in this model are: For each link $a \in L$, the equilibrium marginal cost of emission abatement, τ_a, must satisfy the following system:

$$h_a f_a^* \begin{cases} = & l_a^*, & \text{if } \tau_a^* > 0 \\ \leq & l_a^*, & \text{if } \tau_a^* = 0. \end{cases} \tag{7.22}$$

The following condition for the licenses must also be met at equilibrium: For each link $a \in L$:

$$\tau_a^* \begin{cases} = & p^{L^*}, & \text{if } l_a^* > 0 \\ \leq & p^{L^*}, & \text{if } l_a^* = 0. \end{cases} \tag{7.23}$$

The analogue of the economic quilibrium conditions (7.12) and (7.18) for the link-based system is:

$$\sum_{a \in L} (l_a^0 - l_a^*) \begin{cases} = & 0, & \text{if } p^{L^*} > 0 \\ \geq & 0, & \text{if } p^{L^*} = 0. \end{cases} \tag{7.24}$$

Let $\mathcal{K}^3$ denote the feasible set for this model such that $\mathcal{K}^3 \equiv \{K \times R_+^{2n+1}\}$, where $K \equiv \{(f,d), |\, \text{there exists a vector } x \in R_+^{n_P} \text{ satisfying } (7.2), (7.4)\}$.

The definition of the equilibrium state for the link-based permit system model is:

Definition 7.3 (Link-Based Permit System Equilibrium)
A vector $(f^*, d^*, \tau^{L^*}, l^{L^*}, \rho^{L^*}) \in \mathcal{K}^3$ *is an equilibrium of the traffic network equilibrium path-based emission permits market model if and only if it satisfies the systems of equalities and inequalities (7.21)-(7.24).*

The variational inequality formulation of the equilibrium conditions for this model (see also Theorem 10.1 in Dhanda, Nagurney, and Ramanujam 1999) is now given. Note that, unlike the variational inequality formulations (7.13) and (7.18), this variational inequality is in terms of link flows, rather than paths flows. Indeed, for the preceding two permit system models a link flow formulation is not possible. Although one could provide a path flow formulation of the link-based permit system model, a link formulation was derived in Nagurney, Ramanujam, and Dhanda (1998) and also used therein for computational purposes and, hence, for continuity and consistency we also give it here. In view of (7.4), one can also express the travel disutility function for an O/D pair w as $\hat{\lambda}_w(d), \forall w \in W$.

Theorem 7.3 (Variational Inequality Formulation – Link-Based System)
A vector of link flows, travel demands, marginal costs of emission abatement on links, link licenses, and license price, $(f^*, d^*, \tau^{L^*}, l^{L^*}, \rho^{L^*}) \in \mathcal{K}^3$, *is an equilibrium of the traffic network equilibrium problem with link-based emission pollution permits if and only if it is a solution to the variational inequality problem:*

$$\sum_{a \in L}(c_a(f^*) + h_a\tau_a^*) \times (f_a - f_a^*) - \sum_{w \in W} \hat{\lambda}_w(d^*) \times (d_w - d_w^*)$$

$$+\sum_{a \in L}(l_a^* - h_a f_a^*) \times (\tau_a - \tau_a^*)$$

$$+\sum_{a \in L}(\rho^{L^*} - \tau_a^*) \times (l_a - l_a^*) + \sum_{a \in L}(l_a^0 - l_a^*) \times (\rho^L - \rho^{L^*}) \geq 0,$$

$$\forall (f, d, \tau^L, l^L, \rho^L) \in \mathcal{K}^3. \tag{7.25}$$

Variational inequality (7.25) is now put into standard form (see also (7.14) and (7.20)). Define column vector $X^3 \equiv (f, d, \tau^L, l^L, \rho^L) \in \mathcal{K}^3$ and the column vector $F^3(X^3)$, where:

$$F^3(X^3) \equiv (C^3(X^3), \Lambda^3(X^3), T^3(X^3), L^3(X^3), P^3(X^3)) .$$

$C^3(X^3)$, $T^3(X^3)$, $L^3(X^3)$ are each n-dimensional vectors with component a given, respectively, as follows:

$$C_a^3(X^3) : c_a(f) + h_a\tau_a$$

$$T_a^3(X^3) : l_a - h_a f_a$$
$$L_a^3(X^3) : \rho^L - \tau_a.$$

$\Lambda(X^3)$ is the J-dimensional vector with component w given by:

$$\Lambda_w^3(X^3) : -\lambda_w(d),$$

whereas $P^3(X^3)$ is the one-dimensional vector with the single component:

$$P^3(X^3) : \sum_{a \in L}(l_a^0 - l_a).$$

Thus, variational inequality (7.25) can be expressed as

$$\langle F^3(X^{3^*})^T, X^3 - X^{3^*} \rangle \geq 0, \quad \forall X^3 \in \mathcal{K}^3. \tag{7.26}$$

7.1.4 Sustainability

In this subsection, I establish that a traffic network with elastic demands is sustainable under any of the permit systems describes in Section 7.1, provided that the initial license allocation is set accordingly.

In particular, I now establish that both the O/D pair-based permit system equilibrium pattern and the path-based permit system equilibrium pattern are independent of the initial allocation, respectively, of O/D pair licenses and of path licenses. I also show how to guarantee that the environmental standards are met in equilibrium based on the initial license allocations. The analogous results were established for the link-based permit system model in Nagurney, Ramanujam, and Dhanda (1999).

Corollary 7.1 (Equilibrium Pattern Independence from Initial License Allocation
If $l_w^0 \geq 0$, for all $w \in W$, and $\sum_{w \in W} l_w^0 = \bar{Q}$, with $\bar{Q}$ fixed and positive, then the equilibrium pattern $(x^*, \tau^{W^*}, l^{W^*}, \rho^{W^*})$ for the O/D pair-based permit system is independent of the initial license allocation $l_w^0, \forall w \in W$.

Similarly, if $l_p^0 \geq 0$, for all $p \in P$, and $\sum_{p \in P} l_p^0 = \bar{Q}$, then the equilibrium pattern $(x^*, \tau^{P^*}, l^{P^*}, \rho^{P^*})$ for the path-based permit system is independent of the initial license allocation $l_p^0, \forall p \in P$.

Proof:
The terms in the variational inequality (7.13) are either independent of l_w^0 or depend only on the sum, $\sum_{w \in W} l_w^0$. The conclusion follows for the O/D pair-based system.

Similarly, since the terms in variational inequality (7.19) are either independent of l_p^0 or depend only on the sum, $\sum_{p \in P} l_p^0$. the conclusion follows for the path-based system. □

In the following proposition, I show that the environmental standards are met by both the O/D pair-based permit system equilibrium pattern as well

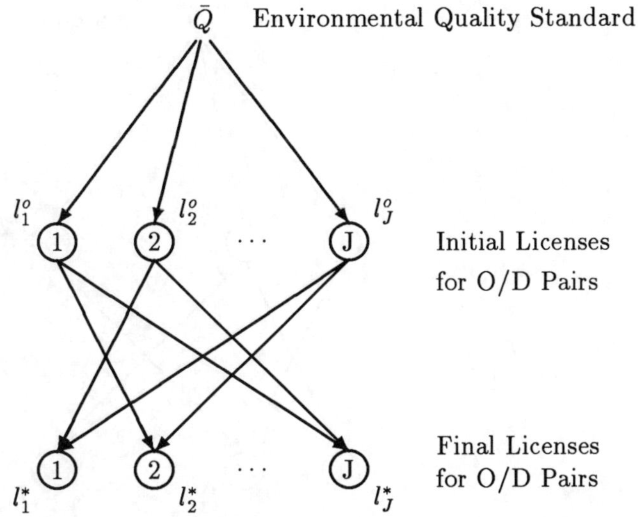

Fig. 7.1. Initial license allocation and final license holdings for the O/D pair-based permit system

as the path-based permit system equilibrium, provided that the sum of the initial allocation of, respectively, O/D pair licenses or path licenses is equal to the imposed environmental standard given by $\bar{Q}$.

Proposition 7.1 (Achievement of Environmental Quality Standard) *If* $\sum_{w\in W} l_w^0 = \bar{Q}$, *the O/D pair-based permit system equilibrium vector achieves the environmental quality standard,* $\bar{Q}$.

Also, if $\sum_{p\in P} l_p^0 = \bar{Q}$, *then the path-based permit system equilibrium vector achieves the environmental quality standard,* $\bar{Q}$.

Proof:
One has from equilibrium conditions (7.10) and (7.12) that:

$$\sum_{w\in W}\sum_{p\in P_w} h_p x_p^* \leq \sum_{w\in W} l_w^* \leq \sum_{w\in W} l_w^0 = \bar{Q}.$$

Similarly, for the path-based permit system one has from equilibrium conditions (7.16) and (7.18) that:

$$\sum_{p\in P} h_p x_p^* \leq \sum_{p\in P} l_p^* \leq \sum_{p\in P} l_p^0 = \bar{Q}.$$

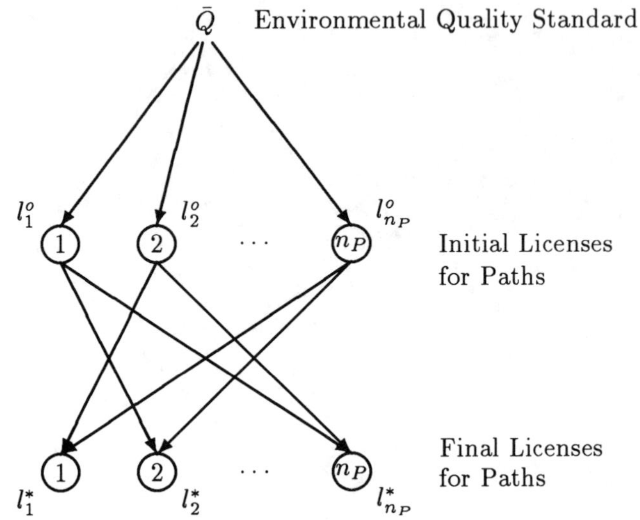

Fig. 7.2. Initial license allocation and final license holdings for the path-based permit system

Hence, the environmental standards are met by either the O/D pair-based or the path-based permit system equilibrium pattern. □

In Figure 7.1, an illustration of the initial O/D pair license allocation summing up to the environmental quality standard plus the final license holdings is given. Figure 7.2 is the analogue of Figure 7.1, but for the path-based permit system.

Remark 7.1

The analogue of Proposition 7.1 for the link-based permit system is (see Proposition 10.2 in Dhanda, Nagurney, and Ramanujam 1999) that $\sum_a l_a^0$ must be equal to the imposed environmental quality standard $\bar{Q}$ in order for the link-based permit system equilibrium to achieve the standard $\bar{Q}$.

Thus, according to Proposition 7.1 an elastic demand traffic network is *sustainable* under the above described permit systems in that an equilibrium pattern is achieved and the environmental quality standard is met.

In the following two propositions it is established, respectively, that, given an equilibrium solution to the O/D pair-based permit system one can construct from it an equilibrium solution to the path-based permit system, and vice versa. For both the propositions, it is assumed that the initial license allocations $\sum_{w \in W} l_w^0$ and $\sum_{p \in P} l_p^0$ have been set equal to the environmental quality standard $\bar{Q}$.

Proposition 7.2

Given an equilibrium solution to the O/D pair-based permit system, that is, one that satisfies equilibrium conditions (7.9)–(7.12) or, equivalently, variational inequality (7.13), one can construct an equilibrium solution to the path-based permit system, that is, one that satisfies equilibrium conditions (7.15)–(7.18) or, equivalently, variational inequality (7.19).

The construction of the path-based equilibrium solution from the O/D pair-based equilibrium solution is as follows: Construct the path flows, thus: $x^{2^*} = x^{1^*}$, where x^{2^*} denotes the equilibrium path flow pattern in the path-based system and x^{1^*} denotes the equilibrium path flow pattern in the O/D pair-based system. Construct the marginal costs of emission abatement on the paths, thus: $\tau_p^* = \rho^{W^*}$, for all paths $p \in P_w$ and all O/D pairs w. Construct the path licenses, thus: $l_p^* = h_p x_p^*$, for all paths p, and, finally, construct the path equilibrium price, thus: $\rho^{P^*} = \rho^{W^*}$.

Proof:

Clearly, by construction, equilibrium condition (7.15) must hold since the path flow patterns are equal and $\tau_p^* = \tau_w^*$ for all paths $p \in P_w$. Also, (7.16) is clearly satisfied since $l_p^* = h_p x_p^{1^*}$, also by construction. System (7.17) is also satisfied since we have set $\tau_p^* = \rho^{W^*} = \rho^{P^*}$.

Finally, (7.18) is satisfied since $\bar{Q} = \sum_{w \in W} l_w^0 - \sum_{p \in P} l_p^0$ and $\sum_{w \in W} l_w^* = \sum_{p \in P} l_p^*$ with $\rho^{P^*} = \rho^{W^*}$. □

I now establish the converse of Proposition 7.2, that is, given an equilibrium solution to the path-based permit system, one can construct an equilibrium solution to the O/D pair-based system.

Proposition 7.3

Given an equilibrium solution to the path-based permit system, that is, one that satisfies equilibrium conditions (7.15)–(7.18), or, equivalently, variational inequality (7.19), one can construct an equilibrium solution to the O/D pair-based system, that is, one that satisfies equilibrium conditions (7.9)–(7.12) or, equivalently, variational inequality (7.13).

The construction of the O/D pair-based equilibrium solution from the path-based solution is as follows: Construct the path flows, thus: $x^{1^*} = x^{2^*}$, where x^{1^*} denotes the equilibrium path flow pattern in the O/D pair-based system and x^{2^*} denotes the equilibrium path flow pattern in the path-based permit system. Construct the marginal costs of emission abatement thus: For each O/D pair w, let $\tau_w^* = \max_{p \in P_w} \tau_p^*$ (which must be equal to ρ^{P^*} if $x_p^{2^*} > 0$). Construct the O/D pair licenses thus: For each O/D pair w, let $l_w^* = \sum_{p \in P_w} h_p x_p^{2^*}$, and, finally, construct the equilibrium license price thus: $\rho^{W^*} = \rho^{P^*}$.

Proof:
It is clear that equilibrium conditions (7.9) will be satisfied based on the construction of the path flows and the marginal costs of emission abatement. Similarly, (7.10) and (7.11) must also be satisfied by construction. Finally, (7.12) also follows since I have set $\sum_{w \in W} l_w^0 = \bar{Q}$ and $\sum_{p \in P} l_p^0 = \bar{Q}$ by assumption. □

7.2 Qualitative Properties

In this section, I present qualitative properties of the equilibrium patterns for both models. In particular, I provide some discussion of existence results and also establish properties of the functions $F^1(X^1)$ and $F^2(X^2)$ under which convergence of the algorithm in Section 7.3 is guaranteed.

I first discuss existence of solutions to variational inequalities (7.14) (equivalently (7.13)) and (7.20) (equivalently (7.19)). One knows from the standard theory of variational inequalities (Kinderlehrer and Stampacchia 1980; Nagurney 1999a; see also Appendix B) that if a solution can be shown to lie in a bounded set of the feasible set then a solution exists. Note, from variational inequality (7.13), that since l^{W*} satisfies equilibrium conditions (7.12), it must be bounded if the initial allocation $\sum_{w \in W} l_w^0$ is finite. This, in turn, implies from (7.10) that the path flow pattern x^* is also bounded and thus, from (7.9), one can infer that the marginal emission abatement costs for the O/D pairs must be bounded, which then implies, from (7.11), that the equilibrium price ρ^{W*} is also bounded. Similar arguments are used to establish that the solution to (7.20) must lie in a bounded set. Hence, it has been proved:

Theorem 7.4 (Existence)
The solution X^{1*} to variational inequality (7.14) and the solution X^{2*} to variational inequality (7.20) are guaranteed to exist.

Certain qualitative properties of the function $F^1(\cdot)$ and $F^2(\cdot)$ are now investigated. Specifically, I first establish that these functions are monotone and then I establish that they are Lipschitz continuous. These two properties are required for convergence of the algorithmic scheme I discuss in Section 7.3 and apply in Section 7.4.

Lemma 7.1
Assume that the user link cost functions are monotone increasing in the link flows and that the travel disutility functions are monotone decreasing in the travel demands, that is, for every $(f', d'), (f'', d'') \in K$, one has that:

$$\langle (c(f') - c(f''))^T, f' - f'' \rangle - \langle (\lambda(d') - \lambda(d''))^T, d' - d'' \rangle \geq 0,$$

$$\forall (f', d'), (f'', d'') \in K. \tag{7.27}$$

Then $F^1(X^1)$ is monotone, that is:

$$\langle (F^1(X') - F(X''))^T, X' - X'' \rangle \geq 0, \quad \forall X', X'' \in \mathcal{K}^1 \tag{7.28}$$

and:

$$\langle (F^2(X') - F(X''))^T, X' - X'' \rangle \geq 0, \quad \forall X', X'' \in \mathcal{K}^2. \tag{7.29}$$

Proof:
From the definition of $F^1(X)$ for the O/D pair-based permit system model, the left-hand side of expression (7.28) takes, after algebraic simplifications, the form:

$$\sum_{w \in} \sum_{p \in P_w} (c_a(f'_a) - c_a(f''_a)) \times (f'_a - f''_a) - \sum_{w \in W} (\lambda_w(d') - \lambda_w(d'')) \times (d'_w - d''_w), \tag{7.30}$$

which must be $\geq 0, \forall (f', d'), (f'', d'') \in K$, by the assumption that the link travel cost functions and the travel disutility functions are each monotone.

Similarly, from the definition of $F^2(X)$ for the path-based permit system model, the left-hand side of expression (7.29) takes, after algebraic simplification, exactly the form given by (7.30), which must hold $\forall (f', d'), (f'', d'') \in K$.

Hence, both $F^1(\cdot)$ and $F^2(\cdot)$ are monotone functions. □

A uniqueness result is presented in the subsequent theorem.

Theorem 7.5 (Uniqueness)
Assume that the user link cost functions and minus the travel disutility functions are strictly monotone in f and d, respectively, that is:

$$\langle (c(f') - c(f''))^T, f' - f'' \rangle - \langle (\lambda(d') - \lambda(d''))^T, d' - d'' \rangle > 0,$$

$$\forall (f', d''), (f', d'') \in K.$$

Then the equilibrium link flow and travel demand pattern (f^*, d^*) induced by either X^{1^*} or X^{2^*} is unique, respectively, in the case of variational inequality governing the O/D pair-based system and the path-based permit system.

Proof:
I first consider variational inequality (7.14) (equivalently (7.13)) and then variational inequality (7.20) (equivalently (7.19)). Assume, on the contrary, that there are two distinct equilibrium patterns for variational inequality (7.14), denoted by $\hat{X}^1$ and $\hat{X}^2$. Then, both must satisfy the variational inequality (7.14). Hence, one has that:

$$\langle F^1(\hat{X}^1)^T, X - \hat{X}^1 \rangle \geq 0, \quad \forall X \in \mathcal{K}^1 \tag{7.31}$$

and:

$$\langle F(\hat{X}^2)^T, X - \hat{X}^2 \rangle \geq 0, \quad \forall X \in \mathcal{K}^1. \tag{7.32}$$

Substituting $\hat{X}^2$ for X in (7.31) and $\hat{X}^1$ for X in (7.32) and adding the two resultant inequalities, after algebraic simplifications, yields:

$$\sum_{a\in L}(c_a(f^1) - c_a(f^2)) \times (f_a^2 - f_a^1) - \sum_{w\in W}(\lambda_w(d^1) - \lambda_w(d^2)) \times (d_w^2 - d_w^1) \geq 0, \tag{7.33}$$

but due to the assumption of strict monotonicity this implies that this inequality must hold as an equality and, hence, one must have that $f^1 = f^2$ and $d^1 = d^2$.

Analogously, one reaches the same conclusion in the case of variational inequality (7.20). □

Theorem 7.6 (Lipschitz Continuity)
If the travel cost functions and the travel disutility functions have bounded first-order derivatives, then the functions $F^1(\cdot)$ and $F^2(\cdot)$ are Lipschitz continuous, that is, there exists a positive constant $\bar{L}^1$, such that:

$$\|F^1(X^1) - F^1(X)\| \leq \bar{L}^1\|X^1 - X\|, \quad \forall X^1, X \in \mathcal{K}^1 \tag{7.34}$$

and a positive constant $\bar{L}^2$, such that:

$$\|F^2(X^2) - F^2(X)\| \leq \bar{L}^2\|X^2 - X\|, \quad \forall X^2, X \in \mathcal{K}^2. \tag{7.35}$$

Proof:
Follows along the same arguments as the proof of Lemma 3 in Nagurney (1994). □

7.3 Computational Procedure

In this section, the modified projection method of Korpelevich (1977) is proposed for the solution of both variational inequality (7.13) (equivalently, (7.14)) and variational inequality (7.19) (equivalently, (7.20)). It was also used to compute the equilibrium pattern for the link-based permit system model in the case of fixed travel demands in Chapter 6 (see Section 5.4 for the general statement of the algorithm).

For both the O/D pair-based model and the path-based model, however, the variables are now no longer link variables but, rather, path variables. Interestingly, this results in even simpler subproblems, each of which can be solved explicitly and in closed form.

For completeness, I present the modified projection method with $F(X) = F^1(X^1)$ and $\mathcal{K} = \mathcal{K}^1$ in expanded form for the O/D pair-based permit system model. I then do the same for when $F(X) = F^2(X^2)$ and $\mathcal{K} = \mathcal{K}^2$ for the path-based permit system model.

Modified Projection Method for the O/D Pair-Based Permit System Model Satisfying Variational Inequality (7.13)

Step 0: Initialization

Set $(x^0, \tau^{W^0}, l^{W^0}, \rho^{W^0}) \in \mathcal{K}^1$. Let $\mathcal{T} = 1$ and set α such that $0 < \alpha < \frac{1}{\bar{L}^1}$, where $\bar{L}^1$ is the Lipschitz constant for the problem (cf. (7.34)).

Step 1: Computation

Compute $(\bar{x}^{\mathcal{T}}, \bar{\tau}^{W\mathcal{T}}, \bar{l}^{W\mathcal{T}}, \bar{\rho}^{W\mathcal{T}}) \in \mathcal{K}^1$ by solving the variational inequality subproblem:

$$\sum_{w\in W}\sum_{p\in P_w}(\bar{x}_p^{\mathcal{T}} + \alpha(C_p(x^{(\mathcal{T}-1)}) + h_p\tau_p^{(\mathcal{T}-1)} - \lambda_w(x^{(\mathcal{T}-1)})) - x_p^{(\mathcal{T}-1)}) \times (x_p - \bar{x}_p^{\mathcal{T}})$$
$$+ \sum_{w\in W}(\bar{\tau}_w^{\mathcal{T}} + \alpha(l_w^{(\mathcal{T}-1)} - \sum_{p\in P_w} h_p x_p^{(\mathcal{T}-1)}) - \tau_w^{(\mathcal{T}-1)}) \times (\tau_w - \bar{\tau}_w^{\mathcal{T}})$$
$$+ \sum_{w\in W}(\bar{l}_w^{\mathcal{T}} + \alpha(\rho^{W(\mathcal{T}-1)} - \tau_w^{(\mathcal{T}-1)}) - l_w^{(\mathcal{T}-1)}) \times (l_w - \bar{l}_w^{\mathcal{T}})$$
$$+(\bar{\rho}^{W\mathcal{T}} + \alpha(\sum_{w\in W} l_w^0 - \sum_{w\in W} l_w^{(\mathcal{T}-1)}) - \rho^{W(\mathcal{T}-1)}) \times (\rho^W - \bar{\rho}^{W\mathcal{T}}) \geq 0,$$
$$\forall (x, \tau^W, l^W, \rho^W) \in \mathcal{K}^1. \tag{7.36}$$

Step 2: Adaptation

Compute $(x^{\mathcal{T}}, \tau^{W\mathcal{T}}, l^{W\mathcal{T}}, \rho^{W\mathcal{T}}) \in \mathcal{K}^1$ by solving the variational inequality subproblem:

$$\sum_{w\in W}\sum_{p\in P_w}(x_p^{\mathcal{T}} + \alpha(C_p(\bar{x}^{\mathcal{T}}) + h_p\bar{\tau}_p^{\mathcal{T}} - \lambda_w(\bar{x}^{\mathcal{T}})) - x_p^{(\mathcal{T}-1)}) \times (x_p - x_p^{\mathcal{T}})$$
$$+ \sum_{w\in W}(\tau_w^{\mathcal{T}} + \alpha(\bar{l}_w^{\mathcal{T}} - \sum_{p\in P_w} h_p \bar{x}_p^{\mathcal{T}}) - \tau_w^{(\mathcal{T}-1)}) \times (\tau_w - \tau_w^{\mathcal{T}})$$
$$+ \sum_{w\in W}(l_w^{\mathcal{T}} + \alpha(\bar{\rho}^{W\mathcal{T}} - \bar{\tau}_w^{\mathcal{T}}) - l_w^{(\mathcal{T}-1)}) \times (l_w - l_w^{\mathcal{T}})$$
$$+(\rho^{W\mathcal{T}} + \alpha(\sum_{w\in W} l_w^0 - \sum_{w\in W} \bar{l}_w^{\mathcal{T}}) - \rho^{W(\mathcal{T}-1)}) \times (\rho^W - \rho^{W\mathcal{T}}) \geq 0,$$
$$\forall (x, \tau^W, l^W, \rho^W) \in \mathcal{K}^1. \tag{7.37}$$

Step 3: Convergence Verification

If $|x_p^{\mathcal{T}} - x_p^{(\mathcal{T}-1)}| \leq \epsilon$, $\forall p \in P$, $|\tau_w^{\mathcal{T}} - \tau_w^{(\mathcal{T}-1)}| \leq \epsilon$, $|l_w^{\mathcal{T}} - l_w^{(\mathcal{T}-1)}| \leq \epsilon$, $\forall w \in W$, and $|\rho^{W\mathcal{T}} - \rho^{W(\mathcal{T}-1)}| \leq \epsilon$, with $\epsilon > 0$, a pre-specified tolerance, then stop; otherwise, set $\mathcal{T} := \mathcal{T} + 1$, and go to Step 1.

I now present the above algorithm with $F(X) = F^2(X^2)$ and $\mathcal{K} = \mathcal{K}^2$ in expanded form for the path-based permit system model.

Modified Projection Method for the Path-Based Permit System Equilibrium Model Satisfying Variational Ineqaulity (7.19)

Step 0: Initialization

Set $(x^0, \tau^{P^0}, l^{P^0}, \rho^{P^0}) \in \mathcal{K}^2$. Let $\mathcal{T} = 1$ and set α such that $0 < \alpha < \frac{1}{\bar{L}^2}$, where $\bar{L}^2$ is the Lipschitz constant for the problem (cf. (7.35)).

Step 1: Computation

Compute $(\bar{x}^{\mathcal{T}}, \bar{\tau}^{P^{\mathcal{T}}}, \bar{l}^{P^{\mathcal{T}}}, \bar{\rho}^{P^{\mathcal{T}}}) \in \mathcal{K}^2$ by solving the variational inequality subproblem:

$$\sum_{w \in W} \sum_{p \in P_w} (\bar{x}_p^{\mathcal{T}} + \alpha(C_p(x^{(\mathcal{T}-1)}) + h_p \tau_p^{(\mathcal{T}-1)} - \lambda_w(x^{(\mathcal{T}-1)})) - x_p^{(\mathcal{T}-1)}) \times (x_p - \bar{x}_p^{\mathcal{T}})$$

$$+ \sum_{p \in P} (\bar{\tau}_p^{\mathcal{T}} + \alpha(l_p^{(\mathcal{T}-1)} - h_p x_p^{(\mathcal{T}-1)}) - \tau_p^{(\mathcal{T}-1)}) \times (\tau_p - \bar{\tau}_p^{\mathcal{T}})$$

$$+ \sum_{p \in P} (\bar{l}_p^{\mathcal{T}} + \alpha(\rho^{P(\mathcal{T}-1)} - \tau_p^{(\mathcal{T}-1)}) - l_p^{(\mathcal{T}-1)}) \times (l_p - \bar{l}_p^{\mathcal{T}})$$

$$+ (\bar{\rho}^{P\mathcal{T}} + \alpha(\sum_{p \in P} l_p^0 - \sum_{p \in P} l_p^{(\mathcal{T}-1)}) - \rho^{P(\mathcal{T}-1)}) \times (\rho^P - \bar{\rho}^{P\mathcal{T}}) \geq 0,$$

$$\forall (x, \tau^P, l^P, \rho^P) \in \mathcal{K}^2. \tag{7.38}$$

Step 2: Adaptation

Compute $(x^{\mathcal{T}}, \tau^{P^{\mathcal{T}}}, l^{P^{\mathcal{T}}}, \rho^{P^{\mathcal{T}}}) \in \mathcal{K}^2$ by solving the variational inequality subproblem:

$$\sum_{w \in W} \sum_{p \in P_w} (x_p^{\mathcal{T}} + \alpha(C_p(\bar{x}^{(\mathcal{T})}) + h_p \bar{\tau}_p^{(\mathcal{T})} - \lambda_w(\bar{x}^{\mathcal{T}})) - x_p^{(\mathcal{T}-1)}) \times (x_p - x_p^{\mathcal{T}})$$

$$+ \sum_{p \in P} (\tau_p^{\mathcal{T}} + \alpha(\bar{l}_p^{(\mathcal{T})} - h_p \bar{x}_p^{(\mathcal{T})}) - \tau_p^{(\mathcal{T}-1)}) \times (\tau_p - \tau_p^{\mathcal{T}})$$

$$+ \sum_{p \in P} (l_p^{\mathcal{T}} + \alpha(\bar{\rho}^{P\mathcal{T}} - \bar{\tau}_p^{(\mathcal{T})}) - l_p^{(\mathcal{T}-1)}) \times (l_p - l_p^{\mathcal{T}})$$

$$+ (\rho^{P^{\mathcal{T}}} + \alpha(\sum_{p \in P} l_p^0 - \sum_{p \in P} \bar{l}_p^{(\mathcal{T})}) - \rho^{P(\mathcal{T}-1)}) \times (\rho^P - \rho^{P^{\mathcal{T}}}) \geq 0,$$

$$\forall (x, \tau^P, l^P, \rho^P) \in \mathcal{K}^2. \tag{7.39}$$

Step 3: Convergence Verification

If $|x_p^{\mathcal{T}} - x_p^{(\mathcal{T}-1)}| \leq \epsilon$, $\forall p \in P$, $|\tau_p^{\mathcal{T}} - \tau_p^{(\mathcal{T}-1)}| \leq \epsilon$, $|l_p^{\mathcal{T}} - l_p^{(\mathcal{T}-1)}| \leq \epsilon$, $\forall p \in P$, and $|\rho^{P\mathcal{T}} - \rho^{P(\mathcal{T}-1)}| \leq \epsilon$, with $\epsilon > 0$, a pre-specified tolerance, then stop; otherwise, set $\mathcal{T} := \mathcal{T} + 1$, and go to Step 1.

I now discuss the solution of the variational inequality subproblems (7.34) and (7.35) which can be computed very efficiently. For example, in (7.36), the computation of the path flows can be done explicitly and in closed form as follows: For all paths O/D pairs $w \in W$ and and paths $p \in P_w$:

$$\bar{x}_p^{\mathcal{T}} = \max\{0, -\alpha(C_p(x^{(\mathcal{T}-1)}) + h_p \tau_w^{\mathcal{T}-1} - \lambda_w(x^{(\mathcal{T}-1)})) + x_p^{(\mathcal{T}-1)}\}. \quad (7.40)$$

The marginal costs of emission abatement for the O/D pairs, in turn, can be computed as: For all O/D pairs $w \in W$:

$$\bar{\tau}_w^{\mathcal{T}} = \max\{0, -\alpha(l_w^{(\mathcal{T}-1)} - \sum_{p \in P_w} h_p x_p^{(\mathcal{T}-1)}) + \tau_w^{(\mathcal{T}-1)}\}, \quad (7.41)$$

whereas the licenses can be computed according to: For all O/D pairs $w \in W$:

$$\bar{l}_w^{\mathcal{T}} = \max\{0, -\alpha(\rho^{W(\mathcal{T}-1)} - \tau_w^{(\mathcal{T}-1)}) + l_w^{(\mathcal{T}-1)}\}. \quad (7.42)$$

Finally, the price can be computed according to the expression:

$$\bar{\rho}^W = \max\{0, -\alpha(\sum_{w \in W} l_w^0 - \sum_{w \in W} l_w^{(\mathcal{T}-1)}) + \rho^{W(\mathcal{T}-1)}\}. \quad (7.43)$$

In an analogous manner one can obtain closed form expressions for the elements of $x^{\mathcal{T}}, \tau^{W^{\mathcal{T}}}, l^{W^{\mathcal{T}}}$, and $\rho^{W^{\mathcal{T}}}$ as the solution to variational inequality subproblem (7.37).

The solutions to variational inequality subproblems (7.38) and (7.39) induced by the modified projection method applied to the path-based permit system also are obtained exactly and in closed form in a fashion analogous to the statements (7.40)–(7.43).

Convergence for the algorithm is given in the following Theorem.

Theorem 7.7 (Convergence)
If the user link travel cost functions c and the travel disutility functions $-\lambda$ are assumed to be monotone and have bounded first-order derivatives, then the modified projection method described above converges to the solution of the variational inequality (7.14) and (7.20).

Proof:
From Lemma 7.1, it follows that both $F^1(X)$ and $F^2(X)$ are monotone, whereas from Theorem 7.6 it follows that both $F^1(X)$ and $F^2(X)$ are Lipschitz continuous. Hence, according to Korpelevich (1977), the modified projection method is guaranteed to converge. □

7.4 Numerical Example

In this section, I present a numerical example to illustrate both the models and the algorithm. I implemented the modified projection method in

FORTRAN for each of the three permit system models of interest here: the O/D-based, the path-based, and the link-based ones. Again, I utilized the IBM SP2 located at the Computer Science Department at the University of Massachusetts at Amherst for the numerical work.

The modified projection method was initialized by setting the initial demand for each O/D pair equal to 100 and setting the flow on a path equal to the travel demand for the O/D pair that the path belongs to divided by the number of paths. All other variables were initialized to zero. I report the CPU time, exclusive of input/output and setup time, as well as the number of iterations for the example. The convergence tolerance $\epsilon = .0001$ for each code.

I also report the total payment, T, to the government, where:

$$T_1 = \sum_{w \in W} \sum_{p \in P_w} \tau_w^* h_p x_p^*$$

in the case of the O/D pair-based system:

$$T_2 = \sum_{w \in W} \sum_{p \in P_w} \tau_p^* h_p^* x_p^*$$

in the case of the path-based system, and:

$$T_3 = \sum_{p \in P} \sum_{a \in L} \tau_a^* h_a \delta_{ap} x_p^*$$

in the case of the link-based permit system.

Example 7.1

The example depicted in Figure 7.3 had the topology of the Braess (1968) network with user link travel cost functions given by:

$$c_1(f) = .0005 f_1^4 + 10 f_1 + 2 f_2,$$

$$c_2(f) = .00001 f_2^4 + f_2 + .5 f_1 + 50,$$

$$c_3(f) = .0004 f_3^4 + f_3 + .2 f_2 + 10,$$

$$c_4(f) = .0001 f_4^4 + f_4 + .1 f_3 + 50,$$

$$c_5(f) = .0001 f_5^4 + 10 f_5 + 4 f_1.$$

The O/D pair was $w_1 = (1,4)$ with a travel disutility given by $\lambda_{w_1}(d_{w_1}) = -d_{w_1} + 98$.

The paths were $p_1 = (1,3,5)$, $p_2 = (1,4)$, and $p_3 = (2,5)$.

In the example, the emission factors were set as follows: $h_a = a$, for all $a \in L$. The initial licenses for the link-based permit system were as follows: $l_a^0 = a$, for all links $a \in L$ for the link licenses. This initial allocation corresponds to an environmental quality standard of $\sum_{a \in L} l_a^0 = \bar{Q} = 15$.

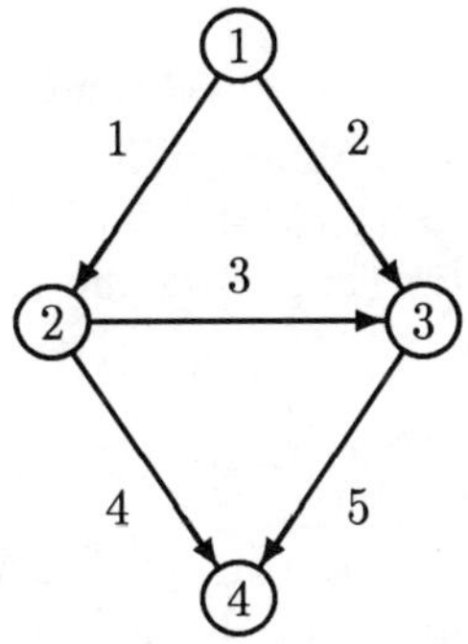

Fig. 7.3. Network topology for Example 7.1

The initial O/D pair licenses for the O/D pair-based system were set to: $l_w^0 = \bar{Q} = 15$, whereas the initial path licenses for the path-based permit system was set thus: $l_{p_1}^0 = l_{p_2}^0 = l_{p_3}^0 = 5$ and, hence, $\sum_{p \in P_w} l_p^0 = \bar{Q} = 15$.

Solution to the O/D-Based Permit System

I set $\alpha = 0.01$ in this version of the modified projection method. The algorithm converged to the following path flow pattern:

$$x_{p_1}^* = 0.00, \quad x_{p_2}^* = 2.99, \quad x_{p_3}^* = 0.30,$$

with induced equilibrium link load pattern:

$$f_1^* = 2.99, \quad f_2^* = 0.30, \quad f_3^* = 0.00, \quad f_4^* = 2.99, \quad f_5^* = 0.30,$$

and travel demand $d_{w_1}^* = 3.29$.

The marginal cost of emission abatement $\tau_{w_1}^* = 2.79$ which was also the equilibrium license price ρ^{W*}. The equilibrium license was $l_{w_1}^* = 15$.

The cost on the used paths, including the costs due to the payment for the pollution permits, that is, $C_p(x) + \tau_{w_1}^* h_p$, were as follows:

$$C_{p_1} + \tau_{w_1}^* h_{p_1} = C_{p_2} + \tau_{w_1}^* h_{p_2} = 94.71$$

and 94.71 was also the valued of the travel disutility λ_{w_1}.

The total payment to the government $T_1 = 41.84$.

Solution to the Path-Based Permit System

I set $\alpha = 0.001$ in the modified projection method. The algorithm converged to the following path flow pattern:

$$x_{p_1}^* = 0.00, \quad x_{p_2}^* = 2.99, \quad x_{p_3}^* = 0.30,$$

with induced equilibrium link load pattern:

$$f_1^* = 2.99, \quad f_2^* = 0.30, \quad f_3^* = 0.00, \quad f_4^* = 2.99, \quad f_5^* = 0.30,$$

and travel demand $d^*_{w_1} = 3.29$.

The marginal costs of emission abatement on used paths were: $\tau^*_{p_2} = \tau^*_{p_3} = 2.79$ which was also the equilibrium license price ρ^{P^*}. The equilibrium licenses were: $l^*_{p_1} = 0.00$, $l^*_{p_2} = 11.95$, and $l^*_{p_3} = 3.05$.

The cost on the used paths, including the costs due to the payment for the pollution permits, that is, $C_p(x) + \tau^*_p h_p$, were as follows:

$$C_{p_2} + \tau^*_{w_1} h_{p_2} = C_{p_3} + \tau^*_{w_1} h_{p_3} = 94.71$$

and 94.71 was also the valued of the travel disutility λ_{w_1}.

The total amount of payments to the government $T_2 = 41.83$.

Solution to the Link-Based Permit System

I set $\alpha = 0.1$ in the link-based version of the modified projection method. The modified projection method computed the following equilibrium path flow pattern:

$$x^*_{p_1} = 1.20, \quad x^*_{p_2} = 0.85, \quad x^*_{p_3} = 0.00,$$

which induced the following equilibrium link load pattern:

$$f^*_1 = 2.04, \quad f^*_2 = 0.00, \quad f^*_3 = 1.20, \quad f^*_4 = 0.85, \quad f^*_5 = 1.20,$$

and the travel demand $d^*_{w_1} = 2.04$.

The cost on a path after the payment was equal to $C_p + \sum_{a \in L} \tau^*_a h_a \delta_{ap}$ and the values for the used paths were:

$$C_{p_1} + \sum_{a \in L} \tau^*_a h_a \delta_{ap_1} = C_{p_2} + \sum_{a \in L} \tau^*_a h_a \delta_{ap_2} = 95.96$$

and this was also the travel disutility λ_{w_1}.

The marginal costs of emission abatement on the used links were equal to 4.91 which was also the equilibrium price ρ^{L^*}. The total payment to the government $T_3 = 75.35$.

Note that the computed equilibrium path flows, the demand, as well as the link flows were identical for both the O/D pair-based and the path-based models. Moreover, note that $\tau^*_{w_1} = \tau^*_{p_2} = \tau^*_{p_3} = 2.79$. Finally, $\rho^{W^*} = \rho^{P^*}$. Moreover, the increased costs for used paths (after payments) were identical for both the O/D pair-based and the path-based permit systems as was (approximately) the payment to the government. These values were higher than the corresponding ones in the case of the link-based permit system model.

In this chapter, I presented a hierarchy of permit systems for elastic demand traffic networks and showed that the networks are sustainable under such permit systems. The results are from Nagurney (1999d).

With this chapter, I conclude Part II of this book. In Table 7.2, I provide a summary of the policy instruments that have been developed in Part II of this book for sustainable user-optimized transportation networks.

Table 7.2. Summary of policy instruments for sustainable U-O networks

Chapter 5	
Emission pricing: Fixed demand networks:	• Known O/D pairs • Known origins • Known destinations • Known total demand
Emission pricing: Elastic demand networks:	• Known O/D pairs
Chapter 6	
Pollution permits: Fixed demand networks:	• link-based system
Chapter 7	
Pollution permits: Elastic demand networks:	• O/D pair-based system • path-based system • link-based system

Part III Policies for Sustainable System-Optimized Transportation Networks

8 Sustainable System-Optimized Networks

With this chapter, I begin the third part of this book, which focuses on policies for sustainable transportation networks, but from a *system-optimized* perspective, rather than from a user-optimized viewpoint, which was the subject of Part II of this book. Recall that, as discussed in Chapter 2, in a system-optimized network, the total cost associated with traveling on the network is minimized. This concept is useful not only in the context of congested urban transportation networks but, in fact, in other networks, including freight networks, in which there exists a central controller who can route traffic on the network in an optimal fashion; optimality here, unlike in the case of user-optimized networks, is represented by the solution of an optimization problem, even in the case of general user link travel cost functions.

Consequently, in this part of the book, I add another dimension to the modeling and analysis of sustainable transportation networks in that I explicitly now handle not only the total emissions generated and guarantee that they do not exceed the imposed environmental quality standard, but also include an explicit objective function whose minimization reflects the minimization of total cost in the network as reflected by the total congestion. Note that in the user-optimized focus of Part II the total congestion was not treated on the networks since it was assumed that the behavior of the users was such that each individual traveler sought to determine his own minimal cost of travel in a noncooperative fashion.

As in the models in Part II, I also assume here that the networks are viable. Furthermore, I consider traffic networks in which the travel demands are fixed. In Table 8.1, I summarize the policy instruments developed for sustainable system-optimized networks in Part III of this book. Here, I consider, in both Chapters 8 and 9, policy instruments not only for pure system-

Table 8.1. Summary of policy instruments for sustainable S-O networks

Chapter 8
Emission/congestion pricing – Fixed demand networks
Emission/congestion tolls for U-O – Fixed demand networks
Chapter 9
Tradable pollution permits – Fixed demand networks
Tradable pollution permits/tolls for U-O – Elastic demand networks

optimization but I also investigate policies in the form of tolls to guarantee that, if the behavior is that of user-optimization but a system-optimum is desired, the S-O pattern is also U-O.

This chapter is organized as follows. In Section 8.1, I develop models of sustainable system-optimized transportation networks, beginning with a simple model. In Section 8.2, I then model the scenario in which travelers behave in a user-optimized manner, but the transportation authority wishes to impose tolls which cover both the emissions as well as guarantee that the travelers also behave in a system-optimized manner. These combined emission and congestion tolls guarantee sustainability of the transportation network in a global sense in that the travelers, after the imposition of the emission/congestion tolls, still behave in a user-optimized fashion, but the generated flow patterns are also system-optimized and, hence, optimal from a societal perspective.

8.1 Modeling of Sustainable System-Optimized Networks

In this section, I develop models for sustainable transportation networks in which the underlying behavior is that of system-optimization and the policy is that of emission tolls. In Subsection 8.1.1, I present a simple model, which is, subsequently, generalized in Section 8.1.2

In Table 8.2, the relationship between a viable, system-optimized transportation network in the presence of emission/congestion tolls, as developed in this section, is highlighted.

8.1.1 A Simple Model

As in earlier chapters, consider a traffic network consisting of the graph $G = [N, L]$, where N denotes the set of nodes and L the set of links. Moreover, assume in this chapter, as given, a vector of travel demands d associated with the origin/destination pairs. In this subsection, hence, I consider the "classical" form of the total link travel cost functions, due to Beckmann,

Table 8.2. Relationship between system-optimization and emission/congestion pricing and sustainability

System-Optimized Viable Network + **Emission/Congestion Pricing**	$\Rightarrow$	**Sustainability**

McGuire, and Winsten (1956), in which the total cost on a link, denoted by $\hat{c}_a$ is equal to the product of the user link travel cost, which is assumed to be a separable function of the link load, times the total load on the link, that is:

$$\hat{c}_a = c_a(f_a) \times f_a, \quad \forall a \in L, \tag{8.1}$$

where, as in the simple model of Section 5.1.1, in which the user-optimized version was presented, it was assumed that the user link travel cost function c_a is increasing in the flow for each link in the network (see also Figure 2.1).

The total travel cost on a path p, hence, is equal to the sum of the total travel costs on links that comprise that path, that is:

$$\hat{C}_p = \sum_{a \in L} \hat{c}_a \delta_{ap}, \quad \forall a \in L. \tag{8.2}$$

The marginal of the total cost on a path p, in turn, which is denoted by $\hat{C}'_p$, for all $p \in P$, is given by the sum of the marginals of the total costs on the links that comprise the path, that is,

$$\hat{C}'_p = \sum_{a \in L} \hat{c}'_a \delta_{ap} = \sum_{a \in L} \frac{\partial \hat{c}_a(f_a)}{\partial f_a} \delta_{ap}. \tag{8.3}$$

Recall that in the system-optimization problem one seeks to minimize the total cost in the network, where the objective function is given by:

$$\text{Minimize} \sum_{a \in L} \hat{c}_a(f_a) = \text{Minimize} \sum_{a \in L} c_a(f_a) \times f_a \tag{8.4}$$

or, equivalently, in path flows by:

$$\text{Minimize} \sum_{p \in P} \hat{C}_p = \text{Minimize} \sum_{p \in P} C_p(x) \times x_p. \tag{8.5}$$

I am now ready to state the system-optimization problem, whose solution will guarantee that the transportation network is sustainable. I utilize the path flow form of the objective function given by (8.5). Hence, I retain the objective function in the classical traffic network system-optimization model due to Beckmann, McGuire, and Winsten (1956), as well as the constraints, but now I add the environmental quality constraint, as was also done in the user-optimized models (cf. (5.6)).

The system-optimization problem can, therefore, be expressed as:

$$\text{Minimize} \quad S(x) = \sum_{p \in P} \hat{C}_p \tag{8.6}$$

subject to:

$$\sum_{p \in P_w} x_p = d_w, \quad \forall w \in W, \tag{8.7}$$

$$\sum_{a \in L} h_a \sum_{p \in P} x_p \delta_{ap} \leq \bar{Q}, \tag{8.8}$$

$$x_p \geq 0, \quad \forall p \in P. \tag{8.9}$$

Observe that conditions (8.7)–(8.9) correspond precisely to Linear System 4.1, the existence of a solution to which guarantees viability of a transportation network with given O/D pairs and travel demands.

Optimality Conditions

I now derive the optimality conditions for the system-optimization problem given by (8.6)–(8.9). These are optimality conditions, rather than equilibrium conditions, as is the case where the travelers behave in a user-optimizing manner, since here one now has an explicit objective function, which represents the total cost or congestion to be minimized.

Note that, since the user travel cost functions are increasing functions of the flow, the objective function is convex and the constraints, which are linear, are also convex. Thus, the Kuhn-Tucker optimality conditions (see Appendix A) can be stated as follows: $x^* \in R^{n_P}_+$ is an optimal solution if it satisfies the travel demands, and satisfies the following system of equalities and inequalities: For each O/D pair $w \in W$, and each path $p \in P_w$:

$$\bar{\hat{C}}'_p(x^*, \tau^*) = \hat{C}'_p(x^*) + \tau^* \sum_{a \in L} h_a \delta_{ap} \begin{cases} = & \mu_w, & \text{if } x^*_p > 0 \\ \geq & \mu_w, & \text{if } x^*_p = 0, \end{cases} \tag{8.10}$$

where τ^* is the Lagrange multiplier associated with the environmental quality constraint (8.8) with τ^* having the interpretation here as being the marginal cost of emission abatement, as in the case of the user-optimized models.

In addition, one must have that:

$$\bar{Q} - \sum_{a \in L} h_a \sum_{p \in P} x^*_p \delta_{ap} \begin{cases} = & 0, & \text{if } \tau^* > 0 \\ \geq & 0, & \text{if } \tau^* = 0, \end{cases} \tag{8.11}$$

Observe that $\hat{C}'_p = \frac{\partial S(x)}{\partial x_p}$, $\forall p \in P$. Note that $\bar{\hat{C}}'_p$ in (8.10) denotes the *generalized* marginal cost associated with traveling now on path p, where the term: $\tau^* \sum_{a\in L} h_a\delta_{ap}$ represents the, de facto, marginal of the total cost on path p due to the emissions generated by traveling on path p. Hence, this term may also be interpreted as a "price" which is associated with traveling on the path. There exists a similar interpretation of the term arising in the case of the user-optimized model of Section 5.1.1 (see, e. g., (5.8)). Consequently, the higher the emission factors on a utilized path, the higher this term for travelers on that path. Condition (8.11) has precisely the same form as condition (5.9) for the analogous U-O problem, but here the flow pattern is system-optimized, rather than user-optimized. Similarly, conditions (8.10) are analogous to conditions (5.8) for the U-O problem, but there the flow pattern is user-optimized, rather than system-optimized, as it is here.

Note that, in the case of system-optimization, it is the generalized marginal travel costs on used paths for each O/D pair that get equalized (or equilibrated), rather than the generalized user travel costs, as is the case in the models in Chapter 5.

Pricing Policies

As already stated, in the case of system-optimized networks, the central authority controls the flows, be they flows which correspond to motor vehicles, freight, or others. Hence, the solution to the sustainable system-optimization problem is implemented by the authority or central controller.

Nevertheless, one may interpret the costs associated with emissions so that one may assign the following price policies which reflect the cost of emitting. Specifically, one can construct pricing policies, in links, and in paths, respectively, which satisfy optimality conditions (8.10) and (8.11), and which are analogous to those for the user-optimized problem described in Section 5.1.1, but which are interpreted there as tolls, since the users in that case do not control the system and act independently. Here, however, the total cost in the network is also minimized simultaneously.

The following emission pricing policies satisfy the conditions (8.10) and (8.11).

Link Pricing Policy

The link pricing policy given by $t_a = \tau^* h_a$, $\forall a \in L$, where τ^* is the equilibrium marginal cost of emission abatement and t_a denotes the payment on link a, guarantees that the transportation network is sustainable.

Path Pricing Policy

The path pricing policy given by $t_p = \tau^* \sum_{a\in L} h_a\delta_{ap}$ for all $p \in P$, where t_p denotes the payment on path p, guarantees that the network will be sustainable.

Note that here τ^* does not correspond to the marginal cost of emission abatement resulting from the solution of the policy problem in the case of user-optimization described in Chapter 5. The similar notation is used simply for convenience and is clear from the context of the problem under study.

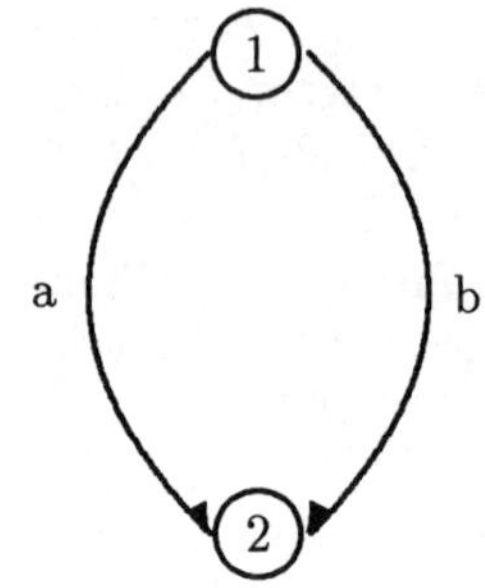

Fig. 8.1. Network topology for Example 8.1

I now present an example, for which the sustainable system-optimized flow pattern can be solved for explicitly.

Example 8.1

Consider the network depicted in Figure 8.1, consisting of two nodes: 1 and 2, and two links: a and b. There is a single O/D pair $w_1 = (1,2)$. Let path $p_1 = a$ and path $p_2 = b$. The travel demand $d_{w_1} = 10$. The user link travel cost functions are:

$$c_a(f_a) = f_a + 7, \quad c_b(f_b) = 2f_b + 4.$$

Hence, the total cost functions on the links are:

$$\hat{c}_a(f_a) = f_a^2 + 7f_a, \quad \hat{c}_b(f_b) = 2f_b^2 + 4f_b.$$

The marginals of the total costs on the links, in turn, are given by the expressions:

$$\hat{c}'_a(f_a) = 2f_a + 7, \quad \hat{c}'_b(f_b) = 4f_b + 4,$$

which also correspond to the path marginals of the total costs, since each path consists of a single link:

$$\hat{C}'_{p_1} = 2x_{p_1} + 7, \quad \hat{C}'_{p_2} = 4x_{p_2} + 4.$$

Suppose that the emission factors are $h_a = 0.1$ and $h_b = 0.5$, and the environmental quality standard $\bar{Q} = 3$. It is easy to verify that the network is viable (for example, one may simply let $x_{p_1} = 10$ and $x_{p_2} = 0$ and the Linear System 4.1 is satisfied).

Due to the simplicity of the example, one can solve explicitly for the solution. Indeed, note that the path flow pattern $x^*_{p_1} = 6\frac{1}{6}$, $x^*_{p_2} = 3\frac{5}{6}$ with $\tau^* = 0$, yields:

$$\hat{C}'_{p_1} = \hat{C}'_{p_2} = 19\frac{1}{3}.$$

Hence, there are no tolls needed in this transportation network example, and the system-optimized solution is also sustainable, with the total emissions generated by the flow pattern equal to 2.533, which is less than $\bar{Q} = 3$.

Suppose now that one tightens the environmental quality standard so that the new $\bar{Q} = 1.5$. The preceding pattern violates the environmental quality condition and, hence, a new sustainable system-optimized flow pattern needs to be determined. The new system-optimal flow pattern is:

$$x^*_{p_1} = 8.75, \quad x^*_{p_2} = 1.25,$$

and the equilibrium marginal cost of emission abatement $\tau^* = 36.25$, yielding a link pricing policy (which also corresponds to a path pricing policy in this case) given by:

$$t_a = .1(36.25) = 3.625, \quad t_b = .5(36.25) = 18.125,$$

and with generalized marginals of the total costs on paths equal to:

$$\bar{\hat{C}}'_{p_1} = \bar{\hat{C}}'_{p_2} = 28.125.$$

Indeed, the environmental quality standard is precisely met by this pattern.

Remark 8.1

One might be tempted to construct an optimization problem which has as its objective function to minimize both the total cost in the network as well as the total emissions. For example, one may consider the following problem:

$$\text{Minimize} \quad \sum_{p \in P} C_p(x) x_p + \sum_{a \in L} h_a \sum_{p \in P} x_p$$

subject to:

$$\sum_{p \in P_w} x_p = d_w, \quad \forall w \in W,$$

$$x_p \geq 0, \quad \forall p \in P.$$

Note that the Kuhn-Tucker conditions for this problem can be stated as, assuming that the flow pattern is feasible: For all O/D pairs $w \in W$ and all paths $p \in P_w$:

$$\bar{\hat{C}}'_p(x^*) = \hat{C}'_p(x^*) + \sum_{a \in L} h_a \delta_{ap} \begin{cases} = & \mu_w, & \text{if } x^*_p > 0 \\ \geq & \mu_w, & \text{if } x^*_p = 0. \end{cases} \tag{8.12}$$

However, although the objective function includes the expression for the total emissions, the environmental quality standard may not be met by the solution to this problem and, consequently, the resulting flow pattern may not correspond to a sustainable one.

Indeed, consider the following example.

Example 8.2

The network topology is given in Figure 8.1 and consists of two nodes: 1 and 2 and two links: a and b, and a single O/D pair $w_1 = (1,2)$. Let $p_1 = a$ and $p_2 = b$. Assume that the emission factors are $h_a = 0.1$ and $h_b = 0.5$. The travel demand $d_{w_1} = 10$ and the user link cost functions are:

$$c_a(f_a) = f_a + 5, \quad c_b(f_b) = f_b + 5,$$

so the total cost functions are:

$$\hat{c}_a(f_a) = f_a^2 + 5f_a, \quad \hat{c}_b(f_b) = f_b^2 + 5f_b,$$

with marginals of the total cost functions given by:

$$\hat{c}_a'(f_a) = 2f_a + 5 \quad \hat{c}_b'(f_b) = 2f_b + 5,$$

which corresponds to the marginals of the total costs on the paths:

$$\hat{C}_{p_1}' = 2x_{p_1} + 5, \quad \hat{C}_{p_2}' = 2x_{p_2} + 5.$$

Assuming that both paths are used and using the expression for the travel demand being equal to the sum of the paths for the O/D pair, one obtains a single equation corresponding to the Kuhn-Tucker condition above:

$$2f_a + 5 + 0.1 = 2(10 - f_a) + 5 + 0.5,$$

the solution of which yields:

$$f_a^* = 5.1, \quad f_b^* = 4.9,$$

with $\hat{C}_{p_1}' + \sum_{a \in p_1} h_a = \hat{C}_{p_2}' + \sum_{a \in p_2} h_a = 15.3$.

Note, however, that this flow pattern yields total emissions equal to 2.96, which exceed $\bar{Q} = 2$! Therefore, the solution of the optimization problem satisfying optimality conditions (8.12) does not guarantee a sustainable transportation network.

8.1.2 The General Model

In this section, I now consider traffic networks which are sustainable and system-optimized, but on which the user link travel cost functions are no longer separable. Hence, I assume the general situation in which the user link travel cost on link a is given by:

$$c_a = c_a(f), \quad \forall a \in L, \tag{8.13}$$

and, consequently, the total cost expression on a link a, denoted by $\hat{c}_a$, is given by:

$$\hat{c}_a = c_a(f) \times f_a, \quad \forall a \in L. \tag{8.14}$$

Note that, in the simple model of Section 8.1.1, $\frac{\partial S(x)}{\partial x_p}$, where $S(x)$ denoted the total cost on the network, was precisely equal to $\hat{C}'_p = \sum_{a\in L} \hat{c}'_a$, since the user link cost travel functions, and, hence, the total link travel cost functions were separable. In the general case, however, one can still define the "marginal of the total cost" on path p, denoted, again, by $\hat{C}'_p$ to be equal to $\frac{\partial S(x)}{\partial x_p}$, in which case the optimality conditions (8.10) and (8.11) coincide with the optimality conditions for the general problem, whose objective function remains that of (8.6), subject to constraints: (8.7)–(8.9).

Clearly, one can also derive a variational inequality formulation of the Kuhn-Tucker optimality conditions for this problem but this is not necessary since the problem, even in the general case, remains an *optimization problem* in the case of system-optimization, rather than an *equilibrium problem* as is the case in user-optimization. Indeed, recall that in the case of nonseparable and asymmetric user link travel cost functions (see also Section 2.2.3), one can no longer reformulate the traffic network equilibrium conditions as the optimality conditions of a convex optimization problem. Consequently, in order to formulate, analyze, and solve such problems, one must appeal to variational inequality theory.

For completeness, however, as well as for the flexibility in applying, for example, such an algorithm as the modified projection method, which can be used to solve the sustainable S-O problem above, I also give the variational inequality formulation of conditions (8.10) and (8.11). Of course, I emphasize that any general convex programming algorithm can be applied, at least in principle, to compute the solution to the system-optimization problem for sustainable transportation networks given by (8.6)–(8.9). Since the proof of the theorem is so similar to that of Theorem 5.1, it is presented without proof.

Theorem 8.1 (Variational Inequality Formulation of a Sustainable System-Optimized Solution)
A traffic flow pattern and marginal cost of emission abatement $(x^*, \tau^*) \in \mathcal{K}^1$ is a solution of the sustainable system-optimized model described above if and only if it is a solution to the variational inequality problem:

Path Flow Formulation:

$$\sum_{w\in W}\sum_{p\in P_w}\left[\hat{C}'_p(x^*) + \tau^* \sum_{a\in L} h_a \delta_{ap}\right] \times \left[x_p - x^*_p\right]$$

$$+\left[\bar{Q}-\sum_{a\in L}h_a\sum_{p\in P}x_p^*\delta_{ap}\right]\times[\tau-\tau^*]\geq 0,\quad \forall(x,\tau)\in\mathcal{K}^1, \tag{8.15}$$

where $\mathcal{K}^1\equiv\bar{K}_1\times R^1_+$, *and* $\bar{K}_1\equiv\{x|x\geq 0$, *and satisfies* (8.7)$\}$ *and, equivalently,* $(f^*,\tau^*)\in\mathcal{K}^2$ *is a solution of the sustainable S-O problem if and only if it satisfies the variational inequality problem:*

Link Load Formulation:

$$\sum_{a\in L}[\hat{c}'_a(f^*)+\tau^*h_a]\times[f_a-f_a^*]$$

$$+\left[\bar{Q}-\sum_{a\in L}h_af_a^*\right]\times[\tau-\tau^*]\geq 0,\quad \forall(f,\tau)\in\mathcal{K}^2, \tag{8.16}$$

where $\mathcal{K}^2\equiv\bar{K}_2\times R_+$ *and* $\bar{K}^2\equiv\{f|$ *there exists an* $x\geq 0$, *satisfying* (8.7)$\}$.

8.2 Emission/Congestion Tolls for Sustainability

In this section, I develop a framework for the construction of tolls, which serves the twofold purpose of alleviating congestion in that the total cost in the network as reflected by the total congestion is minimized, while, at the same time, guaranteeing that the environmental quality standard is satisfied, even though the travelers are now assumed to adopt, once again, as in the models of Part II, user-optimizing behavior. Hence, here I assume that travelers seek to determine their paths from their origins to their destinations so as to minimize their travel "cost" where here cost is interpreted in a general manner to include not only, for example, travel time, but also the outlay of any necessary payments for use of the path. The relationship between the tolls proposed in this section and sustainability of the transportation network is highlighted in Table 8.3.

The Procedure

I now describe a procedure for the allocation of tolls which guarantees that the system-optimized flow pattern for a sustainable network, that is, one that satisfies optimality conditions (8.10) and the corresponding marginal cost of emission abatement, which satisfies, in turn, optimality conditions (8.11), is also a user-optimized pattern, after the imposition of the appropriate toll policy.

Note that, for the system-optimal solution, denoted by (x^*,τ^*), to also be user-optimized, it must satisfy the conditions: For each O/D pair $w\in W$, and each path $p\in P_w$:

$$C_p(x^*)+t_p\begin{cases} = & \lambda_w, \quad \text{if } x_p^*>0\\ \geq & \lambda_w, \quad \text{if } x_p^*=0,\end{cases} \tag{8.17}$$

Table 8.3. Relationship between system-optimization with user-optimized behavior in the presence of emission/congestion tolls and sustainability

System-Optimized Viable Network + **User-Optimized Behavior** + **Emission/Congestion Tolls**	$\Rightarrow$	**Sustainability**

where t_p here denotes a path-toll policy.

Furthermore, the system-optimized flow pattern already satisfies conditions (8.10); that is: For each O/D pair $w \in W$, and each path $p \in P_w$:

$$\hat{C}'_p(x^*) + \tau^* \sum_{a \in L} h_a \delta_{ap} \begin{cases} = & \mu_w, & \text{if } x^*_p > 0 \\ \geq & \mu_w, & \text{if } x^*_p = 0, \end{cases} \tag{8.18}$$

For a solution to (8.18) to coincide with that of (8.17) implies that, for each path $p \in P$, one must have that:

$$t_p = \hat{C}'_p(x^*) - C_p(x^*) + \tau^* \sum_{a \in L} h_a \delta_{ap}. \tag{8.19}$$

Path-Toll Policy

Hence, equation (8.19) implies a procedure by which one can construct a path-toll policy. In particular, one first solves the problem (8.6)–(8.9) and then determines, for each path p in the network, the path-toll policy according to equation (8.19).

Link-Toll Policy

A link-toll policy, in turn, can also be determined according to:

$$t_a = \hat{c}'_a(f^*) - c_a(f^*) + \tau^* h_a, \quad \forall a \in L. \tag{8.20}$$

Remark 8.2

It is worth highlighting the similarities between expressions (8.19) and (8.20) and the analogous expressions for path tolls and link tolls, respectively, arising in the classical toll policies described in Chapter 2, in which only congestion is considered and not pollution due to emissions (cf. (2.25), (2.26), and (2.31)). Indeed, in the latter framework, there would be no such terms $\tau^* \sum_{a \in L} h_a \delta_{ap}$ and $\tau^* h_a$, and the flow pattern x^* and the link load pattern f^* would simply correspond to the patterns obtained by the solution of the system-optimization problem (8.6), subject only to (8.7) and (8.9) (when the link load/path flow expression is substituted directly into the formulation). These terms reflect precisely the cost associated with the emissions.

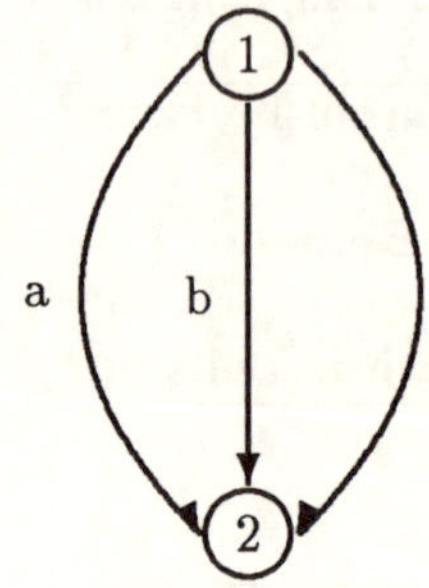

Fig. 8.2. Network topology for Example 8.3

8.3 Numerical Example

In this section, I present numerical examples of sustainable S-O transportation networks, to which the solutions are computed using the modified projection method outlined in Section 5.4, whose specific steps are given by (5.40) and (5.41). Due to the similarities between variational inequalities (5.12) and (8.16), it is easy to adapt the code for the former to solve the latter. Indeed, this is precisely what I did, noting that now one needs to also formulate the marginals of the total costs on the links, rather than simply the user link costs. The code, as all the other codes, was written in FORTRAN and the computer system used for the numerical work was the IBM SP2 located at the Computer Science Department at the University of Massachusetts at Amherst.

Example 8.3: Example 5.4 Revisited

For purposes of comparison, I selected the same network and data as in Example 5.4, which was, in turn, a variant of Example 5.1. The network topology if reproduced in Figure 8.2, for convenience.

The network consists of two nodes, denoted by 1 and 2; three links, denoted by a, b, and c, and a single O/D pair $w_1 = (1,2)$. I let $p_1 = a$, $p_2 = b$, and $p_3 = c$. The travel demand $d_{w_1} = 10$. Recall that the user link travel cost functions are:

$$c_a(f_a) = 2f_a + 5, \quad c_b(f_b) = f_b + 8, \quad c_c(f_c) = 1.5f_c + 5.$$

The emissions are: $h_a = 0.1$, $h_b = 0.2$, and $h_c = 0.3$, with the environmental quality standard $\bar{Q} = 1.5$.

I set $\alpha = 0.4$ in the modified projection method with $\epsilon = .001$. An application of the modified projection method yielded the following sustainable S-O solution:

$$f_a^* = 5.40, \quad f_b^* = 4.20, \quad f_c^* = 0.40$$

This optimal link load pattern was induced by the optimal path flow pattern:

$$x_{p_1}^* = 5.40, \quad x_{p_2}^* = 4.20, \quad x_{p_3}^* = 0.40.$$

The optimal marginal cost of emission abatement was

$$\tau^* = 102.03.$$

The total cost in the network, as represented by the objective function $\sum_{a \in L} \hat{c}_a \times f_a$, was equal to 138.79. Note that the total cost computed under the equilibrium flow pattern for Example 5.4 was 140.00, which is clearly higher than that under system-optimization.

The results presented in this chapter are original and are discussed here for the first time.

9 Tradable Permits for System-Optimized Networks

In this chapter, I return to the policy mechanism of pollution permits which was discussed for user-optimized transportation networks in Chapters 6 and 7. In this chapter, however, I model explicitly distinct transportation jurisdictions, each with its own responsible authority for its transportation network. Moreover, I assume that there is an environmental quality standard that cannot be exceeded by the total emissions generated by the flows in all the transportation networks under consideration. Hence, the transportation networks may correspond to regions with the standard being imposed by, for example, a state government or the federal government to ensure that the environmental quality standard is upheld. Moreover, one can also consider the individual entities to be nations, each responsible for its own transportation network and the total emissions generated by the vehicles on its network.

Specifically, in Section 9.1, I develop the pollution permit model, in the case of fixed travel demands, which assumes that there is a central controller in each transportation network under consideration. Each controller or authority is given an initial license allocation and seeks to now minimize not only the total cost in the network but also to maximize its net revenue from the license trades. The entire network system, however, must (after the trading takes place) adhere to the imposed environmental quality standard. Hence, those jurisdictions with higher emissions may need to purchase licenses from other jurisdictions. I derive the equilibrium conditions which state the optimality conditions for each transportation authority, and the equilibrium conditions for the licenses, the marginal costs of emission abatement, and the license prices.

In Section 9.2, I provide an algorithm for computational purposes and then apply the algorithm to several numerical examples.

In Section 9.3, I subsequently consider that the travelers on the respective networks behave in a user-optimizing manner and the transportation authorities seek to determine the sustainable system-optimized flow pattern according to the model developed in Section 9.1, and to induce the travelers, through the use of tolls, to travel so that their behavior coincides with the system-optimum. I describe tolling policies which accomplish precisely this and conclude with several numerical examples in which the toll policies guarantee that the sustainable system-optimized flow pattern is also user-optimized.

9.1 The Model with Tradable Pollution Permits

I now introduce the notation for the permit system model which assumes that there are I transportation jurisdictions, with a typical jurisdiction denoted by i. For each jurisdiction i, consider a transportation network $G_i = [N_i, L_i]$ consisting of the set of nodes N_i and a set of directed links L_i. For a typical such network, let a, b, etc., denote the links and let p, q, etc., denote the paths, which are assumed to be acyclic. Assume that there are J_i origin/destination (O/D) pairs in network i, with a typical O/D pair denoted by w, and the set of O/D pairs for network i is denoted by W_i. Let P_w denote the set of paths connecting O/D pair w and let P_i denote the set of paths in the network i.

The flow on a link a is denoted by f_a, and the user cost associated with traveling on link a by c_a. Group the link loads for network i into a column vector $f_i \in R^{n_i}$, and the link user travel costs into a row vector $c_i \in R^{n_i}$, where n_i is the number of links in the network i. Further group the link loads and the user travel costs into the respective column vectors: $f \in R^n_+$ and $c \in R^n$.

Here I am interested in system-optimized networks in which each jurisdiction is faced with its own objective function. I assume that, in general, the user link travel costs associated with a particular network can depend on the flow upon the entire link load pattern on their own network, and, thus, the total link cost for a link $a \in L_i$ can be expressed as follows:

$$\hat{c}_a = \hat{c}_a(f_i) \times f_a, \quad \forall a \in L_i. \tag{9.1}$$

The total travel cost on path p, in turn, denoted by $\hat{C}_p$, is given by:

$$\hat{C}_p(f) = \sum_{a \in L_i} \hat{c}_a(f_i)\delta_{ap}, \quad \forall p \in P_i, \tag{9.2}$$

where $\delta_{ap} = 1$, if link a is contained in path p, and 0, otherwise.

I consider the case of fixed travel demands where the demand for O/D pair $w \in W_i$ is denoted by d_w. The nonnegative flow on path p is denoted by x_p, with the path flows grouped into a column vector $x_i \in R^{Q_i}_+$, where Q_i denotes the number of paths in the network i. Further group the path flows for all the networks into the vector $x \in R_+^{n_P}$, where n_P denotes the number of paths in all the networks. The following conservation of flow equations must be satisfied by the flows in each network i:

$$d_w = \sum_{p \in P_w} x_p, \quad \forall w \in W_i, \tag{9.3}$$

and

$$f_a = \sum_{p \in P_i} x_p \delta_{ap}, \quad \forall a \in L_i. \tag{9.4}$$

The conservation of flow equation (9.3) states that the sum of the path flows on paths connecting an O/D pair must be equal to the travel demand for that O/D pair in network i. Equation (9.4), on the other hand, states that the flow on a link equals the sum of the path flows on paths that use that link. Let K_i denote the feasible set defined as follows:

$$K_i = \{f_i, \text{ such that there exists a vector } x \geq 0, \text{ satisfying (9.3) and (9.4)}\}.$$

Let l_a denote the number of license permits on link a that allows travelers to emit pollutants at a certain rate. Let l_a^0, in turn, denote the initial allocation of licenses on link a, which is assumed to be nonnegative. Group the licenses into the column vector $l_i \in R_+^{n_i}$ for each network i and further group all the licenses into the column vector $l \in R_+^n$. As in the previous chapters, let h_a denote the emission factor associated with link a.

The price and cost structure associated with the marketable pollution permits is now discussed. Let ρ denote the price of a license in the transportation network and let τ_a denote the marginal cost of emission abatement on link a. Group the marginal costs of abatement for network i into the column vector $\tau_i \in R_+^{n_i}$. Further group the marginal costs of emission abatement for the links in all the networks into the column vector $\tau \in R_+^n$, where n is the total number of links.

Next, I derive the equilibrium conditions. They consist of systems of equalities and inequalities which most hold, respectively, for the path flows, the marginal costs of emission abatement, the licenses, and the license price. Subsequently, I derive the variational inequality formulation of the governing equilibrium conditions.

First, however, I present the system-optimization problem facing the central controller in each transportation network i. Specifically, assume, as in Chapter 8, that the objective function must include the total cost in the network which reflects the congestion, but now one needs to also incorporate into the objective function the net revenue due to trading in the permits, which is to be maximized. The net revenue term, assuming a given price for the license ρ^*, is then:

$$\sum_{a \in L_i} \rho^*(l_a^0 - l_a). \tag{9.5}$$

Moreover, one knows that the emissions on each link of the network cannot exceed the license holdings for that link which allow the travelers to emit at that rate. Combining the above, one obtains, hence, for each network $i \in I$, the following system-optimization problem:

$$\text{Minimize} \quad \sum_{p \in P_i} S_i(x_i) - \sum_{a \in L_i} \rho^*(l_a^0 - l_a) = \text{Minimize} \quad \sum_{p \in P_i} \hat{C}_p - \sum_{a \in L_i} \rho^*(l_a^0 - l_a) \tag{9.6}$$

subject to:

$$h_a f_a \leq l_a, \quad \forall a \in L_i, \tag{9.7}$$

$$\sum_{p \in P_w} x_p = d_w, \quad \forall w \in W_i \tag{9.8}$$

$$x_p \geq 0, \quad \forall p \in P_i, \tag{9.9}$$

$$l_a \geq 0, \quad \forall a \in L_i. \tag{9.10}$$

Since the feasible set is convex and, under the assumption that the user link travel cost functions are increasing functions of the flow, the total cost function is also convex, the Kuhn-Tucker optimality conditions are both necessary and sufficient and given by: For network i and all O/D pairs $w \in W_i$ and each path $p \in P_w$:

$$\hat{C}'_p(f_i^*, \tau^*) = \hat{C}'_p(x_i^*) + \sum_{a \in L_i} h_a \tau_a^* \delta_{ap} \begin{cases} = & \mu_w, \quad \text{if } x_p^* > 0 \\ \geq & \mu_w, \quad \text{if } x_p^* = 0, \end{cases} \tag{9.11}$$

where $\hat{C}'_p(x^*)$ denotes the marginal of the total cost on path p and, as described in Section 8.1.2, is given by: $\hat{C}'_p(x) = \frac{\partial S_i(x_i)}{\partial x_p}$. Note that here the decoupled nature of the individual transportation networks is explicitly emphasized, since it is asssumed that each is under the jurisdiction of a distinct transportation authority.

Also, for each link $a \in L_i$, the equilibrium marginal cost of emission abatement τ_a^*, must satisfy:

$$h_a f_a^* \begin{cases} = & l_a^*, \quad \text{if } \tau_a^* > 0 \\ \leq & l_a^*, \quad \text{if } \tau_a^* = 0. \end{cases} \tag{9.12}$$

The following condition must also hold: For each link $a \in L_i$:

$$\tau_a^* \begin{cases} = & \rho^*, \quad \text{if } l_a^* > 0 \\ \leq & \rho^*, \quad \text{if } l_a^* = 0. \end{cases} \tag{9.13}$$

The above conditions are the optimality conditions for a system-optimal solution for transportation network i. Observe that τ_a^* is the marginal cost of emission abatement associated with constraint (9.7).

Table 9.1. Trade in pollution permits

Jurisdiction 1	Jurisdiction 2 ...	Jurisdiction I
Network 1	Network 2 ...	Network I
$G_1 = [N_1, L_1]$	$G_2 = [N_2, L_2] \ldots$	$G_I = [N_I, L_I]$
Initial: $\sum_{a \in L_1} l_a^0$	Initial: $\sum_{a \in L_2} l_a^0 \ldots$	Initial: $\sum_{a \in L_I} l_a^0$
	$\Downarrow$	
$\Rightarrow$	Trade	$\Leftarrow$
	$\Downarrow$	
Final: $\sum_{a \in L_1} l_a^*$	Final: $\sum_{a \in L_2} l_a^* \ldots$	Final: $\sum_{a \in L_I} l_a^*$

Market Equilibrium Condition for Licenses

I now state the market equilibrium conditions for licenses, which say that if the equilibrium price of a license is positive, then the market must clear for the licenses, that is, the total supply of the licenses, which is given by the sum of the initial license allocations, must be equal to the sum of the final (equilibrium license) holdings:

$$\sum_{i \in I} \sum_{a \in L_i} (l_a^0 - l_a^*) \begin{cases} = & 0, \quad \text{if } \rho^* > 0 \\ \geq & 0, \quad \text{if } \rho^* = 0. \end{cases} \tag{9.14}$$

Indeed, expression (9.14) corresponds to the well-known economic equilibrium conditions that state that, in equilibrium, if a price of a good (which in this case is the license) is positive, then the market for that good must clear, that is, the supply of the licenses, which is equal to $\sum_{i \in I} \sum_{a \in L_i} l_a^0$, must be equal to the demand for the licenses in equilibrium, which is given by $\sum_{i \in I} \sum_{a \in L_i} l_a^*$. On the other hand, if the price of a license is zero, then one may have an excess supply of the licenses.

Let $\mathcal{K}$ denote the feasible set such that $\mathcal{K} \equiv \prod_{i \in I} K_i \times R_+^{\sum_{i \in I} 2n_i \times R_+}$. I am now ready to define the equilibrium state.

Definition 9.1 (Sustainable System-Optimum with Tradable Pollution Permits)
A vector $(f^*, \tau^*, l^*, \rho^*) \in \mathcal{K}$ is an equilibrium of the sustainable system-optimal tradable pollution permits model if and only if it satisfies the systems of equalities and inequalities (9.11)–(9.13) for all networks $i \in I$ and (9.14).

In Table 9.1, the structure of the trade problem in licenses is given. Note that the licenses may also be interpreted as flows between the network jurisdictions whereas the transportation flows are internal to each network.

I now present the variational inequality formulation of the equilibrium conditions for the model. The proof is almost identical to that of Theorem 6.1 and, hence, is not given. A path flow version can also be readily obtained.

Theorem 9.1 (Variational Inequality Formulation of Tradable Pollution Permit System Traffic Network Equilibrium with System-Optimized Behavior)
A vector of link loads, marginal costs of emission abatement, licenses, and license price, $(f^*, \tau^*, l^*, \rho^*) \in \mathcal{K}$, is an equilibrium of the tradable pollution permit market equilibrium model in the case of sustainable system-optimized networks if and only if it is a solution to the variational inequality problem:

$$\sum_{i\in I}\sum_{a\in L_i}(\hat{c}'_a(f_i^*)+h_a\tau_a^*)\times(f_a-f_a^*)+\sum_{i\in I}\sum_{a\in L_i}(l_a^*-h_af_a^*)\times(\tau_a-\tau_a^*)$$

$$+\sum_{i\in I}\sum_{a\in L_i}(\rho^*-\tau_a^*)\times(l_a-l_a^*)+\sum_{i\in I}\sum_{a\in L_i}(l_a^0-l_a^*)\times(\rho-\rho^*)\geq 0, \quad \forall (f,\tau,l,\rho)\in\mathcal{K}. \tag{9.15}$$

Variational inequality (9.15) is now put into standard form. Define column vector $X \equiv (f, \tau, l, \rho) \in \mathcal{K}$ and the column vector $F(X)$, where:

$$F(X) \equiv \left(\hat{C}'(X), T(X), L(X), P(X)\right).$$

$\hat{C}'(X)$, $L(X)$, $T(X)$ are each n-dimensional column vectors with component a given, respectively, as follows:

$$\hat{C}'_a(X) : \hat{c}'_a(f) + h_a\tau_a,$$

$$T_a(X) : l_a - h_a f_a,$$

$$L_a(X) : \rho - \tau_a,$$

whereas $P(X)$ is the one-dimensional vector with the single component:

$$P(X) : \sum_{a\in L_i}(l_a^0 - l_a).$$

Thus, variational inequality (9.15) can be expressed as:

$$\langle F(X^*)^T, X - X^*\rangle \geq 0, \quad \forall X \in \mathcal{K}. \tag{9.16}$$

I now turn to studying whether the equilibrium pattern is independent of the initial allocation of the licenses on the links and how to guarantee that the environmental emission standards imposed by the governing body are met in equilibrium. The question as to whether the initial allocation of licenses affects the equilibrium pattern is answered in the following corollary.

Corollary 9.1
If $l_a^0 \geq 0$ for all a, and $\sum_{i\in I}\sum_{a\in L_i} l_a^0 = \bar{Q}$, with $\bar{Q}$ fixed and positive, then the equilibrium pattern $(f^*, \tau^*, l^*, \rho^*)$ is independent of the initial allocation.

Table 9.2. Relationship between a viable system-optimized network, tradable permits, and sustainability

System-Optimized Viable Network + **License Allocation:** $\sum_{i \in I} \sum_{a \in L_i} l_a^0 = \bar{Q}$	$\Rightarrow$	**Sustainability**

Proof:
The terms in the variational inequality (9.15) are either independent of l_a^0 or depend only on the sum, $\sum_{i \in I} \sum_{a \in L_i} l_a^0$. The conclusion follows. □

In the following proposition, I show that the environmental standards are met by the equilibrium pattern, provided that the sum of the initial allocation of licenses is equal to the imposed environmental standard given by $\bar{Q}$.

Proposition 9.1
If $\sum_{i \in I} \sum_{a \in L_i} l_a^0 = \bar{Q}$, the equilibrium vector achieves the environmental quality standard, $\bar{Q}$, provided that the entire transportation network is viable.

Proof:
One has from equilibrium conditions (9.12) and (9.14) that:

$$\sum_{i \in I} \sum_{a \in L_i} h_a f_a^* \leq \sum_{i \in I} \sum_{a \in L_i} l_a^* \leq \sum_{i \in I} \sum_{a \in L_i} l_a^0 = \bar{Q}.$$

Hence, the environmental standards are met by the equilibrium pattern. □

Proposition 9.1 says that the complete transportation network consisting of the I individual transportation networks is sustainable, that is, the environmental quality standard will not be exceeded, provided that the sum of the license allocations are set equal to the target. Of course, as emphasized in Table 9.2, the complete network must be viable in that there must exist a solution to the Linear System 4.1 in order to even be able to achieve sustainability.

Example 9.1

I now present an example which illustrates the basic concepts. Consider the two networks depicted in Figure 9.1, each of which is the responsibility of a separate transportation authority. Each network consists of two links with the first network consisting of links a and b, whereas the second consists of links c and d. The O/D pair for Network 1, denoted by w_1, is $(1,2)$, whereas the O/D pair for Network 2 is $(3,4)$. The user link travel cost functions are:

$$c_a(f_a) = f_a + 5, \quad c_b(f_b) = f_b + 10,$$

$$c_c(f_c) = f_c + 5, \quad c_d(f_d) = f_d + 5.$$

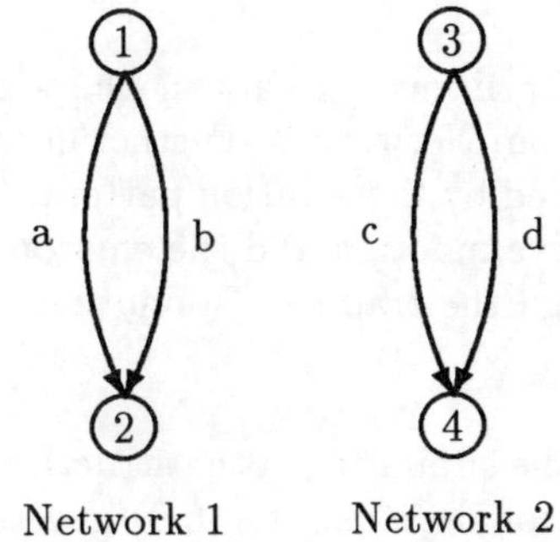

Fig. 9.1. Networks for Example 9.1

The travel demands are: $d_{w_1} = 10$ and $d_{w_2} = 10$. Denote the paths as follows: $p_1 = a$, $p_2 = b$, $p_3 = c$, and $p_4 = d$.

Assume that the emission factors are: $h_a = h_b = 1$, and $h_c = h_d = 0.2$ with the initial license allocation given by: $l_a^0 = l_b^0 = l_c^0 = l_d^0 = 3$. Hence, Network 1 has a total license allocation of 6 for its network links as does Network 2. Moreover, the environmental quality standard $\bar{Q} = 12$.

Note that Network 1 has links with higher emission factors than Network 2 and, in fact, with only an initial license allocation of 6 it cannot, without the trading of licenses, emit less than or equal to its allocation. Indeed, in order to satisfy its fixed demand of 10, 10 units of pollutants will be generated due to its emission factors on its links. Network 2, on the other hand, has links which are characterized by lower emission factors. Indeed, it is easy to verify that it can satisfy its permission to emit at 6 units since its demand is 10 and the emissions generated on its network will be 2. Hence, it can sell several of its licenses to Network 1, which needs to purchase licenses since it cannot sustain its demand with the given allocation.

Since the network structure of both networks is simple, we can solve for the conditions (9.11)–(9.14) to obtain the following solution:
The flows are:

$$x_{p_1}^* = f_a^* = 6.35, \quad x_{p_2}^* = f_b^* = 3.75,$$

$$x_{p_3}^* = f_c^* = 5.00, \quad x_{p_4}^* = f_d^* = 5.00,$$

the marginal costs of emission abatement are:

$$\tau_a^* = \tau_b^* = \tau_c^* = \tau_d^* = 1.94,$$

which is also the price ρ^*;

the licenses are:

$$l_a^* = 6.25, \quad l_b^* = 3.75, \quad l_c^* = 1.00, \quad l_d^* = 1.00.$$

Hence, the market for licenses clears in this example, and Network 1 purchases four licenses from Network 2. Furthermore, the conditions (9.11)–(9.13) are precisely satisfied by the solution pattern. Therefore, each network has minimized its objective function and the environmental quality standard has been achieved through the trading of pollution permits.

Remark 9.1

It is worth emphasizing the similarity in the structures of variational inequality (9.15) and the variational inequality (6.9) governing the user-optimized version of the pollution permit system model (link-based and assuming fixed travel demands). Indeed, one sees that in the system-optimized version one has marginals of the total link travel cost functions appearing in the function $F(\cdot)$ that enters the variational inequality; whereas in the case of user-optimization, one has the user link travel cost functions, instead. The other terms, however, that enter the function are identical. Hence, by making appropriate substitutions, one can adapt the qualitative properties obtained in Section 6.1.1 for the user-optimized model for the model developed above. The same holds for the computational procedure, following the statement of the algorithm in Section 6.2. I now, for completeness, provide the statement of the computational procedure for this model in the next section.

9.2 Algorithm and Numerical Examples

In this section, I show the realization of the modified projection method for the solution of variational inequality problem (9.15). In Section 9.2.1, I state the algorithm and discuss it more fully from a computational perspective. In Section 9.2.2, the algorithm is then applied to several numerical examples.

9.2.1 The Algorithm

Here the algorithm is presented for solving variational inequality (9.15). As noted in the preceding section, due to the similarities between the variational inequalities governing the system-optimized and the user-optimized pollution permit models, one can adapt the statement of the modified projection method given in Section 6.2 to the system-optimized problem as follows.

Modified Projection Method for the Tradable Permit Model for Sustainable System-Optimized Networks

Step 0: Initialization

Set $(f^0, \tau^0, l^0, \rho^0) \in \mathcal{K}$. Let $\mathcal{T} = 1$ and set α such that $0 < \alpha < \frac{1}{\bar{L}}$, where $\bar{L}$ is the Lipschitz constant for the problem.

Step 1: Computation

Compute $(\bar{f}^{\mathcal{T}}, \bar{\tau}^{\mathcal{T}}, \bar{l}^{\mathcal{T}}, \bar{\rho}^{\mathcal{T}}) \in \mathcal{K}$ by solving the variational inequality subproblem:

$$\sum_{i\in I}\sum_{a\in L_i}(\bar{f}_a^{\mathcal{T}} + \alpha(\hat{c}'_a(f_i^{\mathcal{T}-1}) + h_a\tau_a^{\mathcal{T}-1}) - f_a^{\mathcal{T}-1}) \times (f_a - \bar{f}_a^{\mathcal{T}})$$

$$+\sum_{i\in I}\sum_{a\in L_i}(\bar{l}_a^{\mathcal{T}} + \alpha(\rho^{\mathcal{T}-1} - \tau_a^{\mathcal{T}-1}) - l_a^{\mathcal{T}-1}) \times (l_a - \bar{l}_a^{\mathcal{T}})$$

$$+\sum_{i\in I}\sum_{a\in L_i}(\bar{\tau}_a^{\mathcal{T}} + \alpha(l_a^{\mathcal{T}-1} - h_a f_a^{\mathcal{T}-1}) - \tau_a^{\mathcal{T}-1}) \times (\tau_a - \bar{\tau}_a^{\mathcal{T}})$$

$$+(\bar{\rho}^{\mathcal{T}} + \alpha(\sum_{i\in I}\sum_{a\in L_i} l_a^0 - \sum_{i\in I}\sum_{a\in L_i} l_a^{\mathcal{T}-1}) - \rho^{\mathcal{T}-1}) \times (\rho - \bar{\rho}^{\mathcal{T}}) \geq 0, \quad \forall (f,\tau,l,\rho) \in \mathcal{K}. \tag{9.17}$$

Step 2: Adaptation

Compute $(f^{\mathcal{T}}, \tau^{\mathcal{T}}, l^{\mathcal{T}}, \rho^{\mathcal{T}}) \in \mathcal{K}$ by solving the variational inequality subproblem:

$$\sum_{i\in I}\sum_{a\in L_i}(f_a^{\mathcal{T}} + \alpha(\hat{c}'_a(\bar{f}_i^{\mathcal{T}}) + h_a\bar{\tau}_a^{\mathcal{T}}) - f_a^{\mathcal{T}-1}) \times (f_a - f_a^{\mathcal{T}})$$

$$+\sum_{i\in I}\sum_{a\in L_i}(l_a^{\mathcal{T}} + \alpha(\bar{\rho}^{\mathcal{T}} - \bar{\tau}_a^{\mathcal{T}}) - l_a^{\mathcal{T}-1}) \times (l_a - l_a^{\mathcal{T}})$$

$$+\sum_{i\in I}\sum_{a\in L_i}(\tau_a^{\mathcal{T}} + \alpha(\bar{l}_a^{\mathcal{T}} - h_a\bar{f}_a^{\mathcal{T}}) - \tau_a^{\mathcal{T}-1}) \times (\tau_a - \tau_a^{\mathcal{T}})$$

$$+(\rho^{\mathcal{T}} + \alpha(\sum_{i\in I}\sum_{a\in L_i} l_a^0 - \sum_{i\in I}\sum_{a\in L_i} \bar{l}_a^{\mathcal{T}}) - \rho^{\mathcal{T}-1}) \times (\rho - \rho^{\mathcal{T}}) \geq 0, \quad \forall (f,d,l,\tau,\rho) \in \mathcal{K}. \tag{9.18}$$

Step 3: Convergence Verification

If $| f_a^{\mathcal{T}} - f_a^{\mathcal{T}-1} |\leq \epsilon$, $|l_a^{\mathcal{T}} - l_a^{\mathcal{T}-1} |\leq \epsilon$, $| \tau_a^{\mathcal{T}} - \tau_a^{\mathcal{T}-1} |\leq \epsilon$, for all $a \in L$, and $| \rho^{\mathcal{T}} - \rho^{\mathcal{T}-1} |\leq \epsilon$, with $\epsilon > 0$, a pre-specified tolerance, then stop; otherwise, set $\mathcal{T} := \mathcal{T} + 1$, and go to Step 1.

The decomposed subproblems can be computed efficiently. Observe that in the system-optimized problem over several transportation jurisdictions, the feasible set $\mathcal{K}$ is a Cartesian product, such that one can decompose both subproblems (9.17) and (9.18) for each network separately in terms of the flows (as well as the licenses and marginal costs of emission abatement). The flow subproblems are, in fact, separable quadratic programming problems, each of which can be solved using the equilibration algorithm of Dafermos and Sparrow (1969). The subproblems in licenses, marginal costs of emission abatement and, finally, the license price, in turn, have an explicit form solution identical to (6.37)–(6.39) for (9.17) and analogously adapted for the induced subproblems in (9.18).

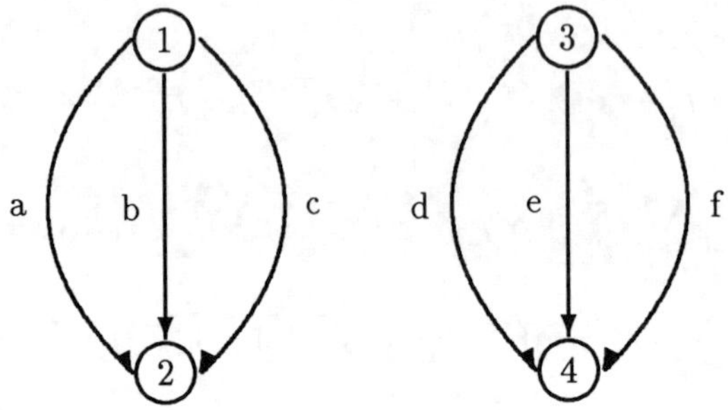

Fig. 9.2. Network topology for Example 9.2

9.2.2 Numerical Examples

In this subsection, numerical examples are presented to illustrate both the pollution permit trading model and the algorithm. The modified projection method was implemented in FORTRAN and the numerical experiments were conducted on the IBM SP2 located in the Computer Science Department at the University of Massachusetts at Amherst.

For the solution of the standard traffic network equilibrium problem encountered in both the computation and adaptation steps (cf. (9.17) and (9.18)) I utilized the equilibration method (cf. Dafermos and Sparrow 1969). The convergence criterion was given by: $|x_p^{\mathcal{T}} - x_p^{\mathcal{T}-1}| \leq \epsilon$, for all $p \in P$, $|\tau_a^{\mathcal{T}} - \tau_a^{\mathcal{T}-1}| \leq \epsilon$, for all $a \in L$, $|l_a^{\mathcal{T}} - l_a^{\mathcal{T}-1}| \leq \epsilon$, for all $a \in L$, and $|\rho^{\mathcal{T}} - \rho^{\mathcal{T}-1}| \leq \epsilon$.

The modified projection method was initialized by setting the flow on a path equal to the travel demand for the O/D pair that the path belongs to, divided by the number of paths. All other variables were initialized to zero.

Example 9.2

The first numerical example in this subsection consisted of the two networks depicted in Figure 9.2, each of which had three links and a single O/D pair, where $w_1 = (1, 2)$ and $w_2 = (3, 4)$.

The user link travel cost functions were:

$$c_a(f_a) = 2f_a + 1, \quad c_b(f_b) = f_b + 5, \quad c_c(f_c) = 2f_c + 3,$$

$$c_d(f_d) = 1.5f_d + 1, \quad c_e(f_e) = 3f_e + 2, \quad c_f(f_f) = f_e + 5.$$

The travel demands were:

$$d_{w_1} = 20, \quad d_{w_2} = 80.$$

The emission factors were:

$$h_a = 3, \quad h_b = 0.2, \quad h_c = 1,$$

$$h_d = 1, \quad h_e = 0.5, \quad h_f = 0.1.$$

The initial license allocations were:

$$l_a^0 = l_b^0 = l_c^0 = l_d^0 = l_e^0 = l_f^0 = 2,$$

and, hence, the environmental quality standard $\bar{Q} = 12$.

I set $\alpha = 0.2$ in the modified projection method. The modified projection method converged in 10,351 iterations and required 1.25 CPU seconds for convergence. It computed the following solution:
The flow pattern was:

$$x_{p_1}^* = f_a^* = 0.00, \quad x_{p_2}^* = f_b^* = 20.00, \quad x_{p_3}^* = f_c^* = 0.00,$$

$$x_{p_4}^* = f_d^* = 0.00, \quad x_{p_5}^* = f_e^* = 0.00, \quad x_{p_6}^* = f_f^* = 80.00.$$

The marginal costs of emission abatement were:

$$\tau_a^* = 41.8327, \quad \tau_b^* = 407.4937, \quad \tau_c^* = 123.5008,$$

$$\tau_d^* = 204.7472, \quad \tau_d^* = 407.4937, \quad \tau_f^* = 407.936.$$

The licenses were:

$$l_a^* = l_c^* = l_d^* = l_e^* = 0.00,$$

$$l_b^* = 4.00, \quad l_f^* = 8.00.$$

The price of the license was:

$$\rho^* = 407.937.$$

The market cleared for the licenses and, hence, the license price was positive. Furthermore, note that for those links with positive license holdings in equilibrium, the marginal cost of emission abatement was positive and equal to the license price. Furthermore, conditions (9.14) were met. Note that the transportation authority for Network 1, which had six initial licenses, sold two of those licenses to Network 2.

Example 9.3

This example was identical to Example 9.2, except that now the initial license allocations were increased so that:

$$l_a^0 = l_b^0 = l_c^0 = l_d^0 = l_e^0 = l_f^0 = 3,$$

which corresponds to a loosening of the environmental quality standard from 12 to $\bar{Q} = 18$.

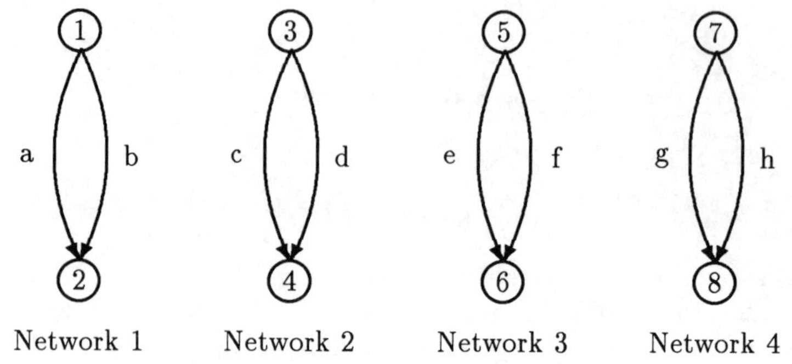

Fig. 9.3. Networks for Example 9.4

The modified projection method converged in 1907 iterations and required 0.29 CPU seconds for convergence. It yielded the following solution:
The new flow pattern was:

$$x^*_{p_1} = f^*_a = 0.00, \quad x^*_{p_2} = f^*_b = 20.00, \quad x^*_{p_3} = f^*_c = 0.00,$$

$$x^*_{p_4} = f^*_d = 1.02, \quad x^*_{p_5} = f^*_e = 12.70, \quad x^*_{p_6} = f^*_f = 66.28.$$

The new marginal costs of emission abatement were:

$$\tau^*_a = 24.5554, \quad \tau^*_b = 148.3249, \quad \tau^*_c = 71.6638,$$

$$\tau^*_d = \tau^*_e = \tau^*_f = 148.3249.$$

The new licenses were:

$$l^*_a = l^*_c = 0.00,$$

$$l^*_b = 4.00, \quad l^*_d = 1.0204, \quad l^*_e = 6.3520, \quad l^*_f = 6.6275.$$

The new price of the license was:

$$\rho^* = 148.3249.$$

The market for licenses cleared in this example and the license price was positive. Note now that since the supply of initial licenses is greater than that in Example 9.2, the equilibrium license price decreased. The authority responsible for Network 2 purchased five licenses from Network 1.

Example 9.4

I then considered the four networks depicted in Figure 9.3, each of which was under the jurisdiction of a separate transportation authority.

Each network consisted of a single O/D pair and two links, where $w_1 = (1,2)$, $w_2 = (3,4)$, $w_3 = (5,6)$, and $w_4 = (7,8)$. The paths were: $p_1 = a$, $p_2 = b$, $p_3 = c$, $p_4 = d$, $p_5 = e$, $p_6 = f$, $p_7 = g$ and $p_8 = h$.

The user link travel cost functions were:

$$c_a(f_a) = f_a + 1, \quad c_b(f_b) = 2f_b + 5, \quad c_c(f_c) = f_c + 2, \quad c_d(f_d) = 3f_d + 4,$$

$$c_e(f_e) = 2f_e + 1, \quad c_f(f_f) = f_f + 3, \quad c_g(f_g) = 3f_g + 5, \quad c_h(f_h) = 2f_h + 2.$$

The travel demands were:

$$d_{w_1} = 20, \quad d_{w_2} = 20, \quad d_{w_3} = 10, \quad d_{w_4} = 10.$$

The emission factors were:

$$h_a = 0.1, \quad h_b = 0.2, \quad h_c = 1, \quad h_d = 0.5,$$

$$h_e = 1, \quad h_f = 0.5, \quad h_g = 0.1, \quad h_h = 1.$$

The environmental quality standard was $\bar{Q} = 20$ and the initial license allocations were evenly distributed so that

$$l_a^0 = l_b^0 = l_c^0 = l_d^0 = l_e^0 = l_f^0 = l_g^0 = l_h^0 = 2.5.$$

I set $\alpha = 0.2$ in the modified projection method. The algorithm converged in 12,022 iterations and 1.99 seconds of CPU time.

The flow pattern was:

$$x_{p_1}^* = f_a^* = 17.15, \quad x_{p_2}^* = f_b^* = 2.85, \quad x_{p_3}^* = f_c^* = 3.43, \quad x_{p_4}^* = f_d^* = 16.57,$$

$$x_{p_5}^* = f_e^* = 0.00, \quad x_{p_6}^* = f_f^* = 10.00, \quad x_{p_7}^* = f_g^* = 10.00, \quad x_{p_8}^* = f_h^* = 0.00.$$

The marginal costs of emission abatement were:

$$\tau_a^* = \tau_b^* = \tau_c^* = \tau_d^* = \tau_f^* = \tau_g^* = 189.1181,$$

$$\tau_e^* = 116.5568, \quad \tau_h^* = 81.9086.$$

The licenses were:

$$l_a^* = 1.7151, \quad l_b^* = 0.5697, \quad l_c^* = 3.4302, \quad l_d^* = 8.2849,$$

$$l_e^* = 0.0000, \quad l_f^* = 5.0000, \quad l_g^* = 1.0000, \quad l_h^* = 0.0000.$$

The price of the license was:

$$\rho^* = 189.1181.$$

The market for licenses cleared in this example and the license price was positive.

9.3 Pricing in the Case of User-Optimized Behavior

Consider now that the transportation authorities are still faced with determining the system-optimal solution, as was done in the preceding section, but now the travelers on the networks behave in a *user-optimized* manner. Hence, the different transportation authorities will need to implement policies to guarantee that the users behave also in a system-optimized fashion in the presence of tradable pollution permits.

Note that for the system-optimal solution with tradable pollution permits to also be user-optimized, it must satisfy the conditions: For each $i \in I$, and for O/D pair $w \in W_i$, and each path $p \in P_w$:

$$C_p(x_i^*) + t_p \begin{cases} = & \lambda_w, \quad \text{if } x_p^* > 0 \\ \geq & \lambda_w, \quad \text{if } x_p^* = 0, \end{cases} \tag{9.19}$$

where t_p here denoted a path toll policy on path p.

Furthermore, the system-optimized flow pattern already satisfies conditions (8.10), that is: For each $i \in I$, and O/D pair $w \in W_i$, and each path $p \in P_w$:

$$\hat{C}'_p(x_i^*) + \tau_a^* \sum_{a \in L} h_a \delta_{ap} \begin{cases} = & \mu_w, \quad \text{if } x_p^* > 0 \\ \geq & \mu_w, \quad \text{if } x_p^* = 0, \end{cases} \tag{9.20}$$

For a solution to (9.20) to coincide with that of (9.19) implies that, for each path $p \in P$, we must have that:

$$t_p = \hat{C}'_p(x^*) - C_p(x^*) + \tau_a^* \sum_{a \in L} h_a \delta_{ap}. \tag{9.21}$$

Hence, (9.21) consists of a procedure in which to construct a path-toll policy, that is, solve the problem (9.6)–(9.10) and determine then for each path p in the network the path-toll policy accoding to the equation (9.21).

A link-toll policy, in turn, can also be determined according to:

$$t_a = \hat{c}'_a(f^*) - c_a(f^*) + \tau_a^* h_a, \quad \forall a \in L. \tag{9.22}$$

In Table 9.3, I depict the relationships between the behavioral principles and the environmental policy instruments just described.

I now present several numerical examples. In particular, I construct tolls for the networks in Examples 9.2–9.4 to guarantee that the system-optimized pattern for a sustainable transportation network is also user-optimized (after the imposition of the tolls).

Table 9.3. Relationship between a viable system-optimized network, user-optimized behavior, tradable permits, tolls, and sustainability

System-Optimized Viable Network		
+		
License Allocation: $\sum_{i \in I} \sum_{a \in L_i} l_a^0 = \bar{Q}$	$\Rightarrow$	**Sustainability**
+		
User-Optimized Behavior		
+		
Tolls		

Example 9.5: Example 9.2 Revisited

I considered Example 9.2 in which the paths consist of single links (as in the subsequent examples). I utilized the computed sustainable S-O solution for Example 9.2 in expression (9.22) to obtain the following toll policy:

$$t_a = 125.4981, \quad t_b = 101.4988, \quad t_c = 123.5008,$$

$$t_d = 204.7472, \quad t_e = 203.7481, \quad t_e = 120.7488.$$

Under this link-toll policy, the user costs, after the imposition of these tolls were: for O/D pair w_1 126.4981 and for O/D pair w_2 205.7482.

Example 9.6: Example 9.3 Revisited

I returned to Example 9.3 and constructed a link-toll policy using formula (9.22) and the computed sustainable S-O flow pattern for Example 9.3. Recall that Example 9.3 was constructed from Example 9.2 by increasing the initial license allocation. Note that in this example the paths consist of single links.

Solving for the link tolls as in (9.22) yields the following toll policy:

$$t_a = 73.6661, \quad t_b = 49.6649, \quad t_c = 71.6638,$$

$$t_d = 149.8554, \quad t_e = 112.2744, \quad t_e = 81.1081.$$

Under this link-toll policy, one has that the user costs, after the imposition of tolls are: for O/D pair w_1, the user cost plus the toll on the path for each of the three paths connecting O/D pair w_1 is equal to 74.66; whereas for O/D pair w_2 the user cost plus the toll on each path is equal to 152.38. Hence, the computed sustainable S-O pattern is also U-O, after the imposition of tolls as described.

Example 9.7: Example 9.4 Revisited

I then considered Example 9.4, in which there are four networks, again, in which each path consists of an individual link. An application of formula

(9.22) into which the sustainable S-O solution was substituted, yielded the following link-toll policy:

$$t_a = 36.0632, \quad t_b = 43.5209, \quad t_c = 192.5484, \quad t_d = 144.2683,$$

$$t_e = 116.5568, \quad t_f = 104.5591, \quad t_g = 48.9118, \quad t_h = 81.9086.$$

The incurred user travel costs with this toll policy were: for O/D pair w_1 54.21; for O/D pair w_2 197.97; for O/D pair w_3 117.55, and for O/D pair w_4 83.91.

The results in this chapter are original and are presented here for the first time.

Part IV Special Topics

10 Spatial Oligopolies and Marketable Pollution Permits

With this chapter, I begin Part IV of this book, entitled "Special Topics." In this part, I present, first, transportation-based models of spatial competition, beginning with an oligopoly model in this chapter, and then focus on spatial price models in the subsequent chapter. I then turn to technology and network design issues and see how they can be handled within the framework developed in this text.

Specifically, in this chapter, a spatial oligopoly network model is developed with pollution permits associated with the emissions due to transporting the commodity from the firms to the demand markets. The model is an example of imperfect competition, rather than perfect competition, as will be the case in the spatial price equilibrium models in Chapter 11. Indeed, here the firms are assumed to be only several in number and each can affect the price of the commodity. The model is based on the spatial oligopoly model of Dafermos and Nagurney (1987), who also established the relationship between oligopolistic market equilibrium problems and spatial price equilibrium problems (without policy instruments such as pollution permits). It is a special case of the spatial oligopoly model of Nagurney (1998) (see also Dhanda, Nagurney, and Ramanujam 1999), who also considered permits associated with pollutants on the production side. Here the focus is on sustainable transportation networks and, consequently, the emphasis is on the transportation issues.

The model serves to illustrate another application of variational inequality theory – that of the formulation of Nash (1950, 1951) equilibria – which is a well-known game theoretic concept.

The chapter is organized as follows. In Section 10.1, I present the spatial price oligopoly model with pollution permits, derive the equilibrium condi-

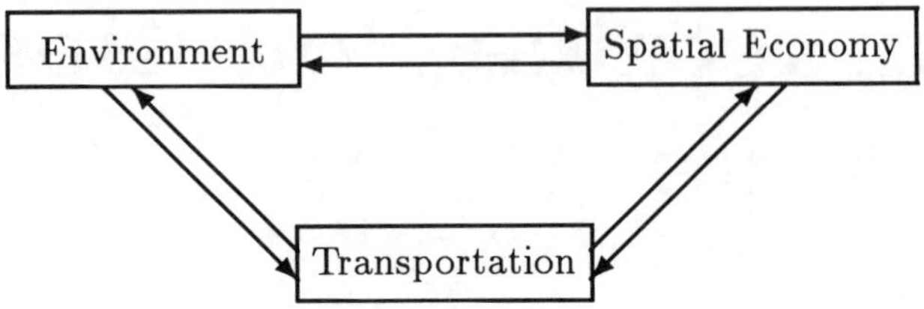

Fig. 10.1. Relationships between transportation, the spatial economy, and the environment

tions, and establish the variational inequality formulation. I also show that the environmental standards can be achieved, provided that the initial license allocations are set accordingly.

In Section 10.2, some qualitative properties of the equilibrium pattern are provided, including an existence result, and some sensitivity analysis results. I also propose an algorithm for the computation of the equilibrium pattern.

Hence, with this and the subsequent chapter, the focus is not only on transportation but also on its role in the organization of economic activity in space and its interaction with the environment. Figure 10.1 graphically emphasizes this point.

10.1 The Spatial Oligopoly Model with Permits

In this section, I present a generalized version of the oligopoly model of Dafermos and Nagurney (1987), which allows for tradable pollution permits associated with the emissions generated through the transportation of the commodity. Assume that there are m firms and n demand markets that are generally spatially separated and are involved, respectively, in the production and consumption of a homogeneous commodity in a noncooperative fashion. Let q_i denote the nonnegative commodity output produced by firm i and group the production outputs into the column vector $q \in R^m_+$. Let d_j denote the demand for the commodity at demand market j and group the demands into the column vector $d \in R^n_+$. Let Q_{ij} denote the nonnegative commodity shipment from supply market i to demand market j and group the commodity shipments for firm i into the column vector $Q_i \in R^n_+$. Finally, group the commodity shipments of all the firms into the column vector $Q \in R^{mn}_+$.

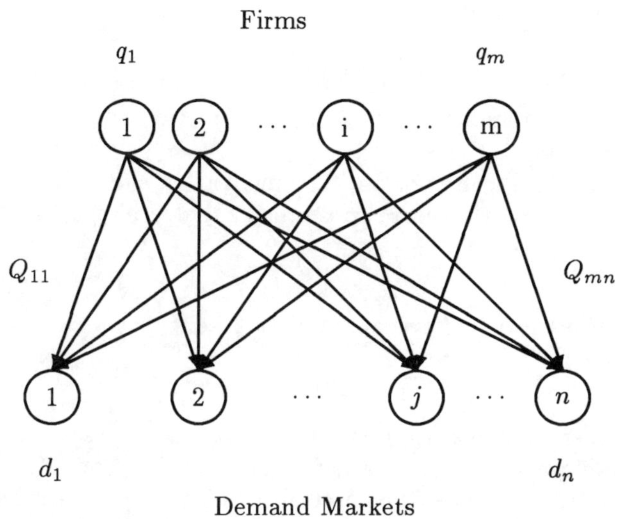

Fig. 10.2. The network structure of the spatial oligopoly problem

The following conservation of flow equations must hold:

$$q_i = \sum_{j=1}^{n} Q_{ij}, \quad i = 1, \ldots, m \tag{10.1}$$

$$d_j = \sum_{i=1}^{m} Q_{ij}, \quad j = 1, \ldots, n, \tag{10.2}$$

where $Q_{ij} \geq 0$, $\forall i, j$. Equation (10.1) states that the production output of the commodity for each firm must be equal to the commodity shipments from that firm to all the demand markets. Equation (10.2) says that the demand for the commodity at each demand market must be equal to the sum of the commodity shipments from all the firms to that demand market.

In Figure 10.2, the network structure of the spatial oligopoly problem is depicted. Note that the network structure is *bipartite* in that there are two sets of nodes: the upper level nodes denoting the firms and the lower level nodes denoting the demand markets, which are joined to the firms through the transportation links.

Associate with each firm i a production cost f_i, and allow for the more general situation where the production cost of a firm i may depend upon the entire production pattern, that is:

$$f_i = f_i(q). \tag{10.3}$$

In view of the conservation of flow equation (10.1), one may define the production cost function $\hat{f}_i$, where:

$$\hat{f}_i \equiv \hat{f}_i(Q). \tag{10.4}$$

Hence, one may reexpress the production cost function as a function of the commodity shipments.

I allow the demand price for the commodity at a demand market to depend, in general, upon the entire consumption pattern, that is:

$$\rho_j = \rho_j(d). \tag{10.5}$$

In view of the conservation of flow equation (10.2), one may define the demand price function $\hat{\rho}$ as:

$$\hat{\rho}_j = \hat{\rho}_j(Q) \tag{10.6}$$

and, therefore, the demand price function can also be expressed in terms of the commodity shipments. Such a transformation of the production cost and demand price functions reduces the number of variables in the model without any loss in generality.

Let c_{ij} denote the transportation cost associated with trading (shipping) the commodity between firm i and demand market j. Note that here I explicitly assume that the firms are spatially separated. Moreover, I allow the transportation cost to depend, in general, upon the entire commodity shipment pattern, that is:

$$c_{ij} = c_{ij}(Q). \tag{10.7}$$

I now introduce the notation for the ambient-based permit system (APS). Assume that there is a single receptor point associated with the emissions generated by the transportation or shipment of the commodity from the firms to the demand markets. Of course, one can consider as many receptor points as are needed in this framework, but with a concomitant increase in notation.

Let h_{ij} denote the contribution that one unit of emission associated with the shipment Q_{ij} makes to the average pollution concentration at the transportation emission receptor point. Note that one can also extend the model herein to the case of multiple receptor points.

Assume that the firms are given an initial endowment of licenses given by l^0_{ij}; $i = 1, \ldots, m; j = 1, \ldots, n$. Let p^* denote the price of a license to pollute at the transportation emission receptor point. Then the value of a firm's initial endowment of licenses is given by $\sum_{j=1}^n p^* l^0_{ij}$.

The profit u_i of firm i is then:

$$u_i = \sum_{j=1}^n \hat{\rho}_j(Q)Q_{ij} - \hat{f}_i(Q) - \sum_{j=1}^n c_{ij}(Q)Q_{ij} - \sum_{j=1}^n p^*(l_{ij} - l^0_{ij}). \tag{10.8}$$

The first term to the right-hand side of the equality in (10.8) expresses the revenue of the firm, whereas the subsequent terms represent, respectively, the production cost, the total cost of shipping the commodity to the demand markets, and the cost associated with purchasing the permits associated with the commodity shipment.

One may write (10.8) as:

$$u_i = u_i(Q, l_i), \tag{10.9}$$

where $l_i = \{l_{i1}, \ldots, l_{in}\}$ denotes the vector of licenses held by firm i associated with the transportation emissions.

An oligopolistic firm's optimization problem is then expressed as:

$$\text{Maximize} \quad u_i(Q, l_i) \tag{10.10}$$

subject to:

$$h_{ij}Q_{ij} \leq l_{ij}, \quad j = 1, \ldots, n, \tag{10.11}$$

and

$$Q_{ij} \geq 0, \quad j = 1, \ldots, n. \tag{10.12}$$

Inequality (10.11) states that a firm cannot emit on the transportation links at a rate higher than it is licensed to emit.

Now consider the usual oligopolistic market mechanism, in which the m firms supply the commodity in a noncooperative fashion, each one trying to maximize its own profit. One seeks to determine a nonnegative commodity shipment and license pattern, (Q^*, l^*), for which the m firms will be in a state of Nash (1950) equilibrium as defined below.

Definition 10.1 (A Spatial Nash Equilibrium with Permits)
A commodity shipment, and license pattern, $(Q^*, l^*) \in R^{2mn}_+$, is said to constitute a Nash equilibrium if for each firm i; $i = 1, \ldots, m$,

$$u_i(Q_i^*, \hat{Q}_i^*, l_i^*) \geq u_i(Q_i, \hat{Q}_i^*, l_i),$$

$$\forall Q_i \in R^n_+, \forall l_i \in R^n_+, \textit{ satisfying } (10.11), (10.12), \forall i, \tag{10.13}$$

where:

$$Q_i \equiv \{Q_{i1}, \ldots, Q_{in}\} \quad \textit{and} \quad \hat{Q}_i^* \equiv (Q_1^*, \ldots, Q_{i-1}^*, Q_{i+1}^*, \ldots, Q_m^*).$$

Let τ_{ij}; j; $j = 1, \ldots, n$, denote the marginal cost of emission abatement associated with constraint (10.11) and group the τ_{ij}s into the vector τ_i and all such vectors for all the firms into the vector $\tau \in R^{mn}_+$.

Observe that the profit function for each firm i is concave with respect to the license vector l_i, since the function is linear in the licenses. Assuming that the profit function $u_i(Q, l_i)$ is concave with respect to Q_i, and that $u_i(Q, l_i)$ is continuously differentiable, then the necessary and sufficient conditions for an optimal product, license, and marginal emission abatement cost pattern (associated with constraint (10.11)), given the license price vector, p^*, is that the pattern, $(Q_i^*, l_i^*, \tau_i^*) \in R_+^{3n}$, and satisfies the inequality:

$$\sum_{j=1}^{n} \left[\frac{\partial \hat{f}_i(Q^*)}{\partial Q_{ij}} + c_{ij}(Q) - \hat{\rho}_j(Q^*) + \sum_{g=1}^{n} \left[\frac{\partial c_{ig}(Q^*)}{\partial Q_{ij}} - \frac{\partial \hat{\rho}_j(Q^*)}{\partial Q_{ij}} \right] Q_{ig}^* + \tau_{ij}^* h_{ij} \right]$$

$$\times \left[Q_{ij} - Q_{ij}^* \right] + \sum_{j=1}^{n} \left[p^* - \tau_{ij}^* \right] \times \left[l_{ij} - l_{ij}^* \right]$$

$$+ \sum_{j=1}^{n} \left[l_{ij}^* - h_{ij} Q_{ij}^* \right] \times \left[\tau_{ij} - \tau_{ij}^* \right] \geq 0, \quad \forall Q_i \in R_+^n, \forall l_i \in R_+^n, \forall \tau_i \in R_+^n. \tag{10.14}$$

In the case of Nash equilibrium, an inequality similar to (10.14) must hold for each of the oligopolistic firms i; $i = 1, \ldots, m$.

The market equilibrium conditions for the licenses are now stated.

Market Equilibrium Conditions for Licenses

The market equilibrium conditions associated with the transportation emission licenses are:

$$\sum_{i=1}^{m} \sum_{j=1}^{n} (l_{ij}^0 - l_{ij}^*) \begin{cases} = & 0, \quad \text{if } p^* > 0, \\ \geq & 0, \quad \text{if } p^* = 0. \end{cases} \tag{10.15}$$

I now define the ambient-based permit system spatial oligopolistic equilibrium.

Definition 10.2 (Pollution Permit Spatial Oligopolistic Equilibrium)
A vector of commodity shipments, licenses, marginal costs of emission abatement, and license price, (Q^*, l^*, τ^*, p^*), is an equilibrium of the ambient-based permit system spatial oligopoly problem if it satisfies inequality (10.14) for all firms i; $i = 1, \ldots, m$, and the market equilibrium conditions (10.15).

The variational inequality formulation of the governing equilibrium conditions for this problem is now given. It is presented without proof since the proof follows using similar arguments as in the variational inequality derivations provided in earlier chapters (see also Nagurney and Dhanda 1996 and Dhanda, Ramanujam, and Nagurney 1999).

Theorem 10.1 (Variational Inequality Formulation of the Pollution Permit Spatial Oligopoly Model)
A vector of commodity shipments, licenses, marginal costs of emission abatement, and license price, $(Q^*, l^*, \tau^*, p^*) \in R_+^{3mn+1}$, is an equilibrium if and only if it satisfies the variational inequality problem:

$$\sum_{i=1}^{m} \sum_{j=1}^{n} \left[\frac{\partial \hat{f}_i(Q^*)}{\partial Q_{ij}} + c_{ij}(Q) - \hat{\rho}_j(Q^*) + \sum_{g=1}^{n} \left[\frac{\partial c_{ig}(Q^*)}{\partial Q_{ij}} - \frac{\partial \hat{\rho}_j(Q^*)}{\partial Q_{ij}} \right] Q_{ig}^* \right.$$

$$+\tau_{ij}^* h_{ij}] \times [Q_{ij} - Q_{ij}^*]$$

$$+\sum_{i=1}^{m}\sum_{j=1}^{n}[p^* - \tau_{ij}^*] \times [l_{ij} - l_{ij}^*]$$

$$+\sum_{i=1}^{m}\sum_{j=1}^{n}[l_{ij}^* - h_{ij}Q_{ij}^*] \times [\tau_{ij} - \tau_{ij}^*]$$

$$+\sum_{i=1}^{m}\sum_{j=1}^{n}[l_{ij}^0 - l_{ij}^*] \times [p - p^*] \geq 0,$$

$$\forall Q \in R_+^{mn}, \forall l \in R_+^{mn}, \forall \tau \in R_+^{mn}, \forall p \in R_+^1. \tag{10.16}$$

I now put variational inequality (10.16) into standard form (cf. (2.32)). Define the column vector $X \equiv (Q, l, \tau, p)$ and the column vector $F(X)$ consisting of the column vectors:

$$(C(X), L(X), T(X), P(X)),$$

where $C(X)$ is the mn-dimensional vector with component (i, j) given by:

$$C_{ij}(X) = \sum_{j=1}^{n}\left[\frac{\partial \hat{f}_i(Q)}{\partial Q_{ij}} + c_{ij}(Q) - \hat{\rho}_j(Q) + \sum_{g=1}^{n}\left[\frac{\partial c_{ig}(Q)}{\partial Q_{ij}} - \frac{\partial \hat{\rho}_j(Q)}{\partial Q_{ij}}\right] Q_{ig}\right.$$

$$\left. + \tau_{ij}h_{ij}\right],$$

$L(X)$ is the mn-dimensional vector with component (i, j) given by:

$$L_{ij}(X) = [p - \tau_{ij}],$$

$T(X)$ is the mn-dimensional vector with component (i, j) given by:

$$T_{ij}(X) = [l_{ij} - h_{ij}Q_{ij}],$$

and $P(X)$ is the one-dimensional vector with component 1 given by:

$$\sum_{i=1}^{m}\sum_{j=1}^{n}[l_{ij}^0 - l_{ij}].$$

Indeed, variational inequality (10.16) can be expressed as: Determine $X^* \in \mathcal{K}$, such that:

$$\langle F(X^*)^T, X - X^*\rangle \geq 0, \quad \forall X \in \mathcal{K}, \tag{10.17}$$

where $\mathcal{K} \equiv \{X = (Q, l, \tau, p) \in R_+^{3mn+1}\}$.

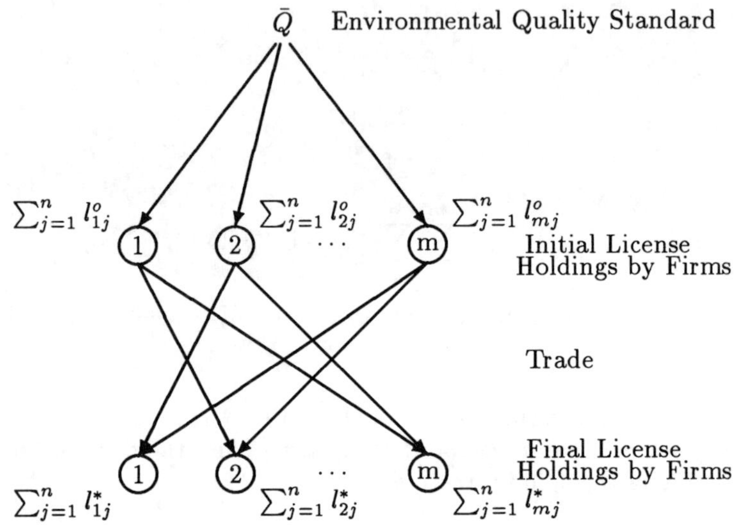

Fig. 10.3. Initial license allocation, trade, and final license holdings

In the subsequent corollary, I establish that the equilibrium pattern is independent of the initial license allocation, provided that the sum of licenses for each receptor point is fixed.

Corollary 10.1 (Equilibrium Pattern Independence from Initial License Allocation)
If $l_{ij}^0 \geq 0$, for all $i = 1, \ldots, m$; $j = 1, \ldots, n$, and $\sum_{i=1}^{m} \sum_{j=1}^{n} l_{ij}^0 = \bar{Q}$, then the equilibrium pattern (Q^*, l^*, τ^*, p^*) is independent of $\{l_{ij}^0\}$.

Proof:
The first three terms of variational inequality (10.16) are independent of $\{l_{ij}^0\}$, whereas the subsequent term depends only on the sum $\sum_{i=1}^{m} \sum_{j=1}^{n} l_{ij}^0$. □

In the next theorem, a mechanism for determining the appropriate sums of the initial licenses is provided. How the licenses should be allocated plus the trade that takes place is depicted in Figure 10.3.

Theorem 10.2 (Achievement of Environmental Quality Standards)
An equilibrium pattern achieves environmental quality standards represented by $\bar{Q}$, provided that $\sum_{i=1}^{m} \sum_{j=1}^{n} l_{ij}^0 = \bar{Q}$.

Proof:
One has from inequality (10.11) that, for each i; $i = 1, \ldots, m$:

$$h_{ij} Q_{ij}^* \leq l_{ij}^*, \quad j = 1, \ldots, n, \tag{10.18}$$

and from equilibrium conditions (10.15) and the assumption of the initial license allocations we can conclude that:

$$\sum_{i=1}^{m}\sum_{j=1}^{n} h_{ij}Q_{ij}^* \leq \sum_{i=1}^{m}\sum_{j=1}^{n} l_{ij}^* \leq \sum_{i=1}^{m}\sum_{j=1}^{n} l_{ij}^0 = \bar{Q}. \tag{10.19}$$

□

10.2 Qualitative Properties

In this section, I provide some qualitative properties of the variational inequality problem. I also establish the convergence of the modified projection method which can be applied to compute the equilibrium pattern for the spatial oligopoly problem with ambient-based pollution permits.

In particular, the existence of a solution pattern is first established. It is then shown that the function $F(\cdot)$ that enters variational inequality (10.17) is monotone. I discuss Lipschitz continuity of the function, present some sensitivity analysis results, and conclude this section with the convergence result.

Theorem 10.3 (Existence)
If $(Q^*, l^*, \tau^*, p^*) \in \mathcal{K}$ satisfies variational inequality (10.16), then the commodity shipment and emission pattern is a solution to the variational inequality problem:

$$\sum_{i=1}^{m}\sum_{j=1}^{n}\left[\frac{\partial \hat{f}_i(Q^*)}{\partial Q_{ij}} + c_{ij}(Q) - \hat{\rho}_j(Q^*) + \sum_{g=1}^{n}\left[\frac{\partial c_{ig}(Q^*)}{\partial Q_{ij}} - \frac{\partial \hat{\rho}_j(Q^*)}{\partial Q_{ij}}\right] Q_{ig}^*\right]$$

$$\times \left[Q_{ij} - Q_{ij}^*\right] \geq 0, \quad \forall Q \in K^1, \tag{10.20}$$

where:

$$K^1 \equiv \left\{ Q | \, Q \in R_+^{mn}; h_{ij}Q_{ij} \leq l_{ij}; l_{ij} \geq 0, \forall i, j; \sum_{i=1}^{m}\sum_{j=1}^{n}(l_{ij}^0 - l_{ij}) \geq 0 \right\}. \tag{10.21}$$

Moreover, a solution to (10.20) is guaranteed to exist provided that $-\nabla u(\cdot)$ is coercive. Furthermore, if Q^* is a solution to (10.20), there exist $l^* \in R_+^{mn}$, $\tau^* \in R_+^{mn}$, and $p^* \in R_+$ with $(Q^* l^*, \tau^*, p^*)$ being a solution to variational inequality (10.16) and, hence, an equilibrium.

Proof:
Assume, on the contrary, that is, for some $Q \in K^1$, we have that:

$$\sum_{i=1}^{m}\sum_{j=1}^{n}\left[\frac{\partial \hat{f}_i(Q^*)}{\partial Q_{ij}} + c_{ij}(Q) - \hat{\rho}_j(Q^*) + \sum_{g=1}^{n}\left[\frac{\partial c_{ig}(Q^*)}{\partial Q_{ij}} - \frac{\partial \hat{\rho}_j(Q^*)}{\partial Q_{ij}}\right] Q_{ig}^*\right.$$

$$\times \left[Q_{ij} - Q_{ij}^*\right] < 0. \tag{10.22}$$

But, according to variational inequality (10.16), it then follows that

$$\sum_{i=1}^{m}\sum_{j=1}^{n}\left[\tau_{ij}^* h_{ij}\right] \times \left[Q_{ij} - Q_{ij}^*\right] + \sum_{i=1}^{m}\sum_{j=1}^{n}\left[p^* - \tau_{ij}^*\right] \times \left[l_{ij} - l_{ij}^*\right]$$

$$+\sum_{i=1}^{m}\sum_{j=1}^{n}\left[l_{ij}^* - h_{ij}Q_{ij}^*\right] \times \left[\tau_{ij} - \tau_{ij}^*\right] + \sum_{i=1}^{m}\sum_{j=1}^{n}\left[l_{ij}^0 - l_{ij}^*\right] \times \left[p - p^*\right]$$

$$\geq -\sum_{i=1}^{m}\sum_{j=1}^{n}\left[\frac{\partial \hat{f}_i(Q^*)}{\partial Q_{ij}} + c_{ij}(Q) - \hat{\rho}_j(Q^*) + \sum_{g=1}^{n}\left[\frac{\partial c_{ig}(Q^*)}{\partial Q_{ij}} - \frac{\partial \hat{\rho}_j(Q^*)}{\partial Q_{ij}}\right] Q_{ig}^*\right]$$

$$\times \left[Q_{ij} - Q_{ij}^*\right] > 0. \tag{10.23}$$

Letting now $\tau_{ij} = 0$, for all i, j, $p = 0$, and substituting these values into the first expression in (10.23) yields, after algebraic simplifications:

$$\sum_{i=1}^{m}\sum_{j=1}^{n}\tau_{ij}^*\left[h_{ij}Q_{ij} - l_{ij}\right] + \sum_{i=1}^{m}\sum_{j=1}^{n}\left[l_{ij}^0 - l_{ij}\right]\left[-p^*\right]. \tag{10.24}$$

Clearly, in view of the feasible set K^1, the expression in (10.24) is nonnegative and, hence, we have obtained a contradiction to (10.22). It thus follows that variational inequality (10.20) must be satisfied.

Furthermore, under the coercivity condition assumption on $-\nabla u$, the existence of a solution to (10.20) is guaranteed from the standard theory of variational inequalities. Moreover, since $\sum_{i=1}^{m}\sum_{j=1}^{n} l_{ij}^0$, l must lie in a compact set and, hence, the existence of the vector l^* is guaranteed. Finally, according to the Lagrange Multiplier Theorem, we are guaranteed the existence of the nonnegative multipliers τ^* and p^* associated, respectively, with the inequality constraints corresponding to the emissions and the licenses that comprise the feasible set K^1 and must satisfy (10.16). □

Lemma 10.1 (Monotonicity)
If the utility functions are concave for each firm i, then $F(X)$ is monotone.

Proof:
In view of the definition of $F(X)$ in this model, the monotonicity condition here takes the form:

$$\langle (F(X^1) - F(X^2))^T, X^1 - X^2\rangle \geq 0, \quad \forall X^1, X^2 \in \mathcal{K}, \tag{10.25}$$

where the left-hand side of (10.25) here, after algebraic simplifications, reduces to:

$$\sum_{i=1}^{m}\sum_{j=1}^{n}\left[\frac{\partial \hat{f}_i(Q^1)}{\partial Q_{ij}} + c_{ij}(Q^1) - \hat{\rho}_j(Q^1) + \sum_{g=1}^{n}\left[\frac{\partial c_{ig}(Q^1)}{\partial Q_{ij}} - \frac{\partial \hat{\rho}_j(Q^1)}{\partial Q_{ij}}\right] Q_{ig}^1\right]$$

$$-\left[\frac{\partial \hat{f}_i(Q^2)}{\partial Q_{ij}} + c_{ij}(Q^2) - \hat{\rho}_j(Q^2) + \sum_{g=1}^{n}\left[\frac{\partial c_{ig}(Q^2)}{\partial Q_{ij}} - \frac{\partial \hat{\rho}_j(Q^2)}{\partial Q_{ij}}\right] Q_{ig}^2\right]$$
$$\times \left[Q_{ij}^1 - Q_{ij}^2\right]. \qquad (10.26)$$

However, the expression in (10.26) is nonnegative under the assumption that the utility function is monotone and, hence, the conclusion follows. □

The subsequent lemma is presented without proof since its proof is similar to the Lipschitz continuity lemma proofs in Part II of this book.

Lemma 10.2 (Lipschitz Continuity)
The function $F(X)$ is Lipschitz continuous under the assumption that the utility functions have bounded second-order derivatives.

I now provide a sensitivity analysis result surrounding changes in the initial license allocation for the transportation licenses.

Corollary 10.2 (Sensitivity Analysis)
Consider the fixed change Δ_{ij}^0, where $-l_{ij}^0 < \Delta_{ij}^0 < \infty$ for a particular transportation link (i,j). Let Δp denote the subsequent change in price of the transportation emission license. Then:

$$-\Delta_{ij}^0 \times \Delta p \geq 0. \qquad (10.27)$$

Proof:
Let $F(X)$ and X^* denote, respectively, the function in (10.17) and the solution of the variational inequality problem (10.17) before the perturbation. Let $\hat{F}(X)$ and $\hat{X}$ denote the perturbed function and the corresponding solution to the resulting variational inequality problem. One, thus, has that:

$$\langle F(X^*)^T, X - X^*\rangle \geq 0, \quad \forall X \in \mathcal{K} \qquad (10.28)$$

and:

$$\langle \hat{F}(\hat{X})^T, X - \hat{X}\rangle \geq 0, \quad \forall X \in \mathcal{K}. \qquad (10.29)$$

Substituting $\hat{X}$ for X in (10.28) and X^* for X in (10.29) and adding the resulting inequalities yields:

$$\langle (F(X^*) - \hat{F}(\hat{X}))^T, \hat{X} - X^*\rangle \geq 0, \qquad (10.30)$$

and, with the use of Lemma 10.1:

$$-\Delta l_{ij}^0 \times \Delta p \geq \langle (F(X^*) - F(\hat{X}))^T, X^* - \hat{X}\rangle \geq 0. \qquad (10.31)$$

□.

Note that from Corollary 10.2, one has that if the initial license for a link is increased (decreased) then the equilibrium price for the license decreases (increases).

Table 10.1. Typology of networks studied in this text

Type:	• congested transportation networks
	• spatial economic networks
	• • oligopolistic
	• • perfectly competitive

As for the numerical computation of the equilibrium pattern, one knows that the modified projection method is guaranteed to converge (Korpelevich 1977), provided that the function $F(\cdot)$ enters the variational inequality problem is monotone and Lipschitz continuous. One, thus, has the following:

Theorem 10.4 (Convergence)
The modified projection method is guaranteed to converge to the solution of the variational inequality problem (10.17).

Proof:
Follows from Lemmas 10.1 and 10.2. □

In this chapter of the book, I presented a spatial oligopoly network model with ambient-based pollution permits that specifically takes into consideration that the demand markets may be spatially separated. The model is an example of imperfect competition. It also allows for the spatial dispersion of emissions in the shipment of the commodity to the demand markets. The formulation and qualitative analysis of the model was done using the theory of variational inequalities. The results from this chapter are adapted from Nagurney (1998). See also Dhanda, Nagurney, and Ramanujam (1999) for an environmental networks approach to this problem in which trading in permits for another pollutant is permitted on the production side.

In the next chapter, I present spatial price network models, which include emissions generated by the supply markets and the demand markets, in addition to emissions generated during the transportation of the commodity from the supply markets to the demand markets. Hence, in the next chapter, I model both *stationary* emitters as well as *mobile* emitters.

Table 10.1 highlights the typology of networks modeled and studied in this text.

11 Spatial Price Networks and Emission Policies

The topic of this chapter is spatial price networks, in which there now exist both stationary and mobile sources of pollutants. For such problems, I develop emission pricing policies which guarantee sustainability of such networks. Hence, it is now assumed that emissions can be generated not only in the transporting of the commodity but also in its production of the good as well as in its consumption. Examples of stationary sources of pollutants include factories and power plants. In this chapter, thus, I present a global approach to sustainability by considering emissions not only associated with transportation, but also with production and consumption.

I first present a simple emission pricing model in which it is assumed that the emissions generated in the production, transport, and consumption of the commodity are identical. The pricing scheme guarantees that the environmental quality standard will be achieved. Subsequently, I extend the model to allow for distinct emissions on the production side, on the shipment side, as well as on the consumption side.

By permitting environmental quality standards to be imposed on the production side as well as on the consumption side, in addition to the transportation links, I extend not only the modeling framework for sustainable networks, but also enhance the flexibility of emission pricing instruments for policy analysis and application. Nagurney (1998) introduced pollution permits for spatial price networks (see also Dhanda, Nagurney, and Ramanujam 1999) but only considered permits on the production side and for the transportation of the commodity.

Sustainability of spatial price networks has been a topic of recent and growing interest (see Verhoef and Van den Bergh 1996; Verhoef, Van den Bergh, and Button 1997; and Verhoef 1996). As noted in Verhoef (1996), an exogeneous global environmental restriction (as is introduced also in the models developed herein), represents the "environmental utilization space"

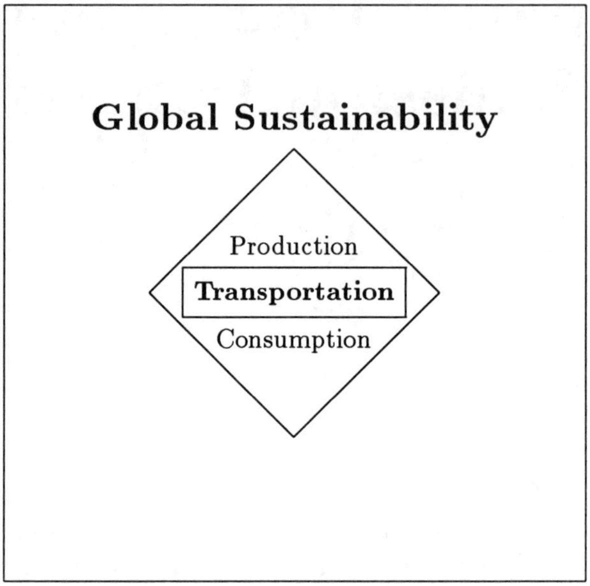

Fig. 11.1. Global sustainability

and, hence, satisfaction of this restriction is a necessary prerequisite for overall sustainability. Furthermore, the analysis here, as emphasized in other models by Verhoef (1996), can refer to any global environmental target, be it sustainability or any other less ambitious goal.

Spatial price equilibrium models, which form the basic setting for the policy models developed in this chapter, date to Samuelson (1952) and Takayama and Judge (1971). They have formed the foundations for the study of agricultural and energy markets, and have also been applied to financial markets. Moreover, their development has given rise to many effective numerical schemes for computational purposes, which exploit, typically, the underlying network structure of the problem (see Nagurney 1999a and the references therein). The assumption underlying spatial price equilibrium problems is that of perfect competition, as opposed to imperfect competition, which was the case in the oligopolistic models of Chapter 11. Hence, here it is assumed that there are many identical producers at each supply market, each of which cannot affect the price of the good. The relationship between spatial oligopolistic market equilibrium problems and spatial price equilibrium problems was established in Dafermos and Nagurney (1987), using game theoretic concepts.

In this chapter, and as depicted in Figure 11.1, the focus is on global sustainability through the development of appropriate policy instruments.

This chapter is organized as follows. In Section 11.1, a simple spatial price equilibrium model with an emission pricing policy that guarantees sustainability of the network system is developed. The model is then generalized to the case of nonseparable and asymmetric functions. In Section 11.2, the model is further extended to allow for distinct pollutants generated in the production of the commodity, the shipment of the commodity, as well as the consumption of the commodity. In this chapter, the focus is on a single commodity; the extension to the multiple commodity case is straightforward, but with an increase in notation. In Section 11.3, the qualitative properties of the model are presented. Section 11.4 then proposes an algorithmic scheme for the computation of the equilibrium patterns in both the single pollutant model as well as the multipollutant model. The algorithm is, subsequently, applied in Section 11.5 to compute solutions to numerical examples of both models.

11.1 Sustainable Spatial Price Network Models

In this section, I develop spatial price network policy models in which pollution, due to emissions generated by the producers, the transporters, and/or the consumers, are guaranteed to not exceed the imposed environmental quality standard. I assume that the emissions generated by the producers, shippers, and/or consumers is of a single pollutant. In Section 11.2, the model is generalized to the case of distinct pollutants emitted, respectively, by the producers, the shippers, and the consumers as regards the single commodity under study. Specifically, in Section 11.1.1, I model the special case in which the supply price functions, the transportation cost functions, as well as the demand price functions are separable, whereas in Section 11.1.2, the case of asymmetric (and, hence, nonseparable) functions is considered.

11.1.1 A Spatial Network Policy Model with Separable Functions

I now describe the spatial network policy model. The model is based on the classical spatial price equilibrium models of Samuelson (1952) and Takayama and Judge (1971), for which an optimization reformulation of the spatial price equilibrium conditions exists.

Specifically, consider m supply markets involved in the production of a homogeneous commodity and n demand markets. Assume that these markets are spatially separated. Denote a typical supply market by i and a typical demand market by j. Let s_i denote the supply at supply market i and let d_j be the demand at demand market j. Group the supplies into a column vector $s \in R^m_+$ and the demands into a column vector $d \in R^n_+$. Let Q_{ij} denote the nonnegative commodity shipment between supply and demand market pair (i, j), and group the commodity shipments into a column vector $Q \in R^{mn}_+$.

The commodity shipments and the supplies and demands must satisfy the

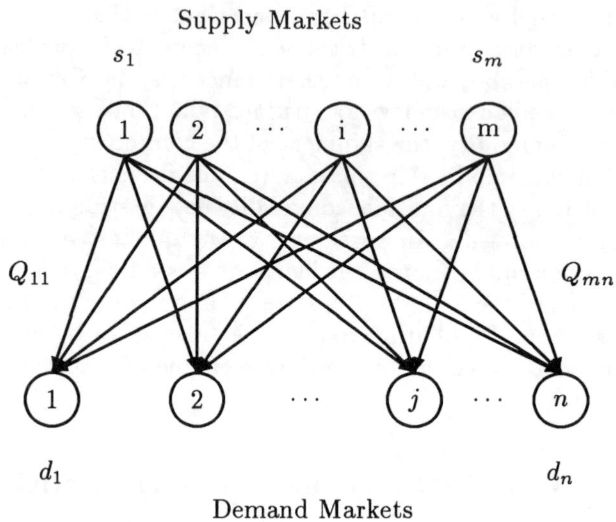

Fig. 11.2. The bipartite network structure of the spatial price equilibrium problem

following conservation of flow equations:

$$s_i = \sum_{j=1}^{n} Q_{ij}, \quad i = 1, \ldots, m \tag{11.1}$$

and:

$$d_j = \sum_{i=1}^{m} Q_{ij}, \quad j = 1, \ldots, n, \tag{11.2}$$

that is, the supply at each supply market must be equal to the sum of the commodity shipments from that market to all the demand markets, and the demand at each demand market must be equal to the sum of the commodity shipments from all supply markets to each demand market.

The bipartite network structure of the spatial price network problem is depicted in Figure 11.2. Note that the structure is identical to that of the spatial oligopoly model given in Figure 10.2. However, economically speaking, the models are distinct since here I consider perfect, rather than imperfect, competition and, hence, the uppermost nodes in Figure 11.2 correspond to supply markets, where at each node there are many identical firms, whereas in the uppermost nodes of Figure 10.2, each node corresponds to an individual firm.

The price and cost structure is now described. Let π_i denote the supply price at supply market i and let ρ_j the demand price at demand market j. Group the supply prices into a column vector $\pi \in R^m$ and the demand prices into a column vector $\rho \in R^n$. The unit transportation cost associated with shipping the commodity between supply market i and demand market j is denoted by c_{ij}. Group the transportation costs into a column vector $c \in R^{mn}$.

I assume, as in the classical models of Samuelson (1952) and Takayama and Judge (1971), that the supply price at a supply market depends upon the supply of the commodity at the supply market, that is:

$$\pi_i = \pi_i(s_i), \quad i = 1, \ldots, m, \tag{11.3}$$

where π is a smooth function.

Similarly, the demand price at a demand market depends upon the demand for the commodity at the demand market, that is:

$$\rho_j = \rho_j(d_j), \quad j = 1, \ldots, n, \tag{11.4}$$

where ρ is a smooth function.

The unit transportation cost, in turn, associated with shipping the commodity between a pair of supply and demand markets is assumed to be a function of the commodity shipment between the pair of markets, that is:

$$c_{ij} = c_{ij}(Q_{ij}), \quad i = 1, \ldots, m; j = 1, \ldots, n. \tag{11.5}$$

In the absence of any policies, and under the assumption of perfect competition, the well-known spatial price equilibrium conditions are stated as:

Definition 11.1 (Spatial Price Equilibrium)
Following Samuelson (1952) and Takayama and Judge (1971), the supply, commodity shipment, and demand pattern (s^*, Q^*, d^*) constitutes a spatial price equilibrium, if it is feasible with respect to (11.1) and (11.2), and for all pairs of supply and demand markets (i, j), it satisfies the conditions:

$$\pi_i(s_i^*) + c_{ij}(Q_{ij}^*) \begin{cases} = \rho_j(d_j^*), & \text{if} \quad Q_{ij}^* > 0 \\ \geq \rho_j(d_j^*), & \text{if} \quad Q_{ij}^* = 0. \end{cases} \tag{11.6}$$

Hence, if the commodity shipment between a pair of supply and demand markets is positive at equilibrium, then the demand price at the demand market must be equal to the supply price at the originating supply market plus the unit transportation cost. If the commodity shipment is zero in equilibrium, then the supply price plus the transportation cost can exceed the demand price.

As established by Samuelson (1952) and Takayama and Judge (1971), the spatial price equilibrium conditions (11.6) can be formulated as the solution to the optimization problem, given by:

$$\text{Minimize} \quad \sum_{i=1}^{m} \int_0^{s_i} \pi_i(x)dx + \sum_{i=1}^{m} \sum_{j=1}^{n} \int_0^{Q_{ij}} c_{ij}(y)dy - \sum_{j=1}^{n} \int_0^{d_j} \rho_j(z)dz, \tag{11.7}$$

subject to:

$$s_i = \sum_{j=1}^{n} Q_{ij}, \quad \forall i = 1, \ldots, m, \tag{11.8}$$

$$d_j = \sum_{i=1}^{m} Q_{ij}, \quad \forall i = 1, \ldots, n, \tag{11.9}$$

$$Q_{ij} \geq 0, \quad \forall i, j. \tag{11.10}$$

Indeed, under the assumption of increasing supply price functions, decreasing demand price functions, and increasing transportation cost functions, the Kuhn-Tucker conditions (see Appendix A) of this optimization problem coincide with the spatial price equilibrium conditions and, moreover, the spatial price equilibrium pattern (s^*, Q^*, d^*) is unique. Furthermore, in the case that the functions are linear, problem (11.7) takes the form of a quadratic objective function.

The notation for the emission pricing policy system is now introduced. Assume that the estimation of pollution dispersion can be modeled as the product of an emission factor times, respectively, the quantity of the commodity produced, the quantity of the commodity transported (see, for example, Glover and Brzezinski 1989; DeCorla-Souza, et al. 1995; Anderson, et al. 1996; and Allen 1996), and the quantity of the commodity consumed. In previous chapters, however, I had focused only on the emissions generated due to transportation. In this chapter, on the other hand, I also consider emissions due to stationary sources associated with the production of a commodity as well as the consumption of the commodity.

In particular, let h_i^s denote the emission factor associated with producing the commodity at supply market i; $i = 1, \ldots, m$. Let h_{ij}, in turn, denote the emission factor associated with transporting the commodity from supply market i to demand market j, where $i = 1, \ldots, m$; $j = 1, \ldots, n$. Finally, let h_j^d denote the emission factor associated with consuming the commodity at demand market j, where $j = 1, \ldots, n$. In this section, I assume that there is only a single pollutant emitted by the producers, shippers, and consumers; in the next section, I relax this assumption. Moreover, I assume that there is a single receptor point for the emissions. As has been the notation in the preceding chapters, let $\bar{Q}$ denote the environmental quality standard.

The emission pricing policy model is now formulated, the solution of which will yield a production, consumption, and commodity shipment pattern, which is guaranteed to be sustainable from an environmental perspective.

Formulation of Emission Pricing Policy Model for Spatial Price Networks

Consider the objective function (11.7) in which one has substituted the conservation of flow equations (11.1) and (11.2) directly, for simplicity, which yields the following optimization problem:

$$\text{Minimize} \quad \sum_{i=1}^{m} \int_0^{\sum_{j=1}^{n} Q_{ij}} \pi_i(x)dx + \sum_{i=1}^{m}\sum_{j=1}^{n} \int_0^{Q_{ij}} c_{ij}(y)dy - \sum_{j=1}^{n} \int_0^{\sum_{i=1}^{m} Q_{ij}} \rho_j(z)dz \tag{11.11}$$

subject to:

$$\sum_{i=1}^{m} h_i^s \sum_{j=1}^{n} Q_{ij} + \sum_{i=1}^{m}\sum_{j=1}^{n} h_{ij}Q_{ij} + \sum_{j=1}^{n} h_j^d \sum_{i=1}^{m} Q_{ij} \le \bar{Q}, \tag{11.12}$$

$$Q_{ij} \ge 0, \quad \forall i, j. \tag{11.13}$$

Note that constraint (11.12) guarantees that the environmental quality standard for the single pollutant emitted will be met.

Remark 11.1

Dafermos and Nagurney (1985) established that a spatial price equilibrium problem is isomorphic to a traffic network equilibrium problem with elastic demands. Refer to the structure of the isomorphic network given in Figure 11.3. Indeed, the origin/destination pairs correspond to the pairings of the super source node (0) with the bottom nodes in the networks. Note that the paths, hence, connecting each origin/destination node are disjoint, that is, they have no links in common. This special networks structure has been exploited for computational purposes (see, e.g., Nagurney 1999a).

Therefore, viability of a spatial price network can, at least, in principle, be reduced to viability of a traffic network with elastic demands, as described in Section 4.3. However, in the case of emissions on spatial price networks I also model emissions generated in the consumption of the commodity, whereas such an issue did not arise on the demand side in traffic networks. Nevertheless, it is easy to verify that one can always obtain a commodity shipment pattern that satisfies the environmental constraint (11.12) and the nonnegativity constraints (11.13), and, hence, a spatial price network is always viable.

I now derive the Kuhn-Tucker optimality conditions for this problem and then give an interpretation of them as equilibrium conditions. Note that the cost of a commodity produced at supply market i and consumed at demand market j is now not only equal to the supply price plus the transportation

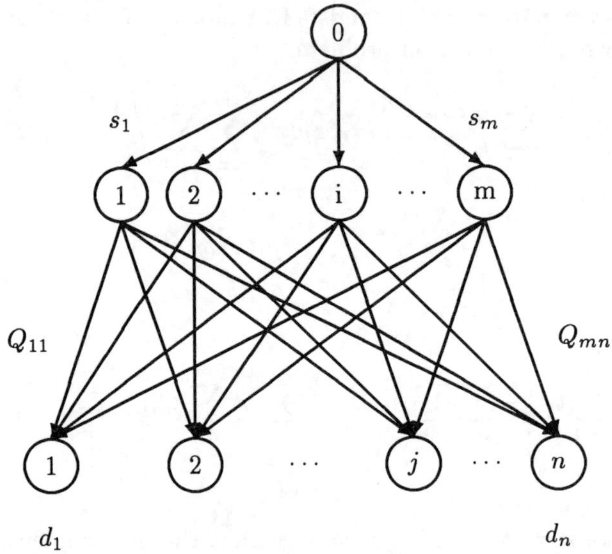

Fig. 11.3. Isomorphic traffic network structure of spatial price equilibrium

cost, but, rather, is now subject to the true cost of emissions and, hence, the *generalized* cost of a commodity produced at supply market i and shipped to demand market j, denoted by $\hat{c}_{ij}$, is given by:

$$\hat{c}_{ij} = \pi_i(s_i) + c_{ij}(Q_{ij}) + (h_i^s + h_{ij} + h_j^d)\tau,$$

where τ is the Lagrange multiplier associated with constraint (12.12) and here also can be interpreted as the marginal cost of emission abatement.

Spatial Price Equilibrium Conditions with Emission Pricing

Consequently, the spatial price equilibrium conditions (see also (11.6)), in the presence of an emission pricing policy, now take the form: For each pair of supply and demand markets (i, j):

$$\hat{c}_{ij} = \pi_i(s_i^*)+c_{ij}(Q_{ij}^*)+(h_i^s+h_{ij}+h_j^d)\tau^* \begin{cases} = & \rho_j(d_j^*), \quad \text{if } Q_{ij}^* > 0 \\ \geq & \rho_j(d_j^*), \quad \text{if } Q_{ij}^* = 0. \end{cases} \tag{11.14}$$

Indeed, conditions (11.14) have an interpretation as *equilibrium* conditions and state that the price of a commodity at a demand market, if consumed, is equal to the supply price at the originating supply market plus the unit transportation cost plus the emissions costs incurred by the supply market, the transportation link, and the demand market. Note that here the consumers "pay" for the costs of emissions associated with production, transportation, and consumption in the form of an "elevated" demand price at the demand market, if they purchase from that particular supply market.

Moreover, one must have the following condition holding as regards the equilibrium emissions and marginal cost of emission abatement:

$$\bar{Q} - \sum_{i=1}^{m} h_i^s s_i^* - \sum_{i=1}^{m}\sum_{j=1}^{n} h_{ij} Q_{ij}^* - \sum_{j=1}^{n} h_j^d d_j^* \begin{cases} = & 0, \quad \text{if } \tau^* > 0 \\ \geq & 0, \quad \text{if } \tau^* = 0. \end{cases} \tag{11.15}$$

11.1.2 A Sustainable Spatial Price Network Policy Model with General Functions

In this subsection, I generalize the model of Subsection 11.1.1 in order to consider general functions. Hence, it is now assumed that the supply price at a supply market may depend, in general, upon the entire vector of supplies, that is:

$$\pi_i = \pi_i(s), \quad i = 1, \ldots, m. \tag{11.16}$$

The unit transportation cost associated with shipping the commodity between a pair of markets, in turn, may depend upon the entire vector of commodity shipments, that is:

$$c_{ij} = c_{ij}(Q), \quad i = 1, \ldots, m; j = 1, \ldots, n, \tag{11.17}$$

whereas the demand price associated with consuming the commodity at a demand market may now, in general, depend upon the entire vector of demands, that is:

$$\rho_j = \rho_j(d), \quad j = 1, \ldots, n. \tag{11.18}$$

Making the substitutions s for s_i; Q for Q_{ij}, and d for d_j for the variables in the functions in (11.14), the equilibrium state is defined as follows:

Definition 11.2 (Spatial Price Market Emission Policy Model Equilibrium)
A vector $(s^*, Q^*, d^*, \tau^*) \in \mathcal{K}$ is an equilibrium of the spatial price network equilibrium emission policy market model if and only if it satisfies the systems of equalities and inequalities (11.14)–(11.15), where $\mathcal{K} \equiv K \times R_+$, and $K \equiv \{(s, Q, d), \text{such that} Q \geq 0, \text{ and} (11.1) \text{ and} (11.2) \text{ hold.}\}$

The variational inequality formulation of the equilibrium conditions for the model is derived in the theorem below.

Theorem 11.1 (Variational Inequality Formulation – Spatial Price Emission Policy Model)
A vector of commodity supplies, shipments, demand, and marginal costs of emission abatement $(s^*, Q^*, d^*, \tau^*) \in \mathcal{K}$ *is an equilibrium of the spatial price network equilibrium problem with the emission pricing policy given above if and only if it is a solution to the variational inequality problem:*

$$\sum_{i=1}^{m} \pi_i(s^*) \times (s_i - s_i^*) + \sum_{i=1}^{m}\sum_{j=1}^{n}(c_{ij}(Q^*) + (h_i^s + h_{ij} + h_j^d)\tau^*) \times (Q_{ij} - Q_{ij}^*)$$

$$-\sum_{j=1}^{n} \rho_j(d^*) \times (d_j - d_j^*)$$

$$+(\bar{Q} - \sum_{i=1}^{m} h_i^s s_i^* - \sum_{i=1}^{m}\sum_{j=1}^{n} h_{ij} Q_{ij}^* - \sum_{j=1}^{n} h_j^d d_j^*) \times (\tau - \tau^*) \geq 0, \quad \forall (s, Q, d, \tau) \in \mathcal{K}. \tag{11.19}$$

Proof:
I first establish that a solution to the equilibrium conditions (11.14)–(11.15) satisfies variational inequality (11.19) in the case of general functions $\pi(s)$, $c(Q)$, and $\rho(d)$.

Equilibrium conditions (11.14) imply that, for a fixed pair of markets (i, j):

$$(\pi_i(s^*) + c_{ij}(Q^*) + (h_i^s + h_{ij} + h_j^d)\tau^*) \times (Q_{ij} - Q_{ij}^*) \geq 0, \quad \forall Q_{ij} \geq 0. \tag{11.20}$$

Indeed, if $Q_{ij}^* = 0$, then $(Q_{ij} - Q_{ij}^*) \geq 0$ and according to (11.14): $(\pi_i(s^*) + c_{ij}(Q^*) + (h_i^s + h_{ij} + h_j^d)\tau^* - \rho_j(d^*)) \geq 0$ and, hence, (11.20) holds true. If $Q_{ij}^* > 0$, then note that the term $(Q_{ij} - Q_{ij}^*)$ may be positive, negative, or zero, depending on Q_{ij}, but since, according to (11.14), in this case, $(\pi_i(s^*) + c_{ij}(Q^*) + (h_i^s + h_{ij} + h_j^d)\tau^* - \rho_j(d^*)) = 0$, inequality (11.20) again holds true.

Summing now (11.20) over all market pairs (i, j) and using (11.1) and (11.2) yields:

$$\sum_{i=1}^{m} \pi_i(s^*) \times (s_i - s_i^*) + \sum_{i=1}^{m}\sum_{j=1}^{n}(c_{ij}(Q^*) + (h_i^s + h_{ij} + h_j^d)\tau^*) \times (Q_{ij} - Q_{ij}^*)$$

$$-\sum_{j=1}^{n} \rho_j(d^*) \times (d_j - d_j^*) \geq 0, \quad \forall (s, Q, d) \in K. \tag{11.21}$$

Moreover, equilibrium conditions (11.15) imply that:

$$(\bar{Q} - \sum_{i=1}^{m} h_i^s s_i^* - \sum_{i=1}^{m}\sum_{j=1}^{n} h_{ij} Q_{ij}^* - \sum_{j=1}^{n} h_j^d d_j^*) \times (\tau - \tau^*) \geq 0, \quad \forall \tau \in R_+. \tag{11.22}$$

Indeed, if $\tau^* = 0$, then $(\tau - \tau^*) \geq 0$, and from (11.15) one concludes that the first term in parentheses in (11.22) is nonnegative, and, hence, the product of the two nonnegative terms on the right-hand side of (11.22) is nonnegative. On the other hand, if $\tau^* > 0$, then, according to conditions (11.15), the first term in (11.22) must be equal to zero and, hence, the product of a zero term times a nonnegative term is zero and the inequality still holds.

Finally, summing inequalities (11.21) and (11.22) yields the variational inequality (11.19).

I now establish that a solution to variational inequality (11.19) satisfies equilibrium conditions (11.14)–(11.15).

Let $(s^*, Q^*, d^*, \tau^*) \in \mathcal{K}$ be a solution to (11.19). Let $s = s^*, Q = Q^*, d = d^*$, and make these substitutions into (11.19), which yields:

$$(\bar{Q} - \sum_{i=1}^{m} h_i^s s_i^* - \sum_{i=1}^{m}\sum_{j=1}^{n} h_{ij} Q_{ij}^* - \sum_{j=1}^{n} h_j^d d_j^*) \times (\tau - \tau^*) \geq 0, \quad \forall \tau \in R_+, \tag{11.23}$$

which implies equilibrium condition (11.15).

Now I turn to the commodity shipment equilibrium conditions. Set $\tau = \tau^*$ and make this substitution into variational inequality (11.19), which yields:

$$\sum_{i=1}^{m} \pi_i(s^*) \times (s_i - s_i^*) + \sum_{i=1}^{m}\sum_{j=1}^{n} (c_{ij}(Q^*) + (h_i^s + h_{ij} + h_j^d)\tau^*) \times (Q_{ij} - Q_{ij}^*)$$

$$- \sum_{j=1}^{n} \rho_j(d^*) \times (d_j - d_j^*) \geq 0, \quad \forall (s, Q, d) \in K, \tag{11.24}$$

which, of course, in view of feasibility constraints (11.1) and (11.2), is equivalent to:

$$\sum_{i=1}^{m}\sum_{j=1}^{n} (\pi_i(s^*) + c_{ij}(Q^*) + (h_i^s + h_{ij} + h_j^d)\tau^* - \rho_j(d^*)) \times (Q_{ij} - Q_{ij}^*) \geq 0,$$

$$\forall Q \in R_+^{mn}. \tag{11.25}$$

Letting now $Q_{kl} = Q_{kl}^*$ for all $kl \neq ij$, and making this substitution into (11.25), one obtains:

$$(\pi_i(s^*) + c_{ij}(Q^*) + (h_i^s + h_{ij} + h_j^d)\tau^* - \rho_j(d^*)) \times (Q_{ij} - Q_{ij}^*) \geq 0, \quad \forall Q_{ij} \geq 0, \tag{11.26}$$

which implies equilibrium condition (11.14) since inequality (11.26) must hold for any (i, j). □

Variational inequality (11.19) is now put into standard form (2.32). Define the column vector $X \equiv (s, Q, d, \tau) \in \mathcal{K}$ and the column vector:

$$F(X) \equiv (\Pi(X), C(X), \mathcal{P}(X), T(X)),$$

where $\Pi(X)$ is an m-dimensional column vectors with component i given, respectively, by:

$$\Pi_i(X) : \pi_i(s).$$

$C(X)$ is an mn-dimensional column vector with component i, j given by:

$$C_{ij}(X) : c_{ij}(Q) + (h_i^s + h_{ij} + h_j^d)\tau.$$

$\mathcal{P}$ is the n-dimensional vector with component j given by:

$$\mathcal{P}_j(X) = \rho_j(d),$$

and $T(X)$ consists of the single element:

$$T(X) = \bar{Q} - \sum_{i=1}^{m} h_i^s s_i - \sum_{i=1}^{m}\sum_{j=1}^{n} h_{ij} Q_{ij} - \sum_{j=1}^{n} h_j^d d_j.$$

Therefore, variational inequality (11.19) may now be expressed as:

$$\langle F(X^*)^T, X - X^* \rangle \geq 0, \quad \forall X \in \mathcal{K}. \tag{11.27}$$

Remark 11.2

Note that in the absence of an emission pricing policy and environmental quality standard the variational inequality (11.19) collapses to the variational inequality formulation of spatial price equilibrium (see Florian and Los 1982) given by:

$$\sum_{i=1}^{m} \pi_i(s^*) \times (s_i - s_i^*) + \sum_{i=1}^{m}\sum_{j=1}^{n} c_{ij}(Q^*) \times (Q_{ij} - Q_{ij}^*) - \sum_{j=1}^{n} \rho_j(d^*) \times (d_j - d_j^*) \geq 0,$$

$$\forall (s, Q, d) \in K,$$

which is the formulation of spatial price equilibrium conditions (11.6) in the case of general supply price, unit transportation cost, and demand price functions.

11.2 A General Sustainable Spatial Network Model

In this section, I develop a general spatial price network model in the presence of an emission policy in which there can now be three distinct pollutants emitted, respectively, by the producers, the shippers, as well as the consumers. I retain the notation of the preceding section, except now I assume, as given, the environmental quality standards $\bar{Q}^s$, $\bar{Q}$, and $\bar{Q}^d$, to denote the environmental quality standard for the emissions generated, respectively, by the producers, by the shippers, and by the consumers in regards to the production, trade, and consumption of the commodity. Without any loss of generality, let

h_i^s denote the emission factor associated with supply market i's emissions; h_{ij} the emission factor associated with the shipment of the commodity between i and j; and h_j^d the emission factor associated with consuming the commodity at demand market j.

I first motivate the general model by deriving the optimality conditions for the case where the underlying functions are separable, that is, given by (11.3), (11.4), and (11.5). Indeed, one can write down immediately, in view of the discussion in the preceding section, the following optimization reformulation of the problem:

$$\text{Minimize} \quad \sum_{i=1}^{m} \int_0^{s_i} \pi_i(x)dx + \sum_{i=1}^{m}\sum_{j=1}^{n} \int_0^{Q_{ij}} c_{ij}(y)dy - \sum_{j=1}^{n} \int_0^{d_j} \rho_j(z)dz \tag{11.28}$$

subject to:

$$\sum_{i=1}^{m} h_i^s s_i \leq \bar{Q}^s, \tag{11.29}$$

$$\sum_{i=1}^{m}\sum_{j=1}^{n} h_{ij} Q_{ij} \leq \bar{Q}, \tag{11.30}$$

$$\sum_{j=1}^{n} h_j^d d_j \leq \bar{Q}^d, \tag{11.31}$$

$$Q_{ij} \geq 0, \quad \forall i, j. \tag{11.32}$$

Spatial Price Equilibrium Conditions with Emission Pricing for Multiple Pollutants

Consequently, the spatial price equilibrium conditions, in the presence of an emission pricing policy in the case of multiple pollutants, as described above, now take the form: For each pair of supply and demand markets (i, j):

$$\pi_i(s_i^*) + h_i^s \tau^{s*} + c_{ij}(Q_{ij}^*) + h_{ij}\tau^* + h_j^d \tau^{d*} \begin{cases} = & \rho_j(d_j^*), \quad \text{if } Q_{ij}^* > 0 \\ \geq & \rho_j(d_j^*), \quad \text{if } Q_{ij}^* = 0. \end{cases} \tag{11.33}$$

Note that here τ^{s*} denotes the Lagrange multiplier associated with the environmental quality constraint (11.29); τ_{ij}^* denotes the Lagrange multiplier associated with the environmental quality constraint (11.30), whereas τ^{d*} denotes the Lagrange multiplier associated with the environmental quality constraint (11.31).

Furthermore, one must have the following conditions holding as regards the emissions and the marginal costs of emission abatement, associated with the production, the transportation, and the consumption of the commodity:

$$\bar{Q}^s - \sum_{i=1}^{m} h_i^s s_i^* \begin{cases} = & 0, \quad \text{if } \tau^{s*} > 0 \\ \geq & 0, \quad \text{if } \tau^{s*} = 0. \end{cases} \tag{11.34}$$

$$\bar{Q} - \sum_{i=1}^{m}\sum_{j=1}^{n} h_{ij}Q_{ij}^* \begin{cases} = & 0, \quad \text{if } \tau^* > 0 \\ \geq & 0, \quad \text{if } \tau^* = 0. \end{cases} \tag{11.35}$$

$$\bar{Q}^d - \sum_{j=1}^{n} h_j^d d_j^* \begin{cases} = & 0, \quad \text{if } \tau^{d^*} > 0 \\ \geq & 0, \quad \text{if } \tau^{d^*} = 0. \end{cases} \tag{11.36}$$

Observe that conditions (11.33)–(11.36) are relevant even in the case of general supply price, demand price, and transportation cost functions, as given by (11.16), (11.17), (11.18). Indeed, one may make the analogous substitutions above to obtain:

Definition 11.3 (Spatial Price Equilibrium with Emission Pricing for Multiple Pollutants)
A pattern is said to be an equilibrium pattern of the multipollutant spatial price equilibrium price emission policy model above if it satisfies conditions (11.33)–(11.36).

The variational inequality formulation of the equilibrium conditions for this model is now given. The result is presented without proof since is it similar to the proof of Theorem 11.2.

Theorem 11.2 (Variational Inequality Formulation – Multipollutant Spatial Price Emission Policy Model)
A vector of commodity supplies, shipments, demand, and marginal costs of emission abatement $(s^*, Q^*, d^*, \tau^{s*}, \tau^*, \tau^{d^*}) \in \mathcal{K}^1$ is an equilibrium of the multipollutant spatial price network equilibrium problem with the emission pricing policy given above if and only if it is a solution to the variational inequality problem:

$$\sum_{i=1}^{m}(\pi_i(s^*) + h_i^s\tau^{s*}) \times (s_i - s_i^*) + \sum_{i=1}^{m}\sum_{j=1}^{n}(c_{ij}(Q^*) + h_{ij}\tau^*) \times (Q_{ij} - Q_{ij}^*)$$

$$-(\sum_{j=1}^{n}\rho_j(d^*) - h_j^d\tau^{d^*}) \times (d_j - d_j^*)$$

$$+(\bar{Q}^s - \sum_{i=1}^{m} h_i^s s_i^*) \times (\tau^s - \tau^{s*}) + (\bar{Q} - \sum_{i=1}^{m}\sum_{j=1}^{n} h_{ij}Q_{ij}^*) \times (\tau - \tau^*)$$

$$+(\bar{Q}^d - \sum_{j=1}^{n} h_j^d d_j^*) \times (\tau^d - \tau^{d^*}) \geq 0, \quad \forall (s, Q, d, \tau^s, \tau, \tau^d) \in \mathcal{K}^1, \tag{11.37}$$

where $\mathcal{K}^1 \equiv K \times R_+^3$.

I now put variational inequality problem (11.37) into standard form. Define the column vector $X \equiv (s, Q, d, \tau^d, \tau, \tau^s)$ and the column vector

$F(X) \equiv (\Pi(X), C(X), \mathcal{P}(X), T^1(X), T^2(X), T^3(X))$, where $\Pi(X)$, $C(X)$, and $\mathcal{P}(X)$ are as defined previously and where $T^1(X)$ is the vector with single component $\bar{Q}^s - \sum_{i=1}^m h_i^s s_i$; $T^2(X)$ consists of the single component $\bar{Q} - \sum_{i=1}^m \sum_{j=1}^n h_{ij} Q_{ij}$; and $T^3(X)$ consists of the single component: $\bar{Q}^d - \sum_{j=1}^n h_j^d d_j$. Hence, the variational inequality problem can be put into standard form (2.32).

11.3 Qualitative Properties

In this section, the focus is on the general model developed in Section 11.2 and the presentation of qualitative properties of the equilibrium pattern, including an existence result. In addition, properties of the function $F(\cdot)$ which enters the variational inequality model for the problem that are needed to establish the convergence of the algorithmic scheme proposed in Section 11.4 are stated. The results are presented without proof since the proofs are similar to analogous proofs earlier in this text.

Theorem 11.3 (Existence)
If $(s^*, Q^*, d^*, \tau^{s*}, \tau^*, \tau^{d^*}) \in \mathcal{K}^1$ satisfies variational inequality (11.37) then the equilibrium commodity supply, shipment, and demand pattern $(s^*, Q^*, d^*) \in K$ is a solution to the variational inequality problem:

$$\sum_{i=1}^m \pi_i(s^*) \times (s_i - s_i^*) + \sum_{i=1}^m \sum_{j=1}^n c_{ij}(Q^*) \times (Q_{ij} - Q_{ij}^*) - \sum_{j=1}^n \rho_j(d^*) \times (d_j - d_j^*) \geq 0,$$

$$\forall (s, Q, d) \in K^1, \tag{11.38}$$

where:

$$K^1 \equiv \{Q \geq 0, \text{ such that} (11.24) - (11.26) \text{ are satisfied}\}.$$

A solution to (11.38) is guaranteed to exist since K^1 is compact, provided that it is nonempty, and π, c, and ρ are assumed to be continuous. Moreover, there exist τ^{s*}, τ^*, and τ^{d^*} with $(s^*, Q^*, d^*, \tau^{s*}, \tau^*, \tau^{d^*}) \in \mathcal{K}^1$ a solution to variational inequality (11.37).

The uniqueness result follows.

Theorem 11.4 (Uniqueness)
Assume that the supply price functions $\pi(s)$, the transportation cost functions $c(Q)$, and minus the demand price functions $-\rho(d)$ are strictly monotone in s, Q, and d, respectively, that is,

$$\langle (\pi(s^1) - \pi(s^2))^T, s^1 - s^2 \rangle + \langle (c(Q^1) - c(Q^2))^T, Q^1 - Q^2 \rangle$$

$$-\langle (\rho(d^1) - \rho(d^2))^T, d^1 - d^2 \rangle > 0,$$

$$\forall (s^1, Q^1, d^1), (s^2, Q^2, d^2) \in K, (s^1, Q^1, d^1) \neq (s^2, Q^2, d^2). \tag{11.39}$$

Then the equilibrium supply, commodity shipment, and demand pattern is unique.

Certain properties of the function $F(\cdot)$ are now provided, which are used to prove convergence of the algorithmic scheme in Section 11.4.

Lemma 11.1 (Monotonicity)
Assume that the supply price functions are monotonically increasing in the supplies, the transportation cost functions are monotonically increasing in the commodity shipments, and the demand prices are monotonically decreasing in the demands; that is, for every $(s^1, Q^2, d^2), (s^2, Q^2, d^2) \in K$, we have that:

$$\langle (\pi(s^1) - \pi(s^2))^T, s^1 - s^2 \rangle + \langle (c(Q^1) - c(Q^2))^T, Q^1 - Q^2 \rangle$$

$$-\langle (\rho(d^1) - \rho(d^2))^T, d^1 - d^2 \rangle \geq 0, \quad \forall (s^1, Q^1, d^1), (s^2, Q^2, d^2) \in K. \quad (11.40)$$

Then $F(X)$ is monotone, that is:

$$\langle (F(X^1) - F(X^2))^T, X^1 - X^2 \rangle \geq 0, \quad \forall X^1, X^2 \in \mathcal{K}^1. \quad (11.41)$$

Lemma 11.2 (Lipschitz Continuity)
If the supply price functions, the transportation cost functions, and the demand price functions have bounded first order derivatives, then the function $F(X)$ is Lipschitz continuous.

11.4 The Algorithm

In this section, the modified projection method of Korpelevich (1977) (see Chapter 5) is proposed for the solution of variational inequality (11.37) and variational inequality (11.19). The algorithm has been applied previously to compute the equilibria in the models in Part II and Part III of this book. Here I state the realization of the algorithm for the general model governed by variational inequality (11.37) and then show its realization for the simpler model governed by variational inequality (11.19).

Modified Projection Method for the Multipollutant Spatial Price Emission Policy Model Satisfying Variational Inequality (11.37)

Step 0: Initialization
Set $(s^0, Q^0, d^0, \tau^{s0}, \tau^0, \tau^{d0}) \in \mathcal{K}^1$. Let $\mathcal{T} = 1$, and set α so that $0 < \alpha < \frac{1}{L}$, where L is the Lipschitz constant for the problem.

Step 1: Computation
Compute $(\bar{s}^{\mathcal{T}}, \bar{Q}^{\mathcal{T}}, \bar{d}^{\mathcal{T}}, \bar{\tau}^{s\mathcal{T}}, \bar{\tau}^{\mathcal{T}}, \bar{\tau}^{d\mathcal{T}}) \in \mathcal{K}^1$ by solving the variational inequality problem:

$$\sum_{i=1}^{m} (\bar{s}_i^{\mathcal{T}} + \alpha(\pi_i(s^{(\mathcal{T}-1)}) + h_i^s \tau^{s(\mathcal{T}-1)}) - s^{(\mathcal{T}-1)}) \times (s_i - \bar{s}_i^{\mathcal{T}})$$

$$+\sum_{i=1}^{m}\sum_{j=1}^{n}(\bar{Q}_{ij}^{\mathcal{T}}+\alpha(c_{ij}(Q^{(\mathcal{T}-1)})+h_{ij}\tau^{(\mathcal{T}-1)})-Q^{(\mathcal{T}-1)})\times(Q_{ij}-\bar{Q}_{ij}^{\mathcal{T}})$$

$$+\sum_{j=1}^{n}\bar{d}_j^{\mathcal{T}}-\alpha(\rho_j(d^{(\mathcal{T}-1)})-h_j^d\tau^{d(\mathcal{T}-1)})-d_j^{(\mathcal{T}-1)})\times(d_j-\bar{d}_j^{\mathcal{T}})$$

$$+(\bar{\tau}^{s\mathcal{T}}+\alpha(\bar{Q}^s-\sum_{i=1}^{m}h_i^s s_i^{(\mathcal{T}-1)})-\tau^{s(\mathcal{T}-1)})\times(\tau^s-\bar{\tau}^{s\mathcal{T}})$$

$$+(\bar{\tau}^{\mathcal{T}}+\alpha(\bar{Q}-\sum_{i=1}^{m}\sum_{j=1}^{n}h_{ij}Q_{ij}^{(\mathcal{T}-1)})-\tau^{(\mathcal{T}-1)})\times(\tau-\bar{\tau}^{\mathcal{T}})$$

$$+(\bar{\tau}^{d\mathcal{T}}+\alpha(\bar{Q}^d-\sum_{j=1}^{n}h_j^d d_j^{(\mathcal{T}-1)})-\tau^{d(\mathcal{T}-1)})\times(\tau^d-\bar{\tau}^{d\mathcal{T}})\geq 0,$$

$$\forall(s,Q,d,\tau^s,\tau,\tau^d)\in\mathcal{K}^1. \quad (11.42)$$

Step 2: Adaptation

Compute $(s^{\mathcal{T}},Q^{\mathcal{T}},d^{\mathcal{T}},\tau^{s\mathcal{T}},\tau^{\mathcal{T}},\tau^{d^{\mathcal{T}}})\in\mathcal{K}^1$ by solving the variational inequality problem:

$$\sum_{i=1}^{m}s_i{}^{\mathcal{T}}+\alpha(\pi_i(\bar{s}^{(\mathcal{T})})+h_i^s\bar{\tau}^{s(\mathcal{T})})-s^{(\mathcal{T}-1)})\times(s_i-s_i{}^{\mathcal{T}})$$

$$+\sum_{i=1}^{m}\sum_{j=1}^{n}(Q_{ij}^{\mathcal{T}}+\alpha(c_{ij}(\bar{Q}^{(\mathcal{T})})+h_{ij}\bar{\tau}^{(\mathcal{T})})-Q^{(\mathcal{T}-1)})\times(Q_{ij}-Q_{ij}^{\mathcal{T}})$$

$$+\sum_{j=1}^{n}d_j{}^{\mathcal{T}}-\alpha(\rho_j(\bar{d}^{(\mathcal{T})})-h_j^d\bar{\tau}^{d(\mathcal{T})})-d_j^{(\mathcal{T}-1)})\times(d_j-d_j^{\mathcal{T}})$$

$$+(\tau^{s\mathcal{T}}+\alpha(\bar{Q}^s-\sum_{i=1}^{m}h_i^s\bar{s}_i^{(\mathcal{T})})-\bar{\tau}^{s(\mathcal{T}-1)})\times(\tau^s-\bar{\tau}^{s\mathcal{T}})$$

$$+(\tau^{\mathcal{T}}+\alpha(\bar{Q}-\sum_{i=1}^{m}\sum_{j=1}^{n}h_{ij}\bar{Q}_{ij}^{(\mathcal{T})})-\tau^{(\mathcal{T}-1)})\times(\tau-\bar{\tau}^{\mathcal{T}})$$

$$+(\tau^{d^{\mathcal{T}}}+\alpha(\bar{Q}^d-\sum_{j=1}^{n}h_j^d\bar{d}_j^{(\mathcal{T})})-\tau^{d(\mathcal{T}-1)})\times(\tau^d-\bar{\tau}^{d\mathcal{T}})\geq 0,$$

$$\forall(s,Q,d,\tau^s,\tau,\tau^d)\in\mathcal{K}^1. \quad (11.43)$$

Step 3: Convergence Verification
If $|Q_{ij}^{\mathcal{T}} - Q_{ij}^{(\mathcal{T}-1)}| \leq \epsilon$, for all (i,j); $|\tau^{s\mathcal{T}} - \tau^{s(\mathcal{T}-1)}| \leq \epsilon$, $|\tau^{\mathcal{T}} - \tau^{(\mathcal{T}-1)}| \leq \epsilon$, and $|\tau^{d^{\mathcal{T}}} - \tau^{d(\mathcal{T}-1)}| \leq \epsilon$, for $\epsilon > 0$, some positive tolerance, then stop; else, set $\mathcal{T} =: \mathcal{T} + 1$, and go to Step 1.

I now state the realization of the modified projection method for the solution of the simpler emission pricing policy model with only a single pollutant and governed by variational inequality (11.19)

Modified Projection Method for the Single Pollutant Spatial Price Equilibrium Model Satisfying Variational Inequality (11.19)

Step 0: Initialization

Set $(s^0, Q^0, d^0, \tau^0) \in \mathcal{K}$. Let $\mathcal{T} = 1$, and set α so that $0 < \alpha < \frac{1}{\bar{L}}$, where $\bar{L}$ is the Lipschitz constant for the problem.

Step 1: Computation
Compute $(\bar{s}^{\mathcal{T}}, \bar{Q}^{\mathcal{T}}, \bar{d}^{\mathcal{T}}, \bar{\tau}^{\mathcal{T}}) \in \mathcal{K}$ by solving the variational inequality problem:

$$\sum_{i=1}^{m}(\bar{s}_i^{\mathcal{T}} + \alpha(\pi_i(s^{(\mathcal{T}-1)})) - s^{(\mathcal{T}-1)}) \times (s_i - \bar{s}_i^{\mathcal{T}})$$

$$+\sum_{i=1}^{m}\sum_{j=1}^{n}(\bar{Q}_{ij}^{\mathcal{T}} + \alpha(c_{ij}(Q^{(\mathcal{T}-1)}) + (h_i^s + h_{ij} + h_j^d)\tau^{(\mathcal{T}-1)}) - Q^{(\mathcal{T}-1)})$$

$$\times(Q_{ij} - \bar{Q}_{ij}^{\mathcal{T}}) + \sum_{j=1}^{n} \bar{d}_j^{\mathcal{T}} - \alpha(\rho_j(d^{(\mathcal{T}-1)})) - d_j^{(\mathcal{T}-1)}) \times (d_j - \bar{d}_j^{\mathcal{T}})$$

$$+(\tau^{\mathcal{T}} + \alpha(\bar{Q} - \sum_{i=1}^{m} h_i^s s_i^{(\mathcal{T}-1)} - \sum_{i=1}^{m}\sum_{j=1}^{n} h_{ij} Q_{ij}^{(\mathcal{T}-1)} - \sum_{j=1}^{n} h_j^d d_j^{(\mathcal{T}-1)}) - \tau^{(\mathcal{T}-1)})$$

$$\times(\tau - \bar{\tau}^{\mathcal{T}}) \geq 0, \quad \forall (s, Q, d, \tau) \in \mathcal{K}. \tag{11.44}$$

Step 2: Adaptation
Compute $(s^{\mathcal{T}}, Q^{\mathcal{T}}, d^{\mathcal{T}}, \tau^{\mathcal{T}}) \in \mathcal{K}$ by solving the variational inequality problem:

$$\sum_{i=1}^{m}(s_i{}^{\mathcal{T}} + \alpha(\pi_i(\bar{s}^{(\mathcal{T})})) - s^{(\mathcal{T}-1)}) \times (s_i - s_i{}^{\mathcal{T}})$$

$$+\sum_{i=1}^{m}\sum_{j=1}^{n}(Q_{ij}^{\mathcal{T}} + \alpha(c_{ij}(\bar{Q}^{(\mathcal{T}-1)}) + (h_i^s + h_{ij} + h_j^d)\bar{\tau}^{(\mathcal{T})}) - Q^{(\mathcal{T})}) \times (Q_{ij} - Q_{ij}^{\mathcal{T}})$$

$$+\sum_{j=1}^{n} d_j{}^{\mathcal{T}} - \alpha(\rho_j(\bar{d}^{(\mathcal{T})})) - d_j^{(\mathcal{T}-1)}) \times (d_j - d_j^{\mathcal{T}})$$

$$+(\tau^{\mathcal{T}} + \alpha(\bar{Q} - \sum_{i=1}^{m} h_i^s \bar{s}_i^{(\mathcal{T})} - \sum_{i=1}^{m}\sum_{j=1}^{n} h_{ij}\bar{Q}_{ij}^{(\mathcal{T})} - \sum_{j=1}^{n} h_j^d \bar{d}_j^{(\mathcal{T})}) - \tau^{(\mathcal{T}-1)})$$

$$\times(\tau - \tau^{\mathcal{T}}) \geq 0, \quad \forall (s, Q, d, \tau) \in \mathcal{K}. \tag{11.45}$$

Step 3: Convergence Verification

If $|Q_{ij}^{\mathcal{T}} - Q_{ij}^{(\mathcal{T}-1)}| \leq \epsilon$, for all (i, j) and $|\tau^{\mathcal{T}} - \tau^{(\mathcal{T}-1)}| \leq \epsilon$, for $\epsilon > 0$, some positive tolerance, then stop; else, set $\mathcal{T} =: \mathcal{T} + 1$, and go to Step 1.

I now discuss more fully the form of the individual variational inequality subproblems occurring in (11.42), (11.43), and (11.44), (11.45). Specifically, since both the feasible sets $\mathcal{K}^1$ and $\mathcal{K}$ are Cartesian products, each of which contains the set K, these subproblems result in classical spatial price equilibrium problems, which can, in turn, be solved using a quadratic programming algorithm, as well as simple subproblems in the marginal costs of emission abatement, each of which can be solved explicitly in closed form. For the former problem, there exist many algorithms, including special-purpose algorithms which exploit the special network structure of the spatial price problem (see Nagurney 1999a and the references therein).

Theorem 11.5 (Convergence)

If the supply price functions, transportation cost functions, and minus demand price functions are assumed to be monotone and to have bounded first-order derivatives, then the modified projection method converges to the solution of variational inequality (11.37) and also (11.19).

Proof:

From Lemma 11.1, one concludes that $F(X)$ is monotone and from Lemma 11.2 that $F(X)$ is Lipschitz continuous. Hence, according to Korpelevich (1977), the modified projection method is guaranteed to converge to a solution of the variational inequality problem.

11.5 Numerical Examples

In this section, numerical results are presented in order to illustrate the behavior of the models as well as the algorithm. The modified projection method was, again, implemented in FORTRAN and the IBM SP2 at the Computer Science Department at the University of Massachusetts at Amherst was utilized for the computational work.

For the solution of the spatial price network equilibrium problem encountered in both the computation and the adaptation steps of the modified projection method, the Euler method (cf. Nagurney, Takayama, and Zhang 1995) was utilized, due to its simplicity.

The convergence tolerance ϵ was set to .00001 for all the examples.

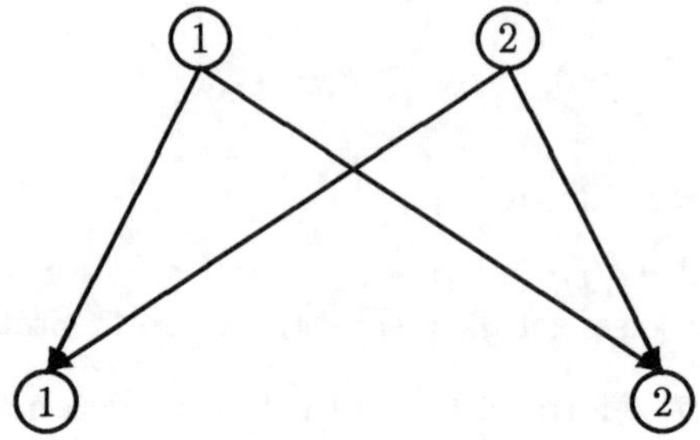

Fig. 11.4. Network structure of two supply market/two demand market examples

The modified projection method was initialized by setting all the variables equal to zero. I report the CPU time, exclusive of input/output times, as well as the number of iterations.

In particular, I solved two sets of examples, corresponding, respectively, to examples of the single pollutant emission policy model governed by variational inequality (11.19) and the multipollutant model governed by variational inequality (11.37). The first set, reported in Subsection 11.5.1, consisting of small-scale examples, and the second set, reported in Subsection 11.5.2, consisted of both small-scale and larger examples. The particular relevant data are reported for each example.

11.5.1 Single Pollutant Model Examples

In this subsection, I report numerical results for small spatial price network examples governed by variational inequality (11.19).

In this set of examples, I considered a spatial price network problem consisting of two supply markets and two demand markets. The network structure is depicted in Figure 11.4.

The common data for all three examples in this set were as follows: The supply price functions were:

$$\pi_1(s) = 5s_1 + 1s_2 + 2, \quad \pi_2(s) = 2s_2 + 1.5s_1 + 1.5,$$

the unit transportation cost functions were:

$$c_{11}(Q) = Q_{11}, \quad c_{12}(Q) = 2Q_{12} + 0.035,$$

$$c_{21}(Q) = 3Q_{21} + 0.162, \quad c_{22}(Q) = 2Q_{22} + 0.115,$$

and the demand price functions were:

$$\rho_1(d) = -2d_1 - 1.5d_2 + 28.75, \quad \rho_2(d) = -4d_2 - d_1 + 41.$$

The emission parameters were: $h_1^s = 0.5$, $h_s^2 = 1$; $h_{11} = 0.5$, $h_{12} = 1.$, $h_{21} = .5$, $h_{22} = 1$; and $h_d^1 = .5$, $h_d^2 = 1$.

In this set of examples, I varied the environmental quality standard $\bar{Q}$ by making it increasingly tighter. I set $\alpha = 0.6$ in the modified projection method for all examples in this set. The convergence criterion was as described for the algorithm in Section 11.4 for this model.

Example 11.1

In the first example, I set $\bar{Q} = 20$.

The algorithm converged in a negligible amount of CPU time and required 43 iterations for convergence. It yielded the following equilibrium pattern:

$$s_1^* = 2.1353, \quad s_2^* = 4.5093,$$

$$Q_{11}^* = 0.6280, \quad Q_{12}^* = 1.5073, \quad Q_{21}^* = 1.3100 \quad Q_{22}^* = 3.1994,$$

$$d_1^* = 1.9380, \quad d_2^* = 4.7066,$$

$$\tau^* = 0.0000.$$

Note that in this example, the environmental quality standard, along with the emission factors, were such that the total emissions were less than the standard by 3.07 units and, hence, $\tau^* = 0$. The commodity production, shipment, and consumption pattern, hence, is actually the spatial price equilibrium pattern satisfying also variational inequality governing the spatial price equilibrium problem without any policy interventions. Indeed, this example serves, hence, as the baseline for the two subsequent examples in which we successively tighten the environmental quality standard.

Example 11.2

In the second example, the data were as in Example 11.1 in this set, except that the environmental quality standard was tightened so that $\bar{Q} = 15$. Note that such a change could represent that there was a tightening of the standard due to a policy agreement.

The algorithm converged in a negligible amount of CPU time and required 41 iterations for convergence. It yielded the following equilibrium pattern:

$$s_1^* = 2.0212, \quad s_2^* = 3.9091,$$

$$Q_{11}^* = 0.6511, \quad Q_{12}^* = 1.3701, \quad Q_{21}^* = 1.1294 \quad Q_{22}^* = 2.7798,$$

$$d_1^* = 1.7805 \quad d_2^* = 4.1499,$$

$$\tau^* = 1.5318.$$

The environmental quality standard was precisely met since τ^* was positive. Moreover, the equilibrium conditions (11.14) were also satisfied (for the case of general functions).

Whereas in the preceding example there were no payments due to the emissions generated, since the environmental quality standard exceeded the total emissions, here there were emission payments as follows:
For the pair of markets $(1,1)$:

$$(h_1^s + h_{11} + h_d^1)\tau^* = 2.2977,$$

for the pair of markets $(1,2)$:

$$(h_1^s + h_{12} + h_d^2)\tau^* = 3.8294,$$

for the pair of markets $(2,1)$:

$$(h_2^s + h_{21} + h_d^1)\tau^* = 3.0635,$$

for the pair of markets $(2,2)$:

$$(h_2^s + h_{22} + h_d^2)\tau^* = 4.5953.$$

Example 11.3

In the third example, the data were as in Example 11.1, except that now the environmental quality standard was tightened even more than was done for Example 11.1. Specifically, I now set $\bar{Q} = 10$.

The algorithm converged in a negligible amount of CPU time and required 40 iterations for convergence. It yielded the following equilibrium pattern:

$$s_1^* = 1.7255, \quad s_2^* = 2.3528,$$

$$Q_{11}^* = 0.7110, \quad Q_{12}^* = 1.0145, \quad Q_{21}^* = 0.6611, \quad Q_{22}^* = 1.6917,$$

$$d_1^* = 1.3720, \quad d_2^* = 2.7062,$$

$$\tau^* = 5.5036.$$

As expected, τ^* increased as $\bar{Q}$ increased. In this example, as in Example 11.2, since τ^* was positive, the environmental quality standard was precisely met. Moreover, the equilibrium conditions (11.14) were also satisfied.

The emission payments were as follows:
For the pair of markets $(1,1)$:

$$(h_1^s + h_{11} + h_d^1)\tau^* = 8.2544,$$

for the pair of markets $(1,2)$:

$$(h_1^s + h_{12} + h_d^2)\tau^* = 13.7590,$$

for the pair of markets $(2,1)$:

$$(h_2^s + h_{21} + h_d^1)\tau^* = 11.0072,$$

for the pair of markets $(2,2)$:

$$(h_2^s + h_{22} + h_d^2)\tau^* = 16.5108.$$

11.5.2 Multipollutant Examples

In this subsection, I computed solutions to multipollutant spatial price examples, whose governing equilibrium conditions coincide with the solution of variational inequality (11.37). In Subsection 11.5.2.1, smaller examples were considered, and, in Subsection 11.5.2.2, larger examples.

11.5.2.1 Small Examples

Specifically, in this subsection, I solved three examples, each of which consisted of two supply markets and two demand markets with the network structure as depicted in Figure 11.4. The supply price, unit transportation cost, as well as the demand price functions were identical to those in the examples of Section 11.5.1. The emission factors were also as described therein. Here, however, in each example, one needed to identify the specific environmental quality standards $\bar{Q}^s$, $\bar{Q}$, and $\bar{Q}^d$ imposed on the emissions generated, respectively, by the supply markets, the transportation of the commodity, as well as by the demand markets, in the production, transportation, and consumption of the commodity. Hence, for each example in this subsection I also report the imposed environmental quality standards.

I set $\alpha = 0.6$ in the modified projection method. Here the convergence tolerance $\epsilon = .00001$, with the convergence verification step as given in the modified projection method in Section 11.4 for this model. The initialization of the data was as previously described.

Example 11.4

In the first example in this subsection, I set $\bar{Q}^s = 10$, $\bar{Q} = 10$, and $\bar{Q}^d = 10$.

The modified projection method converged in a negligible amount of CPU time and required 43 iterations for convergence. It yielded the following the identical equilibrium commodity production, shipment, and consumption pattern to that of Example 11.1, that is:

$$s_1^* = 2.135, \quad s_2^* = 4.5093,$$

$$Q_{11}^* = 0.6280, \quad Q_{12}^* = 1.5073, \quad Q_{21}^* = 1.3100, \quad Q_{22}^* = 3.1994,$$

$$d_1^* = 1.9380, \quad d_2^* = 4.7066,$$

with:

$$\tau^{s*} = 0.0000, \quad \tau^* = 0.0000, \quad \tau^{d^*} = 0.0000.$$

The environmental quality standard at the supply markets exceeded the emissions generated at the supply markets by 4.4230. The environmental quality standard associated with shipping the commodity to the demand markets from the supply markets exceeded the emissions generated in the transportation of the commodity by 4.3244, which was also the value of the difference between the environmental quality standard imposed on the demand markets and the emissions generated by the demand markets.

Hence, this example may serve as the baseline for the two subsequent examples in which we tighten the environmental quality standards.

Example 11.5

In the second example in this set, the data were as in Example 11.4, except that I now tightened the environmental quality standard associated with shipping the commodity so that $\bar{Q} = 5$, with the remainder of the data as in Example 11.4.

The algorithm converged in 0.01 seconds of CPU time and required 114 iterations for convergence. It yielded the following equilibrium pattern:

$$s_1^* = 1.9326, \quad s_2^* = 4.0477,$$

$$Q_{11}^* = 0.7069, \quad Q_{12}^* = 1.2257, \quad Q_{21}^* = 1.2536, \quad Q_{22}^* = 2.7940,$$

$$d_1^* = 1.9605, \quad d_2^* = 4.0197,$$

$$\tau^{s^*} = 0.0000, \quad \tau^* = 4.7632, \quad \tau^{d^*} = 0.0000.$$

Note that now the environmental quality standard was precisely met on the transportation side and the marginal cost of emission abatement associated with transportation was now positive. The marginal costs of emission abatement associated with the supply markets and the demand markets, however, remained at zero since the emissions generated were less than the imposed environmental quality standards for the supply and the demand markets.

The payments associated with transporting the commodity were:
For the pair of markets $(1,1)$:

$$(h_{11})\tau^* = 2.3816,$$

for the pair of markets $(1,2)$:

$$(h_{12})\tau^* = 4.7632,$$

for the pair of markets $(2,1)$:

$$(h_{21})\tau^* = 2.3816,$$

for the pair of markets $(2,2)$:

$$(h_{22})\tau^* = 4.7632.$$

Example 11.6

In the third example in this set, the data were as in Example 11.5, except that now I tightened the environmental quality standards for the supply markets and the demand markets as well. Specifically, I now set $\bar{Q}^s = 5$, $\bar{Q} = 5$, and $\bar{Q}^d = 5$.

The modified projection method converged in 0.01 seconds of CPU time and required 233 iterations for convergence. It yielded the following equilibrium pattern:

$$s_1^* = 1.9410, \quad s_2^* = 4.0295,$$

$$Q_{11}^* = 0.7013, \quad Q_{12}^* = 1.2397, \quad Q_{21}^* = 1.2397, \quad Q_{22}^* = 2.7898,$$

$$d_1^* = 1.9410, \quad d_2^* = 4.0295,$$

$$\tau^{s*} = 0.1678, \quad \tau^* = 2.3040, \quad \tau^{d^*} = 2.3040.$$

Note that now the emissions generated by the supply markets, the shippers, as well as the demand markets were each precisely equal to the respective imposed environmental quality standard for that type of emission. Furthermore, as required by the equilibrium conditions (11.34)–(11.36), the respective marginal costs of emission abatement were, hence, positive.

Moreover, it is worth noting that the equilibrium condition (11.33) was also met by the computed supply, commodity shipment, and demand pattern.

The emission payments were as follows:
For the pair of markets (1, 1):

$$(h_1^s \tau^{s*} + h_{11}\tau^* + h_d^1 \tau^{d^*}) = 2.3879,$$

for the pair of markets (1, 2):

$$(h_1^s \tau^{s*} + h_{12}\tau^* + h_d^2 \tau^{d^*}) = 4.6920,$$

for the pair of markets (2, 1):

$$(h_2^s \tau^{s*} + h_{21}\tau^* + h_d^1 \tau^{d^*}) = 2.4718,$$

for the pair of markets (2, 2):

$$(h_2^s \tau^{s*} + h_{22}\tau^* + h_d^2 \tau^{d^*}) = 4.7758.$$

11.5.2.2 Larger Examples

The data for these examples were generated randomly. The supply price functions were linear and asymmetric as were the demand price functions with five terms in each such function. The transportation costs were linear and separable. The diagonal term in each supply price function lay in the range [10, 30], the diagonal in each demand price function lay in the range [−5, −55]. The fixed terms in the supply price functions lay in the range [10, 100], whereas the fixed term in the demand price function lay in the range [50, 5000]. The fixed term in the transportation cost function lay in the range [0.05, 0.50]. The off-diagonal terms in both the supply price and demand price functions were generated to ensure strict diagonal dominance and, hence, positive definiteness. The emission factors were generated as follows: $h_i^s =$

$0.5 \times i$, for all supply markets i, $h_{ij} = 0.5 \times j$, for all transportation links (i, j), and $h_j^d = j$, for all demand markets j.

For all examples in this set, I let $\alpha = 0.1$ in the modified projection method. In this set, I do not report the equilibrium solutions since the problems are too large. The examples consisted of ten supply markets and ten demand markets. The underlying functions were identical for all three examples in this set, but the environmental quality standards were varied.

Example 11.7

In the first example in this set, I let the environmental quality standards be as follows: $\bar{Q}^s = 30$, $\bar{Q} = 30$, and $\bar{Q}^d = 30$. The modified projection method converged in 2,019 iterations and required 6.90 CPU seconds for convergence. The environmental quality standards were precisely met at the supply markets and at the demand markets with the computed marginal costs of emission abatement equal to $\tau^{s*} = 194.9827$, $\tau^* = 1.0000$, and $\tau^{d^*} = 1338.0352$.

The emissions due to transportation of the commodity were 14.9997 units which are lower than $\bar{Q} = 30$ and, hence, the marginal cost of emission abatement τ^* was equal to zero.

Example 11.8

In the second example in this set, the data were as in Example 11.7, but now I tightened the environmental quality standard associated with the supply markets so that $\bar{Q}^s = 20$.

The modified projection method required 30.86 CPU seconds for convergence and 39,091 iterations. The marginal costs of emission abatement were $\tau^{s*} = 924.9709$, $\tau^* = 0.0000$, and $\tau^{d^*} = 637.8857$.

The environmental quality standard $\bar{Q}$ exceeded the emissions due to transportation of the commodity by 15 units and, hence, τ^* was positive.

Example 11.9

In the third example in this set, I kept the data as in Example 11.8, but now I also tightened the environmental quality standard associated with the demand markets so that $\bar{Q}^d = 20$ and with transportation so that $\bar{Q} = 20$. The algorithm converged in 7,932 iterations and required 6.19 CPU seconds for convergence.

The algorithm computed the following equilibrium marginal costs of emission abatement: $\tau^{s*} = 123.9795$, $\tau^* = 0.0000$, and $\tau^{d^*} = 1729.5646$.

The environmental quality standard $\bar{Q}$ exceeded, as in the previous example, the total emissions due to transportation by 10.2432 units.

Note that, although, in the case of larger problems, the algorithm requires many iterations for convergence, each iteration is simple, consisting of decomposed subproblems with special structure, which are solved efficiently.

In this chapter, I have focused on global sustainability by developing pricing instruments which guarantee the achievement of the environmental quality standard in the presence of production, consumption, and transportation activities.

12 Technology and Network Design Issues

In this chapter, I explore technology and network design issues for sustainable transportation networks. Research and development are progressing in such areas as electric drive vehicles powered by hydrogen-based fuels and vehicles with internal combustion engines operated on alcohol fuels derived from renewable biomass sources (see Transportation Research Board 1997 and Sperling 1995). Although the design of such vehicles in a cost-effective and efficient manner has yet to be realized, such innovations lie on the horizon.

Moreover, the introduction of alternative modes of transportation to an existing network may allow for emission reduction, since it is well-known that, on the average, older vehicles emit more than new vehicles.

Indeed, "super-emitters" – that is, those cars that emit much more now than when they were new, are 10% of those cars and light trucks that account for approximately half of the emissions. Interestingly, the cleanest 50 % produce less than 1% of the emissions. Super-emitters tend to be older vehicles, although some may be newer ones with inappropriately maintained engines, defective emission-control equipment, or with tampered emission controls (cf. Sperling 1995 and the references therein).

Hence, in this chapter, I model technology and network design instruments which can be used in conjunction with the market-based policy instruments of the preceding chapters to explore sustainability of transportation networks. As in the preceding chapters, I emphasize the network topology in the formulations and analyses. Note that technology innovations aimed at emission reduction, in practice, may be grouped in the following categories: new fuels, new vehicles, and/or new travel options.

The chapter is organized as follows. In Section 12.1, both single-modal and multimodal versions of optimal budget allocation models for emission reductions are developed. These models are linear programming models.

Table 12.1. Model summary

• Optimal budget allocation for emission reduction
• Optimal viability achievement
• New mode introduction
• Viable growth
• System optimality under mode allocation control

In Section 12.2, subsequently, the formulation of the optimal viability achievement problem is derived in which one seeks to minimize the total cost associated with emission reduction, subject to the satisfaction of the imposed environmental quality standard. The objective function for this problem is allowed to be nonlinear and, hence, the problem is a nonlinear programming problem.

In Section 12.3, the introduction of a new mode into the transportation network is evaluated where a distinction is made between two cases, in which mode switching is and is not allowed. Here, I formulate the problems which determine the tightest environmental quality standard that can be achieved, given the introduction of a new mode. Policy makers can then evaluate whether or not the introduction of the new mode is reasonable from an environmental perspective. Both problems are linear programming problems.

In Section 12.4, I turn to the question of viable growth of a transportation network in terms of the increase in total demand that can occur, given the desired environmental quality standard. This problem also takes on a linear programming formulation.

This chapter concludes with the presentation of a model for system-optimization which allows for mode allocation control in that the central controller can now allocate the flows on the network across modes.

In Table 12.1, a summary of the models that are developed in this chapter is given.

I must emphasize that advances in intelligent vehicle highway systems as well as in the development of emission sensors are making the realization of the implementation of the policy instruments described in this text possible.

12.1 Optimal Budget Allocation for Emission Reduction

In this section, I construct a model which allows a transportation planner to determine how a given budget should be allocated in order to reduce the total emissions by the greatest possible amount. Let Δh_a denote the change in emission factor on a link a, where Δh_a is assumed to be nonnegative since it represents the reduction in the emission factor h_a on the link a. Let B denote the budget available to the authority for network improvements in the form of emission reductions (due, for example, to technology innovations). Let k_a denote the cost associated with making a reduction on link a.

I assume here that a flow pattern on the transportation network is given and I denote the induced link load pattern by f^*. Note that, for the sake of generality, I do not explicitly state whether the solution f^* is system- or user-optimized (or neither).

Then the optimization problem facing the transportation authority is:

$$\text{Maximize} \quad \sum_{a \in L} f_a^* \Delta h_a \tag{12.1}$$

subject to:

$$\sum_{a \in L} k_a \Delta h_a \leq B, \tag{12.2}$$

$$0 \leq \Delta h_a \leq u_a, \quad \forall a \in L, \tag{12.3}$$

where u_a denotes the upper bound possible on the reduction in the emission factor on link $a \in L$.

The objective function (12.1) represents the total emission reduction. The constraint (12.2) expresses the budget constraint, whereas the constraints (12.3) ensure that the emission reductions are within technologically feasible limits.

Note that in the above framework, one could also investigate a "second best" policy in which only certain links' emission factors can be reduced, in which case one would simply have to sum in constraint (12.2) over those links and bound them according to (12.3).

Observe that the problem is a linear programming problem, which may be solved by the well-known simplex method. Moreover, there exist commercial software codes for this algorithm for practical applications.

I now present a simple example for illustrative purposes.

Example 12.1

The network is the two node, two link network depicted in Figure 12.1.

Let the user link travel cost functions be:

$$c_a(f_a) = f_a + 5, \quad c_b(f_b) = f_b + 5,$$

with a travel demand $d_{w_1} = 10$ associated with O/D pair $w_1 = (1, 2)$. Assume that the travel behavior is that of user-optimization and that the emission factors on the links are:

$$h_a = 0.5, \quad h_b = 0.5.$$

Hence, one has that $f_a^* = f_b^* = 5$, with incurred path costs on path $p_1 = a$, $C_{p_1} = 10$, and on path $p_2 = b$, $C_{p_2} = 10$.

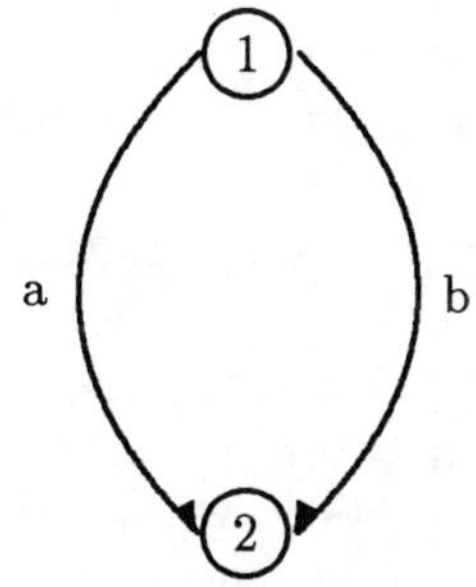

Fig. 12.1. Network topology for Examples 12.1 and 12.2

Suppose that the authority has 1 dollar in his budget for emission reduction and that the unit costs for reduction are $k_a = 2$, $k_b = 2$. Furthermore, assume that the upper bounds on emission factor reductions are $u_a = 0.25$ and $u_b = 0.25$.
The problem can then be formulated as:

$$\text{Maximize} \quad 5\Delta h_a + 5\Delta h_b$$

subject to:

$$2\Delta h_a + 2\Delta h_b \leq 1,$$

$$0 \leq \Delta h_a \leq 0.25,$$

$$0 \leq \Delta h_b \leq 0.25.$$

The solution of this problem yields: $\Delta h_a = 0.25$, $\Delta h_b = 0.25$, with a total reduction in emissions of 2.5 and an exhaustion of the budget.

Multimodal Version

I now construct a multimodal version of the above budget allocation problem. Let j denote a typical mode. Δh_a^j denotes the reduction in the emission factor of the mode, whereas f_a^{j*} denotes the link load of mode j on link a. Note that, again, I permit flexibility in terms of how this load pattern is achieved. Also, let u_a^j denote the upper bound on link a associated with the reduction of the emission factor for mode j.

The multimodal budget allocation problem is then:

$$\text{Maximize} \quad \sum_j \sum_{a \in L} f_a^{j*} \Delta h_a^j \tag{12.4}$$

subject to:

$$\sum_j \sum_{a\in L} k_a^j \Delta h_a^j \le B, \tag{12.5}$$

$$0 \le \Delta h_a^j \le u_a^j, \quad \forall j, \quad \forall a \in L. \tag{12.6}$$

12.2 Optimal Viability Achievement

In this section, I address the cost associated with the achievement of the viability of a transportation network (see also Chapter 4). Specifically, I am interested in formulating the problem whose solution will provide the reduction of the emission factors at minimal total cost so that the environmental quality standard is achieved, given a specific flow pattern, which is denoted, again, by f^*.

For the sake of greater generality, I now assume, as given, a cost function $\hat{k}_a$ associated with reducing the emission factor on link a. The function is a function of the change (reduction) in the emission factor. Using the same notation as in the preceding model (single-modal version), one has the following optimization problem, whose solution yields the optimal emission factor reductions at minimal total cost, given the desired environmental quality standard $\bar{Q}$:

$$\text{Minimize} \quad \sum_{a\in L} \hat{k}_a(\Delta h_a) \tag{12.7}$$

subject to:

$$\sum_{a\in L} f_a^*(h_a - \Delta h_a) \le \bar{Q}, \tag{12.8}$$

$$0 \le \Delta h_a \le u_a, \quad \forall a \in L. \tag{12.9}$$

The objective function (12.7) expresses the total cost associated with emission factor reduction, whereas constraint (12.8) expresses the environmental quality standard achievement. Finally, constraints (12.9) ensure that the emission reductions are within technologically feasible limits.

Note that there may not exist a solution to this problem if the feasible set governed by constraints (12.8) and (12.9) is empty. Indeed, this would mean that there is no technologically feasible manner (given the state of the art) to achieve the standard with the given flow pattern. Of course, one could also formulate the problem which would consist of nonlinear constraints (and a nonlinear objective function) that permits the flows to vary as well. Indeed, this problem would then take the form:

$$\text{Minimize} \quad \sum_{a\in L} \hat{k}_a(\Delta h_a) \tag{12.10}$$

subject to:

$$\sum_{a\in L} (h_a - \Delta h_a) f_a \le \bar{Q}, \tag{12.11}$$

$$f_a = \sum_{p \in P} x_p \delta_{ap}, \quad \forall a \in L, \tag{12.12}$$

$$\sum_{p \in P_w} x_p = d_w, \quad \forall w \in W, \tag{12.13}$$

$$x_p \geq 0, \quad \forall p \in P, \tag{12.14}$$

$$0 \leq \Delta h_a \leq u_a, \quad \forall a \in L. \tag{12.15}$$

The constraint (12.11) is nonlinear whereas the other constraints are linear.

Example 12.2

An example for the model (12.7)–(12.9) is now presented. The network is the one as depicted in Figure 12.1 with user link cost functions, travel demand, and emission factors as in Example 12.1. Assume that the cost functions $\hat{k}_a$ and $\hat{k}_b$ are linear and fixed, that is, $\hat{k}_a = 10$ and $\hat{k}_b = 10$. The optimization problem is, hence:

$$\text{Minimize} \quad 10\Delta h_a + 10\Delta h_b$$

subject to:

$$(0.5 - \Delta h_a)5 + (0.5 - \Delta h_b)5 \leq 2.5,$$

$$0 \leq \Delta h_a \leq 0.25,$$

$$0 \leq \Delta h_b \leq 0.25.$$

The optimal solution to this problem is:

$$\Delta h_a = 0.25, \quad \Delta h_b = 0.25.$$

The total cost associated with such an emission reduction is 5 and the environmental quality standard is precisely met.

12.3 Introduction of a New Mode

In this section, I present models to assist in the evaluation of whether or not a new mode should be introduced. Two distinct cases are considered:

1. in the first case, mode switching is allowed, that is, a portion of the users of the original mode of transportation can switch to the new mode so as to achieve the tightest possible environmental quality standard and
2. in the second case, no such mode switching is permitted.

I first present some needed notation. Let d_w^0 for all $w \in W$ denote the original travel demands associated with the O/D pairs in the transportation network. Let superscript 1 refer to mode 1 and superscript 2 to mode 2. The problem I am interested in formulating is, hence:

$$\text{Minimize} \quad Q \tag{12.16}$$

subject to:

$$d_w^1 + d_w^2 = d_w^0, \quad \forall w \in W, \tag{12.17}$$

$$\sum_{p \in P_w} x_p^1 = d_w^1, \quad \forall w, \tag{12.18}$$

$$\sum_{p \in P_w} x_p^2 = d_w^2, \quad \forall w \tag{12.19}$$

$$\sum_{a \in L} h_a^1 \sum_{p \in P} x_p^1 \delta_{ap} + \sum_{a \in L} h_a^2 \sum_{p \in P} x_p^2 \delta_{ap} \le Q, \tag{12.20}$$

$$x_p^1 \ge 0, \quad x_p^2 \ge 0, \quad \forall w \in W. \tag{12.21}$$

The objective function (12.16) denotes the tightest environmental quality standard to be achieved. In constraints (12.17), on the other hand, the demands d_w^1 and d_w^2 for all w are variables and they must sum for each O/D pair to the (original) demand for that O/D pair, which is assumed to be given. Moreover, constraints (12.18) and (12.19) ensure that the path flows associated with the original mode and the new mode satisfy the (to be determined) optimal travel demands for each mode. Constraint (12.20) guarantees that the path flow pattern will not exceed the environmental quality standard, which is to be determined at the tightest value possible.

Note that here one can also consider a second best policy in which a new mode of transportation only connects one or more (but not necessarily all) O/D pairs of travel, in which case the constraints (12.17)–(12.20) would be modified accordingly.

Mode Switching Not Permitted

I now consider the case in which the introduction of a new mode generates its own travel demand and no switching takes place from the original mode to the new one. Again, I am interested in determining the tightest environmental quality standard that can be achieved in this situation. The problem is, thus:

$$\text{Minimize} \quad Q \tag{12.22}$$

subject to:

$$\sum_{p \in P_w} x_p^1 = d_w^1, \quad \forall w \in W, \tag{12.23}$$

$$\sum_{p \in P_w} x_p^2 = d_w^2, \quad \forall w \in W, \tag{12.24}$$

$$\sum_{a \in L} h_a^1 \sum_{p \in P} x_p^1 \delta_{ap} + \sum_{a \in L} h_a^2 \sum_{p \in P} x_p^2 \delta_{ap} \le Q, \tag{12.25}$$

$$x_p^1 \ge 0, \quad x_p^2 \ge 0 \quad \forall p \in P. \tag{12.26}$$

Of course, in this case, one can also construct a model in which one has the second-best policy in the sense that only a subset of the O/D pairs are introduced to the new mode.

12.4 Viable Growth

I now turn to the determination of the maximal growth of a transportation network that is possible, in terms of the travel demand, while adhering to the desired environmental quality standard $\bar{Q}$. Specifically, let Δd_w denote the nonnegative change associated with the travel demand for O/D pair $w \in W$. I seek to maximize the total change in the travel demand for the entire network.

The optimization problem is given by:

$$\text{Maximize} \quad \sum_{w \in W} \Delta d_w \tag{12.27}$$

subject to:

$$\sum_{p \in P_w} x_p = d_w + \Delta d_w, \quad \forall w \in W. \tag{12.28}$$

$$\sum_{a \in L} h_a \sum_{p \in P} x_p \delta_{ap} \leq \bar{Q}, \tag{12.29}$$

$$x_p \geq 0, \quad \forall p \in P, \tag{12.30}$$

$$\Delta d_w \geq 0, \quad \forall w \in W. \tag{12.31}$$

The objective function (12.27) represents the total change or growth in travel demand. The constraint (12.28) guarantees that the path flow pattern satisfies the new travel demands, whereas constraint (12.29) ensures that the environemental quality standard will not be exceeded by the path flow pattern. Constraints (12.30) and (12.31) guarantee nonnegativity of the path flows and the travel demand changes.

This optimization problem is a linear programming problem and, hence, amenable to solution via the simplex method.

Example 12.3

The network is depicted in Figure 12.2 and is comprised of three nodes: 1, 2, 3; three links: a, b, c; and a single O/D pair $w_1 = (1, 3)$. Let path $p_1 = (a, c)$ and path $p_2 = (b, c)$.

The travel demand is $d_{w_1} = 100$ and the emission factors on the links are $h_a = 0.1$, $h_b = 0.1$, and $h_c = 0.1$. Assume that the environmental quality standard $\bar{Q} = 30$. The optimization problem for optimal viable growth is then:

$$\text{Maximize} \quad \Delta d_w$$

subject to:

$$x_{p_1} + x_{p_2} = 100 + \Delta d_{w_1},$$

$$0.1 x_{p_1} + 0.1 x_{p_2} + 0.1(x_{p_1} + x_{p_2}) \leq 30,$$

$$x_{p_1} \geq 0, \quad x_{p_2} \geq 0,$$

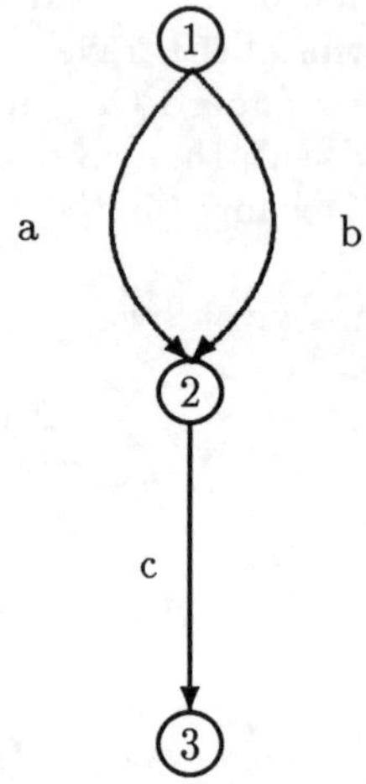

Fig. 12.2. Network for Example 12.3

$$\Delta d_{w_1} \geq 0.$$

A solution to this problem yields $\Delta d_{w_1} = 50$, resulting in a new travel demand of 150. Note that there are alternative optimal path flow patterns, given for example by $x^*_{p_1} = 150$, $x^*_{p_2} = 0$, and $x^*_{p_1} = x^*_{p_2} = 75$.

12.5 System-Optimization with Mode Allocation Control

In this section, I develop a model which allows the controller to allocate the flows on the network across modes while still satisfying the total demand associated with each O/D pair. Hence, one now no longer can assume that the travel demand associated with each mode and each O/D pair are fixed. For example, the controller may select modes of transportation which are lower emitters so as to not violate the environmental quality standard by allocating more of the flows to the lower emitters.

Let j denote mode j, which is used as a superscript for the link cost functions, the path flows and the travel demands. Otherwise, the notation is as in Chapter 8. Here, I present a path flow formulation, akin to (8.6)–(8.9), but now I allow for switching among the modes for an O/D pair. Let D_w denote the total demand for O/D pair.

The multimodal system-optimization problem with mode allocation control is, hence:

$$\text{Minimize} \quad S(x) = \sum_j \sum_{p \in P} \hat{C}_p^j \tag{12.32}$$

subject to:

$$\sum_{p \in P_w} x_p^j = d_w^j, \quad \forall w \in W, \quad \forall j, \tag{12.33}$$

$$\sum_j d_w^j = D_w, \quad \forall w \in W, \tag{12.34}$$

$$x_p^j \geq 0, \quad \forall p \in P, \quad \forall j, \tag{12.35}$$

$$d_w^j \geq 0, \quad \forall w \in W, \quad \forall j. \tag{12.36}$$

The vector x in the objective function in (12.32) is the vector of path flows for all the modes. Note that constraint (12.34) reflects that mode allocation is permitted across the modes for each O/D pair.

In this chapter, I have proposed model formulations which allow environmental and transportation planners to determine the cost-effectiveness of various technology and network design instruments. The models developed here are by no means exhaustive but only serve as fundamental ones for the investigation of some basic ideas. Additional models can be developed which address such questions as the effect of the addition of a new road(s) on the emissions generated (assuming certain behavior of the travelers) as well as the addition of new origins and destinations, coupled with new roads.

Part V Summary and Conclusions

13 Concluding Comments

Transportation is essential for the movement of people and goods over space and fundamental to the functioning of societies and economies. Over time, there has been an evolution of available modes of transportation over land, water, and air with the automobile revolution providing the principal mode of transport used by individuals in modern societies today. The automobile has added not only to the freedom and ability of humans to select their places of residence and of employment but has helped to transform the urban and suburban landscapes. Coupled with the advantages of automobile use for many have come, nevertheless, such associated problems or externalities as congestion and pollution. Indeed, over the past several decades, congestion has increased globally, especially in urban settings, and people as well as governments have become increasingly aware of the deleterious environmental effects of emissions due to automobiles and other vehicles.

This book was written in order to lay the foundations for the study of the sustainability of transportation networks in this environment of growing concern for the externalities associated with transportation. The approach taken in this book was to build upon the extensive research already laid in the study of transportation networks, and to introduce and develop a variety of policy instruments to guarantee sustainability. The major theme of this book is the emphasis on alternative behaviors of the users of transportation networks in the design the policy instruments aimed at congestion and/or emission abatement.

13.1 Contributions

The ideas set forth in this book explicitly recognize the network structure of the transportation systems as well as the behavior of the users of the networks, be they system-optimized or user-optimized networks. Moreover, the ideas in this book are developed rigorously through the presentation of definitions, models, theoretical analyses, as well as computational procedures,

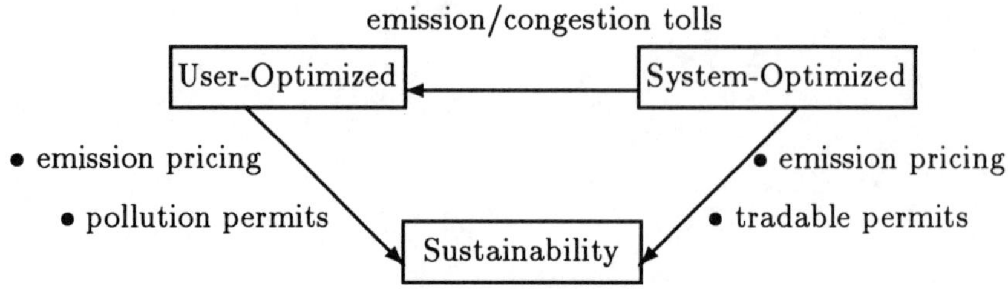

Fig. 13.1. Policy instruments for sustainability of transportation networks

accompanied by numerical examples for illustration purposes. It is my belief that only through the explicit identification of the basic components of the transportation network systems and their effects on the environment, and through their utilization, can the topic of sustainable transportation systems be addressed and studied.

Part I of this book lays the foundations of the subject by defining such principal concepts as viability and sustainability of a transportation network. Moreover, it shows that the network structure of the transportation system, along with the underlying demand and cost structure and the behavior of the users, must be incorporated into any policy schema since so-called "improvements" to a transportation network may actually result in an increase in the total emissions. Here several emission paradoxes are presented to emphasize this point.

Part II and Part III of this book then focus on the development of policy models for sustainable transportation networks, with Part II concentrating on user-optimized networks and Part III on system-optimized networks. Here such economic-incentive based approaches as alternative pollution permit systems are developed as well as a spectrum of pricing schemes associated with emission (and congestion) abatement. The models are constructed in an integrative manner and their development is presented at a level of increasing generality. Particular emphasis is placed on the conceptualization of the models and their theoretical underpinnings. This book, hence, aims to present a unified treatment of sustainable transportation networks through policy design and analysis. In Figure 13.1, a summary of the policy instruments developed in Parts II and III of the book is given.

In Part IV, I turn to spatial economic networks, with transportation being the critical link in joining producers and consumers. Hence, here I consider transportation as pivotal to economic activity in terms of trade and the shipment of goods from the producers to the consumers. Figure 13.2 summarizes the policy instruments developed in this part of the book for the sustainabil-

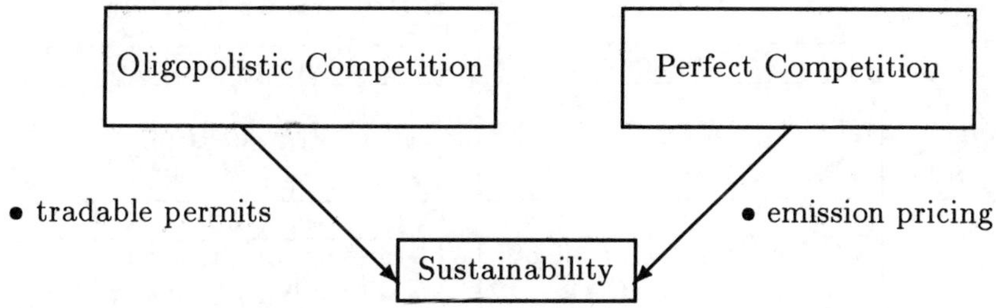

Fig. 13.2. Policy instruments for sustainability of spatial economic networks

ity of spatial economic networks. In Part IV, I am concerned not only with emissions generated due to transportation but also due to the production and/or the consumption of commodities. Consequently, Part IV directs the research to that of global sustainability.

Part IV also addresses technology and network design issues related to sustainable transportation networks. For example, such innovations as low or zero-emitting vehicles are currently under development as are fuels which generate lower emissions. Furthermore, the design of a network can also affect emissions generated through the network topology and the users' behavior. Moreover, the design of a network can include new modes of transportation and can provide new travel options.

In Table 13.1, technology and network design innovations and their effects on the transportation network system are identified. Part IV of this book focuses on such issues through models aimed at investigating the relationships of different innovations on sustainability.

In addition, innovations in technology, such as the much publicized intelligent vehicle highway systems as well as electronic tolls, can be used in conjunction with the policies proposed in this book. Indeed, there have been assumptions made throughout the modeling processes in this book and these include, among others: the availability of sensors to measure emissions; the availability of information to the transportation network users as to the routes and other network characteristics; and the availability of emission factors as inputs into the models.

Table 13.1. Technology and network design innovations and their effects

Technology	Network Design
⇓	⇓
• New fuels • New vehicles	• New travel options
⇓	⇓
• • emission factor effects • • supply side effects • • demand side effects	• • emission factors effects • • supply side effects • • demand side effects

13.2 Research Directions

Of course, the policy models developed in this book are by no means exhaustive nor are they all-inclusive. For example, possible research directions from this point on include:

• developing models which can handle nonlinear relationships between the congestion on a link and the emissions generated;
• developing sustainable transportation network policy models in which time is an explicit variable;
• further empirical evaluation of the models and algorithms;
• developing a synthesis of communication and transportation networks to assist in sustainability;
• investigating the relative feasibility of the policy instruments from political perspectives.

13.3 Personal Comments

This book was written while I was on sabbatical in Sweden, living at the Wenner Gren Centre, a community designated for international researchers, in Stockholm and bordering the majestic Haga Park. This was the second time that I had returned with my family to Stockholm for an extended period of time, having also lived at the centre in 1996. The centre provided an ideal community for scholarly exchange with its residents from numerous countries and its proximity to universities and libraries, as well as the amenities of Stockholm, which could be reached through a variety of modes of transportation, including bicycling, walking, driving, taking the bus and/or subway.

The beauty of the city with its parks, lovely architecture, easily accessible stores, shops, and museums and the convenient location of our housing arrangement provided the perfect ambience for writing this book. Indeed, simply the view from one's porch which included: a resplendent fountain;

a playground filled with children from around the world; strawberry, raspberry, and lingonberry bushes and flowers, stimulated the thought processes and the importance of the preservation of the natural environment. Walks through Haga Park, which was filled with people of all ages (along with the native residents such as birds, ducks, swans, rabbits, and deer) enjoying the beauty and serenity of the fields, ocean inlets, and woods, helped greatly in the conceptualization of the ideas in this book.

The hospitality of the Royal Institute of Technology (KTH), and especially the Division of Transportation and Location Analysis, with colleagues such as Lars-Goran Mattsson, Lars Lundqvist, and Farideh Ramjerdi, along with excellent coffee, enabled the translation of the ideas onto paper. Discussions with Borje Johansson and Folke Snickars supplied further intellectual stimulation. Moreover, the Stockholm School of Economics provided the library resources to enable the writing of this book.

The University of Massachusetts at Amherst and, in particular, the Isenberg School of Management deserve special thanks for granting me the sabbatical that made the writing of this book possible. The sabbatical also enabled additional travel which helped to further synthesize the ideas in this book. Of special note was my participation in the Transatlantic Research Conference on Social Change and Sustainable Transport held at the University of California at Berkeley in March of 1999 and co-chaired by William Black and Peter Nijkamp. Special thanks go to the organizers and to Ken Button, Eric Verhoef, and David Boyce, whose presentations reinforced the importance of the topic. In addition, thanks are extended to Gilbert Laporte, Sophie Lapierre, and Michel Gendreau for organizing of Optimization Days held in Montreal, Canada in May, 1999 during which the celebratory festschrift in honor of Michael Florian organized by Michel Gendreau and Patrice Marcotte was held.

Finally, sincere thanks are extended to Jack Smith, the CEO and Chairman of the Board of General Motors, for his vision of the automobile industry and its future, and for his support of women in professional endeavors both in industry and in academia.

Appendix A Optimization Theory

Concepts such as optimization as well as equilibrium are fundamental to the study of transportation systems and economics, in general, and to environmental economics, in particular.

In this appendix, the basics of the tools of optimization theory are provided at a level utilized in Parts I – IV of this book. The goal of this appendix, along with Appendix B, is to provide the minimal mathematical background needed for an adequate understanding of the models in this book. The reader may skip this appendix at first reading and may refer back to it as needed.

Here I review basic definitions and results from convexity theory and mathematical optimization, at a level that is relevant to the material presented in this book. The results are standard. For a more detailed presentation of the aforementioned areas, refer to the books by Bradley, Hax, and Magnanti (1977), Bazaraa, Jarvis, and Sherali (1990), and Bazaraa, Sherali, and Shetty (1993). I begin with some basic concepts from convexity theory and then proceed to optimization theory.

Convexity theory plays an essential role in optimization theory and I begin with some basic definitions.

Definition A.1 (A Convex Set)
A set $K \subset R^n$ is called a convex set if, given any two vectors X_1 and X_2 in K, $\lambda X_1 + (1-\lambda)X_2 \in K$, for every $\lambda \in [0,1]$.

In the special case of two dimensions, that is, when one is dealing with a set $K \in R^2$, simply stated, a set is convex if the line that connects any two points in that set also lies in the interior of that set.

Example A.1 – A Convex Set

For example, consider the set K consisting of x_1, x_2, such that $x_1 \geq 0$ and

$x_2 \geq 0$. Moreover, assume that x_1 and x_2 must also satisfy the constraint:

$$x_1 + x_2 \leq 2.$$

Clearly, the set K is convex.

Certain functions that arise often in the models developed in this book are now defined.

Definition A.2 (A Continuous Function)
A function $f : K \mapsto R$ is said to be continuous at $X \in K$, if for any given $\epsilon > 0$, there is a $\delta > 0$, such that $\psi \in K$ and $\|\psi - X\| < \delta$, imply that $|f(\psi) - f(X)| < \epsilon$.

Definition A.3 (A Differentiable Function)
Consider a nonempty set K such that $K \subset R^n$, a column vector X lying in the interior of K, and let f be a function such that $f : K \mapsto R$. Then f is said to be differentiable, if there exists a column vector $\nabla f(X) \in R^n$, called the gradient of f at X, and defined as:

$$\nabla f(X)^T = \left(\frac{\partial f(X)}{\partial X_1}, \frac{\partial f(X)}{\partial X_2}, \ldots, \frac{\partial f(X)}{\partial X_n} \right), \tag{A.1}$$

and a function $\beta(X; y) \to 0$ as $y \to x$ such that

$$f(y) = f(X) + \langle \nabla f(X)^T, (y - X) \rangle + \|y - X\| \beta(X; y), \quad \forall y \in K, \tag{A.2}$$

where $\langle \cdot, \cdot \rangle$ denotes the inner product in the n-dimensional Euclidean space.

Definition A.4 (A Twice Differentiable Function)
The function f is said to be twice differentiable at X if, in addition to the gradient vector, there exists an $n \times n$ matrix $H(X)$, called the Hessian matrix of the function f at X, defined as:

$$H = \begin{pmatrix} \frac{\partial^2 f}{\partial X_1 \partial X_1} & \frac{\partial^2 f}{\partial X_1 \partial X_2} & \cdots & \frac{\partial^2 f}{\partial X_1 \partial X_n} \\ \frac{\partial^2 f}{\partial X_2 \partial X_1} & \frac{\partial^2 f}{\partial X_2 \partial X_2} & \cdots & \frac{\partial^2 f}{\partial X_2 \partial X_n} \\ \vdots & \ddots & \ddots & \vdots \\ \frac{\partial^2 f}{\partial X_n \partial X_1} & \cdots & \cdots & \frac{\partial^2 f}{\partial X_n \partial X_n} \end{pmatrix}, \tag{A.3}$$

and a function $\beta(X; y) \to 0$ as $y \to X$ such that:

$$f(y) = f(X) + \langle \nabla f(X)^T, (y - X) \rangle$$

$$+ \frac{1}{2} (y - X)^T H(X) (y - X) + \|y - X\|^2 \beta(X; y), \quad \forall y \in K. \tag{A.4}$$

Example A.2

An example of a twice differentiable function in two dimensions is: $f(x) = 3x_1^2 + 5x_2^2$.

Definition A.5 (Convex and Concave Functions)
Let K be a nonempty convex set and consider a function $f : K \mapsto R$. Then the function $f(X)$ is said to be a convex function on K if for any two distinct points $X_1, X_2 \in K$, and for all $\lambda \in [0,1]$, the following holds:

$$f\left[\lambda X_2 + (1-\lambda) X_1\right] \leq \lambda f(X_2) + (1-\lambda) f(X_1). \qquad (A.5)$$

The function f is said to be strictly convex on K if the above inequality holds as a strict inequality. A function $f(X)$ is said to be concave (strictly concave) if $-f(X)$ is convex (strictly convex).

In other words, in two dimensions, a function $f(X)$ is convex (concave) if a line segment joining any two points $[X_1, f(X_1)]$, $[X_2, f(X_2)]$ on the surface of $f(X)$ lies on or above (below) that surface.

The previous definition can be used directly to establish whether a function is convex or not. For example, if one assumes that the function $f(X)$ is continuous and that it has second-order partial derivatives over K, then an alternative way to determine whether a function is convex or not is to evaluate whether the Hessian of the function is positive definite or not. In particular, if the Hessian matrix H of second-order partial derivatives is positive definite, then $f(X)$ is convex, and if H is negative definite, then $f(x)$ is concave. Recall that a matrix is positive (negative) definite if all its eigenvalues are positive (negative) or, equivalently, if all of its principal determinants have positive (negative) value. A matrix is positive semidefinite if all its eigenvalues are nonnegative as are all of its principal determinants.

Example A.3 – A Convex Function

Consider the function $f(x_1, x_2) = 2x_1^2 + 3x_2^2$, whose Hessian matrix is:

$$H = \begin{pmatrix} 2 & 0 \\ 0 & 3 \end{pmatrix}.$$

This Hessian matrix is a diagonal matrix with positive elements on the diagonal and, hence, positive definite so f is clearly convex.

Definition A.6 (Quasiconvex and Quasiconcave Functions)
Let K be a nonempty convex set and consider a function $f : K \mapsto R$. The function $f(X)$ is said to be a quasiconvex function on K, if for any two distinct points $X_1, X_2 \in K$, and $\forall \lambda \in [0,1]$, we have:

$$f\left[\lambda X_2 + (1-\lambda) X_1\right] \leq \textit{maximum}\ \left(f(X_1), f(X_2)\right).$$

The function $f(X)$ is said to be quasiconcave on K if $-f(X)$ is quasiconvex.

Definition A.7 (Pseudoconvex and Pseudoconcave Functions)
Let K be a nonempty convex set and consider a function $f : K \mapsto R$, which is differentiable on K. Then the function $f(X)$ is said to be a pseudoconvex function on K, if for any two distinct points $X_1, X_2 \in K$, with $\langle \nabla f(X_1)^T, X_2 - X_1 \rangle \geq 0$, we have $f(X_2) \geq f(X_1)$.

The function $f(X)$ is said to be pseudoconcave on K if $-f(X)$ is pseudoconvex.

One of the principal goals of economic theory is the determination of an optimal solution for a series of different problems. I now present the basics of optimization theory in addition to some of the concepts and ideas that are utilized throughout this book. I also present some examples for illustrative purposes.

An optimization problem in R^n is a problem in which one seeks to optimize a function f, which is said to be the *objective function*, subject to some constraints. For example, an objective function may represent profits to be maximized or costs to be minimized, whereas constraints can reflect budget or other resource constraints. A point $X^0 \in R^n$ is called a *feasible solution* to the optimization problem if it satisfies all the constraints of the problem. Moreover, a point $X^* \in R^n$ is called an *optimal solution* to the optimization problem if it is a feasible solution and it provides the best possible value for the objective function.

There are different classes of optimization problems, depending on the structure of the objective function and the constraints. For example, as is the case in several models in Chapter 12, if the objective function is linear, as are the constraints, and the variables are continuous (rather than discrete), then the problem is a *linear* programming problem, whose principal method of solution is the simplex method (see Bazaraa, Jarvis, and Sherali 1990). On the other hand, if either the objective function or the constraints are nonlinear expressions of the variables, then the problem is a *nonlinear* programming problem. For further details, see Bazaraa, Sherali, and Shetty (1993). Clearly, the classical system-optimization problems as well as the optimization reformulation of the symmetric user-optimization problem (see Chapter 2) are nonlinear programming problems.

A well-known case of a nonlinear programming problem occurs when the objective function is quadratic and the constraints are linear, in which case we have a quadratic programming problem. The classical spatial price equilibrium problems (see Chapter 11) with linear and symmetric supply price, demand price, and unit transportation cost functions, as well as traffic network equilibrium problems with linear and symmetric user link cost functions (for which an optimization reformulation exists (see Chapter 2))are examples of quadratic programming problems. In Appendix B, I provide equilibration algorithms which can be applied to solve quadratic programming problems with network structure, such as those encountered in problems in this text.

On the other hand, if one or more of the variables in a problem are constrained to be discrete, that is, to take on integer values, then one has an *integer* programming problem at hand.

A.1 Karush-Kuhn-Tucker Optimization Conditions

In this subsection, I discuss important conditions for optimality, but I first present some basic definitions.

Definition A.8 (Global Maximum and Minimum)
The function $f : K \mapsto R^n$ is said to take its global maximum at point X^* if

$$f(X) \leq f(X^*), \quad \forall X \in K. \tag{A.6}$$

Similarly, the function $f : K \mapsto R^n$ is said to take its global minimum at point ψ^* if:

$$f(\psi) \geq f(\psi^*), \quad \forall \psi \in K. \tag{A.7}$$

Definition A.9 (Local Maximum and Minimum)
The function $f : K \mapsto R^n$ is said to take its local maximum at point X^* if there exists a $\delta > 0$ such that for every $X \neq X^*$ that belongs to K and is in a δ-neighborhood of X^*, the following holds:

$$f(X) \leq f(X^*), \quad \forall X \in (K \cap B(X^*, \delta)), \tag{A.8}$$

where $B(X^*, \delta)$ denotes the ball with center X^* and radius δ.

Simiiarly, the function $f : K \mapsto R^n$ is said to take its local minimum at point ψ^* if there exists a $\delta > 0$ such that for every $\psi \neq \psi^*$ that belongs to K and is in a δ-neighborhood of ψ^*, the following holds:

$$f(\psi) \geq f(\psi^*), \quad \forall \psi \in (K \cap B(\psi^*, \delta)). \tag{A.9}$$

Karush-Kuhn-Tucker (KKT) Conditions

Karush (1939) and Kuhn and Tucker (1951) independently proposed a set of necessary and sufficient conditions for an optimal solution of a general mathematical optimization problem. Their work provided the mathematical framework upon which the qualitative theory as well as the computational methods in optimization have been based. In this subsection, a compact presentation of these conditions is given for reference purposes.

Karush-Kuhn-Tucker Necessary Conditions

Let $\mathcal{K}$ be a nonempty open set such that $\mathcal{K} \subset R^n$, and let $\{f : R^n \mapsto R\}$, $\{g_i : R^n \mapsto R\}$ for $i = 1, 2, \ldots, m$, and $\{h_j : R^n \mapsto R\}$ for $j = 1, 2, \ldots, t$. Moreover, consider the general optimization problem of the following form:

$$\text{Minimize} \quad f(X)$$

subject to:

$$g_i(X) \leq 0, \quad \text{for} \quad i = 1, 2, \ldots, m,$$

$$h_j(X) = 0, \quad \text{for} \quad j = 1, 2, \ldots, t,$$

$$X \in \mathcal{K}.$$

Let X^* be a feasible solution and let $I = \{i : g_i(X^*) = 0\}$. Furthermore, assume that f and g_i are differentiable at X^* for $i \in I$, and that the g_i are continuous at X^* for $i \in I$. Finally, assume that the h_j are continuously differentiable at X^* for all $j = 1, 2, \ldots, t$. Further, suppose that $\nabla g_i(X^*)$ for $i \in I$ and $\nabla h_j(X^*)$ for $j = 1, 2, \ldots, t$, are linearly independent. If X^* locally solves the minimization problem then there exist unique scalars v_i^* for $i \in I$, and w_j^* for $j = 1, 2, \ldots, t$, such that:

$$\nabla f(X^*) + \sum_{i \in I} v_i^* \nabla g_i(X^*) + \sum_{j=1}^{t} w_j^* \nabla h_j(X^*) = 0 \tag{A.10}$$

$$v_i^* g_i(X^*) = 0, \text{ for } i \in I \tag{A.11}$$

$$v_i^* \geq 0, \text{ for } i \in I. \tag{A.12}$$

The scalars v_i^* and w_j^* are called *Lagrange* multipliers. Note that there is one Lagrange multiplier associated with each constraint and that they represent the marginal rate of change in the objective function f with respect to each per unit change in the right-hand side of the corresponding constraint. Lagrange multipliers have important economic interpretations, which will be revealed in the environmental network policy models that are presented in the subsequent parts of this book.

Any point that satisfies the KKT conditions is called a *KKT point*.

An optimization problem sometimes includes nonnegativity constraints for the variables involved, that is, $X \geq 0$. Such inequality constraints are especially relevant in transportation since we need to ensure, for example, that the flows on the network, which are physical entities be they vehicle or goods, are nonnegative. Moreover, in an environmental setting, such nonnegativity constraints may also apply to emissions. Clearly, the KKT conditions that were just presented will still hold. Many times, however, for reasons of convenience and simplification, the Lagrange multipliers associated with the nonnegativity constraints are eliminated, and the conditions are reduced to:

$$\nabla f(X^*) + \sum_{i \in I} v_i^* \nabla g_i(X^*) + \sum_{j=1}^{t} w_j^* \nabla h_j(X^*) \geq 0 \tag{A.13}$$

$$\left[\nabla f(X^*) + \sum_{i \in I} v_i^* \nabla g_i(X^*) + \sum_{j=1}^{t} w_j^* \nabla h_j(X^*)\right]^T X^* = 0 \qquad (A.14)$$

$$v_i^* g_i(X^*) = 0, \text{ for } i \in I \qquad (A.15)$$

$$v_i^* \geq 0, \text{ for } i \in I. \qquad (A.16)$$

A geometric interpretation of the KKT conditions is that a vector X^* is a KKT point if and only if $-\nabla f(X^*)$ lies in the cone spanned by the gradients of the binding constraints, that is, those constraints that hold as equalities.

Karush-Kuhn-Tucker Sufficient Conditions

Let, again, $\mathcal{K}$ be a nonempty open set such that $\mathcal{K} \subset R^n$, and let $\{f : R^n \mapsto R\}$, $\{g_i : R^n \mapsto R\}$ for $i = 1, 2, \ldots, m$ and $\{h_j : R^n \mapsto R\}$ for $j = 1, 2, \ldots, t$. Moreover, consider, once again, the general optimization problem of the following form:

$$\text{Minimize} \quad f(X)$$

subject to:

$$g_i(X) \leq 0, \quad \text{for} \quad i = 1, 2, \ldots, m$$
$$h_j(X) = 0, \quad \text{for} \quad j = 1, 2, \ldots, t,$$
$$X \in \mathcal{K}.$$

Let X^* be a feasible solution, and let $I = \{i : g_i(X^*) = 0\}$. Assume that the KKT conditions hold at X^*. In other words, assume that there exist scalars $\overline{v}_i \geq 0$ with $i \in I$ and $\overline{w}_j$ with $j = 1, 2, \ldots, t$, such that

$$\nabla f(X^*) + \sum_{i \in I} \overline{v}_i \nabla g_i(X^*) + \sum_{j=1}^{t} \overline{w}_j \nabla h_j(X^*) = 0. \qquad (A.17)$$

Let $J = \{j : \bar{w}_j > 0\}$ and $L = \{j : \bar{w}_j < 0\}$. Further, suppose that f is pseudoconvex at X^*, the constraints g_i are quasiconvex at X^* for $i \in I$, h_j is quasiconvex for the $j \in J$ and quasiconcave for the $j \in L$. Then X^* is a global optimal solution to the general minimization problem.

For a maximization problem, the KKT conditions are similar, where now the function f has to be pseudoconcave.

Definition A.10 (Lagrangian Function)

Consider, once again, the general minimization problem used in the previous section. Then the function such that:

$$\phi(X, v, w) = f(X) + \sum_{i=1}^{m} v_i g_i(X) + \sum_{j=1}^{t} w_j h_j(X) \qquad (A.18)$$

is said to be the Lagrangian function of the general optimization problem.

If we let X^* be a KKT point to the general optimization problem with v^*, w^* being the Lagrange multipliers that correspond to the constraints of the problem, then the function:

$$L(X) \equiv \phi(X, v^*, w^*) = f(X) + \sum_{i \in I} v_i^* g_i(X) + \sum_{j=1}^{t} w_j^* h_j(X) \qquad (A.19)$$

is said to be the restricted Lagrangian function.

Let $\nabla^2 L$ denote the Hessian of (A.19). Then if $\nabla^2 L$ is:

- positive semidefinite for all X in the feasible set, X^* is a global minimum;
- positive semidefinite for all X in the feasible set and in a δ-neighborhood $B(X^*, \delta)$, for a $\delta > 0$, X^* is a local minimum;
- positive definite, X^* is a strict local minimum.

A.2 Optimization Examples

In this subsection, several examples are presented in order to illustrate some of the above concepts.

Example A.4 - Profit Maximization

Consider a perfectly competitive firm that produces a single product, where q denotes the production output of the firm, and $f(q)$ denotes the production cost associated with producing q. Assume that the production cost function is convex in the production output. Let π denote the price of the product. Assuming that the firm wishes to maximize profits, then the optimization problem faced by the firm is:

$$\text{Maximize} \quad \pi q - f(q)$$

subject to:

$$q \geq 0.$$

Since the objective function that is being maximized is concave and the feasible set is convex, the Karush-Kuhn-Tucker optimality conditions here, which are both necessary and sufficient for an optimal q^*, take the form:

$$\left[\frac{\partial f(q^*)}{\partial q} - \pi\right] \geq 0,$$

$$\left[\frac{\partial f(q^*)}{\partial q} - \pi\right] q^* = 0,$$

$$q^* \geq 0.$$

Indeed, the conditions have the following interpretation: The firm will produce, that is, $q^* > 0$, if the marginal cost of production, given by $\frac{\partial f(q^*)}{\partial q}$ is precisely equal to the price of the good π; if the marginal cost of production exceeds the price that the consumers are willing to pay for the product, then the firm will not produce the product.

Example A.5 – Cost Minimization Subject to Environmental Quality Constraints

Consider a shipper overseeing a network consisting of three links: a, b, and c, with the flows on the links denoted, respectively, by f_a, f_b, and f_c. Let d denote the demand which must be equal to the sum of the shipments. Let $\hat{c}_a$, $\hat{c}_b$, and $\hat{c}_c$ denote the total costs associated with shipping the flows over the links a, b, and c, respectively. Assume that the total cost functions, which are functions of the flow on each link, are convex and continuously differentiable. Furthermore, let h_a, h_b, and h_c denote the emission factors on the links, which, when multiplied by the flow on the link, provide the emissions of the pollutant due to the flows on the links. These factors are assumed to be positive.

Assume now that one wishes to restrain the emissions on each link individually to guarantee that the emissions on the links do not exceed a certain bound. Let $\bar{Q}_a$, $\bar{Q}_b$, and $\bar{Q}_c$ denote the environmental emission bound on links a, b, and c, respectively.

Then the shipper's optimization problem is to:

$$\text{Minimize} \quad \hat{c}_a(f_a) + \hat{c}_b(f_b) + \hat{c}_c(f_c)$$

subject to:

$$h_a f_a \leq \bar{Q}_a,$$

$$h_b f_b \leq \bar{Q}_b,$$

$$h_c f_c \leq \bar{Q}_c,$$

$$f_a + f_b + f_c = d,$$

$$f_a \geq 0, \quad f_b \geq 0, \quad f_c \geq 0.$$

Since the objective function that one wishes to minimize is convex and continuously differentiable and the feasible set is convex, the KKT optimality conditions are both necessary and sufficient and are given by:

$$\left[\frac{\partial \hat{c}_a(f_a^*)}{\partial f_a} + v_a^* h_a + w^*\right] \geq 0, \quad \left[\frac{\partial \hat{c}_a(f_a^*))}{\partial f_a} + v_a^* h_a + w^*\right] f_a^* = 0,$$

$$\left[\frac{\partial \hat{c}_b(f_b^*)}{\partial f_b} + v_b^* h_b + w^*\right] \geq 0, \quad \left[\frac{\partial \hat{c}_b(f_b^*)}{\partial f_b} + v_b^* h_b + w^*\right] f_b^* = 0,$$

$$\left[\frac{\partial \hat{c}_c(f_c^*)}{\partial f_c} + v_c^* h_c + w^*\right] \geq 0, \quad \left[\frac{\partial \hat{c}_c(f_c^*)}{\partial f_c} + v_c^* h_c + w^*\right] f_c^* = 0,$$

$$v_i^* \left[\bar{Q}_i - h_i f_i^*\right] = 0, \quad i = a, b, c,$$

$$v_i^* \geq 0, \quad i = a, b, c,$$

$$f_a^* + f_b^* + f_c^* = d,$$

$$f_a^* \geq 0, \quad f_b^* \geq 0, \quad f_c^* \geq 0,$$

where v_i^*; $i = a, b, c$, is the Lagrange multiplier associated with the emission constraint a, b, and c, respectively and w^* is the Lagrange multiplier associated with the demand constraint.

Appendix B Variational Inequality Theory

In this appendix, I provide a brief overview of finite-dimensional variational inequality theory. For a more thorough treatment of the theory, algorithms, as well as applications to network economics, see the book by Nagurney (1999a). For applications to environmental networks, see the book by Dhanda, Nagurney, and Ramanujam (1999). For applications to financial networks, see the book by Nagurney and Siokos (1997).

Variational inequalities were introduced by Hartman and Stampacchia (1966), principally for the study of problems arising in the field of mechanics. The research focused on infinite-dimensional variational inequalities, rather than on finite-dimensional variational inequalities, which are the ones utilized in this book. The book by Kinderlehrer and Stampacchia (1980) provides an introduction to infinite-dimensional variational inequality problems.

Smith (1979) presented a formulation of the equilibrium conditions of the traffic network equilibrium problem that were then identified as a finite-dimensional variational inequality by Dafermos (1980). From this connection, much research has been conducted on such variational inequality problems and many applications, ranging from oligopolistic market equilibrium problems to general economic and financial equilibrium problems, have been studied, both qualitatively and computationally, using this methodology.

The power of variational inequality theory is that it provides a unifying framework for the study of many equilibrium problems, since the variational inequality problem contains, as special cases, important problem classes which are widely utilized in economics, such as systems of nonlinear equations, optimization problems, and complementarity problems. Moreover, the problem is related to fixed point problems. Indeed, it has been utilized to formulate equilibrium problems governed by entirely distinct equilibrium concepts, including: Wardrop (1952) equilibrium governing congested urban traffic networks (cf. Smith 1979 and Dafermos 1980), spatial price equilib-

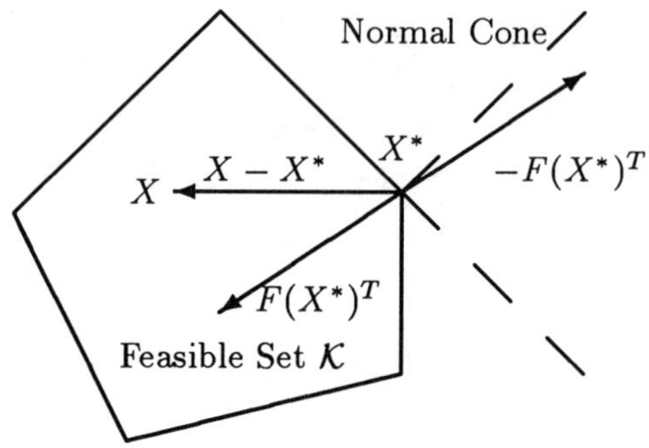

Fig. B.1. Geometric interpretation of VI($F, \mathcal{K}$)

rium (cf. Samuelson 1952; Takayama and Judge 1971; Florian and Los 1982), and oligopolistic market equilibrium (cf. Gabay and Moulin 1980), governed by the Cournot (1838)–Nash (1950) equilibrium. In this book, we show how variational inequality theory can be utilized in the study of sustainable transportation networks.

I will first present the definition of a variational inequality problem and will then discuss the relationship between the variational inequality problem and optimization problems.

Definition B.1 (The Variational Inequality Problem)
The finite-dimensional variational inequality problem, VI($F, \mathcal{K}$)*, is to determine a vector $X^* \in K$, such that:*

$$\langle F(X^*)^T, X - X^* \rangle \geq 0, \quad \forall X \in \mathcal{K}, \tag{B.1}$$

where F is a given continuous function from $\mathcal{K}$ to R^N, $\mathcal{K}$ is a given closed convex set, and $\langle \cdot, \cdot \rangle$ denotes the inner product in R^N.

The variational inequality problem has a geometric interpretation. In particular, it states that $F(X^*)^T$ is "orthogonal" to the feasible set $\mathcal{K}$ at the point X^*. In Figure B.1, the geometric interpretation is provided.

In order to emphasize the relationship between the variational inequality problem and optimization problems, we now present the following results. Proofs can be found in Kinderlehrer and Stampacchia (1980) and in Nagurney (1999a).

Relationship Between the Variational Inequality Problem and Optimization Problems

I now present the relationship between variational inequality problems and optimization problems. Specifically, note that a variational inequality problem contains an optimization problem as a special case.

Proposition B.1
Let X^* be the solution the following optimization problem:

$$\text{Minimize} \quad f(X) \tag{B.2}$$

subject to:

$$X \in \mathcal{K},$$

where f is a continuously differentiable function, and $\mathcal{K}$ is closed and convex. Then X^* is a solution of the variational inequality problem:

$$\langle \nabla f(X^*)^T, X - X^* \rangle \geq 0, \quad \forall X \in \mathcal{K}, \tag{B.3}$$

where $\nabla f(X^*)$ denotes the gradient of f with respect to X with components:

$$\left(\frac{\partial f_1(X^*)}{\partial X_1}, \frac{\partial f_2(X^*)}{\partial X_2}, \ldots, \frac{\partial f_N(X^*)}{\partial X_N}\right).$$

Proposition B.2
If $f(X)$ is a convex function and X^* is a solution to VI$(\nabla f, \mathcal{K})$ *given by (B.3), then X^* is a solution to the optimization problem (B.2).*

In the special case, when $\mathcal{K} = R^N$, then the above optimization problem (B.2) is an unconstrained problem.

On the other hand, if a certain symmetry condition holds, the variational inequality problem can also be reformulated as an optimization problem.

Theorem B.1
Assume that $F(X)$ is continuously differentiable on $\mathcal{K}$ and that the Jacobian matrix:

$$\nabla F(X) = \left\{ \begin{array}{ccc} \frac{\partial F_1}{\partial X_1} & \cdots & \frac{\partial F_1}{\partial X_N} \\ \vdots & & \vdots \\ \frac{\partial F_N}{\partial X_1} & \cdots & \frac{\partial F_N}{\partial X_N} \end{array} \right\} \tag{B.4}$$

is symmetric and positive semidefinite, so that F is convex. Then there exists a real-valued function $f : \mathcal{K} \mapsto R$ satisfying

$$\nabla f(X) = F(X) \tag{B.5}$$

with X^* the solution of VI$(F, \mathcal{K})$ *also being the solution of the optimization problem (B.2).*

Hence, one can see that the variational inequality problem encompasses the optimization problem and that the variational inequality problem can be reformulated as a convex optimization problem only when the symmetry and the positive semidefiniteness conditions hold.

Therefore, the variational inequality problem is a more general problem in that it can also handle a function $F(X)$ with an asymmetric Jacobian, that is, when (cf. (B.4)): $\frac{\partial F_i}{\partial X_j} \neq \frac{\partial F_j}{\partial X_i}$, for i, j. Historically, many equilibrium problems were reformulated as optimization problems under the symmetry and positive semidefiniteness condition, including the spatial price equilibrium problem (cf. Samuelson 1952; Takayama and Judge 1971) and the traffic network equilibrium problem (cf. Beckmann, McGuire, and Winsten 1956). This assumption, however, is restrictive in many application settings, specifically, in the case of transportation networks since it cannot adequately handle asymmetric cost functions as well as multimodal/multiclass transportation networks.

Variational Inequality Formulation of a Separable Constrained Optimization Problem

I now present a result (see Bertsekas and Tsitsiklis 1989) that demonstrates how separable constrained optimization problems over specific types of constraints can be formulated as variational inequality problems. This type of problem is encountered several times in the text and we use the realization as a variational inequality problem for the sake of consistency and to also explore more general models with asymmetric functions through this linkage.

Consider the separable, convex constrained optimization problem:

$$\text{Minimize} \quad \sum_{i=1}^{m} f_i(X_i) \tag{B.6}$$

subject to:

$$a_j^T X \leq b_j, \quad j = 1, \ldots, r$$
$$X_i \in K_i, \quad i = 1, \ldots, m,$$

where $f_i : R^{n_i} \mapsto R$ is a convex differentiable function and a_j^T is a row vector of coefficients corresponding to the j-th constraint, and X is vector consisting of the vectors; $\{X_1, \ldots, X_m\}$. Then this problem is equivalent to the variational inequality problem of finding $X_i^* \in K_i$ and $u_j^* \geq 0$, such that

$$\sum_{i=1}^{m} \langle (\nabla f_i(X_i^*) + \sum_{j=1}^{r} u_j^* a_{ji})^T, (X_i - X_i^*) \rangle + \sum_{j=1}^{r} (b_j - a_j^T X^*) \times (u_j - u_j^*) \geq 0, \tag{B.7}$$

$$\forall X_i \in K_i, \quad u_j \geq 0, \quad \forall j.$$

Note that u_j^* is the Lagrange ultiplier in the solution associated with inequality constraint j in the minimization problem. The coefficient a_{ji} corresponds to the ith component of the vector a_j. This problem can be solved using the modified projection method discussed in Section B.5.

B.1 An Example

In this subsection, I present an example of a variational inequality problem for illustrative purposes. Specifically, I present a market equilibrium example.

Example B.1 - Market Equilibrium

Assume that there are N commodities, which are produced and consumed, with a typical commodity denoted by i. Let p denote the N-dimensional column vector of the commodity prices with components $\{p_1, \ldots, p_N\}$.

Let D_i denote the demand in the economy for commodity i and let S_i denote the supply in the economy of commodity i. Assume that, in general, the demand for a commodity i may depend upon the prices of all the commodities, that is:

$$D_i = D_i(p), \quad \forall i.$$

Similarly, the supply of commodity i may, in general, depend upon the prices of all the commodites, that is:

$$S_i = S_i(p), \quad \forall i.$$

Group the demands for the commodities into the N-dimensional column vector D with components $\{D_1, \ldots, D_N\}$ and the supplies of the commodities into the N-dimensional column vector S with components: $\{S_1, \ldots, S_N\}$.

The economic equilibrium conditions are then: For each commodity i; $i = 1, \ldots, N$:

$$S_i(p^*) - D_i(p^*) \begin{cases} = 0, & \text{if } p_i^* > 0 \\ \geq 0, & \text{if } p_i^* = 0. \end{cases}$$

Note that equilibrium conditions state that if the price of a commodity is positive in equilibrium then the supply of that commodity must be equal to the demand for that commodity. On the other hand, if the price of a commodity at equilibrium is zero, then there may be an excess supply of that commodity at equilibrium, that is, $S_i(p^*) - D_i(p^*) > 0$, or the market clears. Furthermore, the equilibrium conditions guarantee that the prices of the commodities do not take on negative values.

The variational inequality formulation of this problem is given by: Determine $p^* \in R^N_+$, such that

$$\langle (S(p^*) - D(p^*))^T, p - p^* \rangle \geq 0, \quad \forall p \in R^N_+.$$

Observe that this variational inequality problem can be put into standard form (B.1) if we define the column vectors: $X \equiv p$ and $F(X) = S(p) - D(p)$, and the feasible set $\mathcal{K} = R^N_+$.

Furthermore, in the *special* case where the demand functions are separable, that is, $D_i = D_i(p_i)$ and supply functions are also separable, that is, $S_i = S_i(p_i)$, for all $i = 1, \ldots, N$, then the Jacobians (cf. (B.4)) of these functions are symmetric since they are diagonal and given, respectively, by:

$$\nabla S(p) = \begin{pmatrix} \frac{\partial S_1}{\partial p_1} & 0 & 0 & \cdots & 0 \\ 0 & \frac{\partial S_2}{\partial p_2} & 0 & \cdots & 0 \\ \vdots & \ddots & \ddots & \ddots & \vdots \\ 0 & 0 & 0 & \cdots & \frac{\partial S_N}{\partial S_N} \end{pmatrix},$$

$$\nabla D(p) = \begin{pmatrix} \frac{\partial D_1}{\partial p_1} & 0 & 0 & \cdots & 0 \\ 0 & \frac{\partial D_2}{\partial p_2} & 0 & \cdots & 0 \\ \vdots & \ddots & \ddots & \ddots & \vdots \\ 0 & 0 & 0 & \cdots & \frac{\partial D_N}{\partial p_N} \end{pmatrix}.$$

In this special case, the price vector p^* that satisfies the equilibrium conditions can be obtained, in view of (B.5), by solving the following optimization problem:

$$\text{Minimize} \sum_{i=1}^{N} \int_0^{p_i} S_i(x)dx - \sum_{i=1}^{N} \int_0^{p_i} D_i(y)dy$$

subject to:

$$p_i \geq 0, \quad i = 1, \ldots, N.$$

Note that one also obtains an optimization reformulation of the equilibrium conditions, provided that the following symmetry condition holds: $\frac{\partial S_i}{\partial p_k} = \frac{\partial S_k}{\partial p_i}$ and $\frac{\partial D_i}{\partial p_k} = \frac{\partial D_k}{\partial p_i}$ for all commodities i, k. In other words, the price of a commodity k affects the supply of a commodity i in the same way that the price of a commodity i affects the supply of a commodity k. A similar situation must hold for the demands for the commodities.

However, such conditions are clearly limiting from the application standpoint. Consequently, the appeal of variational inequality theory, which allows for the formulation and computation of equilibria where such restrictive symmetry assumptions on the underlying functions need no longer hold.

B.2 Qualitative Properties

I now present some basic qualitative properties of variational inequality problems. Specifically, I discuss the issues of existence and uniqueness of a solution. Definitions which are referred to in discussions of the convergence of algorithms are also included. All the theoretical results presented in this subsection, along with all the corresponding proofs, can be found in Kinderlehrer and Stampacchia (1980) and Nagurney (1999a).

The existence of a solution to a variational inequality problem follows from continuity of the function F entering the variational inequality, provided that the feasible set $\mathcal{K}$ is compact (that is, closed and bounded, in the case of R^N), as stated in the following theorem.

Theorem B.2 (Existence Under Compactness and Continuity)
If $\mathcal{K}$ is a compact convex set and $F(X)$ is continuous on $\mathcal{K}$, then the variational inequality problem VI$(F, \mathcal{K})$ admits at least one solution X^*.

Note that in the traffic network equilibrium problem with fixed demands (see Dafermos 1980), the feasible set underlying the problem is compact and, hence, existence of a solution to the variational inequality formulation of the problem follows solely from the assumption that the link travel cost functions are continuous functions of the flows.

If the feasible set $\mathcal{K}$ is unbounded, then we have:

Theorem B.3
VI$(F, \mathcal{K})$ admits a solution if and only if there exists an $R > 0$ and a solution X_R^* of VI(F, S), such that $\|X_R^*\| < R$, where $S = \{X : \|X\| \leq R\}$.

Such a condition was utilized by Dafermos (1986) to establish the existence of a solution to the variational inequality governing the elastic demand traffic network equilibrium problem in which the travel demands, rather than the travel disutilities are given (see also Nagurney 1999a).

Under the coercivity condition, the existence of a solution to a variational inequality problem is stated in the following theorem:

Theorem B.4 (Existence Under Coercivity)
Suppose that F(X) satisfies the coercivity condition:

$$\frac{\langle (F(X) - F(X_0))^T, (X - X_0) \rangle}{\|X - X_0\|} \to \infty, \tag{B.8}$$

as $\|X\| \to \infty$, for $X \in \mathcal{K}$, and for some $X_0 \in \mathcal{K}$. Then VI$(F, \mathcal{K})$ always has a solution.

A coercivity condition was imposed on minus the gradients of the utility functions by Gabay and Moulin (1980) in order to establish the existence of a solution to the variational inequality formulation of Nash equilibria, in particular, in the case of oligopolies.

The existence, as well as the uniqueness, of a solution to a variational inequality problem is directly related to certain monotonicity conditions. Indeed, monotonicity plays a role in variational inequality theory that is similar to the role that convexity plays in optimization theory.

I recall some basic definitions and will later discuss some qualitative results.

Definition B.2 (Monotonicity)
$F(X)$ is said to be monotone on $\mathcal{K}$ if:

$$\langle (F(X^1) - F(X^2))^T, X^1 - X^2 \rangle \geq 0, \quad \forall X^1, X^2 \in \mathcal{K}. \tag{B.9}$$

Definition B.3 (Strict Monotonicity)
$F(X)$ is strictly monotone on $\mathcal{K}$ if:

$$\langle (F(X^1) - F(X^2))^T, X^1 - X^2 \rangle \geq 0, \quad \forall X^1, X^2 \in \mathcal{K}, \quad X^1 \neq X^2. \quad (B.10)$$

Definition B.4 (Strong Monotonicity)
$F(X)$ is strongly monotone on $\mathcal{K}$, if for some $\alpha \geq 0$:

$$\langle (F(X^1) - F(X^2))^T, X^1 - X^2 \rangle \geq \alpha \|X^1 - X^2\|, \quad \forall X^1, X^2 \in \mathcal{K}. \quad (B.11)$$

I now present the first uniqueness result in the following theorem.

Theorem B.5 (Uniqueness Under Strict Monotonicity)
If $F(X)$ is strictly monotone on the feasible set $\mathcal{K}$, then if a solution to VI$(F, \mathcal{K})$ *exists, it is unique.*

For example, uniqueness of the equilibrium link load pattern in a fixed demand traffic network equilibrium problem (see Dafermos 1980 and Nagurney 1999a) is guaranteed under the assumption of strict monotonicity of the user link travel cost functions.

Under the strong monotonicity assumption on the function $F(\cdot)$, one obtains both the existence and the uniqueness of a solution:

Theorem B.6 (Existence and Uniqueness Under Strong Monotonicity)
If $F(X)$ is strongly monotone on the feasible set $\mathcal{K}$, then there exists precisely one solution X^* to VI$(F, \mathcal{K})$.

Strong monotonicity of the user link travel cost functions as well as minus the travel disutility functions guarantees in the case of the elastic demand traffic network equilibrium problem (see Dafermos 1982 and Nagurney 1999a) both the existence and the uniqueness of an equilibrium link load and travel demand pattern. In the case of the elastic demand traffic network equilibrium problem, the feasible set is no longer compact, as was the case in the fixed demand traffic network equilibrium problem and, hence, a stronger condition (such as strong monotonicity) is needed to guarantee the existence of a solution. Strong monotonicity, in addition, however, guarantees uniqueness of the solution.

In many cases computational algorithms require the function F that enters the variational inequality problem to be Lipschitz continuous, that is:

Definition B.5 (Lipschitz Continuity)
$F(X)$ is Lipschitz continuous on $\mathcal{K}$ if there exists a constant $L > 0$, such that:

$$\|F(X^1) - F(X^2)\| \leq L\|X^1 - X^2\|, \quad \forall X^1, X^2 \in \mathcal{K}, \quad (B.12).$$

where L is referred to as the Lipschitz constant.

B.3 Algorithms

The results in the previous section are useful not only in the qualitative analysis of solutions to variational inequality problems, but also in providing conditions for establishing the convergence of algorithms. In this section, I present some of the basic algorithmic schemes, with special emphasis on algorithms that are used to compute equilibrium patterns in models discussed in this book. These algorithms resolve a variational inequality problem, typically, into a series of simpler variational inequality problems, which in turn can usually be reformulated as optimization problems. The conditions of convergence are also discussed. For a variety of different algorithms applied to a plethora of equilibrium problems, including traffic network equilibrium problems, spatial price equilibrium problems, as well as oligopolistic market equilibrium problems, see Nagurney (1999a).

As already mentioned, variational inequality algorithms resolve the variational inequality subproblem into simpler variational inequality subproblems, which are, typically, optimization problems. Hence, the overall efficiency of a variational inequality algorithm will depend upon the optimization algorithm used at each iteration. The subproblems often have a special structure and special-purpose algorithms that unveil the structure can be used to solve the embedded mathematical programming problems to achieve further efficiencies. In particular, in the problems considered in this text, the underlying structure is that of a network and, for completeness, and easy reference, I also present some network-based optimization algorithms in Section B.3.2.

In this subsection, I present two computational algorithms, the projection method and the modified projection method, along with their convergence conditions.

B.3.1 Projection Methods

Projection methods resolve a variational inequality problem (B.1) into, typically, a series of quadratic programming problems. Projection methods have been successfully implemented for the computation of a variety of equilibrium problems, including traffic network equilibrium problems (cf. Dafermos 1980, 1982, 1983; Nagurney 1999a; and the references therein).

I now present a typical iteration of the projection method.

The Projection Method

The typical iteration, $\mathcal{T}$, of a projection method, following the initialization step, can be stated as follows:

$$X^{\mathcal{T}} = P_{\mathcal{K}}(X^{\mathcal{T}-1} - \alpha G^{-1} F(X^{\mathcal{T}-1})), \qquad (B.13)$$

where G is a symmetric $N \times N$ positive definite matrix, $\alpha > 0$, and $P_{\mathcal{K}}X$ is the orthogonal projection of X on the set $\mathcal{K}$, where:

$$y = P_{\mathcal{K}}X = \arg\min_{z \in \mathcal{K}} \|X - z\|.$$

The subproblem, at an iteration $\mathcal{T}$, induced by (B.13), consists of the solution of the following minimum norm problem:

$$\min_{X\in\mathcal{K}}\|X-(X^{\mathcal{T}-1}-\alpha G^{-1}F(X^{\mathcal{T}-1}))\|, \tag{B.14}$$

or, equivalently, to the solution of the strictly convex quadratic programming problem:

$$\min_{X\in\mathcal{K}}\frac{1}{2}\langle X^T,X\rangle-\langle (X^{\mathcal{T}-1}-\alpha G^{-1}F(X^{\mathcal{T}-1}))^T,X\rangle. \tag{B.15}$$

In the special case, where $\mathcal{K}$ is the nonnegative orthant, that is, when $\mathcal{K}=R^N_+$, then the projection operation becomes particularly simple. In this case, an iteration of the projection method (B.13) takes on the following closed form expression:

$$(X^{\mathcal{T}})_i=\begin{cases}(X^{\mathcal{T}-1}-\alpha G^{-1}F(X^{\mathcal{T}-1}))_i, & \text{if } (X^{\mathcal{T}-1}-\alpha G^{-1}F(X^{\mathcal{T}-1}))_i\geq 0,\\ 0, & \text{otherwise,}\end{cases} \tag{B.16}$$

for $i=1,\ldots,N$.

In the case that the feasible set $\mathcal{K}$ is the nonnegative orthant, a simple formula is required in order to compute the iterate $\{X^{\mathcal{T}}\}$. It should also be noted that the evaluation of each $(X^{\mathcal{T}})_i; i=1,\ldots,N$, can be done both independently and simultaneously.

The convergence of the projection method is guaranteed (cf. Bertsekas and Tsitsiklis 1989) provided that the function F is both strongly monotone (see Definition B.4) and Lipschitz continuous (see Definition B.5), for any $\alpha\in(0,\alpha^0]$, such that the mapping induced by the projection is a contraction mapping with respect to the norm $\|\cdot\|_G$. The sequence $\{X^{\mathcal{T}}\}$ generated by the projection algorithm then converges to the solution of X^*.

On the other hand, if the function F is not strongly monotone, but, rather, is only monotone (see Definition B.2) and satisfies the Lipschitz continuity condition, then the modified method of Korpelevich (1977) guarantees a convergence of the solution to the variational inequality problem, provided, of course, that a solution exists. However, if the function F is monotone, rather than strongly monotone, then a unique solution is no longer guaranteed.

The modified projection method is presented next since it is used frequently in this book.

The Modified Projection Method

The typical iteration of the modified projection method, following the initialization with a feasible solution, is as follows:

$$X^{\mathcal{T}}=P_{\mathcal{K}}(X^{\mathcal{T}-1}-\alpha F(\bar{X}^{\mathcal{T}-1})), \tag{B.17}$$

where $\bar{X}^{\mathcal{T}-1}$ is given by:

$$\bar{X}^{\mathcal{T}-1}=P_{\mathcal{K}}(X^{\mathcal{T}-1}-\alpha F(X^{\mathcal{T}-1})), \tag{B.18}$$

and α is a positive scalar, such that $\alpha \in (0, \frac{1}{L}]$, where L is the Lipschitz constant in Definition B.5. Also, note that $G^{-1} = I$ (see (B.13) in the Projection Method).

Other variational inequality algorithms, such as the relaxation method, as well as a variety of decomposition methods, both serial and parallel, can be found in Nagurney (1999a) and the references therein.

B.3.2 Network Equilibration Algorithms

Traffic network equilibrium problems are variational inequality problems in which the feasible set has a network structure. Hence, such problems are best solved as variational inequality problems in which, typically, at each iteration one applies a network-based algorithm to solve the embedded mathematical programming problems. Indeed, if one applies, for example, either the projection method (cf. (B.13)) (in the case of a strongly monotone and Lipschitz continuous $F(\cdot)$) or the modified projection method (cf. (B.17) and (B.18)) (in the case of a monotone and Lipschitz continuous $F(\cdot)$), then one obtains a sequence of quadratic programming problems (diagonal in the case of the modified projection method and in the case of the projection method if G in (B.13) is selected to be diagonal). These quadratic programming problems are network optimization problems in which the feasible set has a characteristic network structure. Hence, such variational inequality algorithms applied to network equilibrium problems solve a sequence of symmetric network equilibrium problems.

Consequently, the algorithms given in the preceding section for the solution of finite-dimensional variational inequality problems can, at least in principle, be applied for the computation of network equilibria, provided that the conditions for convergence are satisfied by the problem under study.

However, the overall efficiency of the projection method for the computation of network equilibria depends on the efficiency and effectiveness of the utilized network-based algorithm for the solution of the embedded mathematical programming problems.

Towards that end, I present now an equilibration algorithm for the solution of the traffic network equilibrium problem in the case of linear and separable user link travel cost functions. The algorithm is due to Dafermos and Sparrow (1969). This algorithm is applicable to any network topology. The equilibration algorithm is a path equilibration algorithm for the solution of the symmetric and separable network equilibrium problem in the case of linear user costs on the links. This equilibration algorithm can be embedded in projection methods, for example, for the computation of traffic network equilibria in the case of nonseparable and asymmetric user link travel costs.

B.3.2.1 An Equilibration Algorithm for Linear and Separable Link Cost Functions

I now present an equilibration algorithm for the solution of problem (2.16)–(2.19), where the user cost on a link (cf. (2.3)) is given by:

$$c_a = g_a f_a + h_a, \quad \forall a \in L,$$

where we assume that g_a and h_a are positive for all links a. Explicitly, the problem that is solved is:

$$\text{Minimize} \quad \sum_{a \in \mathcal{L}} \frac{1}{2} g_a f_a^2 + h_a f_a \qquad (B.19)$$

subject to (2.17), (2.18), and the nonnegativity assumption on the path flows (2.19).

The algorithm is called an equilibration algorithm since it utilizes the network equilibrium conditions (2.15), which in this case are equivalent to the Kuhn-Tucker conditions of problem (2.16)–(2.19), for its motivation. I first present the Single O/D Pair Equilibration Algorithm, and then two alternative Multiple O/D Pair Equilibration Algorithms, which utilize the single/pair equilibration algorithm.

The single pair equilibration algorithm proceeds as follows. One selects the most costly *used* path connecting the O/D pair and the cheapest path. One then distributes the flow from the most expensive used path to the cheapest path using an explicit formula which is actually obtained by solving a minimization problem over a reduced feasible set. One continues in this fashion until the equilibrium conditions (2.15) hold within a prespecified tolerance. For further details, and proof of convergence, see Dafermos and Sparrow (1969).

Single O/D Pair Equilibration

Step 0: Initialization

Construct an initial feasible link load pattern induced by a feasible path flow pattern. Set $k = 1$.

Step 1: Selection and Convergence Verification

Determine:

$$r = \{p | \max_p C_p \quad \text{and} \quad x_p^{k-1} > 0\}$$

$$q = \{p | \min_p C_p\}.$$

If $|C_r - C_q| \leq \epsilon$, with $\epsilon > 0$, a prespecified tolerance, then stop; else, go to Step 2.

Step 2: Computation

Compute:

$$\Delta' = \frac{[C_r - C_q]}{\sum_{a \in \mathcal{L}} g_a(\delta_{aq} - \delta_{ar})^2} \tag{B.20}$$

$$\Delta = \min\{\Delta', x_r^{k-1}\}. \tag{B.21}$$

Set:

$$x_r^k = x_r^{k-1} - \Delta$$

$$x_q^k = x_q^{k-1} + \Delta$$

$$x_p^k = x_p^{k-1}, \quad \forall p \neq q \cup r.$$

Let $k = k + 1$, and go to Step 1.

In the case that a tie exists for the selection of path r and/or q, then any such selection is appropriate.

On a network in which there are now J O/D pairs, the above single O/D pair equilibration procedure is applicable as well.

I term Step 1 (without the convergence check) and Step 2 of the above equilibration operator E_{w_i}. Now two possibilities for equilibration present themselves. In Equilibration Algorithm I, one equilibrates the costs on the most expensive and cheapest paths for the first O/D pair, then does the same for the second O/D pair, and so on, until the Jth O/D pair. One then verifies convergence; if the algorithm has not converged, one continues in the same manner. In Equilibration Algorithm II, one keeps on equilibrating the most expensive and the cheapest paths for the first O/D pair, until optimality has been reached for this O/D pair. One then does the same for the second O/D pair, and so on through the Jth O/D pair. If convergence has not been reached for all O/D pairs, then one proceeds as above again for all O/D pairs.

Multiple O/D Pair Equilibration Algorithm I

Let $E^1 \equiv E_{w_J} \circ \ldots \circ E_{w_1}$.

Step 0: Initialization

Construct an initial feasible flow pattern which induces a feasible link load pattern. Set $\mathcal{T} = 1$.

Step 1: Equilibration

Apply E^1.

Step 2: Convergence Verification

If convergence holds, stop; else, set $\mathcal{T} = \mathcal{T} + 1$, and go to Step 1.

Multiple O/D Pair Equilibration Algorithm II

Let $E^2 = (E_{w_J} \circ (\ldots \circ (E_{w_J}))) \circ \ldots \circ (E_{w_1} \circ (\ldots \circ (E_{w_1})))$.

Step 0: Initialization (as above).

Step 1: Equilibration

Apply E^2.

Step 2: Convergence Verification (as above).

The difference between E^1 and E^2 is as follows. E^1 equilibrates only one pair of paths for an O/D pair before proceeding to the next O/D pair, and so on, whereas E^2 equilibrates the costs on all the paths connecting an O/D pair using the two-path procedure above, before proceeding to the next O/D pair, and so on.

Appendix C Problems

In this appendix, I provide sample problems for self-study and/or pedagogical purposes to supplement the material in this book.

Problems for Chapter 2

Problem 2.1

Consider the system-optimization problem (2.6)–(2.9). Derive the Karush--Kuhn-Tucker conditions for this problem and show that they coincide with conditions (2.13).

Problem 2.2

Consider user link travel cost functions of the form of the Bureau of Public Roads (BPR) cost functions described in Remark 2.1. Obtain the optimization reformulation of the traffic network equilibrium conditions (2.15) (akin to (2.16)–(2.19)) for a transportation network with such user link travel cost functions.

Problem 2.3

Consider Example 2.1 but assume that the travel demand has now doubled to $d_{w_1} = 20$. Determine a link-toll policy, which renders the S-O pattern also a U-O pattern.

Problem 2.4

Consider the transportation network depicted in Figure 2.3 and assume that the user link travel cost functions are given by:

$$c_a(f) = 2f_a + f_b + 11, \quad c_b(f) = 3f_b + 2f_a + 5.$$

Asssume that the O/D pair $w_1 = (1,2)$ and that the travel demand $d_{w_1} = 10$.

a. Is there an optimization reformulation of the U-O conditions for this problem? Why or why not?

b. Determine the U-O flow pattern for this problem.

Problem 2.5

Consider a traffic network with the topology depicted in Figure 2.4 with a single O/D pair $w_1 = (1,3)$. Assume that the user link travel cost functions are:

$$c_a(f_a) = 3f_a + 5, \quad c_b(f_b) = 2f_b + 4, \quad c_c(f_c) = 10f_c + 10,$$

and the travel disutility function is:

$$\lambda_{w_1}(d_{w_1}) = -2d_{w_1} + 50.$$

Determine the traffic network equilibrium flow and demand pattern satisfying conditions (2.41).

Problems for Chapter 3

Problem 3.1

Consider the Braess network example with the network as depicted in Figure 3.1 and with the data as described in Section 3.1.1 for the Braess paradox. Assume that the travel demand now doubles so that $d_{w_1} = 12$ with the remainder of the data remaining unchanged. If the new road e is built will it be used? Discuss.

Problem 3.2

Consider the Braess network example, again, as depicted in Figure 3.1 with the identical data as described in Section 3.1.1, except that now we assume that the demand is no longer fixed, but instead we have a travel disutility function for the O/D pair given by $\lambda = -d_{w_1} + 89$. Does the Braess paradox carry through in the case of the elastic demand function, that is, will the addition of road e increas the travel costs for the users?

Problem 3.3

Assume that the travel behavior is that of user-optimization. Determine how to construct a road between an O/D pair so that, if it is utilized, the user travel costs incurred in equilibrium cannot exceed those incurred for the O/D pair in equilibrium prior to the addition of the road.

Problem 3.4

Describe a network topology with a user travel cost structure and demands such that a decrease in travel demand can never result in an increase in total emissions, assuming user-optimized behavior.

Problem 3.5

Describe a heuristic for determining which links on a transportation network should be "improved," that is, their travel cost functions decreased, so that one does not obtain an associated increase in total emissions. Assume user-optimizing behavior.

Problems for Chapter 4

Problem 4.1

Consider a transportation network with a topology as given in Figure 4.1. Assume that the O/D pair $w_1 = (1, 2)$, the travel demand $d_{w_1} = 10$, and the emission factors are: $h_a = 0.2$, $h_b = 0.3$, and $h_c = 0.4$. Let the environmental quality standard be $\bar{Q} = 3$.
a. Is this network viable? Why or why not?
b. Suppose that the environmental quality standard is tightened to $\bar{Q} = 1.5$. Is the network then viable? Why or why not?

Problem 4.2

Consider a transportation network with a topology as given in Figure 4.2. Assume that the emission factors are: $h_a = 0.1$, $h_b = 0.5$, $h_c = 0.5$, and $h_d = 0.1$. Assume that $w_1 = (1, 2)$ and $d_{w_1} = 10$. Assume also that $w_2 = (1, 3)$ and $d_{w_2} = 5$. Let the environmental quality standard be $\bar{Q} = 1.5$. Is the transportation network viable?
a. Is the network viable in Situation 1? Why or why not?
b. What is the tightest environmental quality standard that can be achieved for this network in Situation 2?

Problem 4.3

Consider a transportation network with topology as given in Figure 4.3. Assume that there are two O/D pairs $w_1 = (1, 3)$ and $w_2 = (2, 4)$. Let $d_{w_1} = 20$ and $d_{w_1} = 10$. Assume that the emission factors are: $h_a = 0.2$, $h_b = 0.2$, $h_e = 0.01$, $h_c = 0.05$, $h_d = 0.05$. Let the environmental quality standard be $\bar{Q} = 2$.
a. Is the transportation network viable?
b. Is the transportation network viable in Situation 1?
c. Is the transportation network viable in Situation 3?

Problem 4.4

Assume that we have multiple modes of transportation but that each mode emits the same pollutant.
a. Determine the multimodal analogue of Linear System 4.1.
b. Define viability of such a multimodal traffic network.

Problem 4.5

Consider a single-modal traffic network but one in which the vehicles emit multiple pollutants. Suppose that there is a distinct environmental quality standard for each pollutant emitted.
a. Determine the extension of Linear System 4.1 to the multipollutant case and define viability of such a transportation network.

b. Give a small numerical example illustrating a viable multipollutant transportation network.

Problems for Chapter 5

Problem 5.1

In Section 5.2, it was shown how to construct expanded networks in order to reduce single-modal traffic networks in alternative situations to the case of a single-modal traffic network problem with known O/D pairs and travel demands. Consider the case of multimodal traffic networks and show how to construct the analogous expanded networks for Situations 1 through 3.

Problem 5.2

Consider Example 5.1, but assume that the travel demand d_{w_1} has decreased to 5 with all other data remaining unchanged. Determine an emission pricing policy that will guarantee that the network is sutainable, assuming user-optimized behavior of the travelers.

Problem 5.3

Consider Example 5.3 and assume that the environmental quality standard is relaxed so that $\bar{Q} = 1.2$. Is the transportation network viable? Is it sustainable in the absence of any emission pricing policies? Why or why not? If not, determine an emission pricing policy to guarantee sustainability.

Problem 5.4

Consider the elastic demand traffic network example, operating under user-optimization, described in Example 2.2. Assume now that we are also given emission factors: $h_a = 0.1$, $h_b = 0.2$, and $h_c = 0.4$. Let the environmental quality standard $\bar{Q} = 3$. Determine an emission pricing policy which will guarantee that this network is sustainable.

Problem 5.5

In Chapter 5, the expanded network constructions were given for Situations 1–3 for the case of fixed travel demand networks. Assume that the travel demands are now elastic, rather than fixed. Show how one can construct expanded networks for Situations 1–3 for elastic demand networks.

Problems for Chapter 6

Problem 6.1

Consider variational inequality (6.9) and assume that the sum of the initial license allocations, $\sum_{a \in L} l_a^0$, has increased. What will happen to the new equilibrium license price? State the proof formally.

Problem 6.2

As noted in the numerical example section, Section 6.3, the equilibrium solutions to the pollution permit examples coincide with the equilibrium solutions to the analogous examples in the emission pricing problems of Section 5.5. Discuss why this is so.

Problem 6.3

Develop a multipollutant version of the model described in Chapter 6, assuming that, as in Chapter 6, there is only a single mode of transportation. Note that now one needs a separate environmental quality standard for each pollutant as well as an emission factor for each pollutant on each link. Be sure to state the equilibrium conditions and to derive the variational inequality formulation.

Problem 6.4

Construct a multimodal version of the model of Chapter 6, assuming that there is, as in the model of Chapter 6, only a single pollutant emitted. Present the equilibrium conditions and derive the variational inequality formulation.

Problem 6.5

Discuss how the pollution permit system developed in this chapter could be implemented in practice.

Problems for Chapter 7

Problem 7.1

In Chapter 7, I presented a hierarchy of pollution permit system models for user-optimized elastic demand traffic networks. Develop an analogous hierarchy for fixed demand traffic networks, including the variational inequality formulations, using the link-based permit system model of Chapter 6 as a baseline.

Problem 7.2

Discuss the relative advantages and disadvantages of the pollution permit systems presented in Chapter 7. What system(s) would be easier to implement in practice? Justify your statements.

Problem 7.3

Discuss the relative fairness of the alternative pollution permit schemes described in Chapter 7 in terms of the payment(s) of the users of the transportation networks.

Problem 7.4

Assume that, rather than having the travel disutility functions associated with the O/D pairs as being given, one now has instead their inverses, that is, the demand functions $d_w(\lambda)$, $\forall w \in W$. Discuss how one would go about developing a link-based pollution permit system model, assuming that now the travel demand functions associated with the O/D pairs are given, rather than the travel disutility functions.

Problem 7.5

Construct a simple numerical example and for it determine the link-based, the path-based, as well as the O/D pair-based equilibrium solution, assuming user-optimized behavior, and given travel disutility functions.

Problems for Chapter 8

Problem 8.1

Give an example of a transportation network in which the system-optimized flow pattern coincides with the user-optimized flow pattern. Be sure to give the topology, the demand, and the cost structure.

Problem 8.2

Consider Example 8.2 and determine emission/congestion tolls to guarantee that the environmental quality standard $\bar{Q} = 2$ is met and, hence, the network is sustainable, assuming system-optimized behavior.

Problem 8.3

Give three applications of system-optimized networks in which emission/congestion tolls could be applicable.

Problem 8.4

Consider Example 8.1 and suppose that the travel demand is now $d_{w_1} = 5$ with the rest of the data remaining unchanged. Determine the emission/congestion toll pattern to guarantee that the network is sustainable, assuming system-optimizing behavior.

Problem 8.5

Consider the variational inequality formulation (8.16) in link loads. Derive a formula expressing the change in link loads, given a change in the environmental quality standard $\bar{Q}$. Discuss the formula.

Problems for Chapter 9

Problem 9.1

The model developed in Chapter 9 assumed that each jurisdiction or transportation authority had control over its transportation network in the form of links and only flows which it controlled flowed over such links. Assume now that that there may be "transborder effects" in that flows controlled by one authority may use links belonging to a network under another authority.

Discuss how a model of tradable pollution permits would be developed in such a situation.

Problem 9.2

Construct a simple numerical example to illustrate the model of Section 9.1.

Problem 9.3

Consider Example 9.1 but assume now that the environmental quality standard is relaxed so that $\bar{Q} = 16$ and the initial license allocation is now: $l_a^0 = l_b^0 = l_c^0 = l_d^0 = 4$. The remainder of the data are unchanged. Compute the new equilibrium flow, license, marginal cost of emission abatement and price pattern.

Problem 9.4

Consider Problem 9.3, but assume that travelers now behave in a user-optimized fashion. Construct the toll policy which renders the solution to Problem 9.3 also a user-optimized one following the procedure described in Section 9.3.

Problem 9.5

Compare the model developed in Section 9.1 with the model proposed in Section 8.1.2. What are the relative advantages/disadvantages of each?

Problems for Chapter 10

Problem 10.1

Extend the oligopoly model with marketable pollution permits discussed in Chapter 10 to the case where there are multiple pollutants associated with shipping the commodity from the firms to the demand markets. Give the equilibrium conditions and derive the variational inequality formulation.

Problem 10.2

Develop an extension of the oligopoly model in Chapter 10 to one in which the stationary firms emit a pollutant which is distinct from the pollutant associated with the shipment of the commodity. Assume that there is now also a market for pollution permits associated with the pollutant emitted by the firms. Determine the equilibrium conditions and derive the variational inequality formulation of the model.

Problem 10.3

Develop a special case of the model constructed in Section 10.1 where the oligopoly is aspatial and the firms are the only emitters. Furthermore, there are no costs associated with shipping the commodity.

Problem 10.4

Discuss what happens to the marginal costs of emission abatement in the model developed in Chapter 10 when the initial allocation of licenses is increased? Is decreased? Support your answers rigorously.

Problem 10.5

Discuss an application of the spatial oligopoly pollution permit system model.

Problems for Chapter 11

Problem 11.1

Consider the spatial price equilibrium problem consisting of a single supply market and two demand markets. Assume that the supply price function is given by:

$$\pi_1(s_1) = 5s_1 + 5,$$

the unit transportation costs associated with shipping the commodity to the demand markets are given by:

$$c_{11}(Q_{11}) = Q_{11} + 2, \quad c_{12}(Q_{12}) + 3,$$

and the demand price functions are given by:

$$\rho_1(d_1) = -d_1 + 20, \quad \rho_2(d_2) = -2d_2 + 30.$$

Determine the spatial price equilibrium production, trade, and consumption pattern satisfying equilibrium conditions (11.6).

Problem 11.2

Consider a special case of the model developed in Section 11.1.2 in which there is only an environmental quality standard associated with the shipment of the commodity. Give the equilibrium conditions and the variational inequality formulation for this special case.

Problem 11.3

Discuss an application of the model described in Section 11.2. Support your arguments fully.

Problem 11.4

Develop a marketable pollution permit system model using the model of Section 11.2 as a guide. In the model, there should be tradable pollution permits on the production side, on the consumption side, as well as on the shipment side.

Problem 11.5

Discuss the challenges associated with the development of an oligopolistic (imperfectly competitive) version of the perfectly competitive sustainable spatial price model of Section 11.2.

Problems for Chapter 12

Problem 12.1

Consider Example 12.1 but assume now that the budget is doubled from 1 to 2.
a. What is the new optimal budget allocation for emission reduction?
b. What is the new solution if, instead, the user travel link cost function on link a is modified so that:

$$c_a(f_a) = f_a + 1.$$

Problem 12.2

Consider Example 12.2 but assume now that $\hat{k}_a = 5$, with the remainder of the data as described. Determine the solution to the optimal viability achievement model for this problem.

Problem 12.3

Describe practical applications in which the introduction of a new mode could result in mode switching. In what kind of transportation situation would you expect that even if a new mode is introduced there may be no or only minimal mode switching to the new mode?

Problem 12.4

Develop a multimodal/multipollutant analogue of the viable growth model of Section 12.4.

Problem 12.5

a. Derive the Karush-Kuhn-Tucker conditions for the multimodal system-optimization problem with mode allocation control given by (12.32)–(12.36).
b. Present two distinct possible applications of the model of Section 12.5.

Bibliography

Allen, W. G. Jr. (1996), "Model Improvements for Evaluating Pricing Strategies, *Transportation Research Record* **1498**, 75-81.

American Automobile Manufacturers Association (1996), *Motor Vehicle Facts and Figures*, Washington, DC.

Anderson, W. P., Kanaroglou, P. S., Miller, E. J., and Buliung, R. N. (1996), "Simulating Automobile Emissions in an Integrated Urban Model, *Transportation Research Record* **1520**, 71-80.

Arnott, R., Arrow, K., Atkinson, A. B., and Dreze, J. H., editors (1994), *Public Economics: Selected Papers by William Vickrey*, Cambridge University Press, Cambridge, England.

Banister, D., and Button, K. J. (1993), "Environmental Policy and Transport: An Overview," in *Transport, the Environment, and Sustainable Development*, D. Banister and K. J. Button, editors, E. & F.N., London, England.

Baumol, W. J., and Oates, W. E. (1988), *The Theory of Environmental Policy*, Cambridge University Press, New York.

Bazaraa, M. S., Jarvis, J. J., and Sherali, H. D. (1990), *Linear Programming and Network Flows*, second edition, John Wiley, New York.

Bazaraa, M. S., Sherali, H. D., and Shetty, C. M. (1993), *Nonlinear Programming: Theory and Algorithms*, second edition, John Wiley, New York.

Beckmann, M. J., McGuire, C. B., and Winsten, C. B. (1956), *Studies in the Economics of Transportation*, Yale University Press, New Haven, Connecticut.

Bergendorff, P., Hearn, D. W., and Ramana, M. V. (1997), "Congestion Toll Pricing of Traffic Networks," in *Network Optimization*, *Lecture Notes in Economics and Mathematical Systems* **450**, pp. 51-71, P. M. Pardalos, D. W. Hearn, and W. W. Hager, editors, Springer-Verlag, Berlin, Germany.

Bertsekas, D. P., and Tsitsiklis, J. N. (1989), *Parallel and Distributed Computation*, Prentice Hall, Englewood Cliffs, New Jersey.

Boyce, D. E., Kirson, A. M., and Schofer, J. L. (1994), "ADVANCE - The llinois Dynamic Navigation and Route Guidance Demonstration Program," in *Advanced Tehcnologies for Road Transport*, pp. 247-270, I. Catling, editor, Artech House, Boston, Massachusetts.

Bradley, S. P., Hax, A., and Magnanti, T. L. (1977), *Applied Mathematical Programming*, Addison-Wesley, Reading, Massachusetts.

Braess, D. (1968), "Uber ein Paradoxon der Verkehrsplanung," *Unternehmenforschung* **12**, 258-268.

Button, K. J. (1990), "Environmental Externalities and Transport Policy," *Oxford Review of Economic Policy* **6**, 61-75.

Button K. J. (1993), *Transport, the Environment and Economic Policy*, Edward Elgar, Aldershot, United Kingdom.

Button, K. J., and Verhoef, E. T., editors (1998), *Road Pricing, Traffic Congestion and the Environment*, Edward Elgar, Cheltenham, United Kingdom.

Clean Air Act, C. 360, 69, Statutory 322, July 14, 1955.

Clean Air Act Amendments of 1970, Public Law No. 91-804, 84 Statutory 1676, December 31, 1970.

Clean Air Act Amendments of 1990, Public Law, No. 101-549 (Senate 1360), 104 Statutory 2399, November 15, 1990.

Coase, R. (1960), "The Problem of Social Cost," *Journal of Law and Economics*, 1-44.

Commission of the European Communities (1995), *Green Paper Towards Fair and Efficient Pricing in Transport: Policy Options for Internalising the External Costs of Transport in the European Union*, Directorate-General for Transport, Brussels, Belgium.

Council on Environmental Quality (1991), *Environmental Quality*, Government Printing Office, Washington, DC.

Cournot, A. A. (1838), *Researches into the Mathematical Principles of the Theory of Wealth*, English translation, Macmillan, London, England, 1897.

Crocker, T. D. (1966), "The Structuring of Atmospheric Pollution Control Systems," in *The Economics of Air Pollution*, pp. 61-86, H. Wolozin, editor, W. W. Norton, New York.

Cropper, M. L., and Oates, W. E. (1992),"Environmental Economics: A Survey," *Journal of Economic Literature* **30**, 675-750.

Dafermos, S. (1976), "Integrated Equilibrium Flow Models for Transportation Planning," in *Traffic Equilibrium Methods*, *Lecture Notes in Economics and Mathematical Sysems* **118**, pp. 106-118, M. A. Florian, editor, Springer-Verlag, New York.

Dafermos, S. (1980), "Traffic Equilibrium and Variational Inequalities," *Transportation Science* **14**, 42-54.

Dafermos, S. (1982), "The General Multimodal Network Equilibrium Problem with Elastic Demand," *Networks* **12**, 57-72.

Dafermos, S. (1983), "An Iterative Scheme for Variational Inequalities," *Mathematical Programming* **26**, 40-47.

Dafermos, S. (1986), "Equilibria on Nonlinear Networks," LCDS #86-1, Lefschetz Center for Dynamical Systems, Brown University, Providence, Rhode Island.

Dafermos, S., and Nagurney, A. (1985), "Isomorphism Between Spatial Price and Traffic Network Equilibrium Models," LCDS # 85-17, Lefschetz Center for Dynamical Systems, Brown University, Providence, Rhode Island.

Dafermos, S., and Nagurney, A. (1987), "Oligopolistic and Competitive Behavor of Spatially Separated Markets," *Regional Science and Urban Economics* **17**, 245-254.

Dafermos, S. C. (1973), "Toll Patterns for Multiclass-User Transportation Networks," *Transportation Science* **7**, 211-223.

Dafermos, S. C., and Sparrow, F. T. (1969), "The Traffic Assignment Problem for a General Network," *Journal of Research of the National Bureau of Standards* **73B**, 91-118.

Dales, J. H. (1968), *Pollution, Property, and Prices*, University of Toronto Press, Toronto, Ontario, Canada.

DeCorla-Souza, P., Everett, J., Cosby, J. and Lim, P. (1995), "Trip-Based Approach to Estimate Emissions with Environmental Protection Agency's MOBILE Model, *Transportation Research Record* **1444**, 118-125.

Dhanda, K. K., Nagurney, A., and Ramanujam, P. (1999), *Environmental Networks: A Framework for Economic Decision-Making and Policy Analysis*, Edward Elgar, Cheltenham, United Kingdom.

Dower, R., Ditz, D., Faeth, P., Johnson, N., Kozloff, K., and MacKenzie, J. J. (1997), *Frontiers of Sustainability*, World Resources Institute, Island Press, Washington, DC.

Dupuit, J. (1844), "On the Measurement of the Utility of Public Works," in *Transport* (1968), D. Murphy, editor, Penguin, London, England.

The Economist (1996), "Living with the Car," June 22, 3-18.

The Economist (1997), "Living with the Car," December 26, 21-23.

Florian, M., and Hearn, D. (1995), "Network Equilibrium Models and Algorithms," in *Network Routing*, *Handbooks in Operations Research and Management Science* **8**, pp. 485-550, M. O. Ball, T. L. Magnanti, C. L. Monma, and G. L. Nemhauser, editors, Elsevier Science, Amsterdam, The Netherlands.

Florian, M., and Los, M. (1982), "A New Look at Static Spatial Price Equilibrium Models," *Regional Science and Urban Economics* **12**, 579-597.

Gabay, D., and Moulin, H. (1980), "On the Uniqueness and Stability of Nash Equilibria in Noncooperative Games," in *Applied Stochastic Control in Econometrics and Management Science*, pp. 271-294, A. Bensoussan, P. Kleindorfer, and C. S. Tapiero, editors, North-Holland, Amsterdam, The Netherlands.

Gartner, N. H. (1980), "Optimal Traffic Assignment with Elastic Demands: A Review. Part I: Analysis Framework," *Transportation Science* **14**, 174-191.

Glover, E. L. and Brzezinski, D. J. (1989), "MOBILE4 Exhaust Emission Factors and Inspection/Maintenance Benefits for Passenger Cars," Technical Report, **EPA-AA-TSS-I/M-89-3**.

Goddard, H. C. (1997), "Optimal Restrictions of Vehicle Use for Urban Sustainability for Mexico City," *International Journal for Environment and Pollution* **7**, 357-374.

Hahn, R. W. (1989), "Economic Prescriptions for Environmental Problems: How the Patient Followed the Doctor's Orders, *Journal of Economic Perspectives* **3**, 95-114.

Hall, J. V. (1995), "The Role of Transport Control Measures in Jointly Reducing Congestion and Air Pollution," *Journal of Transport Economics and Policy* January, 93-103.

Hartman, P. and Stampacchia, G. (1966), "On Some Nonlinear Elliptic Differential Functional Equations," *Acta Mathematica* **115**, 271-310.

Hau, T. D. (1998), "Congestion Pricing and Road Investment," in *Road Pricing, Traffic Congestion and the Environment*, pp. 39-78, K. J. Button and E. T. Verhoef, editors, Edward Elgar Publishing Inc., Cheltenham, United Kingdom.

Ingalls, M. N. (1989), "On Road Vehicle Emission Factors from Measurements in a Los Angeles Area Tunnel, *Paper 89-137.3, Air Waste and Management Association Annual Meeting.*

Johansson, B., and Mattsson, L. G. (1995), "Principles of Road Pricing," in *Road Pricing: Theory, Empirical Assessment and Policy*, pp. 7-33, B. Johansson and L. G. Mattsson, editors, Kluwer Academic Publishers, Boston, Massachusetts.

Jones, P., and Hervik, A. (1992), "Restraining Car Traffic in European Cities: An Emerging Role for Road Pricing, *Transportation Research* **26A**, 133-145.

Karush, W. (1939), "Minima of Functions of Several Variables with Inequalities as Side Conditions," M.S. Thesis, Department of Mathematics, University of Chicago, Chicago, Illinois.

Kinderlehrer, D., and Stampacchia, G. (1980), *An Introduction to Variational Inequalities and Their Applications*, Academic Press, New York.

Knight, F. H. (1924), "Some Fallacies in the Interpretation of Social Cost," *Quarterly Journal of Economics* **38**, 582-606.

Koh, W. T. H., and Lee, D. K. C. (1994), "The Vehicle Quota System in Singapore: An Assessment," *Transportation Research* **28A**, 31-47.

Korpelevich, G. M. (1977), "The Extragradient Method for Finding Saddle Points and Other Problems," *Matekon* **13**, 35-49.

Kuhn, H. W., and Tucker A. W. (1951), "Nonlinear Programming," in *Proceedings of Second Berkeley Symposium on Mathematical Statistics and Probability,* pp. 481-492, J. Neyman, editor, University of California Press, Berkeley, California.

Lawson, D. R., Groblicki, P. J., Stedman, D. H., Bishop, G. A., and Guenther, P. L. (1990), "Emissions from In-Use Motor Vehicles in Los Angeles: A Pilot Study of Remote Sensing and the Inspection and Maintenance Program," *Journal of Air Waste Management Association* **40**, 1096-1105.

Mahmassani, H. S., Peeta, S., Hu, T. Y., and Ziliaskopoulos, A. (1993), "Dynamic Traffic Assignment with Multiple User Classes for Real-Time ATIS /ATMS Applications," in *Large Urban Systems, Proceedings of the Advanced Traffic Management Conference*, pp. 91-114, Federal Highway Administration, US Department of Transportation, Washington, DC.

Meadows, D. H., Meadows, D. L., Randers, J., and Behrens III, W. W. (1974), *The Limits to Growth*, Universe Books, New York.

Montgomery, W. D. (1972), "Markets in Licenses and Efficient Pollution Control Programs," *Journal of Economic Theory* **5**, 395-418.

Morrison, S. A. (1986), "A Survey of Road Pricing," *Transportation Research* **20A**, 87-98.

Nagurney, A. (1994), "Variational Inequalities in the Analysis and Computation of Multi-Sector, Multi-Instrument Financial Equilibria," *Journal of Economic Dynamics and Control* **18**, 161-184.

Nagurney, A. (1998), "Pollution Permits and Spatial Oligopolies," Isenberg School of Management, University of Massachusetts, Amherst, Massachusetts.

Nagurney, A. (1999a), *Network Economics: A Variational Inequality Approach*, second and revised edition, Kluwer Academic Publishers, Dordrecht, The Netherlands.

Nagurney, A. (1999b), "Congested Urban Transportation Networks and Emission Paradoxes," to appear in *Transportation Research D*.

Nagurney, A. (1999c), "Sustainable Transportation Systems and Pollution Permits," Isenberg School of Management, University of Massachusetts, Amherst, Massachusetts.

Nagurney, A. (1999d), "Alternative Pollution Permit Systems for Transportation Networks Based on Origin/Destination Pairs and Paths," *Transportation Research D* **5**, 37-58.

Nagurney, A., and Dhanda, K. (1996), "A Variational Inequality Approach for Marketable Pollution Permits," *Computational Economics* **9**, 363-384.

Nagurney A., and Dhanda, K. K. (1997a), "Variational Inequalities for Marketable Pollution Permits with Technological Investment Opportunities: The Case of Oligopolistic Markets," *Mathematical and Computer Modelling* **26**, 1-25.

Nagurney, A., and Dhanda, K. K. (1997b), "Noncompliant Oligopolistic Firms and Marketable Pollution Permits: Statics and Dynamics," Isenberg School of Management, University of Massachusetts, Amherst, Massachusetts.

Nagurney, A., and Dhanda, K. K. (1997c), "Marketable Pollution Permits in Oligopolistic Markets with Transaction Costs," to appear in *Operations Research*.

Nagurney, A., Dhanda, K. K., and Stranlund, J. (1997), "A General Multiproduct, Multipollutant Market Pollution Permit Model: A Variational Inequality Approach," *Energy Economics* **19**, 57-76.

Nagurney, A., Ramanujam, P., and Dhanda K. K. (1998), "A Multimodal Traffic Network Equilibrium Model with Emission Pollution Permits: Compliance Versus Noncompliance," *Transportation Research D* **3**, 349-374.

Nagurney, A., and Siokos, S. (1997), *Financial Networks: Statics and Dynamics*, Springer-Verlag, Berlin, Germany.

Nagurney, A., Takayama, T., and Zhang, D. (1995), "Massively Parallel Computation of Spatial Price Equilibrium Problems as Dynamical Systems," *Journal of Economic Dynamics and Control* **18**, 3-37.

Nagurney, A., and Zhang, D. (1996), *Projected Dynamical Systems and Variational Inequalities with Applications*, Kluwer Academic Publishers, Boston, Massachusetts.

Nash, J. F. (1950), "Equilibrium Points in N-Person Games," *Proceedings of the National Academy of Sciences* **36**, 48-49.

Nash, J. F. (1951), "Noncooperative Games," *Annals of Mathematics* **54**, 286-298.

Nijkamp, P., Rienstra, S. A., and Vleugel, J. M. (1998), "Design and Assessment of Long Term Sustainable Transport System Scenarios," in *Transport Networks in Europe*, pp. 307-332, K. J. Button, P. Nijkamp, and H. Priemus, editors, Edward Elgar, Cheltenham, United Kingdom.

Oak Ridge National Laboratory (1993), *Transportation Energy Data Book*, volume 13, US Department of Transportation, Federal Highway Administration, Oak Ridge, Tennessee.

OECD (1995), *Urban Travel and Sustainable Development*, European Conference of Ministers of Transport, Paris, France.

Pearce, D. W., and Turner, R. K. (1990), *Economics of Natural Resources and the Environment*, Johns Hopkins University Press, Baltimore, Maryland.

Pigou, A. C. (1920), *The Economics of Welfare*, Macmillan, London, England.

President's Council on Sustainable Development (1996a), *Energy and Transportation Task Force Report.*

President's Council on Sustainable Development (1996b), *Sustainable America: A New Consensus for Prosperity, Opportunity, and a Healthy Environment for the Future.*

Ran, B., and Boyce, D. E. (1996), *Modeling Dynamic Transportation Networks*, Springer-Verlag, Berlin, Germany.

Replogle, M. (1991), "Sustainability: A Vital Concept for Transportation Planning and Development," *Journal for Advanced Transportation* **25**, 3-17.

Roseland, M. (1992), *Toward Sustainable Communities: A Resource Book for Municipal and Local Governments*, National Round Table on the Environment and the Economy, Ottawa, Ontario, Canada.

Samuelson, P. A. (1952), "Spatial Price Equilibrium and Linear Programming," *American Economic Review* **42**, 283-303.

Sevigny, M. (1998), *Taxing Automobile Emissions for Pollution Control*, Edward Elgar, Cheltenham, United Kingdom.

Sheffi, Y. (1985), *Urban Transportation Networks – Equilibrium Analysis with Mathematical Programming Methods*, Prentice-Hall, Englewood Cliffs, New Jersey.

Small, K. A., and Gomez-Ibanez, J. A. (1998), "Road Pricing for Congestion Management: The Transition from Theory to Policy," in *Road Pricing, Traffic Congestion and the Environment*, pp. 213-246, K. J. Button and E. T. Verhoef, editors, Edward Elgar Publishing, Cheltenham, United Kingdom.

Smith, M. J. (1979), "Existence, Uniqueness, and Stability of Traffic Equilibria," *Transportation Research* **13B**, 259-304.

Sperling, D. (1995), *Future Drive*, Island Press, Washington, DC.

Sperling, D., and Shaheen, S. A. editors (1995), *Transportation and Energy: Strategies for a Sustainable Transportation System*, American Council for an Energy-Efficient Economy, Washington, DC, and Berkeley, California; Institute for Transportation Studies, University of California, Davis.

Takayama, T., and Judge, G. G. (1971), *Spatial and Temporal Price and Allocation Models*, North-Holland, Amsterdam, The Netherlands.

Tietenberg, T. H. (1980), "Transferable Discharge Permits and Control of Stationary Air Pollution: A Survey and Synthesis," *Land Economics* **56**, 391-416.

Tietenberg, T. H. (1985), *Emissions Trading, An Exercise in Reforming Pollution Policy*, Resources for the Future, Washington, DC.

Tietenberg, T. (1996), *Environmental and Natural Resource Economics*, fourth edition, HarperCollins, New York.

Toh, R. S. (1992), "Experimental Measures to Curb Road Congestion in Singapore: Pricing and Quotas," *Logistics and Transportation Review* **28**, 289-317.

Train, K. E., Davis, W. B., and Levine, M. K. (1997), "Fuels and Rebates on New Vehicles: Impacts on Fuel Efficiency, Carbon Dioxide Emissions, and Consumer Surplus," *Transportation Research* **33E**, 1-13.

Transportation Research Board (1995), *Expanding Metropolitan Highways: Implications for Air Quality and Energy Use*, Special Report 245, National Research Council, Washington, DC.

Transportation Research Board (1997), *Toward A Sustainable Future: Addressing the Long-Term Effects of Motor Vehicle Transportation on Climate and Ecology*, Special Report 251, National Academy Press, Washington, DC.

United States Department of Transportation (1992a), "A Summary: Transportation Programs and Provisions of the Clean Air Act Ammendments of 1990," Publication Number: FHWA-PD-92-023.

United States Department of Transportation (1992b), "A Summary: Air Quality Programs and Provisions of the Intermodal Surface Transportation Efficiency Act of 1991, 1992, Publication Number: FHWA-PD-92-022.

United States Environmental Protection Agency (1997), *The Benefits and Costs of the Clean Air Act, 1970-1990*, EE-0295, Washington, DC.

Verhoef, E. T. (1996), *The Economics of Regulating Road Transport*, Edward Elgar, Chelthenham, United Kingdom.

Verhoef, E. T., and van den Bergh, J. C. J. M. (1996), "A Spatial Price Equilibrium Model for Environmental Policy Analysis of Mobile and Immobile Sources of Pollution," in *Recent Advances in Spatial Equilibrium Modelling: Methodology and Applications*, pp. 201-220, J. C. J. M. van den Bergh, P. Nijkamp, and P. Rietveld, editors, Springer-Verlag, Heidelberg, Germany,

Verhoef, E. T., van den Bergh, J. C. J. M., and Button, K. J. (1997), "Transport, Spatial Economy and the Global Environment," *Environment and Planning* **29 A**, 1195-1213.

Vickrey, W. S. (1960), "Statement to the Joint Committee on Washington Metropolitan Problems," *Transportation Plan for the National Capital Region*, Hearings, Joint Committee on Washington Metropolitan Problems, November 8-14, 1959, pp. 454-490. Excerpt reprinted in *Journal of Urban Economics* **36** (1994), 42-65.

Vickrey, W. S. (1963), "Pricing in Urban and Suburban Transport," *American Economic Review, Papers and Proceedings* **53**, 452-465.

Walters, A. A. (1961), "The Theory and Measurement of Private and Social Cost of Highway Congestion," *Econometrica* **29**, 676-699.

Wardrop, J. G. (1952), "Some Theoretical Aspects of Road Traffic Research," *Proceedings of the Institute of Civil Engineers*, Part II, pp. 325-378.

Whitelegg, J. (1993), *Transport for a Sustainable Future: The Case of Europe*, Belhaven Press, London, England.

World Bank (1996), *Sustainable Transport: Priorities for Policy Reform*, World Bank, Washington, DC.

World Commission on Environment and Development (1987), *Our Common Future*, Oxford University Press, New York.

Glossary of Notation

This is a glossary of symbols used in this book. Other symbols are defined in the book as needed. A vector is assumed to be a column vector, unless noted otherwise.

$\in$	an element of
$\subset$	subset of
$\cup, \cap$	union, intersection
$\forall$	for all
$\exists$	there exists
R	the real line
R^n	Euclidean n-dimensional space
R^n_+	Euclidean n-dimensional space on the nonnegative orthant
$:$	such that; also $\vert$
$\equiv$	is equivalent to
$\mapsto$	maps to
$\longrightarrow$	tends to
$\circ$	composition
$\Vert x\Vert = (\sum_{i=1}^n x_i^2)^{\frac{1}{2}}$	length of $x \in R^n$ with components $(x_1, x_2, \ldots, x_n)$
x^T	transpose of a vector x
$\langle x^T, x\rangle$	inner product of vector x where $\langle x^T, x\rangle = x_1^2 + \ldots + x_n^2$
$x^T \cdot x$	also denotes the inner product of x
$\vert y\vert$	absolute value of y
$[a, b]\,; (a, b)$	a closed interval; an open interval in R
∇f	gradient of $f : R^n \mapsto R$
∇F	the $n \times n$ Jacobian of a mapping $F : R^n \mapsto R^n$
$\frac{\partial f}{\partial x}$	partial derivative of f with respect to x
$\text{argmin}_{x\in K} f(x)$	the set of $x \in K$ attaining the minimum of $f(x)$
A^T	transpose of the matrix A
A^{-1}	the inverse of the matrix A
I	the identity matrix

Index